COMMON CORE
CURRICULUM MAPS
IN ENGLISH LANGUAGE ARTS

Grades 9–12

COMMON
CORE

JOSSEY-BASS
A Wiley Imprint
www.josseybass.com

OTHER BOOKS IN THE COMMON CORE SERIES:

Common Core Curriculum Maps in English Language Arts, Grades K–5

Common Core Curriculum Maps in English Language Arts, Grades 6–8

Published by Jossey-Bass
A Wiley Imprint
989 Market Street, San Francisco, CA 94103–1741—www.josseybass.com

Readers should be aware that Internet websites offered as citations and/or sources for further information may have changed or disappeared between the time this was written and when it is read.

Limit of Liability/Disclaimer of Warranty: While the publisher and author have used their best efforts in preparing this book, they make no representations or warranties with respect to the accuracy or completeness of the contents of this book and specifically disclaim any implied warranties of merchantability or fitness for a particular purpose. No warranty may be created or extended by sales representatives or written sales materials. The advice and strategies contained herein may not be suitable for your situation. You should consult with a professional where appropriate. Neither the publisher nor author shall be liable for any loss of profit or any other commercial damages, including but not limited to special, incidental, consequential, or other damages.

Jossey-Bass books and products are available through most bookstores. To contact Jossey-Bass directly call our Customer Care Department within the U.S. at 800-956-7739, outside the U.S. at 317-572-3986, or fax 317-572-4002.

Jossey-Bass also publishes its books in a variety of electronic formats. Some content that appears in print may not be available in electronic books.

Library of Congress Cataloging-in-Publication Data
Common Core curriculum maps in English language arts, grades 9–12.—1st ed.
    p.cm.—(The Common Core Series)
Includes index.
ISBN 978-1-118-10820-8 (pbk.)
ISBN 978-1-1-181-5759-6 (ebk.)
ISBN 978-1-1-181-5760-2 (ebk.)
ISBN 978-1-1-181-5761-9 (ebk.)
1. Language arts (Secondary)—Curricula—United States—States. 2. Language arts (Secondary)—Standards—United States—States. I. Common Core, Inc.
LB1631.C657 2012
428.0071′273—dc23

2011029323

Printed in the United States of America
FIRST EDITION
PB Printing   10 9 8 7 6 5 4 3 2 1

CONTENTS

Foreword by Carol Jago   vii

Written by Teachers, for Teachers   xi

Introduction by Lynne Munson   xiii

How to Use the Common Core Curriculum Maps   xvii

Grade 9   1
Unit 1 Literary Elements and the Short Story   3
Unit 2 The Novel—Honor   13
Unit 3 Poetry—Beauty   23
Unit 4 Drama—Fate   37
Unit 5 Epic Poetry—Heroism   47
Unit 6 Literary Nonfiction—Reflection (the Memoir,
       the Essay, and the Speech)   57

Grade 10   67
Unit 1 World Literature: Latin and Central America   69
Unit 2 World Literature: Asia   81
Unit 3 World Literature: Africa and the Middle East   95
Unit 4 World Literature: Russia   107

Grade 11   119
Unit 1 The New World   121
Unit 2 A New Nation   129
Unit 3 American Romanticism   139
Unit 4 A Troubled Young Nation   151
Unit 5 Emerging Modernism   163
Unit 6 Challenges and Successes of the Twentieth Century   173

Grade 12   185

Unit 1 European Literature: Middle Ages   187
Unit 2 European Literature: Renaissance and Reformation   201
Unit 3 European Literature: Seventeenth Century   211
Unit 4 European Literature: Eighteenth and Early
        Nineteenth Century   221
Unit 5 European Literature: Nineteenth Century   231
Unit 6 European Literature: Twentieth Century   243

Appendix: Scoring Rubric   255

About Common Core   257

Acknowledgments   259

Index of Suggested Works   261

Good Schools: The Salt of Society

Carol Jago

Three hundred years ago Cotton Mather preached, "A Good School deserves to be call'd the very Salt of the Town that hath it." Without a school "wherein the Youth may by able Masters be Taught the Things that are necessary to qualify them for future Serviceableness," a community will founder.[1] Mather's advice to townspeople in Puritan New England reflects one of the philosophical underpinnings of the Common Core Curriculum Maps in English Language Arts: Schools matter. Curriculum matters. Teachers matter.

In order to determine which things should be taught, we must of course first define what it means to be serviceable in a twenty-first-century democratic society. To ensure a capable workforce and build a strong economy, high levels of literacy and numeracy are obviously essential. But what about the need for students to develop empathy and thoughtfulness? It is short-sighted to equate the value of education with economic growth. Like salt, good schools with rich curricula enhance the community by adding depth—and piquancy. Like salt, they are a preservative, ensuring that a society's values endure.

Many of the benefits we've come to demand as our rights in a modern society depend upon high levels of employment, but if we shift the discussion of the purpose of school from job training to preparing America's children to lead a worthwhile life, the calculus changes. Is simply working nine-to-five for forty years what you most aspire to for your children? Or do you want them to have an education that invites exploration of essential questions, inspires challenges to the status quo, and somehow prepares them for what we cannot yet know? Most parents want both.

The conundrum for curriculum developers is to avoid becoming so caught up in preparing students to make a living—which starts with paying attention in kindergarten; earning good grades through elementary school, middle school, and high school; achieving competitive SAT and ACT scores; and winning a place in college or in the workplace—that we lose sight of educating students to enrich their lives.

In *Not for Profit: Why Democracy Needs the Humanities,* philosopher Martha Nussbaum warns that, "With the rush to profitability in the global market, values precious for the future of democracy, especially in an era of religious and economic anxiety, are in danger of getting lost."[2] I share her concern. The movement to reform education primarily in order to make the United States more globally competitive seems wrong-headed and even counterproductive. Maybe I lack a competitive spirit, but I have always wanted more for my students than just coming in first. I want them to learn

---

[1] Cotton Mather, "The Education of Children," http://www.spurgeon.org/~phil/mather/edkids.htm.
[2] Martha Nussbaum, *Not for Profit: Why Democracy Needs the Humanities* (Princeton: Princeton University Press, 2010), 6.

about and to think about the world—today's world and yesterday's. Nussbaum explains, "World history and economic understanding must be humanistic and critical if they are to be at all useful in forming intelligent global citizens, and they must be taught alongside the study of religion and of philosophical theories of justice. Only then will they supply a useful foundation for the public debates that we must have if we are to cooperate in solving major human problems."[3] One means of learning about the problems that have beset and continue to bedevil humanity is through the study of the humanities—literature and art, history and philosophy. This is the kind of education the Common Core Curriculum Maps offer. I believe it is the education that every generation of citizens needs.

Unit Three of the Grade One curriculum map, Life Lessons, offers young children opportunities to explore the kind of education Martha Nussbaum recommends. As they work through the unit, "Students read and listen to fables with morals. They learn about rules for life in a book of manners. Reading the life story of George Washington Carver, students learn about a man who had to overcome obstacles in life to make important contributions to science and agriculture. Students learn about Thomas Edison's work with electricity and the rules for its safe use. Descriptive words are the focus of a lesson centered on the artwork of Georgia O'Keeffe. Finally, the children write narratives focused on life lessons and create informative posters focused on electrical safety." This interdisciplinary approach integrates the study of science and builds students' background knowledge. In so doing, it strengthens their reading comprehension and develops their facility with reading informational texts—a key expectation of the Common Core State Standards. It also invites children to investigate Georgia O'Keeffe's paintings and build their cultural literacy.

Some readers of the Common Core Curriculum Maps may argue that their students won't read nineteenth-century novels, that twenty-first-century students raised on Twitter need a faster pace and different kinds of text. I say language arts classrooms may be the last place where young people can unplug themselves from the solipsism of Facebook postings and enter a milieu different from their own. "But my students won't do the homework reading I assign," teachers wail. It isn't as though students don't have the time. A 2010 study by the Kaiser Family Foundation reports that children aged eight to eighteen spend an average of seven and a half hours daily "consuming entertainment media."[4] And this does not include the hour and a half a day they spend texting friends. Today's students have the time to read; many of them simply choose not to.

To those who look at the suggested works for the high school Common Core Curriculum Maps and think, "Our students could never read those books," I urge perusal of the primary grade curriculum maps. If children were immersed in rich literature and nonfiction from the first days of kindergarten and engaged in classroom conversations that encouraged them to think deeply about what they read, then negotiating Ralph Ellison's *Invisible Man* in eleventh grade and Jane Austen's *Sense and Sensibility* in twelfth is certainly possible. Though such books pose textual challenges for young readers, as part of a continuum and under the tutelage of an "able Master," the work is achievable. In our effort to provide students with readings that they can relate to, we sometimes end up teaching works that students can read on their own at the expense of teaching more worthwhile texts that they most certainly need assistance negotiating.

We need to remind ourselves that curriculum should be aimed at what Lev Vygotsky calls students' zone of proximal development. Writing in 1962, Vygotsky said, "the only good kind of instruction is that which marches ahead of development and leads it."[5] Classroom texts should pose intellectual challenges for readers and invite them to stretch and grow. Students also need books that feed their personal interests and allow them to explore "the road not taken." Reading a broad range of books makes students stronger readers and, over time, stronger people. Rigor versus relevance doesn't need to be an

---

[3] Ibid., 94.

[4] Ulla G. Foehr, Victoria J. Rideout, and Donald F. Roberts, "Generation M²: Media in the Lives of 8- to 18-Year-Olds," (Menlo Park, CA: Kaiser Family Foundation, January 2010), http://www.kff.org/entmedia/8010.cfm.

[5] Lev Vygotsky, *Thought and Language*, trans. Eugenia Hanfmann and Gertrude Vakar (Cambridge, MA: MIT Press, 1962), 104.

either-or proposition. With artful instruction by able masters, students can acquire the literacy skills they need—not only to meet the Common Core State Standards, but also to meet the challenges this brave new world is sure to deal them.

Reading literature also helps students explore hypothetical scenarios and consider the ramifications of what might prima facie seem to be a good or profitable idea. Consider the Common Core Curriculum Maps' final Grade Seven unit, Literature Reflects Life: Making Sense of Our World. Addressing Common Core Reading Standard RL.7.6, "Analyze how an author develops and contrasts the points of view of different characters or narrators in a text," the map recommends students read Robert Louis Stevenson's *The Strange Case of Dr. Jekyll and Mr. Hyde*. This nineteenth-century novella invites young readers to reflect upon their own conflicting natures and offers a cautionary tale regarding experimentation. When we consider how best to prepare tomorrow's doctors, scientists, programmers, and engineers for the twenty-first century, it seems to me that reading stories about investigations that go very wrong is quite a good idea.

Later in his sermon, Cotton Mather states that "the Devil cannot give a greater Blow to the Reformation among us, than by causing Schools to Languish under Discouragements." The Common Core Curriculum Maps offer hope to discouraged teachers. They offer a plan for developing young minds, a plan that is both rigorous and has never been more relevant. It may seem odd to be taking guidance from a seventeenth-century Puritan, but I know I couldn't say it better. "Where schools are not vigorously and Honourably Encouraged, whole Colonies will sink apace into a Degenerate and Contemptible Condition, and at last become horribly Barbarous. If you would not betray your Posterity into the very Circumstances of Savages, let Schools have more Encouragement." Amen.

WRITTEN BY TEACHERS, FOR TEACHERS

To my fellow teachers:

The development of these curriculum Maps has enlivened my professional life and rekindled my interest in teaching in remarkable ways. As you well know, developing curriculum is far from easy: it is a never-ending, iterative, and sometimes frustrating process. It can be joyful, though, when you collaborate with wise and cheerful colleagues who only want the best for students. If you are also free to select only the finest literature and literary nonfiction, developing curriculum becomes an inspirational assignment. Finally, if you are open to new technologies, creating a content-rich ELA curriculum is great fun. Technology allows us to consider provocative ways for students to experience and convey their appreciation for classic and contemporary literature and nonfiction; it also offers amazing new ways for students to create and share their original work. We had the liberty to do all these things.

After wrestling with various formats and levels of detail, we have struck what we think is a helpful balance for you in these curriculum Maps, which are designed to jumpstart your own implementation of the CCSS. By providing suggested texts and sample activities, we offer guidance but not prescription. We also provide links to a variety of related and background materials for the thematic units—so you don't have to spend so much time doing that research independently. Links to interviews with authors and footage of poets reading their poetry are among the many embellishments we offer to make your job easier. We also reference related works of visual art, music, and film to help you enhance teaching and learning in your classrooms.

I am profoundly grateful for the definitive contributions of my fellow high school Map drafters. Diana Senechal laid the groundwork for the grade 10 and 12 Maps, which focus on world and European literature. She provided terrific guidance about great works (both old and new) from other countries and cultures, some of which may be new to teachers, but which will no doubt enthuse teachers and students alike. Carol Jago, Melissa Mejias, Leslie Skelton, and Ruthie Stern all provided essential critiques and helped shape the core of many of the units. My colleagues who worked on the elementary and middle school Maps, Lorraine Griffiths and Cyndi Wells, offered much-needed perspective and inspiration, particularly on the inclusion of digital resources and differentiation.

What an amazing learning experience this has been, and I firmly believe that in order to be great teachers, we must be eager students! We hope you will share your experiences with us as you use the Maps so we may continue to refine them over time.

Sheila Byrd Carmichael
Education Policy Consultant
Project Coordinator and Writer, Grades 9–12, Common Core Curriculum Maps in ELA

To My Fellow Teachers:

For years we have been deluged with reform initiatives from on high that claimed they would improve student achievement. Few have actually brought progress. I joined the Common Core team of teachers out of conviction that the Common Core State Standards (CCSS) would make a difference and have a positive impact on our work in the classroom. The standards provide a framework for composing a rich, well-planned curriculum that guides our instruction.

Classroom teachers know that imaginative planning is at the heart of any successful lesson. The seventy-six Sample Lesson Plans (SLP), one for each of the units, are instructional road maps. The purpose of each SLP is to demonstrate how to create the necessary link between the literary and informational texts and the CCSS. The SLPs vary in focus and content—from a novel or selection of poems to a play or informational text. Each has a clear topic, a set of objectives, and suggested activities, as well as helpful guides for differentiated instruction. Consider these plans as a place to start. Use them directly or as a model for developing your own lessons.

Writing the maps and the SLPs has been both intellectually rewarding and joyful to us as classroom teachers. I hope you find that working with these volumes becomes equally joyful and useful in your own classrooms.

Dr. Ruthie Stern
High school teacher, New York City
Lead writer, Sample Lesson Plans, Common Core Curriculum Maps in ELA

INTRODUCTION

Few educators or policymakers would have guessed, even a year or so ago, that nearly all states would jettison their standards and embrace new, largely uniform standards for the teaching of ELA and math. Fewer still would have expected all of this to happen as quickly as it has.

The rapid rise of the Common Core State Standards (CCSS) is an unprecedented event at the national level—and more importantly, at the school level, where its implications are profound. For educators in most states, the CCSS raise the bar for what students should know and be able to do.[1] If you are reading this, you are probably responsible for implementing the CCSS in your school, district, or state. You will find that the CCSS contain explicit guidance about the reading, writing, speaking, listening, and language skills students are expected to master. Almost any single standard in the CCSS illustrates this. Here's one of the reading standards from seventh grade:

> Determine two or more central ideas in a text and analyze their development over the course of the text; provide an objective summary of the text. (RI.7.2)

The CCSS call for the new standards to be taught within the context of a "content-rich curriculum." But the CCSS do not specify what content students need to master, as this fell outside the scope of the standards-setting project. Here is how this is explained in the introduction to the CCSS:

> [W]hile the Standards make references to some particular forms of content, including mythology, foundational U.S. documents, and Shakespeare, they do not—indeed, cannot—enumerate all or even most of the content that students should learn. The Standards must therefore be complemented by a well-developed, content-rich curriculum consistent with the expectations laid out in this document.[2]

Responsibility for developing such a curriculum falls to schools, districts, and states. Common Core's Curriculum Maps in ELA are designed to meet the needs of the teacher, principal, curriculum director, superintendent, or state official who is striving to develop, or to help teachers to develop, new ELA curricula aligned with the CCSS. The Maps can also

---

1. Sheila Byrd Carmichael, Gabrielle Martino, Kathleen Porter-Magee, and W. Stephen Wilson, "The State of State Standards—and the Common Core—in 2010" (Washington, DC: Thomas B. Fordham Institute, July 2010), 13.

2. *Common Core State Standards for English Language Arts & Literacy in History/Social Studies, Science, and Technical Subjects* (Washington, DC: Common Core State Standards Initiative), 6.

serve as a resource for those endeavoring to conduct professional development related to the standards.

The Maps provide a coherent sequence of thematic curriculum units, roughly six per grade level, K–12. The units connect the skills outlined in the CCSS in ELA with suggested works of literature and informational texts and provide activities teachers could use in their classrooms. You will also find suggested student objectives in each unit, along with lists of relevant terminology and links to high quality additional resources. *Every standard in the CCSS is covered in the Maps*, most more than once. Standards citations are included after each sample activity/assessment to indicate alignment. Each grade includes a "standards checklist" showing which standards are covered in which unit. And most of the works the CCSS lists as "exemplar texts" are included in the Maps.

Moreover, each unit in this print edition of the Maps features a Sample Lesson Plan, a road map showing how to use one or more of the suggested texts in that unit to meet specific standards. Each Sample Lesson Plan includes step-by-step guidance for classroom activities tied to the lesson, questions that engage students in a deeper analysis and appreciation of the texts, and even suggestions for differentiated instruction. Many of the Sample Lesson Plans, particularly in the earlier grades, also include detailed guidance for connecting ELA lessons to other subjects, including math, science, history, geography, music, and art.

An important feature of Common Core's curriculum Maps is their attention to building students' background knowledge of a diverse array of events, people, places, and ideas. Cognitive science has demonstrated that students read better if they know something about the subject they are studying.[3] With this in mind, Common Core incorporated into its Maps themes, texts, and activities that teach students about "The Great Big World," as one of the kindergarten Maps is called. The content cloud shown in Figure I.1 includes much of the key content knowledge in the Maps. The larger an event, name, or idea appears in the cloud, the more emphasis it receives in the Maps. As you examine this cloud, do keep in mind that the Maps contain much that is not included here.

Figure I.1

Common Core's Maps were written by teachers for teachers. More than three dozen public school teachers had a hand in drafting, writing, reviewing, or revising the Maps. Collectively, these teachers

3. Daniel T. Willingham, *Why Don't Students Like School? A Cognitive Scientist Answers Questions About How the Mind Works and What It Means for the Classroom* (San Francisco: Jossey-Bass, 2009).

brought dozens of years of experience to the mapping project. Each of the lead writers is deeply knowledgeable about the CCSS; some even served as feedback providers to the standards' writers. These teachers looked to model curricula, including the International Baccalaureate, and at excellent, content-specific standards, such as the Massachusetts English Language Arts Curriculum Frameworks, for suggestions of what topics and titles to include at each grade. Most importantly, the teachers drew on their own considerable experience of what students enjoy learning about, and infused the Maps with that knowledge.

The Maps also reflect the contributions and perspective of the many teachers who reviewed them. Twice, the American Federation of Teachers convened the same panel of teachers that reviewed the CCSS to review Common Core's Maps. The Milken Family Foundation connected us with a dozen winners of the Milken Educator Award. These teachers, nationally recognized for excellence in the classroom, provided invaluable input and insight. And the National Alliance of Black School Educators identified superintendents, teachers, and content area specialists from across the country who reviewed the Maps in draft form. A public review of our draft Maps, conducted in the fall of 2010, elicited numerous helpful comments.

And the Maps will continue to evolve and improve. The second online edition of the Maps is open to public comment twenty-four hours a day, seven days a week. Anyone is able to critique any aspect of the Maps—any essential question, any student objective, any text suggestion. Viewers can rate each unit Map as a whole, and many other Map elements, such as suggested works and sample activities. Comments on the Maps are open for public view. Also, teachers can submit sample lesson plans that will be reviewed by a committee of teachers who will decide which ones to add to the official Maps website. In these ways and more, Common Core's Curriculum Maps in ELA are living documents, expanding and improving over time as they absorb and reflect the experience and perspective of educators across the nation.

We are thrilled that, as of this writing, the website featuring the maps (www.commoncore.org) has attracted more than three million visitors and that six state departments of education have recommended the Maps for use by districts statewide. The publication of the Maps is a momentous step for the mapping project. If you find this volume of interest we hope you will follow our project as we develop more inspiring and instrumental Maps-related resources for America's educators.

September 2011

Lynne Munson
President and Executive Director, Common Core

HOW TO USE THE COMMON CORE CURRICULUM MAPS

Common Core's Curriculum Maps in ELA are brand-new curriculum materials, built around the Common Core State Standards (CCSS) in English Language Arts. The CCSS dictated both the goals and contours of our Maps. The "exemplar texts" listed in the CCSS figure significantly in our unit Maps, which break down each grade, K–12, into a series of themed units. Each unit pairs standards with suggested student objectives, texts, activities, and more.

The Maps are intended to serve as "road maps" for the school year, as aids for jump-starting the lesson planning process. As common planning tools, these Maps can facilitate school and district-wide collaboration. They also can become the backbone of rich, content-based professional development as teachers work together to create and then refine curricula for their particular schools and classrooms.

The units are designed to be taught in sequence (particularly in elementary school), but teachers could certainly modify the units if they need to be taught in a different order. We do not expect teachers to use every text, nor to do every sample activity or assessment. The suggested texts simply offer a range of rich and relevant materials from which teachers may choose. The suggested activities or assessments are neither prescriptive nor exhaustive. Teachers can select from among them, modify them to meet their students' needs, and/or use them as inspiration for creating their own activities.

Each unit Map contains the following elements:

Overview. This is a brief description of the unit. It explains the unit's theme and provides a summary of what students will learn. It explains the structure, progression, and various components of the unit. It may offer some guidance regarding the selection of texts. The unit descriptions illuminate the connections between the skills identified in the standards and the content of the suggested works.

Essential question. The "essential question" highlights the usefulness, the relevance, and the greater benefit of a unit. It is often the "so what?" question about material covered. It should be answerable, at least to some degree, by the end of the unit, but it should also have more than one possible answer. It should prompt intellectual exploration by generating other questions. Here's an example from eighth grade: "How does learning history through literature differ from learning through informational text?"

Focus standards. These standards are taken directly from the CCSS and have been identified as especially important for the unit. Other standards are covered in each unit as well, but the focus standards are the ones that the unit has been designed to address specifically.

Suggested student objectives. These are the specific student outcomes for the unit. They describe the transferable ELA content and skills that students should possess when the unit is completed. The objectives are often components of more broadly worded standards and sometimes address content and skills necessarily related to the standards. The lists are not exhaustive, and the objectives should not supplant the standards themselves. Rather, they are designed to help teachers "drill down" from the standards and augment as necessary, providing added focus and clarity for lesson planning purposes.

Suggested works. These are substantial lists of suggested literary and informational texts. In most cases (particularly in the middle and high school grades), this list contains more texts than a unit could cover; it is meant to offer a range of options to teachers. Several permutations of the list could meet the goals of the unit. The suggested texts draw heavily from the "exemplar texts" listed in the CCSS. Exemplars are works the CCSS identified as meeting the levels of complexity and rigor described in the standards. These texts are identified with an (E) after the title of an exemplar text. An (EA) indicates a work by an author who has another work cited as an exemplar text.

Art, music, and media. These sections list works of visual art, music, film, and other media that reflect the theme of the unit and that a teacher can use to extend students' knowledge in these areas. Each unit includes at least one sample activity involving the works listed under this heading. ELA teachers who choose to use this material may do so on their own, by team teaching with an art or music teacher, or perhaps by sharing the material with the art or music teacher, who could reinforce what students are learning during the ELA block in their classroom. The inclusion of these works in our ELA Maps is *not* intended to substitute for or infringe in any way upon instruction that students should receive in separate art and music classes.

Sample activities and assessments. These items have been written particularly for the unit, with specific standards and often with specific texts in mind. Each activity addresses at least one standard in the CCSS; the applicable standard(s) are cited in parentheses following the description of each activity. The suggested activities or assessments are not intended to be prescriptive, exhaustive, or sequential; they simply demonstrate how specific content can be used to help students learn the skills described in the standards. They are designed to generate evidence of student understanding and give teachers ideas for developing their own activities and assessments. Teachers should use, refine, and/or augment these activities as desired, in order to ensure that they will have addressed all the standards intended for the unit and, in the aggregate, for the year.

Reading foundations. Our kindergarten through second-grade Maps include a section titled Reading Foundations that provides a pacing guide of instructional goals for the teaching of the CCSS reading Foundational Skills. This guide complements our Maps and was prepared by reading expert Louisa Moats, who also helped develop the reading standards for the CCSS.

Additional resources. These are links to lesson plans, activities, related background information, author interviews, and other instructional materials for teachers from a variety of resources, including the National Endowment for the Humanities and ReadWriteThink. The standards that could be addressed by each additional resource are cited at the end of each description.

Terminology. These are concepts and terms that students will encounter—often for the first time—over the course of the unit. The list is not comprehensive; it is meant to highlight terms that either are particular to the unit, are introduced there, or that play a large role in the work or content of the unit. These terms and concepts are usually implied by the standards, but not always made explicit in them.

Making interdisciplinary connections. This is a section included only in our Maps for the elementary grades. Here we very broadly list the content areas the unit covers and then suggest opportunities for making interdisciplinary connections from the Common Core ELA Maps to other subjects, including history, civics, geography, and the arts. We hope this section will be particularly helpful for K–5 teachers, who typically teach all subjects.

Sample lesson plans. Each unit includes a supplementary document that outlines a possible sequence of lessons, using one or more suggested unit texts to meet focus standards. Many of the texts used in the sample lesson plans are also CCSS exemplar texts. These sample lessons include guidance for differentiated instruction.

Standards checklist. Each grade includes a standards checklist that indicates which standards are covered in which unit—providing teachers an overview of standards coverage for the entire school year.

Addressing all of the CCSS. The curriculum writers worked carefully to ensure that the content and skills in each unit would build on one another so that in the aggregate, all standards would be addressed in a coherent, logical way. They grouped standards that they could envision fitting together in one unit. For example, if a unit were focused on asking and answering questions in informational text, then standards for shared research and expository writing were included in that unit as well. *All standards are addressed at least once,* if not a number of times, in the activities and assessments sections.

Interpreting CCSS citations. Our citations for the standards follow the format established by the CCSS (found in the upper right-hand corners of the pages in the CCSS ELA document):

strand.grade.number

For example, the first Reading Literature (RL) standard in grade four would be cited as RL.4.1. You will find our citations in the front of each focus standard and at the end of each sample activity/assessment. Where standards clearly corresponded to lessons listed under Additional Resources, standards also have been cited.

Understanding unit themes. The unit themes grew organically out of the process of selecting which standards would be the focus of each unit and consulting the list of exemplar texts. The teachers who wrote the Maps intentionally chose themes that would resonate with students, as well as lend coherence to the skills and content addressed. Some of the themes introduced in the early elementary grades, such as courage, re-emerge in later years. We have done so in a deliberate attempt to invite students to wrestle with some of the "great ideas," a hallmark of a liberal education. We hope that as students progress through school, they will consider the themes at greater levels of depth.

Teaching reading. Under the Reading Foundations sections for the kindergarten through second-grade Maps (and embedded into the third- through fifth-grade Maps) is a pacing guide for reading instruction. This guide is aligned with the CCSS reading Foundational Skills. The guide paces instruction in reading foundations logically across the grades. Concepts of print, phonological awareness, phonics, and text reading fluency are all addressed and woven into a developmental progression that leads to word recognition and text reading. Accomplishment of these milestones can be achieved with daily practice and brief activities that would require thirty to forty minutes of instructional time per day. A sample of those activities is also provided. Explicit, sequential, and cumulative teaching of these skills in no way should detract from, substitute for, or prevent the teaching of the oral language, comprehension, and literature-focused instruction, also described in the units.

The curriculum Maps are not tailored for any specific reading instruction method or management technique. *It is up to local school districts and teachers to determine how reading will be taught.* The sample activities and assessments reflect a mix of teacher- and student-centered instruction, but emphasize eliciting evidence of student understanding through authentic assessments.

Selecting materials. Many of the texts listed as exemplars in the CCSS Appendix B are included in our Maps. These texts take priority in our units and indeed shape unit themes. Like the exemplar texts themselves, the additional texts suggested in our Maps include literary works and informational texts that have stood the test of time, as well as excellent contemporary titles. The suggested texts include novels, short stories, poetry, essays, speeches, memoirs, biographies, autobiographies, fables, folktales, and mythology. Teachers will find texts written by authors of wide-ranging diversity: young and old, living and dead, male and female, American and foreign.

In the early grades, the Maps prioritize students' exposure to traditional stories and poetry, Mother Goose rhymes, and award-winning fiction and nonfiction chosen for quality of writing and relevance to themes. They also emphasize concepts of print, phonological awareness, phonics, and text reading fluency. In upper elementary and middle school grades, students read a variety of fiction and nonfiction on science and history topics, as well as diverse selections of classic and contemporary literature. High school begins by establishing in ninth grade a common understanding of literary and informational genres, subgenres, and their characteristics. Grades ten through twelve each focus on a different literary tradition, both American and international. Along the way, the Maps highlight numerous points of connection with history, science, and the arts.

Much consideration has been given to readability. Whenever possible, we have used Lexile level ranges, as described in the CCSS Appendix A, as a guide. We realize that there still will be a range of texts within each grade span. We also recognize that simple texts may be read at upper grades with more nuanced analysis. For this reason, some texts appear in more than one grade. Texts that fall outside the CCSS-recommended grade span are noted.

At the elementary and middle school levels, the text availability and readability levels also were cross-checked with the Scholastic Reading Wizard Reading Levels section, Amazon.com, and the Lexile levels (as available) on the Barnes & Noble website.

Evaluating student work. Aside from the inclusion of a scoring rubric for high school seminars, the Maps do not provide sample student work or scoring rubrics. We do hope that the interactivity feature of the online edition of the Maps may allow teachers to submit these kinds of materials, if they so desire. We expect to develop such additional tools as teachers and curriculum developers use and customize the Maps, and as we conduct ongoing professional development.

Differentiating instruction. The sample lesson plans provide specific guidance for differentiated instruction for advanced and struggling students. As with student work and scoring rubrics, we expect to develop further guidance on differentiation as the Maps are implemented and customized.

Incorporating art, music, and media. While literature is of course a vital component of the standards, some standards in the CCSS address the arts as well. Because Common Core promotes the importance of all students studying the arts, we have highlighted places where ELA instruction could be enhanced by connecting a work of literature or an objective of the unit to art, music, or film. For example, students might compare a novel, story, or play to its film or musical rendition. Where a particular period of literature or the literature of a particular region or country is addressed, works of art from that period or country may also be examined. We suggest, for example, that students study self-portraiture when they are encountering memoirs. In each case, connections are made to the standards themselves.

Promoting student understanding through recitation and memorization. Recitation requires close reading and therefore nurtures deeper levels of students' understanding. Students also benefit from the satisfaction of making a poem or piece of prose one's own for life. In addition, many teachers observe that memorization and recitation help develop a student's experience and confidence in public speaking, which could help students marshal evidence and make effective arguments in other contexts. Keep in mind that our suggestions for memorization activities are not meant to be mandatory in every unit.

GRADE 9

Students who have followed the curriculum Maps for grades K–8 will enter ninth grade with a foundation in fiction, drama, poetry, mythology, and literary nonfiction. In addition, they will have begun to analyze literature from various angles, to view literature in historical context, and to observe connections between literature and the arts. The ninth-grade course is an overview of excellent literature across the major forms and genres (short story, novel, poetry, drama, epic poetry, and literary nonfiction). Each unit focuses on a genre and a related theme: for instance, drama and fate. In their essays, students might compare the use of symbolism in a short story and a painting, or examine the role of free will in a certain play. They begin to read and respond to literary criticism. For instance, they might write about how two works reflect the thesis of William Faulkner's Nobel Prize acceptance speech. In formal seminar discussions, students further investigate philosophical and literary questions that arise in the texts. For example, in the unit on the novel, a seminar question asks whether Boo Radley (of *To Kill a Mockingbird)* is an honorable man. In addition to discussing and writing about works, students memorize poems and excerpts of speeches and learn to deliver them with expression. By the end of ninth grade, students are prepared for focused literary study: world literature in tenth grade, American literature in eleventh grade, and European literature in twelfth.

Standards Checklist for Grade Nine

Standard	Unit 1	Unit 2	Unit 3	Unit 4	Unit 5	Unit 6	Standard	Unit 1	Unit 2	Unit 3	Unit 4	Unit 5	Unit 6
Reading—Literature							3d						
1	FA	A		A			3e						
2		A	FA		A	FA	A					
3		A	FA	A	FA	FA	4						
4		A	A	FA	A		F	5						
5	FA	A	A	FA	A		6						
6				A		A	7	A		A			
7		A	A	A	A	A	8	A		FA			
8 n/a							9					F	
9				A	F		9a						
10		A			A		A	9b					
Reading—Informational Text							10						
1	A			A	F		Speaking and Listening						
2		A	F				1	FA	A	A	FA	A	A
3			F			F	1a						
4			A				1b						
5			A			A	1c						
6			A				1d						
7		A			FA		2	FA	FA	A	A	A	A
8		A					3	A	A	A		FA	FA
9						FA	4	A	A	A	A	A	
10							5		A	FA	A		A
Writing							6	A	A	A	A	A	A
1					A	A	Language						
1a							1	F	FA	FA	F	FA	FA
1b							1a						
1c							1b				A		
1d							2	A	A	A	A	A	A
1e							2a						
2	FA	FA	A	FA	A	A	2b						
2a							3	A	A	FA	A		
2b							3a						
2c							4		F		A		A
2d							4a						
2e							4b						
2f							4c						
3			A		A	FA	4d						
3a							5	F			A		A
3b							5a						
3c							6				F		

F = Focus Standard; A = Activity/Assessment

Literary Elements and the Short Story

This unit, the first of six, uses the short story as the vehicle for reviewing common literary elements, as well as for appreciating the art of great storytelling.

ESSENTIAL QUESTION

? Why do we tell stories?

OVERVIEW

This unit enables students to confirm and hone a common understanding of important literary elements, as well as a shared vocabulary for discussing them. Each story may be used to focus especially on a particular element, such as point of view in "The Cask of Amontillado" by Edgar Allan Poe or symbolism in "The Scarlet Ibis" by James Hurst. Teachers should choose stories that exemplify great storytelling and that they think are best for their students. The range of suggested works provides exposure to literature from a variety of cultures.

FOCUS STANDARDS

These Focus Standards have been selected for the unit from the Common Core State Standards.

RL.9–10.1: Cite strong and thorough textual evidence to support analysis of what the text says explicitly as well as inferences drawn from the text.

RL.9–10.5: Analyze how an author's choices concerning how to structure a text, order events within it (e.g., parallel plots), and manipulate time (e.g., pacing, flashbacks) create such effects as mystery, tension, or surprise.

W.9–10.2: Write informative/explanatory texts to examine and convey complex ideas, concepts, and information clearly and accurately through the effective selection, organization, and analysis of content.

SL.9–10.1: Initiate and participate effectively in a range of collaborative discussions (one-on-one, in groups, and teacher-led) with diverse partners on grades 9–10 topics, texts, and issues, building on others' ideas and expressing their own clearly and persuasively.

L.9–10.1: Demonstrate command of the conventions of Standard English grammar and usage when writing or speaking.

L.9–10.5: Demonstrate understanding of figurative language, word relationships, and nuances in word meanings.

SUGGESTED STUDENT OBJECTIVES

- Identify and explain plot structure (i.e., exposition, rising action, crisis/climax, falling action, resolution/denouement) in short stories.
- Understand and explain why plots in short stories usually focus on a single event.
- Analyze how authors create the setting in a short story.
- Define the concept of theme and identify the theme(s) in stories read.
- Identify and explain characterization techniques in short stories.
- Identify and explain the use of figurative language in short stories.
- Analyze how authors create tone in short stories.
- Identify the point of view in a short story and analyze how point of view affects the reader's interpretation of the story.
- Write a coherent essay of literary analysis with a clear thesis statement, at least three pieces of evidence from texts, and a strong introduction and conclusion.
- Define and refine research questions; cite sources accurately, distinguishing between paraphrasing and quoting.

SUGGESTED WORKS

(E) indicates a CCSS exemplar text; (EA) indicates a text from a writer with other works identified as exemplars.

LITERARY TEXTS

Short Stories

- "The Gift of the Magi" (O. Henry) (E)
- "The Overcoat" (Nikolai Gogol) (EA)
- "The Most Dangerous Game" (Richard Connell)
- "The Kitchen Boy" (Alaa Al Aswany)
- "The Secret Life of Walter Mitty" (James Thurber) (EA)
- "The Cask of Amontillado" (Edgar Allan Poe) (EA)
- "The Black Cat" (Edgar Allan Poe) (EA)
- "The Tell-Tale Heart" (Edgar Allan Poe) (EA)
- "The Scarlet Ibis" (James Hurst)
- "Everyday Use" (Alice Walker) (EA)
- "The Minister's Black Veil" (Nathaniel Hawthorne) (EA)
- "How Much Land Does a Man Need?" (Leo Tolstoy)
- *Points of View: An Anthology of Short Stories* (James Moffett and Kenneth L. McElheny, eds.) (1968 edition)
- *Drinking Coffee Elsewhere: Stories* (ZZ Packer)

INFORMATIONAL TEXTS

None for this unit

ART, MUSIC, AND MEDIA

Art

- Michelangelo, *The Creation of Adam*, Sistine Chapel (c. 1511)
- Sultan Muhammad, *From a Khamsa of Nizamia* (1539 – 1543)
- Jacob Lawrence, *On The Way* (1990)
- Emanuel Leutze, *Washington Crossing the Delaware* (1851)
- Pablo Picasso, *Young Acrobat on a Ball* (1905)
- Tina Barney, *Marina's Room* (1987)
- Roy DeCarava, *Untitled* (1950)

Music and Lyrics

- "Clothesline Saga" (Bob Dylan)
- "Me and Bobby McGee" (Kris Kristofferson and Fred Foster)
- "Peter and The Wolf" (Sergei Prokofiev)
- "The Bonnie Lass o' Fyvie" ("Peggy-O")
- "Variations on an Original Theme ('Enigma')" (Edward Elgar)

Film

- Ken Burns, dir., *Brooklyn Bridge* (1981)
- Ang Lee, dir., "Chosen" (2001) (and other BMW short films)
- Martin Scorsese, dir., *No Direction Home* (2005)

SAMPLE ACTIVITIES AND ASSESSMENTS

For a full Scoring Rubric, see the Appendix.

Note: Textual evidence should be used to support all arguments advanced in seminars and in all essays. Page and word counts for essays are not provided, but attention should be paid to the requirements regarding the use of evidence, for example, to determine the likely length of good essays.

1. INFORMATIVE/EXPLANATORY WRITING

Select a short story and write an essay that analyzes how a particular literary element plays a part in the essence and workings of one of the chosen stories. State your thesis clearly and include at least three pieces of evidence to support it. Your teacher may give you the opportunity to write your first draft on a shared online document and receive feedback from classmates before publication. (RL.9 – 10.1, W.9 – 10.2)

2. ART/CLASS DISCUSSION

How do artists create narratives? Select two works of art to view as a class. Compare the two works, focusing the discussion on the relationship between character and setting, and on how the artists combined these to suggest a narrative. (SL.9 – 10.1, SL.9 – 10.2)

3. ART AND INFORMATIVE/EXPLANATORY WRITING

Select a short story and an artwork and write an essay in which you discuss the use of symbolism in each. State your thesis clearly and include at least three pieces of evidence to support it. An optional extension is to create a digital slide presentation in which you set up a visual comparison between the two works. (RL.9–10.4, W.9–10.2, SL.9–10.6)

4. INFORMATIVE/EXPLANATORY WRITING

Discuss the "slow motion" depiction of the murder in Poe's "The Tell-Tale Heart" and consider how Poe's craft affects the relationship between the narrator and his victim. State your thesis clearly and include at least three pieces of evidence to support it. (RL.9–10.4, W.9–10.2)

5. SPEECH

Select a one-minute passage from one of the short stories and recite it from memory. Include an introduction that states:

- What the excerpt is from
- Who wrote it
- Which literary element it exemplifies and why (RL.9–10.2, SL.9–10.6)

   Record your recitation using a video camera so you can evaluate your performance for accuracy.

6. SEMINAR QUESTION AND WRITING (ARGUMENT)

Is Montresor (from Poe's "The Cask of Amontillado") a reliable narrator? Cite at least three reasons to support your argument. The seminar question may also be used as an essay topic. Your teacher may give you the opportunity to share your initial thoughts on the classroom blog in order to get feedback from your classmates. (RL.9–10.2, RL.9–10.3, SL.9–10.1, SL.9–10.3, SL.9–10.4, SL.9–10.6)

7. RESEARCH AND INFORMATIVE/EXPLANATORY WRITING

Select one of the authors from the short story unit and conduct an author study. Begin by defining a research question and refine it as necessary. The research should include an autobiographical or biographical text, another story by the same author, and/or a critical essay that addresses a specific aspect of the author's style. Include at least three references to the author's work and to other sources. Cite sources carefully and distinguish clearly between paraphrasing and quoting. (RL.9–10.1, RI.9–10.1, W.9–10.2, W.9–10.7, W.9–10.8)

8. GRAMMAR AND USAGE

Parts of Speech Review

Verbs: principal parts of verbs, especially irregular past and past participles; simple, perfect, and progressive tenses; agreement of subject and verb, especially with collective nouns
Nouns: common, proper, concrete, abstract, countable, collective, compound, possessive, gerunds

   Select a paragraph from the novel and identify all the verbs. Name the tense of each verb you find. (L.9–10.3)
   Look at a photograph, painting, or magazine advertisement for at least three minutes. On a piece of paper, draw two intersecting lines to make four squares (one for each category: people, places, things, and ideas). In each square, list the nouns by category that you see in the image. Note whether they are abstract or concrete nouns. (L.9–10.3)

9. MECHANICS

Capitalization of Common and Proper Nouns

Identify the nouns in Activity 8 and determine whether they are common or proper nouns; capitalize them if necessary. (L.9–10.2)

ADDITIONAL RESOURCES

- *Analyzing Irony and Symbolism in a Short Story* (Louisiana Department of Education) (RL.9–10.4, RL.9–10.5)
- Lesson Plans for "The Scarlet Ibis" (WebEnglishTeacher) (RL.9–10.2)
- "The Minister's Black Veil" Study Questions (Mr. Burnett's Classroom) (RL.9–10.1, RL.9–10.2, RL.9–10.3)

TERMINOLOGY

Character, characterization

Figurative language

Irony (e.g., dramatic, situational, verbal)

Narrator

Parable

Plot (i.e., exposition, rising action, crisis/climax, falling action, resolution/denoument)

Point of view

Sensory imagery

Setting

Style

Symbol, symbolism

Theme

Tone

Grade Nine, Unit One Sample Lesson Plan

"The Gift of the Magi" by O. Henry

In this series of three lessons, students read "The Gift of the Magi" by O. Henry, and they:

Perform a close reading of "The Gift of the Magi" (RL.9-10.1, RL.9-10.3, RL.9-10.4, RL.9-10.5, L.9-10.5)

Examine the elements of the short story (RL.9-10.1, RL.9-10.3, RL.9-10.4, RL.9-10.5, SL.9-10.1)

Explore the themes of "The Gift of the Magi" (RL.9-10.2, W.9-10.1, SL.9-10.1)

Summary

Lesson I: "The Gift of the Magi": A Close Reading

Annotate "The Gift of the Magi" for literary style (RL.9-10.1, RL.9-10.4, RL.9-10.5)

Note:

Narrator's voice

Use of humor

Presence and purpose of alliterations

Repetitions

Colors (RL.9-10.1, RL.9-10.4, RL.9-10.5, L.9-10.5)

Review annotations (RL.9-10.1, RL.9-10.4, RL.9-10.5, SL.9-10.1, SL.9-10.3)

Lesson II: The Elements of the Short Story

Incorporate annotations while revisiting the plot of "The Gift of the Magi" (RL.9-10.1, RL.9-10.3, RL.9-10.4, RL.9-10.5, SL.9-10.1, SL.9-10.3)

Note the setting of the story (RL.9-10.1)

Explore the development of the conflict in the story (RL.9-10.1, RL.9-10.5, SL.9-10.1)

Examine O. Henry's depiction of the relationship between Della and Jim (RL.9-10.1, RL.9-10.3, SL.9-10.1)

Lesson III: Themes in "The Gift of the Magi"

Identify the source of the title of the story (RL.9-10.9)

Probe the nature of the couple's gifts (RL.9-10.1, RL.9-10.2, RL.9-10.3, SL.9-10.1)

Explore the purpose of the final paragraph of the story (RL.9-10.1, RL.9-10.9, SL.9-10.1)

Examine the claim by William Saroyan that O. Henry "cleverly … told his story, concealing behind laughing language a profcund love for the great masses of people who are frequently called the little people" (RL.9-10.1, RL.9-10.2, W.9-10.1, SL.9-10.1)

Lesson I: "The Gift of the Magi": A Close Reading

Objectives

Annotate "The Gift of the Magi" for literary style (RL.9-10.1, RL.9-10.4, RL.9-10.5)

Note:

- Narrator's voice
- Use of humor
- Presence and purpose of alliterations
- Repetitions
- Colors (RL.9-10.1, RL.9-10.4, RL.9-10.5, L.9-10.5)

Review annotations (RL.9-10.1, RL.9-10.4, RL.9-10.5, SL.9-10.1, SL.9-10.3)

Required Materials

☐ Class set of "The Gift of the Magi" by O. Henry

Procedures

1. Lead-In:
Students examine annotation guidelines (teachers can use interactive whiteboards, overhead projectors, etc.).

"There was clearly nothing to do but flop down on the shabby little couch and howl. So

humor alliteration

Della did it. Which instigates the moral reflection that life is made up of <u>sobs</u>, <u>sniffles</u>, <u>and smiles</u>, with <u>sniffles</u> predominating." [*What is the narrator's attitude here?*]

"Della finished her cry and attended to her cheeks with the powder rag. She stood by the [*Investigate the use of gray — set up to paragraph?*]
window and looked out dully at a <u>gray</u> fence in a <u>gray</u> backyard."

[metaphor interesting view]

"Oh, and the next two hours tripped <u>by on rosy wings</u>. Forget the hashed metaphor. She was ransacking the stores for Jim's present." [*Narrator is critical of his own metaphor — what does that do?*]

2. Step by Step:
   a. Students, individually or in pairs, annotate "The Gift of the Magi" for:
      - Narrator's voice
      - Use of humor
      - Presence and purpose of alliterations
      - Repetitions
      - Colors
   b. The class discussion that follows closely reflects the students' annotations.
   c. During the class discussion, the students continue to take notes and annotate the story.

3. Closure:
   Remind the students to reread "The Gift of the Magi" in preparation for further discussion.

Differentiation

Advanced

- Select student volunteers to practice reading sections aloud prior to this lesson, or while other students are still working on annotations. The students should practice reading dramatically, recorded with a video camera, so they can evaluate and improve their performances. Students should also research what inspired O. Henry to write "The Gift of the Magi" and present this information as a podcast or an online poster.

- Encourage students to research O. Henry and prepare a biography of his life for classmates.

- Allow students to choose another short story by O. Henry to annotate, and compare and contrast it with "The Gift of the Magi."

- Encourage students to create a modern-day interpretation of the short story. They must be able to justify how the modern version stays true to the original intent of the story, while also changing its style. Perhaps challenge them to create a movie presentation of their modern-day interpretation.

Struggling

- Read/reread the short story to students, and allow them to listen to a pre-recorded version on an MP3 player.
- Be prepared with a list of guiding questions to support students in their annotations (e.g., How do we distinguish the narrator's voice? Where do you think he is using humor or other literary devices?). Students can mark their story with sticky notes prior to class discussion. Alternatively, have the elements you want annotated underlined on the story and have students explain the underlining.
- Give students a worksheet of the story to write on during class discussion, possibly even with sketches (or other nonlinguistic representations) to help aid memory and understanding. Alternatively, allow them to annotate in a text document.

Homework/Assessment
Reread "The Gift of the Magi."

Grade 9 ▶ Unit 2

The Novel—Honor

This unit, the second of six, focuses on the novel as a literary form and explores the unifying theme of honor in the classic American novel *To Kill a Mockingbird*.

OVERVIEW

Students apply the knowledge of literary elements explored in the short story unit to a new literary form—the novel. They discuss the similarities and differences between how those elements are developed in short stories and in novels. Setting and characterization are highlighted, with particular attention paid to the question of which characters in *To Kill a Mockingbird* may be called honorable. Informational texts illuminate the historical context of the Great Depression and the Jim Crow South.

FOCUS STANDARDS

These Focus Standards have been selected for the unit from the Common Core State Standards.

RL.9–10.2: Determine a theme or central idea of a text and analyze in detail its development over the course of the text, including how it emerges and is shaped and refined by specific details; provide an objective summary of the text.

RL.9–10.3: Analyze how complex characters (e.g., those with multiple or conflicting motivations) develop over the course of a text, interact with other characters, and advance the plot or develop the theme.

RI.9–10.3: Analyze how the author unfolds an analysis or series of ideas or events, including the order in which the points are made, how they are introduced and developed, and the connections that are drawn between them.

W.9–10.2: Write informative/explanatory texts to examine and convey complex ideas, concepts, and information clearly and accurately through the effective selection, organization, and analysis of content.

SL.9–10.2: Integrate multiple sources of information presented in diverse media or formats (e.g., visually, quantitatively, orally), evaluating the credibility and accuracy of each source.

L.9–10.1: Demonstrate command of the conventions of Standard English grammar and usage when writing or speaking.

L.9–10.4: Determine or clarify the meaning of unknown and multiple-meaning words and phrases based on grades 9–10 reading and content, choosing flexibly from a range of strategies.

SUGGESTED STUDENT OBJECTIVES

- Learn about the history of the novel as a literary form.
- Recognize the importance of historical context to the appreciation of setting and character.
- Identify major and minor characters.
- Analyze and explain characterization techniques for major and minor characters.
- Explain that novels may have more than one plot and explain the use of multiple plots (e.g., in *To Kill a Mockingbird*).
- Recognize the importance of point of view in a novel (e.g., in *To Kill a Mockingbird*) and why it wouldn't be the same story told from someone else's point of view.

SUGGESTED WORKS

(E) indicates a CCSS exemplar text; (EA) indicates a text from a writer with other works identified as exemplars.

LITERARY TEXTS

Note: Alternatives to *To Kill a Mockingbird* are provided. The theme of honor could be considered in any of the texts listed here.

Novels
- *To Kill a Mockingbird* (Harper Lee) (E)

Alternative Selections
- *The Killer Angels* (Michael Shaara) (E)
- *All Quiet on the Western Front* (Erich Maria Remarque)
- *The Color Purple* (Alice Walker) (EA)
- *Of Mice and Men* (John Steinbeck) (EA)
- *Black Boy* (Richard Wright) (E) *Note:* This is an exemplar text in grades 11 and 12.

INFORMATIONAL TEXTS
- *Brother, Can You Spare a Dime? The Great Depression of 1929–1933* (Milton Meltzer)
- *Only Yesterday* (Frederick Lewis Allen) (excerpts, e.g., Chapters XII through XIV)
- First Inaugural Speech, March 4, 1933 (Franklin D. Roosevelt)

Memoir/Essay (to accompany *The Color Purple*)
- "In Search of Our Mothers' Gardens" (Alice Walker) (EA)

ART, MUSIC, AND MEDIA

Art

- Selected photographs by Dorothea Lange, taken for the Farm Security Administration during the Great Depression (Library of Congress)
- "America from the Great Depression to World War II: Photographs from the FSA-OWI, 1935 – 1945" (Library of Congress)

Film

- Robert Mulligan, dir., *To Kill a Mockingbird* (1962)

SAMPLE ACTIVITIES AND ASSESSMENTS

For a full Scoring Rubric, see the Appendix.

Note: Textual evidence should be used to support all arguments advanced in seminars and in all essays. Page and word counts for essays are not provided here, but attention should be paid to the requirements regarding the use of evidence, for example, to determine the likely length of good essays.

1. INFORMATIVE/EXPLANATORY WRITING

Select a quotation from one of the characters in *To Kill a Mockingbird* (or other novel, if applicable) and write an informative/explanatory essay that explains what the quotation reveals about the theme of honor in the book. State your thesis clearly and include at least three pieces of evidence to support it. Your teacher may give you the opportunity to post your first draft on a shared online document and receive feedback from classmates before publication. (RL.9 – 10.1, RL.9 – 10.2, RL.9 – 10.3)

2. INFORMATIVE/EXPLANATORY WRITING

Write an informative/explanatory essay that compares primary source accounts of the Scottsboro Boys trials with Scout's account of the trial in *To Kill a Mockingbird*. Discuss how novels can reveal dimensions of history even though they are fictional. State your thesis clearly and include at least three pieces of evidence to support it. Your teacher may give you the option of adding a multimedia component to your paper, such as a digital slide presentation that highlights the paper's essential points. (RL.9 – 10.1, RI.9 – 10.7, W.9 – 10.2, SL.9 – 10.6)

3. ART/INFORMATIVE/EXPLANATORY WRITING

Select a documentary photograph from the Library of Congress's Farm Security Administration-Office of War Information Collection (FSA-OWI) website. In a well-developed essay, explain how the image helps illuminate your understanding of life in the American South during the Depression. State your thesis clearly and include at least three pieces of evidence to support it. (RI.9 – 10.7, W.9 – 10.2)

4. SPEECH

Select a descriptive passage from *To Kill a Mockingbird* and recite it from memory. The passage should take one minute to recite. Include an introduction that states:

- The title and author of the book
- Why the book is significant
- How the passage exemplifies one of the book's themes (RL.9 – 10.2, SL.9 – 10.4)

5. SEMINAR QUESTION AND WRITING (ARGUMENT)

Is Boo Radley (from *To Kill a Mockingbird*) an honorable man? Begin by answering the question, "What is honor?" This seminar question may also be used as an essay topic. Be sure to include at least three reasons or illustrative examples from the text to support your thesis. Your teacher may give you the opportunity to share your initial thoughts on the classroom blog in order to get feedback from your classmates. (RL.9–10.2, SL.9–10.1, SL.9–10.4, SL.9–10.6)

6. SEMINAR QUESTION AND WRITING (ARGUMENT)

Is Atticus Finch a hero, or was he just doing his job? This seminar question may also be used as an essay topic. Be sure to include at least three reasons or illustrative examples from the text to support your thesis. Your teacher may give you the opportunity to share your initial thoughts on the classroom blog in order to get feedback from your classmates. (RL.9–10.2, SL.9–10.1, SL.9–10.4, SL.9–10.6)

7. SEMINAR QUESTION AND WRITING (ARGUMENT)

Is Scout a reliable narrator? Why or why not? This seminar question may also be used as an essay topic. Be sure to include at least three reasons or illustrative examples from the text to support your thesis. Your teacher may give you the opportunity to share your initial thoughts on the classroom blog in order to get feedback from your classmates. (RL.9–10.3, SL.9–10.1, SL.9–10.3)

8. ORAL PRESENTATION

Describe whether the 1962 film version of *To Kill a Mockingbird* is faithful to the novel. Cite evidence for why or why not, explaining why you think the film's director chose to omit or emphasize certain events. State your thesis clearly and include at least three pieces of evidence to support your thesis. (RL.9–10.7, SL.9–10.2, SL.9–10.4, SL.9–10.6)

9. ART/ORAL PRESENTATION (ARGUMENT)

Present several photographs of small southern towns during the Depression from Dorothea Lange's or the Library of Congress's collections and compare them to the description of Maycomb in *To Kill a Mockingbird*. Explain which rendering is more vivid to you and why. State your thesis clearly and include at least three pieces of evidence to support it. Your teacher may ask you to record your presentation as a podcast for publication on the class web page. (RL.9–10.4, SL.9–10.2, SL.9–10.5)

10. INFORMATIVE/EXPLANATORY WRITING

In "In Search of Our Mothers' Gardens," Alice Walker writes, "Guided by my heritage of a love of beauty and a respect for strength—in search of my mother's garden, I found my own." Write an informative/explanatory essay in which you answer the question, "How is *The Color Purple* a portrayal of Walker's search?" (RL.9–10.1, RL.9–10.2, RL.9–10.5, W.9–10.2)

11. GRAMMAR AND USAGE

Parts of Speech Review

Verbs: transitive and intransitive (action, linking), helping

Adjectives: including correct forms of irregular comparative and superlative adjectives; articles; nouns and pronouns used as adjectives; proper and compound adjectives

Adverbs: of place, time, manner, frequency, manner, duration, degree, reason; adverbs that modify adjectives; adverbs vs. adjectives (e.g., "fast"); regular and irregular comparative and superlative adverbs

Select three paragraphs from the novel. In one paragraph, highlight each verb and describe what kind of verb it is—transitive or intransitive. (If transitive, identify the direct object.) In the next paragraph, highlight each adjective and identify what type of adjective it is. In the third paragraph, highlight each adverb and identify what type it is. (L.9–10.1, L.9–10.3)

12. MECHANICS

Commas with Adjectives in a Series, Subordinate Clauses

Select a newspaper or magazine article and highlight all the commas that are used in a series or for subordinate clauses. (L.9–10.1, L.9–10.2)

ADDITIONAL RESOURCES

- Harper Lee's *To Kill a Mockingbird*: Profiles in Courage (National Endowment for the Humanities) (RL.9–10.2, RL.9–10.3)
- *To Kill a Mockingbird* and the Scottsboro Boys Trial: Profiles in Courage (National Endowment for the Humanities) (RI.9–10.7, RI.9–10.8)
- *The History of Jim Crow* (JimCrowHistory.org) (RI.9–10.2)
- St. Louis Federal Reserve Resources and References for The Great Depression
- Famous American Trials: "The Scottsboro Boys" Trials (1931–1937) (University of Missouri-Kansas School of Law) (*Note:* This website contains both primary and secondary source accounts of the trial.)
- American Life Histories: Manuscripts from Federal Writers Project (The Library of Congress)

TERMINOLOGY

Antagonist	Extended metaphor	Setting
Characterization	Motif	Theme
Characters: major and minor	Parallel plots	
Conflict	Protagonist	

Grade Nine, Unit Two Sample Lesson Plan

To Kill a Mockingbird by Harper Lee

In this series of seven lessons, students read *To Kill a Mockingbird* by Harper Lee, and they:

Assign titles for the book's chapters (RL.9-10.2, RL.9-10.10, SL.9-10.1)

Conduct a character study (RL.9-10.3, RL.9-10.4, RL.9-10.1, SL.9-10.4, L.9-10.5, L.9-10.3)

Explore how the character that was the focus of the study contributes to the reader's understanding of the complex relationships in the novel (RL.9-10.3, RL.9-10.4, SL.9-10.4, L.9-10.5)

Summary

<table>
<tr><td>

Lesson I: *To Kill a Mockingbird*

Explore the students' chapter titles (in preparation for the study of *To Kill a Mockingbird*, the students have read the novel and have assigned the chapters titles that reflect the chapters' content) (RL.9-10.2, RL.9-10.10, SL.9-10.1)

Recall the story of *To Kill a Mockingbird* (RL.9-10.1, RL.9-10.2, RL.9-10.3, SL.9-10.1, L.9-10.3)

</td><td>

Lesson II: Character Studies—The Beginning

Select a character to study (RL.9-10.3, SL.9-10.1)

Identify key components of character studies (RL.9-10.5, SL.9-10.1, W.9-10.7)

Skim the novel for appearances of the selected character (RL.9-10.1, RL.9-10.4, W.9-10.9a)

Annotate key passages that depict the components identified in the second objective of the lesson (RL.9-10.1, RL.9-10.2, RL.9-10.3, RL.9-10.4, SL.9-10.1, L.9-10.4)

</td></tr>
</table>

Lessons III, IV, V: Character Study*

In small groups, review annotations (RL.9-10.1, SL.9-10.4)

In small groups, explore new details about the selected characters (RL.9-10.1, RL.9-10.3, L.9-10.5)

As a class discussion, analyze the new information in the context of the events in the novel (RL.9-10.1, RL.9-10.3, L.9-10.5, SL.9-10.4, W.9-10.9a)

Continue to annotate (RL.9-10.1, RL.9-10.2, RL.9-10.3, RL.9-10.4, SL.9-10.1, L.9-10.4)

   *These three lessons should follow a similar format, while the students continue to identify new passages about the character that they research.

Lesson VI: Preparing to Write

Revisit notes (RL.9-10.1, SL.9-10.4)

Compose a working thesis[†] (W.9-10.4, SL.9-10.1)

Draft an outline for the essay[†] (W.9-10.5, SL.9-10.1, L.9-10.6)

   [†]In preparation for Lesson VII.

Lesson VII: The Characters of *To Kill a Mockingbird*

Compose an essay in response to the following prompt: How does Harper Lee's depiction of the character contribute to the reader's ability to evaluate the complex relationships in the novel? (W.9-10.2, W.9-10.5, SL.9-10.4, L.9-10.1, L.9-10.2, L.9-10.3, L.9-10.6)

Lesson II: Character Studies—The Beginning

Objectives

Select a character to study (RL.9-10.3, SL.9-10.1)

Identify key components of character studies (RL.9-10.5, SL.9-10.1, W.9-10.7)

Skim the novel for appearances of the selected character (RL.9-10.1, RL.9-10.4, W.9-10.9a)

Annotate key passages that depict the components that were identified in the second objective of the lesson (RL.9-10.1, RL.9-10.2, RL.9-10.3, RL.9-10.4, SL.9-10.1, L.9-10.4)

Required Materials

☐ Class set of *To Kill a Mockingbird* by Harper Lee

☐ Sticky notes

Procedures

1. Lead-In:

Instruct the students to conduct a close study of one of the characters from the novel. (You may choose to assign characters to the students.)

2. Step by Step:

a. Guide a class discussion investigating the ways that readers approach the study of a character in a novel. At the conclusion of the discussion, list (and if necessary, add missing details) the essential questions to ask when conducting a character study:

- Who is the character?
- What is his/her relationship to other characters in the novel?
- What does he/she look like?
- How does the character speak?
- What does the character say?
- How does the character act?
- What do other characters say about the character?
- How does the character's actions expose the rising tensions in the novel?

b. Either individually, or in small groups, students skim the novel. They use sticky notes to identify passages to read more closely.

c. Using sticky notes, students begin to annotate the novel for the questions that were identified in step a.

d. Students discuss their findings. This is an opportunity to point to successful annotations; this is also a good time to point to what may be missing.

3. Closure:

Inform the students that the next three lessons will follow a similar structure to the one they just had.

Differentiation

Advanced

- Select student volunteers to practice reading excerpts aloud prior to this lesson. The students should practice reading dramatically, recorded with a video camera, so they can evaluate and improve their performances.

- Students select two or three characters to study, compare, and contrast. As an extension, students create an online poster or other presentation of their characters.

- Allow students to create a web in an online program about a character. This web will require students to think more abstractly, since it is not about one character in particular, although they must be able to justify their thinking using examples from the text.

- Students create blogs from the point of view of the character(s) studied. For more details about introducing this idea, see ReadWriteThink's Creating Character Blogs.

Struggling

- Read/reread the select passages to students, and allow them to listen to a pre-recorded version.
- Encourage students to create character trading cards to help them identify the characters' traits.
- Assign characters to students and analyze. If needed, provide them page numbers on which to find information about their characters. Allow students to create a web in an online program about a character from the text. Students must be able to justify their thinking using examples from the text.
- Provide students with a graphic organizer of the questions listed in the lesson above. Perhaps allow students to type their answers on a shared spreadsheet to facilitate sharing.
- Provide students with a section of the novel, copied, so they can annotate directly on the text.

Homework/Assessment

Compose an essay in response to the following prompt: How coes Harper Lee's depiction of the character you studied contribute to the reader's understanding of the complex relationships in the novel? (This could be a take-home or an in-class assignment.)

Poetry—Beauty

In this unit, the third of six, students encounter a new literary genre—poetry—and focus on poetic forms, rhyme, and meter.

ESSENTIAL QUESTION

? How does poetry reveal what we might not otherwise recognize?

OVERVIEW

Having studied both the short story and the novel, students now consider why poetry is different from prose. In particular, they examine the power and expressive potential of imagery and other kinds of figurative language. They encounter poetry from a variety of cultures, noting the ways in which the poetic form is universal. As a way of being introduced to literary criticism, students read several authors' reflections on poetry and discuss whether they agree or disagree with their critiques. Finally, the unit is an opportunity to introduce students to the idea of "form" in art, examining masterpieces of art and architecture that, like poems, exhibit an excellent distillation of formal elements.

FOCUS STANDARDS

These Focus Standards have been selected for the unit from the Common Core State Standards.

RL.9–10.4: Determine the meaning of words and phrases as they are used in the text, including figurative and connotative meanings; analyze the cumulative impact of several word choices on meaning and tone (e.g., how the language evokes a sense of time and place; how it sets a formal or informal tone).

RI.9–10.2: Determine a central idea of a text and analyze its development over the course of the text, including how it emerges and is shaped and refined by specific details; provide an objective summary of the text.

W.9–10.8: Gather relevant information from multiple authoritative print and digital sources, using advanced searches effectively; assess the usefulness of each source in answering the research question; integrate information into the text selectively to maintain the flow of ideas, avoiding plagiarism and following a standard format for citation.

SL.9–10.5: Make strategic use of digital media (e.g., textual, graphical, audio, visual, and interactive elements) in presentations to enhance understanding of findings, reasoning, and evidence and to add interest.

L.9–10.1: Demonstrate command of the conventions of Standard English grammar and usage when writing or speaking.

L.9–10.3: Apply knowledge of language to understand how language functions in different contexts, to make effective choices for meaning or style, and to comprehend more fully when reading or listening.

SUGGESTED STUDENT OBJECTIVES

- Define and offer examples of various forms of poetry.
- Identify the form, rhyme scheme, and meter of poems studied.
- Define and explain poetic devices, such as alliteration, assonance, consonance, and enjambment, and describe the ways in which they help reveal the theme(s) of the poem.
- Recognize and explain the distinguishing characteristics of various kinds of poetry, such as ballads, odes, lyric poetry, blank verse, haiku, and sonnets.
- Describe how poetry differs from prose and explain why authors would choose one form over another for a particular purpose.
- Complete a literary research paper, citing at least three sources.

SUGGESTED WORKS

(E) indicates a CCSS exemplar text; (EA) indicates a text from a writer with other works identified as exemplars.

LITERARY TEXTS

Poetry
- "Ozymandias" (Percy Bysshe Shelley) (E)
- "The Raven" (Edgar Allan Poe) (E)
- Sonnet 73 (William Shakespeare) (E)
- "Ode on a Grecian Urn" (John Keats) (E) (*This is a CCSS exemplar text for grades 11 and 12.*)
- "We Grow Accustomed to the Dark" (Emily Dickinson) (E)
- "Mending Wall" (Robert Frost) (E) (*This is a CCSS exemplar text for grades 11 and 12.*)
- "Homecoming" (Julia Alvarez) (EA)
- "Love Is" (Nikki Giovanni) (EA)
- "A Lemon" (Pablo Neruda) (EA)
- "Saturday's Child" (Countee Cullen) (EA)
- "Dream Variations," "In Time of Silver Rain" (Langston Hughes) (EA)
- "I Ask My Mother to Sing," "The Gift" (Li-Young Lee)
- "Phantom Limbs" (Anne Michaels)
- Psalm 96 (King James Bible)
- "Lord Randall" (Anonymous)
- "Campo di Fiori" (Czeslaw Milosz)

- "The Darkling Thrush" (Thomas Hardy)
- "Poetry" (Marianne Moore)
- "Elegy Written in A Country Churchyard" (Thomas Gray)
- "The Sound of the Sea" (Henry Wadsworth Longfellow) (EA)
- "I Wandered Lonely as a Cloud" (William Wordsworth)
- "The Lady of Shalott" (Alfred, Lord Tennyson)
- "Bogland," "Digging," and/or "The Underground" (Seamus Heaney)
- "The Reader," "In Trackless Woods" (Richard Wilbur)
- "Walking Distance" (Debra Allbery)
- "Morning Glory" (Naomi Shihab Nye)
- Haiku selections

INFORMATIONAL TEXTS

- *Faulkner in the University: Class Conferences at the University of Virginia 1957–1958* (William Faulkner, Frederick L. Gwynn, ed.) (excerpts)
- "Crediting Poetry," Nobel Prize Acceptance Speech (1995), [Seamus Heaney] (excerpts)

ART, MUSIC, AND MEDIA

Art and Architecture

- Greek, *Terracotta Hydria* (ca. 510 BCE)
- Leonardo da Vinci, *Mona Lisa* (1503–1506)
- Sandro Botticelli, *The Birth of Venus* (1486)
- Vincent van Gogh, *The Starry Night* (1889)
- Michelangelo, *David* (1504)
- The Parthenon (447–432 BCE)
- Frank Lloyd Wright, Frederick C. Robie House (1909)
- Chartres Cathedral (1193–1250)

Music

- Giacomo Puccini, "Un bel di, vedremo" (*Madama Butterfly*, 1904)
- Giacomo Puccini, "O mio babbino caro" (*Gianni Schicchi*, 1918)

SAMPLE ACTIVITIES AND ASSESSMENTS

For a full Scoring Rubric, see the Appendix.

Note: Textual evidence should be used to support all arguments advanced in seminars and in all essays. Page and word counts for essays are not provided here, but attention should be paid to the requirements regarding the use of evidence, for example, to determine the likely length of good essays.

1. INFORMATIVE/EXPLANATORY WRITING

Write an informative/explanatory essay that compares and contrasts the use of a literary device in two different poems. Discuss at least three aspects. Your teacher may give you the opportunity to write your first draft on a shared online document and receive feedback from classmates before publication. (RL.9–10.4, W.9–10.2)

2. ART/INFORMATIVE/EXPLANATORY WRITING

What similarities can we find between great poems and masterpieces of visual art? Choose one of the following formal elements of poetry: rhythm, tone, structure, or imagery. How might these poetic elements compare to the formal elements of art, such as line, shape, space, color, or texture? Choose a painting such as *The Starry Night* or *The Birth of Venus* and examine its formal elements. How does the artist utilize each element in the artwork? Now think of one of the poems that you've read. Select a formal element in each work and write an essay discussing how the author and the painter develop those elements, comparing the two when appropriate. Cite at least three pieces of evidence for each work. (RL.9–10.7, W.9–10.2)

3. ART/CLASS DISCUSSION

Most great poems explore one idea or concept, often distilling it to its essence. Look carefully at three masterpieces of art (e.g., the *Mona Lisa*, the *David*, the Parthenon). After looking at these works of art, do you believe that the artists who made them did similar things? (SL.9–10.1, SL.9–10.2)

4. ART/INFORMATIVE/EXPLANATORY WRITING

View the image of the terracotta urn from the Archaic age of Greece. Write an essay in which you discuss the ways in which reading Keats's description of the urn is a different experience from viewing it. Discuss at least three differences. (RL.9–10.7, W.9–10.2)

5. RESEARCH

Select a poet and write a research paper in which you analyze the development of the writer's poetry in his/her lifetime, using at least three poems and citing at least three secondary sources. Begin by defining a research question and refine it as necessary as you conduct your research. Cite sources carefully and distinguish clearly between paraphrasing and quoting. Your teacher may give you the option of adding a multimedia component to your paper, such as a digital slide presentation, to highlight your key points. You might include links to online images that illustrate the information you want to share. (RI.9–10.1, RI.9–10.5, RI.9–10.6, W.9–10.2, W.9–10.7, W.9–10.8, SL.9–10.2)

6. SPEECH

Select a poem and recite it from memory. Include an introduction that states:

- Title, author, and type of poem
- How the poem exemplifies the stated type of poetry (SL.9–10.6)

   Record your recitation using a video camera so you can evaluate your performance for accuracy.

7. WRITING (ARGUMENT) AND SEMINAR QUESTION

Are poems better when they follow a strict rhyme or meter? Why or why not? This seminar question may also be used as an essay topic. Be sure to include at least three reasons or examples from the texts to support your argument. Your teacher may give you the opportunity to share your initial thoughts on the classroom blog in order to get feedback from your classmates. (SL.9–10.1, RL.9–10.3, RL.9–10.4, RL.9–10.6, SL.9–10.1, SL.9–10.3)

8. WRITING (ARGUMENT) AND SEMINAR QUESTION

Which is a more effective form of communication—literal language or figurative language? This seminar question may also be used as an essay topic. Be sure to include at least three reasons or examples from texts to support your argument. Your teacher may give you the opportunity to share your initial thoughts on the classroom blog in order to get feedback from your classmates. (SL.9–10.1, RL.9–10.3, RL.9–10.4, RL.9–10.6, SL.9–10.1, SL.9–10.3)

9. ORAL PRESENTATION

Discuss whether you agree with Seamus Heaney when he credits poetry "because credit is due to it, in our time and in all time, for its truth to life, in every sense of that phrase." Say why or why not, and give examples from poems studied or other poems to illustrate your position. State your thesis clearly and include at least three pieces of evidence to support it. Your teacher may ask you to record your presentation as a podcast for publication on the class web page. (RI.9–10.4, RI.9–10.5, RI.9–10.6, SL.9–10.4, SL.9–10.2, SL.9–10.6)

10. RESEARCH AND INFORMATIVE/EXPLANATORY WRITING

Read and listen to or watch Seamus Heaney read "The Underground." Identify and read more about the literary and other allusions in the poem and explain why they might enhance appreciation of the poem. (*Extension:* Discuss how the use of enjambment adds layers of meaning to the poem. Try writing a poem using enjambment to achieve the same effect.) (RL.9–10.4, RL.9–10.9, W.9–10.2, W.9–10.7, SL.9–10.5)

11. NOTE TAKING AND NARRATIVE WRITING

Select a poem (from the list of Exemplar Texts) and perform the following tasks:

- Annotate the poem for the poet's use of poetic devices
- Using your annotations, explicate the poem

In a single paragraph (at least one hundred words long), discuss the poem's theme and the way in which the poet's use of these devices illuminates the theme. (RL.9–10.4, W.9–10.2)

12. NARRATIVE WRITING

(The creative writing assignment below follows the reading and close study of "Mending Wall," by Robert Frost.)

In "Mending Wall," Frost uses an extended metaphor (the wall) to convey an idea. Consider an idea that you want to express and then think of a metaphor that will enable you to convey your idea in a poem.

- Once you select the metaphor, create a web that depicts the metaphor (e.g., a volcano would likely generate words like: *noisy, ash, red, burn, majestic*)
- Begin to string words (e.g., "the burning ash of morning/creeps into my aching heart . . . ")
- Using the generated phrases, compose a poem (RL.9–10.4, W.9–10.3)

13. GRAMMAR AND USAGE

Parts of Speech Review

Prepositions: position, direction, time, purpose and means, possession, accompaniment, comparison, support or opposition, exception, concession; combining prepositions (e.g., *in front of*)

Prepositions Versus Adverbs: Look at a photograph taken during a basketball game or other sporting event (e.g., in the school newspaper or other newspaper). Then, using adverbs and prepositions listed by your teacher, write two sentences for each event that describe what is happening in the picture (e.g., use the words *up, through,* or *behind*). The first sentence should use the word as a preposition, and the second as an adverb. (L.9–10.1, L.9–10.3)

14. MECHANICS

Colons

Select a newspaper or magazine article that uses colons. Highlight where they are used and explain why. (L.9–10.2)

ADDITIONAL RESOURCES

- *Listening to Poetry: Sounds of the Sonnet* (National Endowment for the Humanities) (RL.9–10.4, RL.9–10.5)
- Seamus Heaney reads "The Underground"
- Seamus Heaney reads "Digging"
- Seamus Heaney reads "Bogland"
- Lesson Plan for Robert Frost's "Mending Wall" (National Endowment for the Humanities)
- Robert Frost reads "Mending Wall"

TERMINOLOGY

Alliteration	Dramatic poetry	Lyric poetry	Rhythm
Analogy	Enjambment	Meter	Sestet
Assonance	Figurative language	Narrative poetry	Sonnet (petrarchan, shakespearean)
Ballad	Free verse	Octet	
Blank verse	Haiku	Ode	
Consonance	Heroic couplet	Rhyme	
Diction	Imagery	Rhyme scheme	

Grade Nine, Unit Three Sample Lesson Plan

*"We Grow Accustomed to the Dark" by Emily Dickinson**

"Mending Wall" by Robert Frost

"Ode on a Grecian Urn" by John Keats

"The Raven" by Edgar Allan Poe

Sonnet 73 by William Shakespeare

"Ozymandias" by Percy Bysshe Shelley

"Soul-Making in 'Ode on a Grecian Urn'" by James Shokoff

In this series of ten lessons, students read a selection of poems by William Shakespeare, Percy Bysshe Shelley, Emily Dickinson, Robert Frost, John Keats, and Edgar Allan Poe, and they:

> Identify forms of poems (RL.9-10.1, RL.9-10.5, SL.9-10.1)
>
> Explore the relationship between form and content (RL.9-10.1, RL.9-10.4, RL.9-10.5, SL.9-10.1, L.9-10.3)
>
> Note the role of the speaker in poetry (RL.9-10.1, SL.9-10.3, SL.9-10.1)
>
> Examine use of poetic devices (RL.9-10.1, RL.9-10.2, RL.9-10.4, SL.9-10.1, SL.9-10.4, L.9-10.5)
>
> Explore critics' perspectives (RI.9-10.1, RI.9-10.2, RI.9-10.3, RI.9-10.4, RI.9-10.5, RI.9-10.6, SL.9-10.1)

Summary

Lesson I: Introduction to Poetry and the Sonnets of William Shakespeare	Lesson II: The Sonnets of William Shakespeare: Sonnet 73
Explore the special characteristics of poetry (SL.9-10.1)	Explore the function of the form of the sonnet (RL.9-10.1, RL.9-10.5, SL.9-10.1)
Investigate the relationship between poems' forms and what they depict (SL.9-10.1)	Identify the three ways that the speaker describes himself (RL.9-10.1, SL.9-10.3, L.9-10.6)
Identify the different sonnet forms (SL.9-10.4)	Examine the speaker's presentation of each of the three situations (RL.9-10.1, SL.9-10.3, L.9-10.6)
Examine the form of Shakespeare's Sonnet 73 (RL.9-10.5, SL.9-10.1)	Consider the speaker's point of view and its connection to the couplet (RL.9-10.1, RL.9-10.2, RL.9-10.4, SL.9-10.1, SL.9-10.3)

Lesson III: The Sonnets of Percy Bysshe Shelley: "Ozymandias"

Explore the historical/archaeological origin of the poem (informational/art work) (RL.9, SL.9-10.1)

Identify the sonnet form of "Ozymandias" (SL.9-10.4)

Investigate the speaker's choice to employ the "traveller's" voice (RL.9-10.1, RL.9-10.4, RL.9-10.9, SL.9-10.1, SL.9-10.3)

Examine the poet's ironic presentation of claims of greatness by the "King of Kings" (RL.9-10.1, SL.9-10.1, L.9-10.5)

Assess and critique the speaker's perspective (SL.9-10.3)

Lesson IV: Emily Dickinson's "We Grow Accustomed to the Dark"

Note the speaker of the poem (RL.9-10.1, SL.9-10.3)

Identify the images of darkness (RL.9-10.1, RL.9-10.4, SL.9-10.1, L.9-10.5)

Explicate the poet's use of images of darkness and light (RL.9-10.1, RL.9-10.4, SL.9-10.1, L.9-10.5)

Identify and explain the use of capitalization (L.9-10.1, SL.9-10.4, L.9-10.2)

Lesson V: Emily Dickinson's "We Grow Accustomed to the Dark"

Note the tension between light and darkness (RL.9-10.1, RL.9-10.2, RL.9-10.4, SL.9-10.1)

Explore the connection between darkness and nature (RL.9-10.1, RL.9-10.2, RL.9-10.4, SL.9-10.1, L.9-10.4)

Examine the movement of the image of darkness in the poem (RL.9-10.1, RL.9-10.2, RL.9-10.4, SL.9-10.1, L.9-10.4)

Ponder the greater themes of the poem (RL.9-10.1, RL.9-10.2)

Assess analytical abilities (W.9-10.1, W.9-10.4)

Lesson VI: Robert Frost's "Mending Wall"

Examine the form of "Mending Wall" (RL.9-10.1, SL.9-10.1)

Explore the form's influence on the content of the poem (RL.9-10.1, RL.9-10.5)

Examine the cyclical tensions between natural forces and man's actions (RL.9-10.1, RL.9-10.2, RL.9-10.4, RL.9-10.5, SL.9-10.1, L.9-10.6)

Consider the possibility that the wall is a metaphor or perhaps a symbol (RL.9-10.1, RL.9-10.2, RL.9-10.4, SL.9-10.1, L.9-10.5)

Lesson VII: Robert Frost's "Mending Wall"

Critically explore the complexity of the speaker's point of view (RL.9-10.1, RL.9-10.2, RL.9-10.3, SL.9-10.3)

Challenge the assertion that "Good fences make good neighbors" (RL.9-10.1, RL.9-10.2, RL.9-10.3, RL.9-10.4, SL.9-10.1, L.9-10.5)

Juxtapose the speaker's point of view with his neighbor's (RL.9-10.1, RL.9-10.2, RL.9-10.3, RL.9-10.4, RL.9-10.5, SL.9-10.1)

Expose the intricate ideas that emerge from these tensions (RL.9-10.1, RL.9-10.2, RL.9-10.4, SL.9-10.1)

Lesson VIII: John Keats's "Ode on a Grecian Urn" and "Soul-Making in 'Ode on a Grecian Urn,'" by James Shokoff*

Note what a Grecian urn is/might look like (RL.9-10.1, SL.9-10.1)

Study pictures of Grecian urns (informational text) (RI.9-10.2, RI.9-10.4)

Identify the term ode (SL.9-10.4)

Explore why "Ode on a Grecian Urn" is an ode (RL.9-10.5, RL.9-10.9, SL.9-10.1)

Assess the value of a critical essay (SL.9-10.4, L.9-10.6)

* James Shokoff, "Soul-Making in 'Ode on a Grecian Urn,'" published in Keats-Shelley Journal, Vol. 24 (1975), pp. 102–107.

Lesson IX: John Keats's "Ode on a Grecian Urn" and "Soul-Making in 'Ode on a Grecian Urn,'" by James Shokoff*

Articulate the main ideas in Shokoff's essay (RI.9-10.1, RI.9-10.2, RI.9-10.3, RI.9-10.4, RI.9-10.5, RI.9-10.6, SL.9-10.1)

Note Shokoff's analytical style (RI.9-10.5, SL.9-10.4)

Explore Shokoff's claim that in this poem Keats is "affirming the value of the real world in which he and we all live" (p. 103) (RI.9-10.2) (RI.9-10.2, SL.9-10.1, L.9-10.5)

* James Shokoff, "Soul-Making in 'Ode on a Grecian Urn,'" published in *Keats-Shelley Journal*, Vol. 24 (1975), pp. 102–107.

Lesson X: "The Raven" by Edgar Allan Poe: An In-Class Assessment

Assess what students have learned about the reading of poetry (RL.9-10.1, RL.9-10.2, RL.9-10.3, RL.9-10.4, RL.9-10.5, L.9-10.6)

Assess students' ability to read and interpret a poem independently (RL.9-10.1, RL.9-10.2, RL.9-10.3, RL.9-10.4, RL.9-10.5, SL.9-10.6)

Assess the integration of poetic terms in the students' writing (RL.9-10.4)

Assess the students' analytical writing skills (W.9-10.1, W.9-10.4)

Integrate lessons learned from Shokoff's essay (SL.9-10.4)

Lesson IV: Emily Dickinson's "We Grow Accustomed to the Dark"

Objectives

Note the speaker of the poem (RL.9-10.1, SL.9-10.3)

Identify the images of darkness (RL.9-10.1, RL.9-10.4, SL.9-10.1)

Explicate the poet's use of images of darkness and light (RL.9-10.1, RL.9-10.4, SL.9-10.1, L.9-10.5)

Identify the use of capitalization (L.9-10.1, SL.9-10.4, L.9-10.2)

Required Materials

☐ Copies of "We Grow Accustomed to the Dark" by Emily Dickinson

Procedures

1. Lead-In:
   a. Read "We Grow Accustomed to the Dark" by Emily Dickinson.

2. Step by Step:

Part I
   a. Instruct students to reread the poem and annotate for all references to darkness, light, or vision. (This is an opportunity to walk around the room and notice what the students are doing.)
   b. With a neighbor, students examine their annotations.

Part II

3. Discussion:
   a. Read the poem aloud.
   b. Discuss findings (since all students annotated, the discussion should be lively). Students will add to their annotations during the discussion. (Remind students at this point in the discussion to avoid interpretations.)

Below is the poem with the light/dark images underlined. All students should have these annotations as well.

We Grow Accustomed to the Dark

by EMILY DICKINSON

We grow accustomed to the _Dark_ —
When a _light_ is put away —
As when the Neighbor holds the _Lamp_
To witness her Goodbye —

A Moment — We uncertain step
For newness of the _night_ —
Then — fit our _Vision_ to the _Dark_ —
And meet the _Road_ — erect —

And so of larger — _Darkness_ —
Those Evenings of the _Brain_ —
When not a _Moon_ disclose a sign —
Or _Star_ — come out — within —

The _Bravest_ — grope a little —
And sometimes hit a Tree
Directly in the Forehead —
But as they learn to _see_ —

Either the _Darkness_ alters —
Or something in the _sight_
Adjusts itself to _Midnight_ —
And Life steps almost straight.

c. Following the discussion, explication of the poem follows; model it in the following manner (and remind the students to take notes since this will be their homework):

The speaker of the poem is a collective "we." We, in the present simple tense, "grow accustomed to the Dark." The word *Dark* is capitalized, calling the reader's attention to that particular image.

Line 2 tells us that "We grow accustomed to the Dark" when the "light is put away." The passive tense here suggests that someone, or perhaps something, puts the light away.

Lines 3 and 4 reveal how the darkness happens. The neighbor seems to walk with the "we" of the poem to a certain spot, and then departs. The word *witness* suggests that the speaker can see the neighbor depart. It is also worth mentioning that Dickinson uses capital letters in several places in an unconventional manner.

Once you have demonstrated the explication of the poem, the students will take turns and orally explicate the poem.

4. Closure:

A student volunteer will reread the poem aloud.

Differentiation

Advanced

- Encourage students to research Emily Dickinson and prepare a biography of her for classmates. Students should also research what inspired Dickinson to write "We Grow Accustomed to the Dark" and perhaps present this information as an online poster.
- Select a student volunteer to read the poem at the end of class; give the student an opportunity to practice reading dramatically, recorded with a video camera, so he/she can evaluate and improve his/her performance.

Struggling

- Read the poem to students, or allow them to listen to a pre-recorded version.
- Give students a choice of writing on the copy of the poem or using sticky notes, possibly even with sketches (or other nonlinguistic representations) to help aid memory and understanding. Allow them to talk through their findings with a partner prior to sharing with the class discussion. A final alternative is to allow students to annotate a text document.
- Record the student volunteer who reads the poem using a video camera so students can (1) review and re-watch it as needed, and (2) practice reading along to aid in fluency and understanding.

Homework/Assessment

Students will explicate the poem based on the class model.

Lesson V: Emily Dickinson's "We Grow Accustomed to the Dark"

Objectives

Note the tension between light and darkness (RL.9-10.1, RL.9-10.2, RL.9-10.4, SL.9-10.1)

Explore the connection between darkness and nature (RL.9-10.1, RL.9-10.2, RL.9-10.4, SL.9-10.1, L.9-10.4)

Examine the movement of the image of darkness in the poem (RL.9-10.1, RL.9-10.2, RL.9-10.4, SL.9-10.4, SL.9-10.1, L.9-10.2)

Ponder the greater themes of the poem (RL.9-10.1, RL.9-10.2)

Assess analytical abilities (W.9-10.1, W.9-10.4)

Required Materials

☐ Copies of "We Grow Accustomed to the Dark" by Emily Dickinson

Procedures

1. Lead-In:
   Reread "We Grow Accustomed to the Dark" by Emily Dickinson. Briefly share explication of the poem (student volunteers will read aloud their explication).

2. Step by Step:
   a. Discussion. Direct the discussion as the class progresses into an analytical mode:
      - What do we hear about the darkness in the first two stanzas?
      - What is the relationship between the speaker and the darkness?
      - Note a shift in the third stanza; what is its nature?
      - Is there a possibility here of inner darkness?
      - How are the "Moon" and "Star" used here?
      - What happens in the fourth stanza? Note the words "But as they learn to see —" at the end of the stanza.
      - How would you characterize the final stanza?
      - Is there a possibility of light?

3. Closure:
   In one to three well-organized paragraphs, discuss Dickinson's use of nature. She seems to move from a literal nature to a figurative one. How does it affect the reading of the poem?

Writing Guidelines

- Clearly establish the topic of the paragraph and contextualize it.
- Insightfully organize the sequence of ideas according to the purpose of the paragraph.
- Present a clear and thorough explication of the passage.
- Cite the text using short quotations.
- Use Standard English form.
- Avoid grammatical and mechanical errors.
- Use present simple tense.

Differentiation

Advanced

- Encourage students to read the poem with a variety of dramatic interpretations and choose the most unique to present to classmates. Students should evaluate the different interpretations and discuss how they enhance the poem or detract from it. These readings may be recorded with a video camera to share with other students, as time permits.

- Choose from the following options:
  - Create a modern-day interpretation of the poem. (They must be able to justify how the modern version stays true to the original while also changing its style. Perhaps challenge them to create a movie to present their interpretation.)
  - Write your own poem of nature, using both literal and figurative language. (Ask students also to explain how Dickinson's poem inspired them to write their own.)
  - Research other poems with "darkness" (literal or figurative) in the title. Discuss with a partner how these poems are similar or different.

Struggling

- Reread the poem to students, or allow them to listen to a pre-recorded version (from the prior lesson).
- Give students a second copy of the poem on a transparency to allow them to write responses to analytical interpretations that differ from the explication. Allow them to talk through their findings with a partner prior to sharing during the class discussion. A final alternative is to allow students to annotate in a text document.
- Provide students a graphic organizer or web where they can organize their thoughts about Dickinson's literal and figurative use of nature. Allow students to create a visual using an online program.

Homework/Assessment
N/A

Drama—Fate

This unit, the fourth of six, uses two classic tragedies to address a new literary form for the grade level: the drama.

OVERVIEW

Students read *Antigone* or *Oedipus the King,* learning about the classic form of the Greek tragedy. Students examine Aristotle's *Poetics* and his definitions of comedy and tragedy to deepen their understanding of tragedy. They read Shakespeare's *Romeo and Juliet* and compare and contrast the ways in which the plays treat the related theme of fate versus free will. Building on the poetry unit, students also will consider Shakespeare's use of rhythm, punctuation, and imagery and the ways in which they help convey the motives, thoughts, and feelings of the characters. This unit will confirm students' shared understanding of the elements of drama, preparing them for the study of other dramatic works throughout high school.

FOCUS STANDARDS

These Focus Standards have been selected for the unit from the Common Core State Standards.

RL.9–10.3: Analyze how complex characters (e.g., those with multiple or conflicting motivations) develop over the course of a text, interact with other characters, and advance the plot or develop the theme.

RL.9–10.5: Analyze how an author's choices concerning how to structure a text, order events within it (e.g., parallel plots), and manipulate time (e.g., pacing, flashbacks) create such effects as mystery, tension, or surprise.

RL.9–10.9: Analyze how an author draws on and transforms source material in a specific work (e.g., how Shakespeare treats a theme or topic from Ovid or the Bible or how a later author draws on a play by Shakespeare).

RI.9–10.1: Cite strong and thorough textual evidence to support analysis of what the text says explicitly as well as inferences drawn from the text.

W.9–10.2: Write informative/explanatory texts to examine and convey complex ideas, concepts, and information clearly and accurately through the effective selection, organization, and analysis of content.

SL.9–10.1: Initiate and participate effectively in a range of collaborative discussions (one-on-one, in groups, and teacher-led) with diverse partners on grades 9–10 topics, texts, and issues, building on others' ideas and expressing their own clearly and persuasively.

L.9–10.1: Demonstrate command of the conventions of Standard English grammar and usage when writing or speaking.

L.9–10.6: Acquire and use accurately general academic and domain-specific words and phrases, sufficient for reading, writing, speaking, and listening at the college and career readiness level; demonstrate independence in gathering vocabulary knowledge when considering a word or phrase important to comprehension or expression.

SUGGESTED STUDENT OBJECTIVES

- Identify and explain the elements of drama in general, and in Greek drama in particular (see Terminology section).
- Explain the structure of the plot(s) and describe the dramatic techniques the playwright uses to advance them.
- Trace the development of major and minor characters and explain how characterization advances the plot or theme.
- Understand Aristotle's definitions of comedy and tragedy and explain how the other works studied exemplify the term *tragedy*.
- Analyze the playwrights' use of irony.
- Identify the poetic devices used in *Romeo and Juliet* and explain their effect.

SUGGESTED WORKS

(E) indicates a CCSS exemplar text; (EA) indicates a text from a writer with other works identified as exemplars.

LITERARY TEXTS

Drama
- *Romeo and Juliet* (William Shakespeare) (E)
- *Antigone* (Sophocles) (EA)
- *Oedipus the King* (Sophocles) (E)

INFORMATIONAL TEXTS

- *Poetics* (Aristotle) (excerpt on comedy and tragedy)
- "The Visual Artistry of *Romeo and Juliet*" (James Black) (*Studies in English Literature, 1500–1900*, Vol. 15, No. 2, Spring 1975: 245–256)

ART, MUSIC, AND MEDIA

Art
- Pablo Picasso, *The Tragedy* (1903)
- Michelangelo Merisi da Caravaggio, *The Death of the Virgin* (1604–1606)
- Artemisia Gentileschi, *Judith and Her Maidservant with the Head of Holofernes* (1625)

SAMPLE ACTIVITIES AND ASSESSMENTS

For a full Scoring Rubric, see the Appendix.

Note: Textual evidence should be used to support all arguments advanced in seminars and in essays. Page and word counts for essays are not provided here, but attention should be paid to the requirements regarding the use of evidence, for example, to determine the likely length of good essays.

1. INFORMATIVE/EXPLANATORY WRITING

Write an informative/explanatory essay that compares and contrasts aspects of tragic illumination in the tragedies of *Romeo and Juliet* and *Antigone* (or *Oedipus the King*). State your thesis clearly and include at least three pieces of evidence to support it. Your teacher may give you the opportunity to write your first draft on a shared online document and receive feedback from classmates before publication. (RL.9–10.2, RL.9–10.3, W.9–10.2)

2. INFORMATIVE/EXPLANATORY WRITING

Write an informative/explanatory essay in which you discuss the extent to which one of the dramas studied adheres to Aristotle's definition of tragedy. State your thesis clearly and include at least three pieces of evidence to support it. Your teacher may give you the opportunity to write your first draft on a shared online document and receive feedback from classmates before publication. (RL.9–10.2, RL.9–10.3, W.9–10.2)

3. SPEECH

Select a one-minute passage from one play and recite it from memory. Include an introduction that states:

- The title of the play and the act and scene of the passage
- Why the passage is significant
- How the passage exemplifies one of the play's themes (RL.9–10.2, SL.9–10.4, SL.9–10.6)

Record your recitation using a video camera so you can evaluate your performance for accuracy.

4. SEMINAR QUESTION AND INFORMATIVE/EXPLANATORY WRITING

How does free will play a part in Romeo and Juliet's destiny? This seminar question may also be used as an essay topic. Be sure to state your thesis clearly and include at least three pieces of evidence to support it. Your teacher may give you the opportunity to share your initial thoughts on the classroom blog in order to get feedback from your classmates. (RL.9–10.1, RL.9–10.4, SL.9–10.1)

5. ART/ORAL PRESENTATION

Examine the rendering of Caravaggio's *The Death of the Virgin*. How does the artist choose to create dramatic effects? For instance, note the nuances of light and shadow, mood, composition of the figures, and illusion of depth. Note the curtain the painter has included to "reveal" the scene. How do these elements direct your eye? Does the curtain draw you into a certain part of the painting? Compare the Caravaggio with the Gentileschi. What are both of these artists doing with color and light? How are these paintings different? Can you find similarities between the Caravaggio and Act V, scene iii, of *Romeo and Juliet*? Describe and explain the significance of at least three examples. (RL.9–10.7, SL.9–10.1, SL.9–10.2)

6. INFORMATIONAL TEXT AND INFORMATIVE/EXPLANATORY WRITING

In his essay "The Visual Artistry of *Romeo and Juliet*," James Black argues that "*Romeo and Juliet* is an especially 'visual' play." He notes that the "story is told and its tragedy unfolded in a series of pictures as well as in dialogue; and indeed the play is a brilliant exercise in suiting the action to the word in such a way that both actions and words are given special intensity." To prepare for writing an informative/explanatory essay, students will:

- Select a specific scene from the play
- Note the action in the scene
- Examine the ways that the dialogue "depicts" the action
- Write an informative/explanatory essay in response to the following prompt: How does the dialogue in the scene that you selected contribute to the visual presentation of the action and, by extension, to the play's theme? (RL.9–10.4, RL.9–10.5, L.9–10.3, L.9–10.4, L.9–10.5)

7. GRAMMAR, USAGE, AND MECHANICS

Parts of Speech Review

Pronouns: personal (nominative and objective), demonstrative, interrogative, possessive, indefinite, reflexive/"intensive," relative

Agreement of Pronouns and Antecedents

Appositives: Commas with appositives, restrictive and nonrestrictive clause

Read a fellow student's essay from one of the preceding activities. Highlight all the pronouns and identify each of them by type. Name their antecedents. Explain why commas are or are not included with clauses. (L.9–10.1b, L.9–10.2)

ADDITIONAL RESOURCES

- Shakespeare's *Romeo and Juliet*: "You Kiss by the Book" (National Endowment for the Humanities) (RL.9–10.4, RL.9–10.10)
- *Antigone* and the Ancient Greek Theater (National Endowment for the Humanities) (RL.9–10.4, RL.9–10.10)
- *Oedipus the King*: An Introduction to Greek Drama (PBS) (RL.9–10.4, RL.9–10.10)

TERMINOLOGY

Aside	Dramatic irony	Irony: dramatic, situational, verbal	Stasimon
Blank verse	Foil		Tragedy
Classical allusions	Greek chorus	Monologue	Tragic flaw
Comedy	Heroic couplet	Protagonist	Tragic hero
Dialogue	Iambic pentameter	Soliloquy	Tragic illumination

Grade Nine, Unit Four Sample Lesson Plan

Antigone by Sophocles

In this series of six lessons, students read *Antigone* by Sophocles, and they:

- Probe the origins of the Greek theater (W.9-10.7, RI.9-10.1, RI.9-10.2, RL.9-10.5, RL.9-10.9, SL.9-10.1, SL.9-10.4)
- Explore the themes in *Antigone* (RL.9-10.2, RL.9-10.3, RL.9-10.5, RL.9-10.9, SL.9-10.1)
- Consider why Sophocles's philosophical ideas are still relevant today (SL.9-10.1)

Summary

Lesson I: The Greek Theater*

Explore the origins of the Greek theater (W.9-10.7, RI.9-10.2, RL.9-10.9, SL.9-10.1)

Identify the physical layout of the Greek theater (W.9-10.7, RI.9-10.1)

Identify the structure of the Greek tragedy (RL.9-10.5, SL.9-10.4)

Lessons IV, V: Themes in *Antigone*

In groups, identify passages that contain key ideas for discussion (RL.9-10.4, RL.9-10.5, SL.9-10.1, L.9-10.6)

Explore the themes that emerge (RL.9-10.2, SL.9-10.1, SL.9-10.5)

Lesson II, III: *Antigone*, by Sophocles*

Contextualize *Antigone* as part of Sophocles's *Oedipus Trilogy* (RL.9-10.3, SL.9-10.4)

Identify the sections of *Antigone* (RL.9-10.5, RL.9-10.9, SL.9-10.4)

Select roles to read (SL.9-10.1)

Participate in the reading of the play (SL.9-10.6)

Listen critically to the reading of the play (SL.9-10.1b, SL.9-10.4)

Lesson VI: Value of the Classics*

Recall ideas from Lessons IV & V (SL.9-10.4)

Compose an essay that explores the universal ideas that *Antigone* explores (W.9-10.2, RL.9-10.2, L.9-10.1, L.9-10.2, L.9-10.3, L.9-10.6)

---

* Reed College's web pages on Ancient Greek Theater (http://academic.reed.edu/humanities/110tech/theater.html) are a helpful resource when preparing to teach Lessons I–V.

Lessons IV, V: Themes in *Antigone*

Objectives

In groups, identify passages that contain key ideas for discussion (RL.9-10.4, RL.9-10.5, SL.9-10.1, L.9-10.6)

Explore the themes that emerge (RL.9-10.2, SL.9-10.1, SL.9-10.5)

Required Materials

☐ Class sets of *Antigone*

Procedures

1. Lead-In:

In groups, students briefly revisit the text and identify significant passages in the play. They may use an outline of the play's sections.

2. Step by Step:

Students explore the ideas that emerge in the selected passages. Below are several suggestions.

First Stasimon: Note the praise of man.

> Many wonders there be, but naught more wondrous than man;
> Over the surging sea, with a whitening south wind wan,
> Through the foam of the firth, man makes his perilous way;

Second Episode (Antigone's arguments when she confronts Creon): Note Antigone's juxtaposition of the laws of man versus the laws of Heaven.

> Yea, for these laws were not ordained of Zeus,
> And she who sits enthroned with gods below,
> Justice, enacted not these human laws.
> Nor did I deem that thou, a mortal man,
> Could'st by a breath annul and override
> The immutable unwritten laws of Heaven.
> They were not born today nor yesterday;
> They die not; and none knoweth whence they sprang.
> I was not like, who feared no mortal's frown,
> To disobey these laws and so provoke
> The wrath of Heaven. I knew that I must die,
> E'en hadst thou not proclaimed it; and if death

Is thereby hastened, I shall count it gain.
For death is gain to him whose life, like mine,
Is full of misery. Thus my lot appears
Not sad, but blissful; for had I endured
To leave my mother's son unburied there,
I should have grieved with reason, but not now.
And if in this thou judgest me a fool,
Methinks the judge of folly's not acquit.

Creon's response is a defense of the law; he also notes that she is a woman and he is a man. He repeats this argument several times throughout the play.

First overstepped the established law, and then —
A second and worse act of insolence —
She boasts and glories in her wickedness.
Now if she thus can flout authority
Unpunished, I am woman, she the man.

Third Episode: In this scene Creon and his son Haemon debate the issue of authority. Creon speaks of dangers of "Anarchy." Note how he uses the female pronoun to describe it.

I warrant such a one in either case
Would shine, as King or subject; such a man
Would in the storm of battle stand his ground,
A comrade leal and true; but Anarchy —
What evils are not wrought by Anarchy!
She ruins States, and overthrows the home,
She dissipates and routs the embattled host;
While discipline preserves the ordered ranks.
Therefore we must maintain authority
And yield to title to a woman's will.
Better, if needs be, men should cast us out
Than hear it said, a woman proved his match.

It is worthwhile to read Haemon's response again. He speaks of his respect for reason. He pleads Antigone's case and reminds his father that wise men listen to others. He uses metaphors to advance his point. The conversation that follows expands the gap between father and son.

Father, the gods implant in mortal men
Reason, the choicest gift bestowed by heaven.
'Tis not for me to say thou errest, nor
Would I arraign thy wisdom, if I could;
And yet wise thoughts may come to other men
And, as thy son, it falls to me to mark
The acts, the words, the comments of the crowd.
The commons stand in terror of thy frown,
And dare not utter aught that might offend,
But I can overhear their muttered plaints,
Know how the people mourn this maiden doomed
For noblest deeds to die the worst of deaths.
When her own brother slain in battle lay
Unsepulchered, she suffered not his corpse
To lie for carrion birds and dogs to maul:
Should not her name (they cry) be writ in gold?
Such the low murmurings that reach my ear.
O father, nothing is by me more prized
Than thy well-being, for what higher good
Can children covet than their sire's fair fame,
As fathers too take pride in glorious sons?
Therefore, my father, cling not to one mood,
And deemed not thou art right, all others wrong.
For whoso thinks that wisdom dwells with him,
That he alone can speak or think aright,
Such oracles are empty breath when tried.
The wisest man will let himself be swayed
By others' wisdom and relax in time.
See how the trees beside a stream in flood
Save, if they yield to force, each spray unharmed,
But by resisting perish root and branch.
The mariner who keeps his mainsheet taut,
And will not slacken in the gale, is like

To sail with thwarts reversed, keel uppermost.
Relent then and repent thee of thy wrath;
For, if one young in years may claim some sense,
I'll say 'tis best of all to be endowed
With absolute wisdom; but, if that's denied,
(And nature takes not readily that ply)
Next wise is he who lists to sage advice.

Fourth Episode: Note the Chorus's words to Antigone. They celebrate her strength, but note that for her actions she must die.

Religion has her chains, 'tis true,
Let rite be paid when rites are due.
Yet is it ill to disobey
The powers who hold by might the sway.
Thou hast withstood authority,
A self-willed rebel, thou must die.

Antigone explains her deed. She juxtaposes the laws of the state with the "law of conscience."

Thus by the law of conscience I was led
To honor thee, dear brother, and was judged
By Creon guilty of a heinous crime.
And now he drags me like a criminal,
A bride unwed, amerced of marriage-song
And marriage-bed and joys of motherhood,
By friends deserted to a living grave.
What ordinance of heaven have I transgressed?
Hereafter can I look to any god
For succor, call on any man for help?
Alas, my piety is impious deemed.
Well, if such justice is approved of heaven,
I shall be taught by suffering my sin;
But if the sin is theirs, O may they suffer
No worse ills than the wrongs they do to me.

Fifth Episode: The prophet Tiresias warns Creon.

> *To all men, but the man who having erred*
> *Hugs not his errors, but repents and seeks*
> *The cure, is not a wastrel nor unwise.*
> *No fool, the saw goes, like the obstinate fool.*

3. Closure:
Remind students to revisit their class notes in preparation for the next lesson.

Differentiation

Advanced

- Pre-assess all students for their knowledge of *Antigone* and other tragedies, such as Shakespeare's *Hamlet*. If students are already familiar with what is needed for this lesson, have students write a comparison/contrast essay between *Antigone* and a Shakespeare play of choice. If two students are familiar with the same play, they can discuss and present their discussion to the class in a creative multimedia format.

- Select student volunteers to read sections of *Antigone* aloud; give the students an opportunity to practice reading with expression, recorded with a video camera, so they can evaluate and improve their performances.

Struggling

- Have students work in small groups to outline an episode of *Antigone*. Give students a paper copy and ask them to annotate (or sketch or use other nonlinguistic representations) to aid in memory and understanding. Students may also work as a group using a document camera. Alternatively, give students an electronic copy to annotate. After analyzing one episode together, divide students into pairs. Partners write their notes on a shared spreadsheet or the classroom blog, so that all students can review the notes prior to the class discussion.

- Allow students to listen to, view, or review episodes of *Antigone* prior to analyzing the themes.

- Provide students with a list of potential themes, and then have them find evidence in the text of where they are addressed. Students should be able to justify their thinking by citing the text.

Homework/Assessment
Review class notes.

Grade 9 ► *Unit 5*

Epic Poetry—Heroism

This unit, the fifth of six, focuses on epic poetry as its own genre and introduces students to classic and more recent epics, as well as to works of contemporary nonfiction that also address themes related to heroism.

OVERVIEW

Students read Homer's *The Odyssey* or Virgil's *The Aeneid,* with special attention to the hero's journey, and learn about the characteristics of an epic hero. They become familiar with classic Greek and Roman mythology and consider the role of the gods in the hero's adventures. Building on themes in the previous unit, they may discuss the role of fate. Through pairings of these works with informational texts, students learn about the ancient city of Troy and the story of the Trojan War for historical context. They may also encounter informational texts that describe the experience of soldiers going to or returning from war in contemporary times; they may compare and contrast these accounts with the experiences of Aeneas or Odysseus. Alfred, Lord Tennyson's "The Lotos-Eaters" is included in the unit so that students may explore how authors draw on the works of other authors to examine related themes. "The Song of Hiawatha" by Henry Wadsworth Longfellow is included so that students can compare a classic epic with a more recent one. As a segue to the next unit on memoir, William Manchester's *Goodbye Darkness* allows students to delve more deeply into the themes of bravery and heroism. Teachers may also choose to read excerpts from the Indian epic *The Ramayana* to explore an epic from yet another culture.

ESSENTIAL QUESTION

Are epic heroes brave, smart, or lucky?

FOCUS STANDARDS

These Focus Standards have been selected for the unit from the Common Core State Standards.

RL.9–10.2: Determine a theme or central idea of a text and analyze in detail its development over the course of the text, including how it emerges and is shaped and refined by specific details; provide an objective summary of the text.

RL.9–10.3: Analyze how complex characters (e.g., those with multiple or conflicting motivations) develop over the course of a text, interact with other characters, and advance the plot or develop the theme.

RI.9–10.7: Analyze various accounts of a subject in different mediums (e.g., a person's life story told in both print and multimedia), determining which details are emphasized in each account.

W.9–10.9: Draw evidence from literary or informational texts to support analysis, reflection, and research.

SL.9–10.3: Evaluate a speaker's point of view, reasoning, and use of evidence and rhetoric, identifying any fallacious reasoning or exaggerated or distorted evidence.

L.9–10.1: Demonstrate command of the conventions of Standard English grammar and usage when writing or speaking.

SUGGESTED STUDENT OBJECTIVES

- Identify and explain the elements of an epic poem.
- Identify and explain the characteristics of an epic hero.
- Analyze the relationship between myths or legends and epic poetry.
- Examine the historical context of literary works.
- Compare and contrast how related themes may be treated in different genres (here, epic poetry and contemporary nonfiction).
- Hone effective listening skills during oral presentations and class discussions.

SUGGESTED WORKS

(E) indicates a CCSS exemplar text; (EA) indicates a text from a writer with other works identified as exemplars.

LITERARY TEXTS

Stories
- *Mythology* (Edith Hamilton)

Poetry
- *The Odyssey* (Homer) (E)
- *The Aeneid* (Virgil)
- "The Lotos-Eaters" (Alfred, Lord Tennyson)
- "Endymion" (John Keats) (EA) (excerpts)
- "The Song of Hiawatha" (Henry Wadsworth Longfellow) (EA)
- *The Ramayana* (Valmiki) (excerpts)

INFORMATIONAL TEXTS
- *Poetics* (Aristotle) (excerpts)
- *The Gold of Troy* (Robert Payne)
- *Odysseus in America: Combat Trauma and the Trials of Homecoming* (Jonathan Shay) (excerpts)

- *Goodbye, Darkness: A Memoir of the Pacific War* (William Manchester) (excerpts)
- *Soldier's Heart: Reading Literature Through Peace and War at West Point* (Elizabeth D. Samet)
- *Operation Homecoming: Iraq, Afghanistan, and the Home Front in the Words of U.S. Troops and Their Families* (Andrew Carroll, ed.)
- *The Hero with a Thousand Faces* (Joseph Campbell)
- "The Devious Narrator of *The Odyssey*" (Scott Richardson, *The Classical Journal*, Vol. 101, No. 4, pp. 337–359)
- "Going to War" (Second Lieutenant Kelley Victor Gasper)

ART, MUSIC, AND MEDIA

Art

- Greece, Relief Plaque (ca. 450 BCE)
- India, *Folio from The Ramayana of Valmiki: Ram a Shatters the Trident of the Demon Viradha* (1597–1605)

Music

- Henry Purcell, *Dido and Aeneas* (1689)

SAMPLE ACTIVITIES AND ASSESSMENTS

For a full Scoring Rubric, see the Appendix.

Note: Textual evidence should be used to support all arguments advanced in seminars and in essays. Page and word counts for essays are not provided here, but attention should be paid to the requirements regarding the use of evidence, for example, to determine the likely length of good essays.

1. INFORMATIVE/EXPLANATORY WRITING

Write an informative/explanatory essay in which you describe how Aeneas or Odysseus (or a contemporary soldier from another reading) exhibits the characteristics of an epic hero. State your thesis clearly and include at least three pieces of evidence to support it. (W.9–10.1)

2. NARRATIVE WRITING

Write a poem or prose narrative about a journey you or someone you know has taken, using epic similes, epithets, and allusions. (W.9–10.3)

3. INFORMATIVE/EXPLANATORY WRITING

Write an informative/explanatory essay in which you compare the treatment of the theme of heroism in *The Aeneid* or *The Odyssey* with its treatment one of the contemporary nonfiction accounts. State your thesis clearly and include at least three pieces of evidence to support it. (RL.9–10.2, RI.9–10.7, W.9–10.2)

4. ORAL PRESENTATION/CLASS DISCUSSION

Play excerpts from Henry Purcell's opera *Dido and Aeneas* and lead the class in a discussion on whether this rendering of an epic in another medium is or is not "faithful" to the original. Discuss why or why not. Ask classmates to provide specific evidence for their opinions. (RL.9–10.7, SL.9–10.2, SL.9–10.3, SL.9–10.4)

5. SPEECH

Select a one-minute passage from *The Odyssey* or *The Aeneid* and recite it from memory. Include an introduction that states:

- What the excerpt is
- Who wrote it
- Why it is significant as an example of an important literary tradition (RL.9–10.6, SL.9–10.6)

6. WRITING (ARGUMENT) AND SEMINAR QUESTION

Is Aeneas (or Odysseus) courageous? The seminar question may also be used as an essay topic. State your thesis clearly and include at least three pieces of evidence to support it. (RL.9–10.3, SL.9–10.1, SL.9–10.4, SL.9–10.6)

7. WRITING (ARGUMENT)

Select someone you know or someone famous in contemporary history, and write an argument that explains why you think this person exemplifies the characteristics of an epic hero. Be sure to include at least three specific characteristics and offer examples from the person's "journey" to support your opinion. (W.9–10.1)

8. INFORMATIONAL TEXT AND INFORMATIVE/EXPLANATORY WRITING (FOR ADVANCED STUDENTS)

Read teacher-selected excerpts of Scott Richardson's essay "The Devious Narrator of *The Odyssey*." Compose an informative/explanatory essay in which you discuss how this depiction of the relationship between you (the audience) and Homer (the author) influences your reading of Odysseus's journey. (RL.9–10.3, RL.9–10.5, W.9–10.2)

9. GRAMMAR AND USAGE

Parts of Speech Review

Conjunctions: coordinating, correlative, subordinating (vs. prepositions)
Conjunctive adverbs

Select three paragraphs from one of the informational texts listed. Highlight all the conjunctions and conjunctive adverbs. Identify what kind of conjunctions they are, and explain when and why conjunctive adverbs are used instead of conjunctions. (L.9–10.1)

10. MECHANICS

Semicolons

Using the same excerpt as in Activity 8, explain the reason for the use of each semicolon in the text. (L.9–10.2)

11. ART/CLASS DISCUSSION

Compare the Greek relief and the page from *The Ramayana*. Both show scenes from epic stories. How do they convey heroism? How would you describe the main characters in the scenes? Do you know who the main characters are? Without knowing any additional information about these images, provide some insight into what you see. How is the artist telling these stories? (SL.9–10.1, SL.9–10.2)

12. ART/WRITING

Describe what the text does to the manuscript page from *The Ramayana*. Even though you cannot read the text, how does it enhance or detract from the image? Write what you believe the text says. If there were text in the Greek relief, what do you think it would say? (W.9–10.1, W.9–10.3)

ADDITIONAL RESOURCES

- *Lessons of the Indian Epics: Following the Dharma* (National Endowment for the Humanities) (RL.9–10.6)

TERMINOLOGY

Allusion	Epic/homeric simile	Invocation
Archetype	Epithet	Narrative
Arete	Evidence	Oral tradition
Chronological order	Hero	Thesis statement
The classical epic poem	Heroic couplet	
Epic poetry	Iambic pentameter	

Grade Nine, Unit Five Sample Lesson Plan

The Odyssey by Homer

Excerpts from Poetics by Aristotle

In this series of eleven lessons, students read Homer's *The Odyssey* and excerpts from Aristotle's *Poetics*, and they:

Explore the legacy of Homer (RI.9-10.7, SL.9-10.1, SL.9-10.2, W.9-10.8)

Examine Aristotle's description of:

The role of the poet (RL.9-10.1, RL.9-10.4, W.9-10.9a, SL.9-10.1, L.9-10.4)

The social function of the epic poem (RL.9-10.6, W.9-10.9a, SL.9-10.1)

The characteristics of epic poetry (W.9-10.7, RL.9-10.1, SL.9-10.1)

Examine the narrative structure of *The Odyssey* (RL.9-10.5, W.9-10.9a, SL.9-10.1, L.9-10.6)

Analyze Odysseus's character (RL.9-10.1, RL.9-10.2, RL.9-10.3, RL.9-10.9a, SL.9-10.4, L.9-10.5)

Produce an *Odyssey* journal (W.9-10.4, W.9-10.6, RL.9-10.10, L.9-10.6)

Summary

Lesson I: Homer and the Epic Poem

Explore the legacy of Homer (RI.9-10.7, SL.9-10.1, SL.9-10.2, W.9-10.8)

Examine Aristotle's description of:

The role of the poet (RL.9-10.1, RL.9-10.4, W.9-10.9a, SL.9-10.1, L.9-10.4)

The social function of the epic poem (RL.9-10.6, W.9-10.9a, SL.9-10.1)

The characteristics of epic poetry (W.9-10.7, RL.9-10.1, SL.9-10.1)

Investigate the story of the Trojan War (RL.9-10.1, RL.9-10.5, W.9-10.9a, SL.9-10.1)

Lesson II: Historical Context of *The Odyssey* and Telemachus's Journey Begins (Books I–IV)

Investigate the story of the Trojan War (RL.9-10.1, RL.9-10.2, RL.9-10.5, W.9-10.9a, SL.9-10.1)

Note the historical context at the beginning of *The Odyssey* (RL.9-10.1, RL.9-10.9, SL.9-10.1)

Explore the details of Telemachus's decision to search for his father, Odysseus (RL.9-10.1, RL.9-10.3, SL.9-10.1, W.9-10.9a)

Record the information that Telemachus learns in Books III–IV (W.9-10.4, RL.9-10.4, L.9-10.6)

Document the elements of the epic poem (RL.9-10.2, W.9-10.4, W.9-10.9a)

Lesson III: Meet Odysseus (Books V–VIII)

Probe the role that the gods play in Odysseus's fate (RL.9-10.1, RL.9-10.2, RL.9-10.3, RL.9-10.5, SL.9-10.4)

Document early impressions of Odysseus (Books V–VI) (W.9-10.4, W.9-10.9a)

Recall details of Books VII-VIII (RL.9-10.1, RL.9-10.3, RL.9-10.5, W.9-10.9a, SL.9-10.1, L.9-10.6)

Explore the narrator's attitude towards Odysseus (RI.9-10.1, RL.9-10.4, L.9-10.5, SL.9-10.1, W.9-10.9a)

Examine the complexity of Odysseus's character (RL.9-10.1, RL.9-10.3, RL.9-10.4, SL.9-10.4, L.9-10.5)

Continue to document the elements of the epic poem (RL.9-10.2, W.9-10.4, W.9-10.9a)

Lesson V: Odysseus Returns to Ithaca (Books XIII–XIV)

Examine the involvement of the gods in the events that unfold (RL.9-10.1, RL.9-10.2, RL.9-10.3, RL.9-10.4, SL.9-10.4, L.9-10.5)

Probe Athena's warning (RL.9-10.1, RL.9-10.3, RL.9-10.5, SL.9-10.4, L.9-10.6)

Explore the function of the deceptions in Books XIII-XIV (RL.9-10.1, RL.9-10.2, RL.9-10.4, L.9-10.5, SL.9-10.1, W.9-10.9a)

Consider the purpose of Odysseus's lies (RL.9-10.1, FL.9-10.3, RL.9-10.5, SL.9-10.4, L.9-10.5)

Continue to document the elements of the epic poem (FL.9-10.2, W.9-10.4, W.9-10.9a)

Lesson IV: Odysseus' Story (Books IX–XII)

Examine why Odysseus hides his true identity (RL.9-10.1, RL.9-10.2, RL.9-10.3, SL.9-10.4, W.9-10.9a)

Question the details of Odysseus's narrative (RL.9-10.1, RL.9-10.5, W.9-10.9a, SL.9-10.1, L.9-10.6)

Examine Odysseus's actions (RL.9-10.3, RL.9-10.4, SL.9-10.4, L.9-10.5)

Explore the meaning of Odysseus's visit to the dead (RI.9-10.1, RL.9-10.2, RL.9-10.4, L.9-10.5, SL.9-10.1, W.9-10.9a)

Continue to document the elements of the epic poem (RL.9-10.2, W.9-10.4, W.9-10.9a)

Lesson VI: Father and Son (Books XV–XX)

Outline events as they unfold in Books XV-XX (RL.9-10.1, RL.9-10.2, RL.9-10.3, RL.9-10.5, W.9-10.9a, SL.9-10.1, L.9-10.6)

Explore Athena's role in these events (RI.9-10.1, RL.9-10.3, L.9-10.5, SL.9-10.1, W.9-10.9a)

Trace the numerous deceptions of the characters (RL.9-10.1, RL.9-10.2, SL.9-10.4, L.9-10.5)

Examine the exchanges between Odysseus and Penelope (RL.9-10.1, RL.9-10.2, RL.9-10.3, RL.9-10.4, SL.9-10.4, L.9-10.5)

Continue to document the elements of the epic poem (RL.9-10.2, W.9-10.4, W.9-10.9a)

Lesson VII: The Journey Ends (Books XXI–XXIV)

Examine the battle scenes between Odysseus and the suitors (RL.9-10.1, RL.9-10.3, RL.9-10.4, SL.9-10.4, L.9-10.5)

Analyze Penelope's reaction to Odysseus's revelation (RL.9-10.1, RL.9-10.3, SL.9-10.4)

Explore the purpose of Book XXIV (RL.9-10.2, RL.9-10.5, SL.9-10.1)

Continue to document the elements of the epic poem (RL.9-10.2, W.9-10.4, W.9-10.9a)

Lesson VIII: Research Journals

Examine Aristotle's statement: "Hence poetry is something more philosophic and of graver import than history, since its statements are of the nature rather of universals, whereas those of history are singulars" in the context of the poem (Ch. 9) (RL.9-10.1, RL.9-10.2, RL.9-10.4, SL.9-10.4, L.9-10.5)

Identify the components of *The Odyssey* Journals (SL.9-10.1)

Assign tasks (SL.9-10.1)

Lesson IX, X: Produce *The Odyssey* Journals

Conduct the work assigned in Lesson VIII

Lay out material in journal form (W.9-10.4, W.9-10.5, W.9-10.6, RL.9-10.10, SL.9-10.4, L.9-10.1, L.9-10.2, L.9-10.3)

Lesson XI: Present *The Odyssey* Journals—A Fair

Display *The Odyssey* Journals (W.9-10.6, SL.9-10.5)

Examine the journals (SL.9-10.3)

Reflect upon the process of producing the journals (SL.9-10.4)

Revisit the lessons learned from *The Odyssey* (SL.9-10.1)

Lesson VIII: Research Journals

Objectives

Examine Aristotle's statement: "Hence poetry is something more philosophic and of graver import than history, since its statements are of the nature rather of universals, whereas those of history are singulars" in the context of the poem (RL.9-10.1, RL.9-10.2, RL.9-10.4, SL.9-10.4, L.9-10.5)

Identify the components of *The Odyssey* Journals (SL.9-10.1)

Assign tasks (SL.9-10.1)

Required Materials

☐ Class set of *The Odyssey*
☐ Class set of excerpts from *Poetics*, or access to online version (Ch. 9)
☐ Internet access
☐ Library access

Procedures

1. Lead-In:

Lead a class discussion prompted by Aristotle's words:

From what we have said, it will be seen that the poet's function is to describe, not the thing that has happened, but a kind of thing that might happen, i.e., what is possible as being probable or necessary. The distinction between historian and poet is not in the one writing prose and the other verse—you might put the work of Herodotus into verse, and it would still be a species of history; it consists really in this, that the one describes the thing that has been, and the other a kind of thing that might be. Hence poetry is something more philosophic and of graver import than history, since its statements are of the nature rather of universals, whereas those of history are singulars. By a universal statement I mean one as to what such or such a kind of man will probably or necessarily say or do—which is the aim of poetry, though it affixes proper names to the characters; by a singular statement, one as to what, say, Alcibiades did or had done to him. (Ch. 9)

A possible prompt: How does *The Odyssey* convey that "its statements are of the nature rather of universals"?

2. Step by Step:

a. Introduce the students to the research project: *The Odyssey* Journals. List (with the students' input) the components of the journals:

   - Maps of Odysseus's voyages
   - Story of the Trojan War
   - Artistic renditions of Homer and the Trojan War (with captions)
   - Short texts introducing Homer and Aristotle
   - Reflective passages about the universal ideas that *The Odyssey* exposes

b. Class breaks into small groups.

c. In groups, students hold editorial meetings. They identify the sections of the journal that they will produce and explore a working layout for the journal. They divide the work amongst themselves, building upon the strengths of individual participants.

d. Research begins. Occasionally, the groups convene to discuss progress. You may choose to conduct some of these meetings in order to evaluate the progress of each of the groups.

e. Once the material has been edited and assembled, the groups lay out their journals.

3. Closure:

The students prepare for *The Odyssey* Journals Fair, which will be held during the next lesson.

Differentiation

Advanced

- Encourage students to prepare a biography of Aristotle and/or Homer for classmates. Students should also research what inspired these authors to write and perhaps present this information as an online poster or podcast.
- Have students find and evaluate the most helpful materials and websites for other classmates. Collect the websites on a web portal.
- Pair students to work collaboratively on this project. Encourage them to present their journals in a multimedia format, such as a movie or a web page. Their work should consistently reflect the highest levels of analysis.
- Encourage students to be editors in specific areas of expertise for their classmates.

Struggling

- Consider pre-teaching the key ideas of Aristotle's *Poetics* to students on the day prior (for example, giving them an outline to read or video to view with important vocabulary highlighted). Alternatively, work with a small group of students to identify significant quotations from Aristotle's *Poetics* that will enable them to participate in class discussion. To aid in memory and understanding, allow students to annotate or sketch (or use other nonlinguistic representations) directly on a paper or electronic copy, and share as a group, possibly using a document camera.
- Students research the information needed for *The Odyssey* beyond the text, using pre-selected websites on a web portal (selected by classmates, above). Encourage students to use a graphic organizer to collect their journal research, either on paper or on a shared spreadsheet so that all students have access to it.

Homework/Assessment
N/A

Literary Nonfiction— Reflection (the Memoir, the Essay, and the Speech)

This unit, the last of six, focuses on three kinds of literary nonfiction: the memoir, the essay, and the speech, with "reflection" as the common aspect of these genres.

OVERVIEW

The unit allows students to recognize and appreciate the effective use of literary devices in nonfiction. Students are exposed to memoirs from various cultures and look for common techniques, such as the emphasis on a particularly significant event or time period in the author's life. Works of art that address similar goals, such as self-portraits, are also examined to compare presentation. Students also consider the ways in which essays and speeches may exhibit the same reflective qualities, whereby the authors or orators engage readers or listeners to think carefully about literature, events, or ideas in a new way.

ESSENTIAL QUESTION

How is reflecting different from remembering?

FOCUS STANDARDS

These Focus Standards have been selected for the unit from the Common Core State Standards.

RL.9–10.4: Determine the meaning of words and phrases as they are used in the text, including figurative and connotative meanings; analyze the cumulative impact of several word choices on meaning and tone (e.g., how the language evokes a sense of time and place; how it sets a formal or informal tone).

RI.9–10.3: Analyze how the author unfolds an analysis or series of ideas or events, including the order in which the points are made, how they are introduced and developed, and the connections that are drawn between them.

RI.9–10.9: Analyze seminal U.S. documents of historical and literary significance (e.g., Washington's Farewell Address, the Gettysburg Address, Roosevelt's Four Freedoms speech, King's "Letter from a Birmingham Jail"), including how they address related themes and concepts.

W.9–10.3: Write narratives to develop real or imagined experiences or events using effective technique, well-chosen details, and well-structured event sequences.

SL.9–10.3: Evaluate a speaker's point of view, reasoning, and use of evidence and rhetoric, identifying any fallacious reasoning or exaggerated or distorted evidence.

L.9–10.1: Demonstrate command of the conventions of Standard English grammar and usage when writing or speaking.

SUGGESTED STUDENT OBJECTIVES

- Identify and explain the characteristics of a memoir
- Distinguish between an autobiography and a memoir.
- Identify and explain the effect of stylistic devices used in memoirs.
- Identify and explain the characteristics of various types of essays (e.g., literary and narrative).
- Identify and analyze the effect of rhetorical strategies in speeches such as alliteration, repetition, and extended metaphors.
- Apply rhetorical strategies learned in this lesson to essay writing projects of their own.

SUGGESTED WORKS

(E) indicates a CCSS exemplar text; (EA) indicates a text from a writer with other works identified as exemplars.

LITERARY TEXTS

None for this unit

INFORMATIONAL TEXTS

Memoirs

- *One Writer's Beginnings* (Eudora Welty)
- *A Childhood: The Biography of a Place* (Harry E. Crews)
- *Running in the Family* (Michael Ondaatje)
- "A Four Hundred Year Old Woman" (Bharati Mukherjee)
- "In Search of Our Mothers' Gardens" (Alice Walker) (EA)
- *The Woman Warrior: Memoirs of a Girlhood Among Ghosts* (Maxine Hong Kingston)
- "Learning to Read and Write" (Frederick Douglass) (EA)
- *Notes of a Native Son* (James Baldwin)
- "A Sketch of the Past" (Virginia Woolf)

Essay

- *Life on the Mississippi* (Mark Twain) (EA) (excerpts)

Speeches

- "Second Inaugural Address" (Abraham Lincoln) (E)
- "Gettysburg Address" (Abraham Lincoln) (E)

- "Address at the March on Washington" (Martin Luther King Jr.) (E)
- "Letter from a Birmingham Jail" (Martin Luther King Jr.) (E)
- Nobel Prize Acceptance Speech, 1949 (William Faulkner) (EA)
- "Sinews of Peace Address" (Winston Churchill)
- "Brandenburg Gate Address" (June 12, 1987) (Ronald Reagan)
- "Letter to Albert G. Hodges"

Essays

- "Politics and the English Language" (George Orwell) (E) (*This is a CCSS exemplar text for grades 11 and 12.*)
- "The Lost Childhood" (Graham Greene)
- Excerpts from *The 100 Most Influential Books Ever Written: The History of Thought from Ancient Times to Today* (Martin Seymour-Smith)
- "Lear, Tolstoy, and The Fool" (George Orwell)
- "Avant-Garde and Kitsch" (Clement Greenberg)
- "Preface to *Lyrical Ballads*" (William Wordsworth)
- "Lincoln and the Gettysburg Awakening" (Glenn LaFantasie) (excerpts)

ART, MUSIC, AND MEDIA

Art

- Vincent van Gogh, *Self-Portrait* (1889)
- Jan van Eyck, *Self-Portrait* (1433)
- Albrecht Dürer, *Self-Portrait at the age of 13* (1484)
- Leonardo da Vinci, *Possible Self-Portrait of Leonardo da Vinci* (ca.1513)
- Rembrandt van Rijn, *Self-Portrait at an early age* (1628)
- Rembrandt van Rijn, *Self-Portrait at the Age of 63* (1669)
- Artemisia Gentileschi, *Self-Portrait as the Allegory of Painting* (1638–1639)
- Jacob Lawrence, *Self-Portrait* (1977)
- Gustave Courbet, *The Desperate Man* (self-portrait) (1843)
- Louisa Matthíasdóttir, *Self-Portrait with Dark Coat* (no date)
- Francis Bacon, *Self-Portrait* (1973)
- Balthus, *Le roi des chats* (*The king of cats*) (1935)
- Pablo Picasso, *Self-Portrait* (1907)

SAMPLE ACTIVITIES AND ASSESSMENTS

For a full Scoring Rubric, see the Appendix.

Note: Textual evidence should be used to support all arguments advanced in seminars and in essays. Page and word counts for essays are not provided here, but attention should be paid to the requirements regarding the use of evidence, for example, to determine the likely length of good essays.

1. NARRATIVE WRITING (MEMOIR)

Write a memoir (perhaps after the style of one of those read) recounting a specific person, place, experience, event, day, moment, work of art, or another specific thing and convey its significance to you. Your teacher may give you the option of adding a multimedia component to your memoir, such as a digital slide presentation, for posting on the class web page. (W.9–10.3, L.9–10.5, SL.9–10.5)

2. INFORMATIVE/EXPLANATORY WRITING

Write an informative/explanatory essay in which you discuss how two literary texts studied this year illustrate Faulkner's thesis in his 1949 Nobel Prize acceptance speech. State your thesis clearly and include at least three pieces of evidence to support it. Your teacher may give you the opportunity to post your first draft on a shared online document and receive feedback from classmates before publication. (RL.9–10.2, RI.9–10.9, W.9–10.2)

3. SPEECH

Select a one-minute passage from one of the speeches here and recite it from memory. Include an introduction that explains:

- The occasion/context of the speech
- Its literary and historical significance

Record your recitation using a video camera so you can evaluate your performance for accuracy. (SL.9–10.6)

4. SEMINAR QUESTION AND INFORMATIVE/EXPLANATORY WRITING

Compare Lincoln's Gettysburg Address with Martin Luther King Jr.'s Address at the March on Washington and explain why these are both considered great speeches. Be specific and cite from the texts. Begin by identifying the elements of a good speech. The seminar question may also be used as an essay topic. State your thesis clearly and include at least three pieces of evidence to support it. Your teacher may give you the opportunity to share your initial thoughts on the classroom blog in order to get feedback from your classmates. (SL.9–10.1, SL.9–10.3)

5. ART/ORAL PRESENTATION

Examine the artworks listed. Begin by comparing Rembrandt's *Self-Portrait at an early age* with his *Self-Portrait at the Age of 63*. How has the artist depicted himself in both paintings? Although you can infer from the titles and dates of the works that the artist has aged, what visual clues is Rembrandt giving you? How is he drawing you, as the viewer, into the work of art? Is he telling a story through these portraits—and if so, how? Now view two very different self-portraits—by Jacob Lawrence and Pablo Picasso. How has self-portraiture changed, and remained the same, over time? What similarities can you find in these self-portraits? (RL.9–10.7, SL.9–10.1, SL.9–10.2, SL.9–10.5)

6. ORAL HISTORY AND NARRATIVE WRITING PROJECT: "IN THEIR VOICES"

First, students will interview an adult member of their family. The interview must be substantive; if transcribed, it should be at least one thousand words. Then, they will compose memoirs in the voice of the relative. (SL.9–10.1, SL.9–10.2, W. 9–10.1, L.9–10.4, L.9–10.5)

7. GRAMMAR AND USAGE/MECHANICS

Parts of Speech Review

Interjections (and their punctuation)

Identify the interjections in a passage from one of the memoirs. Explain why their use is appropriate. Would there have been another way to write the sentence(s) in which the interjections are used—and still have the same effect? Why or why not? (L.9–10.1, L.9–10.2)

8. ART/CLASS DISCUSSION

Examine Courbet's *The Desperate Man* and Matthíasdóttir's *Self Portrait with Dark Coat*. How has each artist chosen to depict himself or herself? What mood is each painter trying to depict, and what visual clues led you to discover this? Why do you believe that painters paint themselves—especially in the case of these two images? Is it similar to why people write memoirs? Are these self-portraits believable—that is, do you think it is a faithful depiction of the painter? What do we mean by "faithful" in portraiture, or in writing? (SL.9–10.1, SL.9–10.2, SL.9–10.5)

ADDITIONAL RESOURCES

- *Introducing the Essay: Twain, Douglass, and American Nonfiction* (National Endowment for the Humanities) (RI.9–10.5)
- *Annotated List of Memoirs* (ReadWriteThink)
- *Online Bank of American Speeches* (americanrhetoric.com)

TERMINOLOGY

Abstract/universal essay	Compare-and-contrast essay	Objective/factual essay
Alliteration	Ethos, pathos, logos	Personal/autobiographical essay
Autobiography	Exemplification	Repetition
Chronological order	Extended metaphor	Satire
Classification and division	Memoir	

Grade Nine, Unit Six Sample Lesson Plan

Abraham Lincoln's Gettysburg Address, Second Inaugural Address, and Letter to Albert G. Hodges

In this series of four lessons, students read Abraham Lincoln's Gettysburg Address, Second Inaugural Address, and Letter to Albert G. Hodges, and they:

Examine the historical context of the Gettysburg Address (RI.9-10.9)

Explore the historical impact of the Gettysburg Address (SL.9-10.1c,d)

Investigate a thematic continuity from the Gettysburg Address to the Second Inaugural Address (RI.9-10.1, RI.9-10.2, RI.9-10.3, RI.9-10.6)

Evaluate the ability of words to impact history (RI.9-10.2, RI.9-10.3, RI.9-10.5, RI.9-10.6)

Summary

Lesson I: Abraham Lincoln and the Civil War

Investigate Lincoln's place in American history (RI.9-10.9)

Explore the background to the Civil War (RI.9-10.9)

Chronicle key events in the Civil War (RI.9-10.9)

Identify the details of the battle of Gettysburg (RI.9-10.2)

Lesson II: The Gettysburg Address

Explore the content of the Gettysburg Address (RI.9-10.9)

Explicate the address (RI.9-10.1)

Analyze the rhetorical moves of the address (RI.9-10.2, RI.9-10.3, RI.9-10.5, RI.9-10.6)

Consider why Gettysburg is regarded as "America's most hallowed ground" (SL.9-10.1c,d)

Evaluate "Lincoln and the Gettysburg Awakening" (W.9-10.2a,b,d,e)

Lesson III: Lincoln's Second Inaugural Address and a Letter to Albert G. Hodges	Lesson IV: The Power of Words
Trace the continuity of themes from the Gettysburg Address to Lincoln's Second Inaugural Address (RI.9-10.1, RI.9-10.2, RI.9-10.3, RI.9-10.6)	(Independently or in groups) research and identify a memorable address (SL.9-10.1a, SL.9-10.2)
(Continue to) trace pivotal themes through Lincoln's letter to Hodges (RL.9-10.1, RL.9-10.2, RL.9-10.3, RI.9-10.6)	Provide historical context to the address (SL.9-10.1a, SL.9-10.2)
Examine the rhetorical and literary skills in the speech and in the letter (RI.9-10.6)	Examine the content of the address (SL.9-10.1a, SL.9-10.2)
	Explore the historical impact of the address
Evaluate the continuing historical relevance of Lincoln's words: "With malice toward none; with charity for all; with firmness in the right … and with all nations." (SL.9-10.1.c,d)	Evaluate the fulfillment of its promise for future "awakening" (similar to Gettysburg's)

Lesson II: The Gettysburg Address

Objectives

Explore the content of the Gettysburg Address (RI.9-10.9)

Explicate the address (RI.9-10.1)

Analyze the rhetorical moves of the address (RI.9-10.2, RI.9-10.3, RI.9-10.5, RI.9-10.6)

Consider why Gettysburg is regarded as "America's most hallowed ground" (SL.9-10.1c,d)

Evaluate "Lincoln and the Gettysburg Awakening" (W.9-10.2a,b,d,e)

Required Materials

☐ The Gettysburg Address (class set)

☐ Excerpt from Glenn LaFantasie's "Lincoln and the Gettysburg Awakening" (class set)

Procedures

1. Lead-In:
Quietly read the Gettysburg address (twice). A student volunteer reads the text aloud.
2. Step by Step:
   a. Students discuss the content of the address and paraphrase Lincoln words.

b. Once the students have a grasp of the address's content, they turn to an evaluation of its structure; an explication of the address highlights Lincoln's rhetorical moves. Emphasize the following:

Paragraph I: The promise of America

Paragraph II: The purpose of the war and the reason why "we" are in the "final resting place" of the soldiers

Paragraph III: Why "we" cannot consecrate this ground; why it is that the soldiers who died consecrate the ground; the promise that their death "shall not be in vain"; why Lincoln asserts that America "under God, shall have a new birth of Freedom."

c. Students discuss the claim that Gettysburg is regarded as "America's most hallowed ground" as they evaluate Lincoln's words in their historical context.

d. Students read the excerpt from the LaFantasie essay. Explicate the content of the passage.

3. Closure:

A student volunteer reads the address aloud. Let the impact of the words provide the closure for the lesson.

Differentiation

Advanced

- Students may perform steps a and b on their own.
- Students will document the results of their study.
- If the class has access to an interactive whiteboard, the students' findings will be typed, projected, and used for step c.
- Students could type their responses into a shared spreadsheet, compare answers, and debate similarities or differences among them.

Struggling

- Assist students in small groups.
- Consider varying the academic level of the groups and having the more advanced students assist.
- (Lead-In) Provide students with an audio or video recording of the Gettysburg Address to listen to or watch as they read along. Alternately, assign this as homework the night before as a preview.

Homework/Assessment

I. Writing Task

In "Lincoln and the Gettysburg Awakening," Glenn LaFantasie (see below) argues that Lincoln, in his Gettysburg Address, "achieved a revolution . . . by putting the central element of the Declaration of Independence — equality — in a new light as a fundamental principle of the Constitution which does not mention equality at all."

Students' task is to write a well-developed paragraph analyzing a specific aspect of Lincoln's Gettysburg Address in the context of LaFantasie's argument.

II. Writing Guidelines

Your paragraph will:

- Contain an analysis — not a summary — of the idea that you choose to discuss
- Be carefully and deliberately developed
- Demonstrate a mastery of organizational skills (topic sentences, transitions, order of ideas, etc.)
- Cite both the Gettysburg Address and LaFantasie
- Integrate the citations
- Use Standard English grammar

Lincoln seemed like a prophet of old at Gettysburg because what he said possessed profound spiritual force. Simply put, Lincoln offered a new definition of old truths—a new perspective on old traditions—that unlocked deep American emotions, the mystic chords of memory that Lincoln referred to in his First Inaugural Address. As Garry Wills has shown, Lincoln achieved a revolution at Gettysburg by putting the central element of the Declaration of Independence—equality—in a new light as a fundamental principle of the Constitution, which does not mention equality at all. Lincoln had once declared, "I have never had a feeling politically that did not spring from the sentiments embodied in the Declaration of Independence."[33] At Gettysburg, his address looked back to those sentiments, which were "dedicated to the proposition that all men are created equal," and then looked forward with hope that those sentiments, those old traditions, could be understood in a new light and could, through a rededication of the American people, produce "a new birth of freedom" in the nation that would be as dramatic and as transforming as the spiritual regeneration of a camp meeting or a great awakening. In this respect, then, Lincoln at Gettysburg resembled the stump preachers whose sermons urged that the old light be shunned and a new light embraced, that each soul find God's new light in the awakening of conversion. With the Gettysburg Address, Lincoln was preaching his own great awakening.[34]

Excerpt from Glenn LaFantasie's "Lincoln and the Gettysburg Awakening"

GRADE 10

In tenth grade, students study literature from around the world. There are four twelve-week units (Latin and Central American literature, Asian literature, African and Middle Eastern literature, and Russian literature). Schools should select three out of the four. Each unit allows for close study of literary works, as well as consideration of historical and cultural context. The units focus not only on geographical regions, but also on themes and literary forms that pertain to them. Thus students come to grasp the relationship between local concerns and universal questions. In the Russian literature unit, students begin by reading short Russian masterpieces of the nineteenth century (including works by Pushkin, Gogol, and Chekhov), and proceed to read select twentieth-century works in historical context. In the Asian literature unit, students observe and describe literary forms in texts ranging from Confucius's *Analects* to works by Rabindranath Tagore. In the unit on Africa and the Middle East, students gain cultural insight as they explore prose and poetry from the *Arabian Nights* to Chinua Achebe's *Things Fall Apart*. When studying the literature of Latin America, students read works by Jorge Luis Borges, Julio Cortázar, Gabriel García Márquez, and others. They become aware of the authors' views of literature itself—its forms, peculiarities, language, and relationship to reality. Throughout the year, students take part in seminars, write essays, and deliver speeches. Having read literature from a variety of cultures, they are ready to embark on eleventh grade and the study of American literature.

Standards Checklist for Grade Ten

Standard	Unit 1	Unit 2	Unit 3	Unit 4	Standard	Unit 1	Unit 2	Unit 3	Unit 4
Reading—Literature					3d				
1	FA	A	FA	A	3e				
2	A	FA	A	A	4	FA		F	
3		A		FA	5	F		FA	
4	FA		FA	A	6	F		FA	
5		FA	A	FA	7	A	FA	A	A
6	FA	A	FA	A	8	A	A	A	A
7		A			9	FA	A	FA	A
8 n/a					9a				
9		A			9b				
10			A		10	A	FA	A	A
Reading—Informational Text					Speaking and Listening				
1	A	F	A		1	A	FA	A	A
2			A		1a				
3			A	FA	1b				
4		F			1c				
5	FA		FA		1d				
6				FA	2	A	A	A	A
7				F	3			A	FA
8	F		F		4	A		A	A
9					5	A			
10					6	FA		FA	A
Writing					Language				
1	A	A	A	FA	1	A			
1a					1a				
1b					1b			A	
1c					2		F		
1d					2a				
1e					2b				
2	A	A	A	FA	3				FA
2a					3a				
2b					4				
2c					4a				
2d					4b				
2e					4c				
2f					4d				
3	A		A		5	FA		F	
3a					5a				
3b					5b				
3c					6	F		FA	

F = Focus Standards; A = Activity/Assessment

World Literature: Latin and Central America

In this twelve-week unit, students read works by Latin American and Central American authors.

ESSENTIAL QUESTION

? How does magical realism reveal new perspectives of reality?

OVERVIEW

Students consider religious, generational, and cultural conflicts, as well as the effects of modernization, political struggle, and other themes common to many literary works. Many works in the unit feature magical realism, and may be compared to those found in the Russian literature unit (Unit Four). Students also recognize that not all literary works make explicit political or cultural statements and that they must be approached on their own terms. In order to enrich their understanding, students investigate the historical background for selected works, as well as author biographies.

Note: The tenth-grade World Literature Maps consist of four twelve-week units, each focusing on literature from a different part of the world. Select three out of the four units. As the middle unit will likely cross from one semester into another, it should be divided accordingly. Alternatively, teachers may choose to teach all four units by shortening each and selecting fewer works.

FOCUS STANDARDS

These Focus Standards have been selected for the unit from the Common Core State Standards.

RL.9–10.1: Cite strong and thorough textual evidence to support analysis of what the text says explicitly as well as inferences drawn from the text.

RL.9–10.4: Determine the meaning of words and phrases as they are used in the text, including figurative and connotative meanings; analyze the cumulative impact of specific word choices on meaning and tone (e.g., how the language evokes a sense of time and place; how it sets a formal or informal tone).

RL.9–10.6: Analyze a particular point of view or cultural experience reflected in a work of literature from outside the United States, drawing on a wide reading of world literature.

RI.9–10.5: Analyze in detail how an author's ideas or claims are developed and refined by particular sentences, paragraphs, or larger portions of a text (e.g., a section or chapter).

RI.9–10.8: Delineate and evaluate the argument and specific claims in a text, assessing whether the reasoning is valid and the evidence is relevant and sufficient; identify false statements and fallacious reasoning.

W.9–10.4: Produce clear and coherent writing in which the development, organization, and style are appropriate to task, purpose, and audience. (Grade-specific expectations for writing types are defined in standards 1–3 above.)

W.9–10.5: Develop and strengthen writing as needed by planning, revising, editing, rewriting, or trying a new approach, focusing on addressing what is most significant for a specific purpose and audience. (Editing for conventions should demonstrate command of Language standards 1–3 up to and including grades 9–10 on page 54 of the Common Core State Standards.)

W.9–10.6: Use technology, including the Internet, to produce, publish, and update individual or shared writing products, taking advantage of technology's capacity to link to other information and to display information flexibly and dynamically.

W.9–10.9: Draw evidence from literary or informational texts to support analysis, reflection, and research.

SL.9–10.6: Adapt speech to a variety of contexts and tasks, demonstrating command of formal English when indicated or appropriate. (See grades 9–10 Language standards 1 and 3 on page 54 of the Common Core State Standards for specific expectations.)

L.9–10.5: Demonstrate understanding of figurative language, word relationships, and nuances in word meanings.

L.9–10.6: Acquire and use accurately grade-appropriate general academic and domain-specific words and phrases; gather vocabulary knowledge when considering a word or phrase important to comprehension or expression.

SUGGESTED STUDENT OBJECTIVES

- Explore the role of the magical and the fantastic in Latin American literature.
- Explore narrative forms and techniques in Latin American literature.
- Analyze the role of time in Latin American narrative.
- Listen to and analyze Latin American poetry in the original and in translation.
- Explore the role of local and universal themes in Latin American literature.
- Consider the challenges of translation, including the different connotations that various cultures attach to given words.
- Offer insightful inferences regarding the themes of the text.
- Create clear, original, specific thesis statements.
- Organize concrete evidence and supporting textual details to support a thesis statement.
- Use precise language, avoiding casual language and clichés.
- Write appropriate transitions to organize paragraphs.
- Analyze how literary devices produce meaning.

SUGGESTED WORKS

(E) indicates a CCSS exemplar text; (EA) indicates a text from a writer with other works identified as exemplars.

LITERARY TEXTS

Note: Texts can be combined in a number of ways. Students, for example, can read either one midlength novel or two short novels, in addition to a play, a selection of poems by various authors, and a nonfiction essay.

Novels

Chile

- *The House of the Spirits* (Isabel Allende and Magda Bogin, trans.)

Mexico

- *The Underdogs: A Novel of the Mexican Revolution* (Mariano Azuela and Sergio Waisman, trans.)
- *The Book of Lamentations* (Rosario Castellanos)
- *Like Water for Chocolate* (Laura Esquivel and Thomas Christensen, trans.)
- *The Old Gringo* (Carlos Fuentes and Margaret Sayers Peden, trans.)

Colombia

- *One Hundred Years of Solitude* (Gabriel García Márquez)

Short Stories

Argentina

- "End of the Game" (Julio Cortázar)
- "Letter to a Young Lady in Paris" (Julio Cortázar)
- "The Secret Miracle" (Jorge Luis Borges)
- "The Garden of Forking Paths" (Jorge Luis Borges)

Chile

- *The Stories of Eva Luna* (Isabel Allende) (selections)

Colombia

- "The Sea of Lost Time" (Gabriel García Márquez)
- "No One Writes to the Colonel" (Gabriel García Márquez)
- "Chronicle of a Death Foretold" (Gabriel García Márquez)

Cuba

- "Journey Back to the Source" (Alejo Carpentier)

Drama

Mexico

- *The Impostor: A Play for Demagogues* (Rodolfo Usigli and Ramon Layera, trans.)

Poetry

Chile

- *Gabriela Mistral: A Reader* (Gabriela Mistral, Maria Giachetti, trans., Marjorie Agosin, ed.) (selections)
- "Book of Twilight" (Pablo Neruda)
- *Twenty Love Poems and a Song of Despair* (Pablo Neruda and W. S. Merwin, trans.) (selections)

Mexico

- *Eagle or Sun?* (prose poems) (Octavio Paz) (selections)

INFORMATIONAL TEXTS

- "Complex Feelings about Borges" in *The Noé Jitrik Reader: Selected Essays on Latin American Literature* (Noé Jitrik and Susan E. Benner, trans.) (selections)
- *The Noé Jitrik Reader: Selected Essays on Latin American Literature* (Noé Jitrik and Susan E. Benner, trans.)
- *The Testimony of Contemporary Latin American Authors* (Doris Meyer, ed.) (excerpts)
- *Against All Hope: A Memoir of Life in Castro's Gulag* (Armando Valladares)

Speech

- "The Solitude of Latin America," Nobel Prize Acceptance Speech, 1982 (Gabriel García Márquez)

ART, MUSIC, AND MEDIA

Art

- Murals from Teotihuacan (Tetitla, ca. 100 BCE to 250 CE)
- Murals at Bonampak (Mayan, ca. 580 to 800 CE)
- Diego Rivera, *The History of Mexico: The Ancient Indian* World (1929 – 1935)
- Bird Pendant (Costa Rica, first century BCE to first century CE)
- Tripod Bird Bowl (Guatemala, third to fourth century)
- Deity Figure (Honduras, third to sixth century)
- Masked Figure Pendant (Colombia, tenth to sixteenth century)
- Drinking Vessel (Peru, late fifteenth to early sixteenth century)

SAMPLE ACTIVITIES AND ASSESSMENTS

For a full Scoring Rubric, see the Appendix.

Note: After reading and discussing a work or pairing of works as a class, students prepare for seminars and essays by reflecting individually, in pairs, and/or in small groups on a given question. In this way, students generate ideas. (Seminar and essay assignments include more than one question. Teachers may choose one or all of the questions to explore in the course of the seminar; students should choose one question for the essay.) Seminars should be held before students write essays so that they may explore their ideas thoroughly and refine their thinking before writing. Textual evidence should be used to support all arguments advanced in seminars and in all essays. Page and word counts for essays are not provided here, but teachers should consider the suggestions regarding the use of evidence, for example, to determine the likely length of good essays.

1. COLLABORATION

Reflect on seminar questions, take notes on your responses, and note the page numbers of the textual evidence you will refer to in your seminar and/or essay answers. Share your notes with a partner for feedback and guidance. Have you interpreted the text correctly? Is your evidence convincing? This collaboration can be done in a journal or on a shared online document. (RL.9 – 10.1, SL.9 – 10.1)

2. SEMINAR AND INFORMATIVE/EXPLANATORY WRITING

How does magical realism in *The Stories of Eva Luna,* "The Secret Miracle," "The Garden of Forking Paths," *The House of the Spirits,* or *Like Water for Chocolate* help the reader gain a deeper understanding of reality? How does magical realism reveal the author's true point of view? Write an informative/explanatory essay in which you use at least three pieces of specific textual evidence to support an original thesis statement. Your teacher may give you the opportunity to share your initial thoughts on the classroom blog in order to get feedback from your classmates. (RI.9–10.5, W.9–10.2, W.9–10.4, W.9–10.9, SL.9–10.1)

3. SEMINAR AND INFORMATIVE/EXPLANATORY WRITING

Consider magical realism in *The Stories of Eva Luna,* "The Secret Miracle," "The Garden of Forking Paths," *The House of the Spirits,* or *Like Water for Chocolate.* How is magical realism a metaphor? What is the relationship between the literal and the metaphoric? Does the reader need to suspend his or her notions of reality to accept the device of magical realism of the text? Defend your response using textual evidence to support your thesis. Write an informative/explanatory essay in which you use at least three pieces of textual evidence to support an original thesis statement. Your teacher may give you the opportunity share your initial thoughts on the classroom blog in order to get feedback from your classmates. (RI.9–10.5, W.9–10.2, W.9–10.4, W.9–10.9, SL.9–10.1)

4. ANALYSIS OF FIGURATIVE LANGUAGE

Your teacher will select passages from the works listed in Activity 3. In your journal or on a shared online spreadsheet, identify the figures of speech and interpret them in complete sentences. Then select the abstract nouns in the passage and discuss the nuances and various connotations of each. Discuss with your classmates which connotations you think the author intends. (L.9–10.5)

5. SEMINAR AND INFORMATIVE/EXPLANATORY WRITING

What does Márquez mean by "solitude" in his Nobel Prize acceptance speech, "The Solitude of Latin America," and his novel *One Hundred Years of Solitude*? How is solitude a metaphor? Is it a fitting metaphor? Why or why not? Use specific textual evidence to discuss. After the seminar, write an informative/explanatory essay using at least two pieces of textual evidence to support a clear thesis from both his speech and his novel. Your teacher may give you the opportunity share your initial thoughts on the classroom blog in order to get feedback from your classmates. (RL.9–10.4, W.9–10.2, W.9–10.4, W.9–10.9, SL.9–10.1)

6. SEMINAR AND WRITING (ARGUMENT)

(*Note:* This assessment is meant especially for bilingual students.)

Read key passages of "The Secret Miracle" or "The Garden of Forking Paths" in English and Spanish. Consider issues of translated texts. What skills does a good translator need to have? What, if anything, is lost in translation between the texts? Write an argument in which you organize three to six pieces (ideally, at least three pieces from each text) of textual evidence to support an original thesis statement. Your teacher may give you the opportunity share your initial thoughts on the classroom blog in order to get feedback from your classmates. (RL.9–10.4, W.9–10.2, W.9–10.4, W.9–10.9, SL.9–10.1)

7. SEMINAR AND INFORMATIVE/EXPLANATORY WRITING

How does love serve as a metaphor? Is there one common statement the texts in this unit all seem to be making about love? If so, what is that statement? After discussion in seminar, write a well-organized informative/explanatory essay using six pieces of textual evidence to support an original thesis statement. Your teacher may give you the opportunity to share your initial thoughts on the classroom blog in order to get feedback from your classmates. (RL.9–10.4, W.9–10.2, W.9–10.4, W.9–10.9, SL.9–10.1, SL.9–10.4)

8. NARRATIVE WRITING

Write a short story inspired by any of the works in the unit. Read it aloud to the class and invite discussion about which work might have inspired it and how. Your teacher may give you the option of adding a multimedia component, either creating a digital slide presentation or a movie where your narrative becomes the audio portion. These stories might be posted on a class web page for sharing with others outside of your class. (W.9–10.3, SL.9–10.1, SL.9–10.5)

9. SPEECH

Choose a poem or a prose passage from this unit (three minutes maximum) and recite it from memory. Include an introduction that discusses:

- Who wrote the poem and when it was written (i.e., historical context)
- What makes it memorable or significant
- Words and phrases that hold special meaning in context (RL.9–10.2, SL.9–10.6, L.9–10.5)

Record your recitation using a video camera so you can evaluate your performance for accuracy.

10. ORAL OR MIXED-MEDIA PRESENTATION

Prepare a ten-minute presentation on the life of a Latin American author, with images, maps, audio recordings, and any other applicable resources. Your teacher may ask you to record your presentation as a podcast or vodcast for publication on the class web page. (RI.9–10.1, SL.9–10.2, SL.9–10.5)

11. RESEARCH AND INFORMATIVE/EXPLANATORY WRITING (AND MULTIMEDIA PRESENTATION)

In 1945, Gabriela Mistral (from Chile) became the first Latin American author to win the Nobel Prize in Literature. Six others followed: Miguel Angel Asturias, Guatemala (1967); Pablo Neruda, Chile (1971); Gabriel García Márquez, Colombia (1982); Octavio Paz, Mexico (1990); Derek Walcott, Saint Lucia (1992); V. S. Naipaul, Trinidad (2001); and Mario Vargas Llosa, Peru (2010). Conduct independent research on one of these Nobel Prize winners. (Teachers may choose to assign authors so that all Nobel winners will be represented.) Then, write an informative/explanatory essay to communicate your findings (*optional:* also prepare a digital presentation). The paper should include the following sections:

- Biographical information
- The author's position and contribution in his/her country of origin
- Key ideas (including passages) from the author's Nobel Prize acceptance speech
- A survey of the author's work
- An analysis of a single text
- Reflective conclusion about the author and his/her contribution to twentieth-century literature

The essay should reflect the synthesis and/or adjudication among sources consulted, a balance of paraphrasing and quoting from sources, and proper citation of sources. (W.9–10.1, W.9–10.7, W.9–10.8, W.9–10.9, W.9–10.10)

12. GRAMMAR AND USAGE

Share a page of your research essay (see Activity 11) with a partner and identify (by type) all the clauses you can find. (L.9–10.1)

13. LANGUAGE

Your teacher will select passages from the works in Activity 3 (or others). Find all the figures of speech in the passages. In your journal or on a shared online document, explain what you think each means in the context of the story as a whole. (L.9–10.5)

14. ART/CLASS DISCUSSION

View the images painted in prehistoric Latin America. What do you see in the murals? What colors and symbols are prominent? Why do you think the artist used these colors and these symbols? What do you see in Rivera's mural in comparison to the ancient murals? Do the modern-day murals include any iconography from prehistoric Latin America? Why do you think the artist is interested in the Aztec and Mayan cultures? What symbolism did Rivera use? (SL.9–10.1, SL.9–10.2)

15. ART/CLASS DISCUSSION

Examine the Bird Pendant and Bird Bowl, created in two different Central American cultures. Why does the bird seem to be a relevant symbol for this culture? How has each culture depicted the bird figure— different shapes, forms, or lines? Now examine the Deity Figure from Honduras. What do you see in this figure? Does it look recognizable, or is it distinctively different? Compare the Deity to the Colombian Pendant. What is similar about these two objects? Are they similar in creation as well as style? (SL.9–10.1, SL.9–10.2)

ADDITIONAL RESOURCES

- *Author Gabriel García Márquez Was Born on This Day* (ReadWriteThink) (RL.9–10.6)

TERMINOLOGY

Extended metaphor	Imagery	Paradox	Third-person omniscience
First-person point of view	Irony	Rhetoric	
	Magical realism	Symbolism	
Foreshadowing	Metaphor	Theme	

Grade Ten, Unit One Sample Lesson Plan

Latin American Authors

Nobel Prize Winners

In this series of ten lessons, students read select texts by Gabriela Mistral, Miguel Angel Asturias, Pablo Neruda, Gabriel García Márquez, Octavio Paz, Derek Walcott, V.S. Naipaul, and Mario Vargas Llosa, and they:

Conduct an author study (RI.9-10.1, RI.9-10.2, RI.9-10.5, RI.9-10.7, W.9-10.8, SL.9-10.1, SL.9-10.2)

Explore the characteristics of magical realism (RL.9-10.1, RL.9-10.2, RL.9-10.5)

Produce a six- to eight-page research paper (W.9-10.4, W.9-10.5, W.9-10.7, SL.9-10.4, L.9-10.1, L.9-10.2, L.9-10.3)

Present a digital slide presentation about their author (W.9-10.6, SL.9-10.5, L.9-10.6)

Summary

Lessons I, II: Latin American Authors

Identify Latin American winners of the Nobel Prize in Literature (RI.9-10.1, SL.9-10.1)

Examine the manifestation of magical realism in "The Handsomest Drowned Man in the World," by Gabriel García Márquez (RL.9-10.1, RL.9-10.2, RL.9-10.5)

Explore the legacy of Márquez (RI.9-10.7, RI.9-10.8)

Select an author to study (W.9-10.7, SL.9-10.1, SL.9-10.2)

Select for independent reading and analysis a text that the author wrote (RL.9-10.6, SL.9-10.1, SL.9-10.2)

Note the components of the research paper (SL.9-10.1, W.9-10.7)

Lessons III, IV, V, VI: Research

Conduct online and library research (RI.9-10.7, W.9-10.7, W.9-10.8, SL.9-10.2, L.9-10.6)

Create computer files for each of the research components: (W.9-10.6)

Biographical information

The author's position and contribution in his/her country of origin

Key ideas (including passages) from the author's Nobel Prize Lecture

A survey of the author's work

An analysis of a single text written by the author

Reflective conclusion about the author and his/her contribution to twentieth-century literature

Take notes on each of the topics in the second objective (W.9-10.4)

Revisit notes and identify areas where further research is needed (W.9-10.8, SL.9-10.1)

Lessons VII, VIII: Writing the Essays

Follow the outline provided (W.9-10.4)

Compose the first draft of the research papers (W.9-10.5, L.9-10.6)

Revise the research papers (W.9-10.5, L.9-10.1, L.9-10.2, L.9-10.3)

Prepare a digital slide or keynote presentation (W.9-10.6, SL.9-10.4, SL.9-10.5)

Lessons IX, X: Final Papers and Presentations

Compose a research paper (six to eight pages long) that will include the following sections:

    Biographical information

    The author's position and contribution in his/her country of origin

    Key ideas (including passages) from the author's Nobel Prize Lecture

    A survey of the author's work

    An analysis of a single text

    Reflective conclusion about the author and his/her contribution to twentieth-century literature (W.9-10.2, W.9-10.4)

Present a digital slide or keynote presentation about your author (W.9-10.6, SL.9-10.4, SL.9-10.5)

Lessons I, II: Latin American Authors

Objectives

Identify Latin American winners of the Nobel Prize in Literature (RI.9-10.1, SL.9-10.1)

Examine the manifestation of magical realism in "The Handsomest Drowned Man in the World," by Gabriel García Márquez (RL.9-10.1, RL.9-10.2, RL.9-10.5)

Explore the legacy of Márquez (RI.9-10.7, RI.9-10.8)

Select an author to study (W.9-10.7, SL.9-10.1, SL.9-10.2)

Select for independent reading and analysis a text that the author wrote (RL.9-10.6, SL.9-10.1, SL.9-10.2)

Note the components of the research paper (SL.9-10.1, W 9-10.7)

Required Materials

☐ Computers with Internet access

☐ Library

☐ Class set of "The Handsomest Drowned Man in the World," by Gabriel García Márquez

Procedures

1. Lead-In:

Students conduct online research to identify Latin American winners of the Nobel Prize in Literature.

2. Step by Step, Part A:

   a. Students list the authors:

      Gabriela Mistral, Chile (1945)

      Miguel Angel Asturias, Guatemala (1967)

      Pablo Neruda, Chile (1971)

      Gabriel García Márquez, Colombia (1982)

      Octavio Paz, Mexico (1990)

      Derek Walcott, Saint Lucia (1992)

      V.S. Naipaul, Trinidad (2001)

      Mario Vargas Llosa, Peru (2010)

   b. The teacher distributes "The Handsomest Drowned Man in the World," by Gabriel García Márquez

      Students read the story silently. (Another option is to assign the reading for homework.)

   c. The teacher introduces the students to the key characteristics of magical realism.

   d. The students discuss the use of magical realism in the story. They note the connection between magical realism and the theme of the story. The teacher notes that when the students select one of the authors to study, they will have to conduct analytical reading and writing.

   Step by Step, Part B:

   a. Students conduct preliminary research about the authors listed above.

   b. Students select an author to study in depth.

   c. In groups, students who selected the same author, share their early findings.

   d. With the teacher's guidance, the students (still in their groups) investigate the scope of the research.

   e. In a class discussion, the students explore findings of early research that was done in groups.

3. Closure:

The teacher will summarize and emphasize the areas of research:

   a. Biographical information

      Where was the author born?

      Where did the author study? Work?

      What are some of his or her major works?

   b. The author's position and contribution in his or her country of origin (The teacher may choose to provide an example here–magical realism is regarded as Márquez's contribution to Latin American literature.)

c. What are some key ideas (including passages) from the author's Nobel Prize Lecture?

d. Provide an analysis of a single text written by the author

e. Reflective conclusion about the author and his/her contribution to twentieth-century literature

Differentiation

Advanced

- Students will start researching the broader context of Latin American literature. Have students find and evaluate the most helpful materials and websites. Collect the websites on a web portal.

- Throughout the research, students will analyze and evaluate the effects of the author's contribution to Latin American literature.

- Have students evaluate which author they think made the most significant contributions to Latin American literature. Students select a pivotal passage to read aloud. This gives the students an opportunity to practice reading with expression, recorded with a video camera, so they can evaluate and improve their performances.

Struggling

- Students will brainstorm a list of helpful informational text features to cue importance (e.g., chapter titles, subtitles, picture captions, bold print, Table of Contents, etc.).

- Provide students with a graphic organizer for research, perhaps in a shared spreadsheet, where students can record and share their research. Digital slide presentations can also be collaboratively developed in some shared spreadsheet programs.

- Allow students to listen to audio recordings of select passages of Latin American texts to support their understanding of the text.

Homework/Assessment

Conduct research at home or in the local library.

World Literature: Asia

In this twelve-week unit, students read and discuss ancient and modern Asian literature, especially from China, India, and Japan.

ESSENTIAL QUESTION

? How does Asian literature both honor and challenge cultural traditions?

OVERVIEW

By reading the diverse selections in this unit, students consider the role of ancient philosophies, universal themes, Western influence, and historical change in these works. In addition, students listen to recordings of some of the poems in the original language so that they may appreciate their sounds, structures, and rhythms.

Note: The tenth-grade World Literature Maps consist of four twelve-week units, each focusing on literature from a different part of the world. Select three out of the four units. As the middle unit will likely cross from one semester into another, it should be divided accordingly. Alternatively, teachers may choose to teach all four units by shortening each and selecting fewer works.

FOCUS STANDARDS

These Focus Standards have been selected for the unit from the Common Core State Standards.

RL.9–10.2: Determine a theme or central idea of a text and analyze in detail its development over the course of the text, including how it emerges and is shaped and refined by specific details; provide an objective summary of the text.

RL.9–10.5: Analyze how an author's choices concerning how to structure a text, order events within it (e.g., parallel plots), and manipulate time (e.g., pacing, flashbacks) create such effects as mystery, tension, or surprise.

RI.9–10.1: Cite strong and thorough textual evidence to support analysis of what the text says explicitly as well as inferences drawn from the text.

RI.9–10.4: Determine the meaning of words and phrases as they are used in a text, including figurative, connotative, and technical meanings; analyze the cumulative impact of specific word choices on meaning and tone (e.g., how the language of a court opinion differs from that of a newspaper).

W.9–10.7: Conduct short as well as more sustained research projects to answer a question (including a self-generated question) or solve a problem; narrow or broaden the inquiry when appropriate; synthesize multiple sources on the subject, demonstrating understanding of the subject under investigation.

W.9–10.10: Write routinely over extended time frames (time for research, reflection, and revision) and shorter time frames (a single sitting or a day or two) for a range of tasks, purposes, and audiences.

SL.9–10.1: Initiate and participate effectively in a range of collaborative discussions (one-on-one, in groups, and teacher-led) with diverse partners on grades 9–10 topics, texts, and issues, building on others' ideas and expressing their own clearly and persuasively.

L.9–10.2: Demonstrate command of the conventions of Standard English capitalization, punctuation, and spelling when writing.

SUGGESTED STUDENT OBJECTIVES

- Explore ancient and modern works of literature from Asian countries, particularly China, India, and Japan.
- Consider how Asian literature both draws on and questions cultural traditions.
- Consider how certain Asian authors integrate Western literary influences into their cultural contexts.
- Compare two or more translations of a single poem.
- Write a close literary analysis of a work of poetry, fiction, or drama, considering language use and literary elements.
- Offer insightful inferences regarding the themes of the text.
- Create a clear, original, specific thesis statement.
- Organize concrete evidence and supporting textual details to support a thesis statement.
- Use precise language, avoiding casual language and clichés.
- Write appropriate transitions to organize paragraphs.
- Analyze how philosophy influences literature.
- Understand how literary devices convey theme.

SUGGESTED WORKS

(E) indicates a CCSS exemplar text; (EA) indicates a text from a writer with other works identified as exemplars.

LITERARY TEXTS

Note: Texts can be combined in a number of ways. Students, for example, can read excerpts from an ancient work; one novel; one play; several short stories; and a long poem or selection of poems. Or teachers might choose two novels or two plays instead of one novel and one play. Students should consult informational texts and secondary sources, online and in the library, for their essays.

Novels

China

- *Family* (Pa Jin)

India
- *Midnight's Children* (Salman Rushdie)
- *In Custody* (Anita Desai)
- *Nectar in a Sieve* (Kamala Markandaya)
- *The God of Small Things* (Arundhati Roy)

Japan
- *The Sound of Waves* (Yukio Mishima)
- *After Dark* (Haruki Murakami)
- *Norwegian Wood* (Haruki Murakami)

Short Stories
China
- *Strange Tales from a Chinese Studio* (Pu Songling, ed.)
- *Under The Red Flag* (Ha Jin) (selections)

Japan
- *Rashomon and Other Stories* (Ryunosuke Akutagawa)

Vietnam
- *The General Retires and Other Stories* (Nguyen Huy Thiep)

Drama
China
- *Thunderstorm* (Tsao Yu)

India
- *The Post Office* (Rabindranath Tagore) (EA)

Poetry
- "Lost in Translation" (James Merrill)

Sanskrit
- *The Ramayana* (attributed to the Hindu sage Valmiki)

China
- *The Jade Mountain: A Chinese Anthology, Being Three Hundred Poems of the T'ang Dynasty 618–906* (Kiang Hang-Hu and Witter Bynner, trans.) (selections)
- "A Song of Ch'ang-kan" (Li Bai) (E) (This author is referenced in Appendix B of the CCSS as Li Po, another transliteration of the author's name.) (excerpts)
- "Substance, Shadow, and Spirit" (T'ao Ch'ien) (excerpts)
- "On a Gate-tower at Yuzhou" (Chen Zi'ang) (excerpts)

India
- "Song VII" (Rabindranath Tagore) (E)
- *The Golden Craft* (Rabindranath Tagore) (EA)

INFORMATIONAL TEXTS

- *The Columbia Companion to Modern East Asian Literature* (Joshua Mostow, ed.)
- *Historical Dictionary of Modern Japanese Literature and Theater* (J. Scott Miller)
- *Trading Places: The East India Company and Asia, 1600–1834* (Anthony Farrington)
- *The Scandal of Empire: India and the Creation of Imperial Britain* (Nicholas B. Dirks)
- *The Analects* (Confucius) (selections)
- *The I Ching* (transmitted by Fei Zhi)
- *The Tao Te Ching* (Lao Tzu) (selections)
- *The Tao of Pooh and the Te of Piglet* (Benjamin Hoff) (selections)
- "Li Bai, A Hero among Poets, in the Visual, Dramatic, and Literary Arts of China" (Kathlyn Maurean Liscomb)

Autobiography

- *Six Records of a Floating Life* (Shen Fu) (China)

ART, MUSIC, AND MEDIA

Art

Japan

- Ando Hiroshige, *One Hundred Views of Edo* (1856)
- Arita, Porcelain plate with design of dragon (1690s–1730s)
- Kimono with carp, water lilies, and morning glories (1876)

China

- Ma Lin, wall scroll (1246)
- Moon-shaped flask with birds (1723–1725)
- Han Clothing (pre-seventeenth century)

South Asian and Himalayan

- Box with lid (Indian, late sixteenth century)
- *Four Mandala Vajravali Thangka* (Tibetan, ca. 1430)
- *Scenes from the Life of Buddha* (Pakistan or Afghanistan, ca. late second to early third century)

Media

- *Chinese Poems of the Tang and Sung Dynasties: Read by Lo Kung-Yuan in Northern Chinese, Peking Dialect* (Folkways Records, 1963)

Film

- Akira Kurosawa, dir., *Rashomon* (1950)
- Zhang Yimou, dir., *Curse of the Golden Flower* (2006)

SAMPLE ACTIVITIES AND ASSESSMENTS

For a full Scoring Rubric, see the Appendix.

Note: After reading and discussing a work or pairing of works as a class, students prepare for seminars and essays by reflecting individually, in pairs, and/or in small groups on a given question In this way, students generate ideas. (Seminar and essay assignments include more than one question. Teachers may choose one or all of the questions to explore in the course of the seminar; students should choose one question for the essay.) Seminars should be held before students write essays so that they may explore their ideas thoroughly and refine their thinking before writing. Textual evidence should be used to support all arguments advanced in seminars and in all essays. Page and word counts for essays are not provided here, but teachers should consider the suggestions regarding the use of evidence, for example, to determine the likely length of good essays.

1. COLLABORATION

Reflect on seminar questions, take notes on your responses, and note the page numbers of the textual evidence you will refer to in your seminar and/or essay answers. Share your notes with a partner for feedback and guidance. Have you interpreted the text correctly? Is your evidence convincing? This collaboration can be done in a journal or on a shared spreadsheet. (RL.9–10.1, SL.9–10.1)

2. SEMINAR AND INFORMATIVE/EXPLANATORY WRITING

Analyze Akutagawa's story "In a Bamboo Grove" and Kurosawa's film *Rashomon*. How do the story and the film portray the characters' psychological states? (*Note:* Kurosawa's *Rashomon* is based on Akutagawa's "In a Bamboo Grove," not on his "Rashomon," though a few details from the latter story appear in the film.) Write an informative/explanatory essay using at least three pieces of textual evidence to support an original thesis statement. Your teacher may give you the opportunity to share your initial thoughts on the classroom blog in order to get feedback from your classmates. (RL.9–10.7, SL.9–10.1, W.9–10.2)

3. SEMINAR AND INFORMATIVE/EXPLANATORY WRITING

How does fiction writer Ryunosuke Akutagawa or playwright Tsao Yu integrate Western literary influences into his work? Use textual evidence from the literary and informational texts to support an original thesis. Write an informative/explanatory essay using at least three pieces of textual evidence to support your thesis statement. Your teacher may give you the opportunity to share your initial thoughts on the classroom blog in order to get feedback from your classmates. (RL.9–10.6, RL.9–10.9, SL.9–10.1, W.9–10.2, W.9–10.9)

4. SEMINAR AND INFORMATIVE/EXPLANATORY WRITING

How is the novel *Midnight's Children* or *Nectar in a Sieve* an allegorical text? What does the allegory reveal about the author's point of view? Use evidence from reference texts *Trading Places: The East India Company and Asia, 1600–1834* and *The Scandal of Empire: India and the Creation of Imperial Britain* to enhance your argument. Write an informative/explanatory essay using at least three pieces of evidence from the novels and the reference texts to support an original thesis statement. Your teacher may give you the opportunity to share your initial thoughts on the classroom blog in order to get feedback from your classmates. (SL.9–10.1, W.9–10.2, W.9–10.9)

5. SEMINAR AND INFORMATIVE/EXPLANATORY WRITING

Compare and contrast *Midnight's Children* and *Nectar in a Sieve*. How do they differ in meaning? How are they similar in meaning? Write an informative/explanatory essay using at least two pieces of textual evidence from each text to support an original thesis statement. Your teacher may give you the opportunity to share your initial thoughts on the classroom blog in order to get feedback from your classmates. (RL.9–10.6, RL.9–10.9, SL.9–10.1, W.9–10.2, W.9–10.9)

6. SEMINAR AND WRITING (ARGUMENT)

What does Amal teach the other characters in Rabindranath Tagore's *The Post Office*? Do these teachings reflect the values of Confucianism or Taoism? Write an argument using at least three pieces of textual evidence to support your position. Your teacher may give you the opportunity to share your initial thoughts on the classroom blog in order to get feedback from your classmates. (RL.9–10.1, SL.9–10.1, W.9–10.2,W.9–10.9)

7. SEMINAR AND WRITING (ARGUMENT)

Does the poem "Substance, Shadow, and Spirit" connect to the teachings of Lao Tzu or Confucius? What does the poem reveal about these two philosophies? Write an argument using at least three pieces of textual evidence from multiple sources to support your position. Your teacher may give you the opportunity to share your initial thoughts on the classroom blog in order to get feedback from your classmates. (SL.9–10.1, W.9–10.2, W.9–10.9)

8. SEMINAR AND WRITING (ARGUMENT)

Do the works you have read so far in this unit honor or rebel against cultural tradition? Write an argument that supports an original thesis statement, using at least three pieces of textual evidence to support your position. (The teacher may choose to focus on one or two texts.) Your teacher may give you the opportunity to share your initial thoughts on the classroom blog in order to get feedback from your classmates. (RL.9–10.6, SL.9–10.1, W.9–10.2, W.9–10.9)

9. SEMINAR AND INFORMATIVE/EXPLANATORY WRITING

How do Benjamin Hoff's allegories reveal Asian teachings? Do the allegories accurately illustrate these teachings? Write an informative/explanatory essay that uses textual evidence to support an original thesis statement. Use evidence from more than one text. Your teacher may give you the opportunity to share your initial thoughts on the classroom blog in order to get feedback from your classmates. (RL.9–10.6, SL.9–10.1, W.9–10.2, W.9–10.9)

10. SEMINAR AND WRITING (ARGUMENT)

(This assignment is especially appropriate for bilingual students.) Read James Merrill's poem "Lost in Translation" and discuss it in the context of (one of) the works of Asian literature that you have read in this unit. What skills does a good translator need? In translation, is meaning lost irrevocably to the reader? Write an essay that uses at least three pieces of textual evidence to support your position. Your teacher may give you the opportunity to share your initial thoughts on the classroom blog in order to get feedback from your classmates. (RL.9–10.6, SL.9–10.1, W.9–10.2, W.9–10.9)

11. INFORMATIVE/EXPLANATORY WRITING

Write a close literary analysis of one of the poems in the unit, with attention to its form, figurative language, symbolism, and meaning. Be sure to include any historical context necessary. Use at least three pieces of textual evidence to support your analysis in an informative/explanatory essay. Your teacher may give you the opportunity to share your first draft on a shared online document and receive feedback from classmates before publication. (SL.9–10.1, W.9–10.2, W.9–10.9)

12. MIXED-MEDIA PRESENTATION

(This assignment is especially appropriate for bilingual students.) Choose a recording of a poem from Chinese Poems of the Tang and Sung Dynasties, or find a different recording. Play the recording and explain the literary structure of the poem. Present two translations of the poem and compare the choices the translators have made. (RL.9–10.5)

13. INFORMATIVE/EXPLANATORY WRITING

This writing assignment follows the study of several Asian authors. Included is a recommended selection, but teachers may choose to alter the list. Suggested Texts: *Midnight's Children*, by Salman Rushdie (India); *Rashomon and Other Stories*, by Ryunosuke Akutagawa (Japan); "A Song of Ch'ang-Kan," by Li Bai (China), and *The General Retires and Other Stories*, by Nguyen Huy Thiep (Vietnam). Write an informative/explanatory essay in which you compare the works of two of these authors. Follow these steps as you prepare to write the essay:

- Identify a theme that you wish to examine.
- Select two authors or poets whose works explore this theme.
- Write an introductory paragraph that introduces the authors or poets, names the specific texts that will be discussed, identifies the common theme, and provides a clear thesis.

You may choose to post your paragraph on the classroom blog and discuss it with your classmates prior to writing. Then, following discussions about and revisions to your opening paragraph, compose your essay, citing at least three pieces of evidence from the text to support your thesis. (RL.9–10.2, RL.9–10.9, W.9–10.2)

14. RESEARCH AND INFORMATIVE/EXPLANATORY WRITING

Choose one of the authors in the unit and write a well-researched informative/explanatory essay that discusses the ways in which the author's work reflects or questions one of his or her country's cultural traditions (e.g., arranged marriages or the caste system). Begin by defining a research question (and refining it as necessary as research is conducted). Determine and execute a strategy for locating primary and secondary sources that will enrich your understanding of the cultural tradition in question. The paper should include the following sections:

- Biographical information about the author
- The author's position and contribution in his/her country of origin
- Summary of the cultural tradition in question (i.e., origin, brief history, and significant details)
- Key ideas (including passages) from the author's work that support the thesis about reflecting or questioning the cultural tradition
- Reflective conclusion about the author and his/her contribution to twentieth-century literature

The essay should reflect a synthesis of sources consulted, a balance of paraphrasing and quoting from sources, and proper citation of sources. (W.9–10.1, W.9–10.7, W.9–10.8, W.9–10.9, W.9–10.10)

15. GRAMMAR AND USAGE

Read a draft of another student's essay from an assignment in this unit. Highlight instances of parallel structure and places where parallel structure could strengthen the quality of the writing. Discuss with your partner how and why parallel structure can enhance your writing. (L.9–10.1a)

16. ART/CLASS DISCUSSION

Examine a painting or object from each culture. What iconography do you see in each? Do you see cross-cultural connections in the artwork (i.e., which culture seems to have borrowed ideas from others)? How do you know? What imagery might you interpret as specific to one culture (e.g., designs, patterns, lines, or shapes)? Why does this imagery stand out to you? (SL.9–10.1, SL.9–10.2)

ADDITIONAL RESOURCES

- Lessons of the Indian Epics: The Ramayana (National Endowment for the Humanities) (RL.9–10.3)
- *Being in the Noh:* An Introduction to Two Japanese *Noh* Plays (National Endowment for the Humanities) (RL.9–10.6)
- Poems by Li Bai (Li Po) (PoemHunter.com)

TERMINOLOGY

Absurd	Foreshadowing	Poetic translation	Third-person omniscience
Allegory	Internal monologue	Simile	Tone (Chinese)
Confucianism	Irony	Stream of consciousness	
Figurative language	Metaphor	Symbol	
Filial piety	Paradox	Taoism	
First-person perspective	Perfect rhyme	Theme	
	Perspective		

Grade Ten, Unit Two Sample Lesson Plan

"A Song of Ch'ang" by Li Bai (Li Po)

In this series of four lessons, students read "A Song of Ch'ang" by Li Bai, and they:

- Explore the life of Li Bai (RI.9-10.2, W.9-10.7, W.9-10.8, SL.9-10.1, L.9-10.6)
- Explore the role of the poet in Chinese culture (RI.9-10.2, W.9-10.7, SL.9-10.4, L.9-10.5)
- Examine the poetry of Li Bai (RL.9-10.1, RL.9-10.2, RL.9-10.4, RL.9-10.6, SL.9-10.1, L.9-10.5)

Summary

Lesson I: Li Bai

Explore the life of Li Bai (RI.9-10.2, W.9-10.7, W.9-10.8, SL.9-10.1, L.9-10.6)

Note his place in Chinese culture (SL.9-10.1, RI.9-10.1)

Explore the role of the poet in Chinese culture (RI.9-10.2, W.9-10.7, SL.9-10.4, L.9-10.5)

Examine the artistic renditions of Li Bai (RL.9-10.6)

Document findings (W.9-10.4, RI.9-10.1, RL.9-10.1)

Lesson III: Poetry of Li Bai

Select a poem by Li Bai (SL.9-10.1)

Conduct a close reading of the poem (RL.9-10.1, RL.9-10.2, RL.9-10.3, RL.9-10.4, RL.9-10.6, SL.9-10.6, L.9-10.4, L.9-10.5)

Compose a paragraph that identifies the poem's:

Speaker

Setting

Mood

Theme (W.9-10.2, W.9-10.4)

Lesson II: "A Song of Ch'ang"

Identify the speaker of the poem (RL.9-10.1, RL.9-10.6, SL.9-10.1, W.9-10.9a)

Trace the narrative of the speaker (RL.9-10.1, SL.9-10.1, W.9-10.9a)

Explore the speaker's expressions of love (RL.9-10.3, RL.9-10.4, RL.9-10.6, SL.9-10.4, L.9-10.5)

Note the speaker's use of time and place (W.9-10.9a, SL.9-10.1)

Lesson IV: Poetry of Li Bai

Reread the selected poem (RL.9-10.6, SL.9-10.6)

Revisit paragraph (from Lesson III) (W.9-10.2, W.9-10.5)

View a video and share impressions of the life and poetry of Li Bai (SL.9-10.1, RL.9-10.1)

Lesson I: Li Bai

Objectives

Explore the life of Li Bai (RI.9-10.2, W.9-10.7, W.9-10.8, SL.9-10.1, L.9-10.6)

Note his place in Chinese culture (SL.9-10.1, RI.9-10.1)

Explore the role of the poet in Chinese culture (RI.9-10.2, W.9-10.7, SL.9-10.4, L.9-10.5)

Examine the artistic renditions of Li Bai (RL.9-10.6)

Document findings (W.9-10.4, RI.9-10.1, RL.9-10.1)

Required Materials

☐ Computers with Internet access

☐ Library

☐ Class set of excerpts from "Li Bai, A Hero among Poets, in the Visual, Dramatic, and Literary Arts of China" by Kathlyn Maurean Liscomb (the essay is an excellent source that teachers can use in addition to the students' research)

Procedures

1. Lead-In:

Students view "Classical Chinese Poetry—Tang Li Bai" (available online)

2. Step by Step:

   a. Students discuss their impressions of the video.

   b. Students conduct research about Li Bai's life and his poetry. They also explore his place in Chinese cultural history and the artistic renditions of his life.

   c. Students share their findings. (Teachers will determine the format.)

3. Closure:

Students view another video about Li Bai.

Differentiation

Advanced

- Encourage students to prepare a biography of Li Bai for classmates. Students should also research what inspired Li Bai to write poetry, and perhaps present this information as an online poster or podcast. As an extension, students research a modern-day Chinese poet to compare and contrast with Li Bai.

- Give students an opportunity to evaluate and bookmark the most helpful websites for conducting research about Li Bai. Collect the websites on a web portal.
- Encourage students to compare and contrast Chinese poets and authors with Latin American authors and poets (from the Unit One Map).

Struggling

- Students research Li Bai using pre-selected websites on a web portal (selected by classmates, above) or using an easier article or website. Provide students with a graphic organizer or guiding questions to structure their research of Li Bai.
- Consider pre-teaching key ideas of Chinese poetry to students on the day prior (for example, giving them an outline to read or video to view with key vocabulary highlighted).
- Encourage students to use a graphic organizer to collect their research, such as the ReadWriteThink "Notetaker." Alternatively, students could collaborate to create their own chart or graphic of research questions on a shared spreadsheet that all students can access.

Homework/Assessment
N/A

Lesson II: "A Song of Ch'ang"

Objectives

Identify the speaker of the poem (RL.9-10.1, RL.9-10.6, SL.9-10.1, W.9-10.9a)

Trace the narrative of the speaker (RL.9-10.1, SL.9-10.1, W.9-10.9a)

Explore the speaker's expressions of love (RL.9-10.3, RL.9-10.4, RL.9-10.6, SL.9-10.4, L.9-10.5)

Note the speaker's use of time and place (W.9-10.9a, SL.9-10.1)

Required Materials

☐ Class set of "A Song of Ch'ang" (A Song of Changgan), by Li Bai (Li Po)

Procedures

1. Lead-In:
Students silently read "A Song of Ch'ang".

2. Step by Step:
   a. The teacher instructs the students to reread the poem and annotate it for each of the learning objectives. Below, in italics, are a few examples of the annotations that the teacher will look for:

1 My hair had hardly covered my forehead.
I was picking flowers, playing by my door, *The speaker seems to be a child "playing."*
When you, my lover, on a bamboo horse, *She addresses her "lover, on a bamboo horse."*
Came trotting in circles and throwing green plums.
5 We lived near together on a lane in Ch'ang-kan, *The reader learn that the speaker and the lover*
Both of us young and happy-hearted. *grew up together and that they were "happy hearted."*
...At fourteen I became your wife,
So bashful that I dared not smile, *There is a shift in the relationship when at fourteen the speaker marries.*
And I lowered my head toward a dark corner *There seems to be a shift in her behavior form playful to "bashful,"*
10 And would not turn to your thousand calls; *she lowers her head and does not answer his calls.*
But at fifteen I straightened my brows and laughed, *The speaker is now fifteen and the readers learn that* Learning that no dust
could ever seal our love, *her husband is sometimes away.*
That even unto death I would await you by my post *But the speaker proclaims that her love will not be affected.*
And would never lose heart in the tower of silent watching. *She "would never lose heart."*
15 ...Then when I was sixteen, you left on a long journey
Through the Gorges of Ch'u-t'ang, of rock and whirling water. *Here the reader describes a specific separation.*
And then came the Fifth-month, more than I could bear, *including the length of time.*
And I tried to hear the monkeys in your lofty far-off sky. *The speaker uses her imagination to be with her husband.*
Your footprints by our door, where I had watched you go, *The tone seems to shift here.*
20 Were hidden, every one of them, under green moss, *Her depiction of the setting reflects the pain she fell due to his absence*
Hidden under moss too deep to sweep away.
And the first autumn wind added fallen leaves. *The autumn and the "fallen leaves" continue to represent her feelings* And now,
in the Eighth-month, yellowing butterflies
Hover, two by two, in our west-garden grasses *The butterflies are in twos (unlike her).*
25 And, because of all this, my heart is breaking *And her "heart is breaking."*
And I fear for my bright cheeks, lest they fade.
...Oh, at last, when you return through the three Pa districts,
Send me a message home ahead! *She appeals to her husband to let her know when he will return and*
And I will come and meet you and will never mind the distance, *notes how far she can go to meet him.*
30 All the way to Chang-feng Sha.

b. Once the entire class annotates the poem the students discuss their findings. (It is always useful to refer to line numbers.)

3. Closure:
   A student volunteer reads the poem aloud.

Differentiation

Advanced

- Select student volunteers to read this poem aloud in preparation for future lessons; give the students an opportunity to practice reading dramatically, recorded with a video camera, so they can evaluate and improve their performances.

- Advanced students will be encouraged and expected to provide insightful annotations that go beyond literal interpretation.

Struggling

- Consider pre-teaching this poem to students on the day prior (or let them view their classmates reading the poem).

- While students are working on annotating the teacher may choose to assist some of the struggling students. Class can collaboratively annotate using a shared online document.

Homework/Assessment

N/A

World Literature: Africa and the Middle East

In this twelve-week unit, students read ancient and modern works by African and Middle Eastern authors, as well as select Western perspectives on Africa and the Middle East.

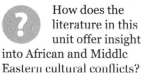

ESSENTIAL QUESTION

How does the literature in this unit offer insight into African and Middle Eastern cultural conflicts?

OVERVIEW

Students consider the beauty and craftsmanship of the works, as well as the effects of the African and Middle Eastern colonial experience—and the subsequent challenges of the postcolonial era. They consider religious, generational, and cultural conflicts, effects of modernization, political struggle, and other themes common to many literary works. At the same time, students recognize that not all literary works make explicit political or cultural statements and that all works must be approached on their own terms. In order to enrich their understanding, students investigate the historical background of selected works, as well as author biographies. They have the opportunity to read additional works of interest.

Note: The tenth-grade World Literature Maps consist of four twelve-week units, each focusing on literature from a different part of the world. Select three out of the four units. As the middle unit will likely cross from one semester into another, it should be divided accordingly. Alternatively, teachers may choose to teach all four units by shortening each and selecting fewer works.

FOCUS STANDARDS

These Focus Standards have been selected for the unit from the Common Core State Standards.

RL.9–10.1: Cite strong and thorough textual evidence to support analysis of what the text says explicitly as well as inferences drawn from the text.

RL.9–10.4: Determine the meaning of words and phrases as they are used in the text, including figurative and connotative meanings; analyze the cumulative impact of specific word choices on meaning and tone (e.g., how the language evokes a sense of time and place; how it sets a formal or informal tone).

RL.9–10.6: Analyze a particular point of view or cultural experience reflected in a work of literature from outside the United States, drawing on a wide reading of world literature.

RI.9–10.5: Analyze in detail how an author's ideas or claims are developed and refined by particular sentences, paragraphs, or larger portions of a text (e.g., a section or chapter).

RI.9–10.8: Delineate and evaluate the argument and specific claims in a text, assessing whether the reasoning is valid and the evidence is relevant and sufficient; identify false statements and fallacious reasoning.

W.9–10.4: Produce clear and coherent writing in which the development, organization, and style are appropriate to task, purpose, and audience. (Grade-specific expectations for writing types are defined in standards 1–3 above.)

W.9–10.5: Develop and strengthen writing as needed by planning, revising, editing, rewriting, or trying a new approach, focusing on addressing what is most significant for a specific purpose and audience. (Editing for conventions should demonstrate command of Language standards 1–3 up to and including grades 9–10 on page 54 of the Common Core State Standards.)

W.9–10.6: Use technology, including the Internet, to produce, publish, and update individual or shared writing products, taking advantage of technology's capacity to link to other information and to display information flexibly and dynamically.

W.9–10.9: Draw evidence from literary or informational texts to support analysis, reflection, and research.

SL.9–10.6: Adapt speech to a variety of contexts and tasks, demonstrating command of formal English when indicated or appropriate. (See grades 9–10 Language standards 1 and 3 on page 54 of the Common Core State Standards for specific expectations.)

L.9–10.5: Demonstrate understanding of figurative language, word relationships, and nuances in word meanings.

L.9–10.6: Acquire and use accurately grade-appropriate general academic and domain-specific words and phrases; gather vocabulary knowledge when considering a word or phrase important to comprehension or expression.

SUGGESTED STUDENT OBJECTIVES

- Read a variety of literary works from Africa and the Middle East, particularly from the postcolonial period.
- Consider the challenges of translation, including the different connotations that various cultures attach to given words.
- Through analysis of literary works, explore the changing social structures of Middle Eastern and African societies.
- Explore various literary devices in plot development such as suspense, foreshadowing, symbolism, and extended metaphor.
- Trace the development of an idea or argument in a work of literary nonfiction.
- Offer insightful inferences regarding the themes of the text.
- Create a clear, original, specific thesis statement.
- Organize concrete evidence and supporting textual details to support a thesis statement.
- Use precise language, avoiding casual language and clichés.
- Write appropriate transitions to organize paragraphs.
- Analyze how literary devices convey theme.

SUGGESTED WORKS

(E) indicates a CCSS exemplar text; (EA) indicates a text from a writer with other works identified as exemplars.

LITERARY TEXTS

Note: Texts can be combined in a number of ways. Students, for example, could read one novel or two short novels, a play, a selection of poems by various authors, and a nonfiction essay. Teachers might choose to include ancient and medieval works, or they may focus on modern works. Where possible, teachers should play audio recordings of the poetry read in the original language, so that the students may become familiar with its sounds.

Novels

Turkey
- *My Name is Red* (Orham Pamuk)

Nigeria
- *Things Fall Apart* (Chinua Achebe) (E)
- *The Joys of Motherhood* (Buchi Emecheta)

South Africa
- *Cry, the Beloved Country* (Alan Paton)
- *Waiting for the Barbarians or Life and Times of Michael K* (J. M. Coetzee)

Egypt
- *The Thief and the Dogs* (Naguib Mahfouz)

Senegal
- *So Long a Letter* (Mariama Ba)

United Kingdom
- *Martha Quest* (Doris Lessing)

Lebanon
- *Beirut Blues* (Hanan al-Shaykh)

Kenya
- *The River Between* (Ngũgĩ wa Thiong'o)

Short Stories

Botswana
- *The Collector of Treasures and Other Botswana Village Tales* (Bessie Head)

South Africa
- *Tales from a Troubled Land* (Alan Paton)

Mozambique
- *We Killed Mangy-Dog and Other Mozambique Stories* (Luis Bernardo Honwana)

Israel

- *The World Is a Room and Other Stories* (Yehuda Amichai)

Egypt

- "The Answer Is No" (Naguib Mahfouz)

Other

- *One Thousand and One Nights or Arabian Nights*

Poetry

- *The Epic of Gilgamesh* (ancient poem from Mesopotamia)
- *Poems of Black Africa* (Wole Soyinka, ed.) (selections)

Palestine

- *The Butterfly's Burden* (Mahmoud Darwish)

Israel

- *Open Closed Open: Poems* (Yehuda Amichai) (selections)

Iran

- *The Conference of the Birds: A Sufi Allegory* (Farīd al Dīn Attār or Attar of Nishapur)
- *The Illuminated Rumi* (Jalal Al-Din Rumi, Michael Green, and Coleman Barks, trans.) (selections)

Drama

South Africa

- *"Master Harold"* ... *and the Boys* (Athol Fugard) (E)
- *Woza Albert!* (Percy Mtwa, Mbongeni Ngema, and Barney Simon)

Nigeria

- *Death and the King's Horseman: A Play* (Wole Soyinka) (E)
- *King Baabu* (Wole Soyinka) (EA)
- *The Lion and the Jewel* (Wole Soyinka) (EA)

INFORMATIONAL TEXTS

Iran

- *Ethics of the Aristocrats and Other Satirical Works* (Nezam al-Din Obeyd-e Zakani)

South Africa

- *Living in Hope and History: Notes From Our Century* (Nadine Gordimer)

Autobiographies

- *Out of Africa* (Isak Dinesen)
- *Long Walk to Freedom: The Autobiography of Nelson Mandela* (Nelson Mandela)

Speech

- Nobel Prize Acceptance Speech, 1993 (Nelson Mandela)

ART, MUSIC, AND MEDIA

Art

Africa

- Gabon, mask for the Okuyi Society (late nineteenth century)
- Burkina Faso, hawk mask (no date)
- Nigeria, House of the Head Shrine: Equestrian, Yoruba (nineteenth to twentieth century)
- Ivory Coast, leopard stool (twentieth century)
- Mali, standing female figure (late nineteenth or early twentieth century)
- Congo, power figure (nineteenth to twentieth century)
- Yinka Shonibare MBE, *Earth* (2010)
- Yinka Shonibare MBE, *Air* (2010)
- Yinka Shonibare MBE, *Fire* (2010)
- Yinka Shonibare MBE, *Water* (2010)

Middle East

- Turkey, dish (second half of the sixteenth century)
- Syria, Qur' an manuscript (late ninth to early tenth century)
- Iran, antique Kurdish rug (no date)
- Shirin Neshat, *Untitled*, (1996)
- Shirin Neshat, *Soliloquy Series (Figure in Front of Steps)* (1999)

SAMPLE ACTIVITIES AND ASSESSMENTS

For a full Scoring Rubric, see the Appendix.

Note: After reading and discussing a work or pairing of works as a class, students prepare for seminars and essays by reflecting individually, in pairs, and/or in small groups on a given question. In this way, students generate ideas. (Seminar and essay assignments include more than one question. Teachers may choose one or all of the questions to explore in the course of the seminar; students should choose one question for the essay.) Seminars should be held before students write essays so that they may explore their ideas thoroughly and refine their thinking before writing. Textual evidence should be used to support all arguments advanced in seminars and in all essays. Page and word counts for essays are not provided here, but teachers should consider the suggestions regarding the use of evidence, for example, to determine the likely length of good essays.

1. COLLABORATION

Reflect on seminar questions, take notes on your responses, and note the page numbers of the textual evidence you will refer to in your seminar and/or essay answers. Share your notes with a partner for feedback and guidance. Have you interpreted the text correctly? Is your evidence convincing? This collaboration can be done in a journal or on a shared online document. (RL.9–10.1, SL.9–10.1)

2. SEMINAR AND INFORMATIVE/EXPLANATORY WRITING

What is satire? What is being satirized in *Ethics of the Aristocrats* or *King Baabu*? What is the author's political point of view as revealed by this satire? Write an essay that uses at least three pieces of textual evidence to support an original thesis statement. Your teacher may give you the opportunity to share your initial thoughts on the classroom blog in order to get feedback from your classmates. (RL.9–10.1, RL.9–10.4, W.9–10.2)

3. SEMINAR AND INFORMATIVE/EXPLANATORY WRITING

Writers are meant to "describe a situation so truthfully that the reader can no longer evade it." Choose an essay by Nadine Gordimer and explain what "truth" she develops in her essay. How does she develop that truth? Use at least three pieces of specific textual evidence from her essay to support an original thesis statement in an essay. Your teacher may give you the opportunity to share your initial thoughts on the classroom blog in order to get feedback from your classmates. (RI.9–10.5, W.9–10.2, W.9–10.4)

4. SEMINAR AND INFORMATIVE/EXPLANATORY WRITING

What is "chi" in its cultural context? Compare the use of "chi" (personal spirit) in *Things Fall Apart* and *The Joys of Motherhood*. After discussion, use two pieces of evidence from *each* text to support an original thesis statement that compares the two texts in an informative/explanatory essay. Your teacher may give you the opportunity to share your initial thoughts on the classroom blog in order to get feedback from your classmates. (RL.9–10.1, RL.9–10.4, W.9–10.1, L.9–10.5)

5. SEMINAR AND WRITING (ARGUMENT)

Do you agree or disagree with this statement? "It is possible to understand this piece of literature outside of its historical context." (Teachers choose the work.) In an organized argument, use textual evidence from the work as well as from historical or reference works to support your position. Your teacher may give you the opportunity to share your initial thoughts on the classroom blog in order to get feedback from your classmates. (W.9–10.1, W.9–10.5, W.9–10.6, W.9–10.7, L.9–10.6)

6. SEMINAR AND WRITING (ARGUMENT)

Is there a common concern of postcolonial literature, as reflected in the works of this unit? Is there one statement they all seem to be making about colonialism? If so, what is that statement? Write an argument using at least three pieces of textual evidence to support your position. Your teacher may give you the opportunity to share your initial thoughts on the classroom blog in order to get feedback from your classmates. (W.9–10.1, SL.9–10.3, SL.9–10.4)

7. SEMINAR AND WRITING (ARGUMENT)

Do you agree or disagree with this statement? "Moral choices are essentially choices between two sets of values: one belonging to one culture or era, one to another." Use textual evidence to support your position. After the seminar, write an organized argument using at least three pieces of textual evidence to support your position. Your teacher may give you the opportunity to share your initial thoughts on the classroom blog in order to get feedback from your classmates. (W.9–10.1, SL.9–10.3, SL.9–10.4)

8. WRITING (ARGUMENT)

This writing assignment follows the reading of *Cry, the Beloved Country* by Alan Paton and *Long Walk to Freedom: The Autobiography of Nelson Mandela*, by Nelson Mandela. Both of these texts depict the experiences of blacks in South Africa during apartheid. Using these texts as examples, compose an argument in which you take the position that fiction is more powerful than nonfiction, or vice versa. Cite at least three pieces of evidence from each text. Your teacher may give you the opportunity to share your initial thoughts on the classroom blog in order to get feedback from your classmates. (RL.9–10.1, RL.9–10.2, RL.9–10.5, RI.19–10.1, RI.9–10.2, RI.9–10.3, RI.9–10.5, W.9–10.1, SL.9–10.3)

9. NARRATIVE WRITING/PERFORMANCE

Write a narrative monologue from the point of view of one of the *secondary* characters in *Things Fall Apart* or *The Lion and the Jewel*. Perform the monologue for the class. Your teacher may give you the option of adding a multimedia component, either creating a digital presentation of illustrations or a movie where your narrative becomes the audio portion. Alternatively, record your presentation using a video camera so you can prepare a podcast for posting on the class web page. (W.9–10.3, SL.9–10.6)

10. RESEARCH AND INFORMATIVE/EXPLANATORY WRITING

Choose one of the authors in the unit and write a well-researched informative/explanatory essay that discusses the ways in which the author explores a changing social structure in a Middle Eastern or African society (e.g., apartheid). Begin by defining a research question (and refining it as necessary as research is conducted). Determine and execute a strategy for locating primary and secondary sources that will enrich the reader's understanding of the changing social structure in question. The paper should include the following sections:

- Biographical information about the author
- The author's position and contribution in his/her country of origin
- Summary of the changing social structure in question (i.e., origin, brief history, and significant details)
- Key ideas (including passages) from the author's work that support the thesis about the changing social structure
- Reflective conclusion about the author and his/her contribution to twentieth-century literature

The essay should reflect a synthesis of sources consulted, a balance of paraphrasing and quoting from sources, and proper citation of sources. (W.9–10.1, W.9–10.7, W.9–10.8, W.9–10.9, W.9–10.10)

11. ORAL PRESENTATION

Working with a partner, choose a work in this unit with a character who faces a difficult choice. Write and perform two monologues, each one defending a particular option. Record your recitation using a video camera so you can evaluate your performance. (W.9–10.3, SL.9–10.6)

12. ORAL PRESENTATION

Choose a poem that you have read in this unit and recite it from memory. Include an introduction that discusses:

- Who wrote the poem and when it was written (i.e., historical context)
- How the form of the poem and its meaning are related

Record your recitation using a video camera so you can evaluate your performance for accuracy. (RL.9–10.2, SL.9–10.4, SL.9–10.6)

13. GRAMMAR AND MECHANICS

Read a classmate's draft essay for one of the activities listed above. Note the places where semicolons are—or could be—used to connect two closely related independent clauses. Discuss why doing so might improve the quality of the writing. (L.9–10.1b)

14. ART/CLASS DISCUSSION

Study the selected traditional African artworks. Compare the two standing figures from Mali and Congo. What do you see? What features are present in both figures? After examining these figures, what characteristics might you think are distinct to the region in which they were created? Now, examine the four works created by contemporary artist Yinka Shonibare. Shonibare was born in Nigeria, heavily affected by colonialism, and moved to study art in the West. Can you see Western influences in his work? Is Shonibare trying to reconcile any conflicts in these figures? Do you see the effects of colonialism (or postcolonialism) in his artwork? If so, what are the evident effects? (SL.9–10.1, SL.9–10.2)

15. ART/CLASS DISCUSSION

View the works of art created in the Middle East. Specifically examine the page from the Qur'an and contemporary Iranian American artist Shirin Neshat's untitled work. How does script play a role in each of these images? What effect does the script have, even though you might not be able to understand the textual references? How does the role of the script change in Neshat's photograph? Examine Neshat's photographs side by side. What do you see? How does she depict the female character? What about Middle Eastern traditions? How do these aspects of her work interact? (SL.9–10.1, SL.9–10.2)

ADDITIONAL RESOURCES

- Chinua Achebe's *Things Fall Apart*: Teaching Through the Novel (National Endowment for the Humanities) (RL.9–10.1, RL.9–10.6, RL.9–10.10) (This lesson can be used alone or in conjunction with the related lesson Chinua Achebe's *Things Fall Apart*: Oral and Literary Strategies.)
- Women in Africa: Tradition and Change (National Endowment for the Humanities) (RL.9–10.1, RL.9–10.6, RL.9–10.10)

TERMINOLOGY

Antagonist	Foreshadowing	Persona	Satire
Colonialism	Irony	Point of view	
Denouement	Mysticism	Postcolonialism	
Extended metaphor	Paradox	Rhetoric	

Grade Ten, Unit Three Sample Lesson Plan

Cry, the Beloved Country by Alan Paton

Long Walk to Freedom: The Autobiography of Nelson Mandela by Nelson Mandela

Nobel Prize Acceptance Speech by Nelson Mandela

In this series of eight lessons, students read *Cry, the Beloved Country* by Alan Paton, *Long Walk to Freedom: The Autobiography of Nelson Mandela* by Nelson Mandela, and Mandela's Nobel Prize Acceptance Speech, and they:

Explore the history of apartheid in South Africa (W.9-10.7, RI.9-10.1, RI.9-10.2, RI.9-10.4, SL.9-10.1, L.9-10.6)

Compare the depiction of apartheid in the texts (W.9-10.8, RI.9-10.1, RI.9-10.6, RI.9-10.7, SL.9-10.1)

Identify the authors' perspectives (RI.9-10.6, SL.9-10.4)

Study Nelson Mandela's Nobel Prize Acceptance Speech (RI.9-10.2, RI.9-10.3, RI.9-10.5, RI.9-10.6, L.9-10.3, L.9-10.4)

Evaluate the texts' strengths (SL.9-10.4, RI.9-10.1)

Summary

Lesson I: South Africa and Apartheid

Conduct online and library research about the history of apartheid in South Africa (W.9-10.7, W.9-10.8, RI.9-10.2, RI.9-10.4, RI.9-10.6, RI.9-10.7, L.9-10.6, SL.9-10.1)

Document findings (RI.9-10.1, W.9-10.4)

Discuss findings (SL.9-10.1)

Lessons II, III, IV: *Cry, the Beloved Country*

Explore the purpose of each of the novel's three parts (RL.9-10.5, SL.9-10.1)

Explore South African society under apartheid (SL.9-10.4, L.9-10.6, RI.9-10.1, RI.9-10.2, RL.9-10.6)

Examine the generational framework of the novel (RL.9-10.5, SL.9-10.1)

Trace the evolution of Stephen Kualo and James Jarvis (RL.9-10.3, SL.9-10.4, L.9-10.5)

Analyze the multiple conflicts in the novel (RL.9-10.2, RL.9-10.3, RL.9-10.6, SL.9-10.4, L.9-10.4)

Critique the novel's resolution (RL.9-10.5, SL.9-10.3, L.9-10.6)

Explore the author's vision for South Africa in the closing words of the novel: "'For it is the dawn that has come, as it has come for a thousand centuries, never failing. But when that dawn will come, of our emancipation, from the fear of bondage and the bondage of fear, why, that is the secret." (RL.9-10.1, RL.9-10.6, SL.9-10.4, L.9-10.6)

Lessons V, VI, VII: *Long Walk to Freedom: The Autobiography of Nelson Mandela*

Explore Mandela's background, childhood, and education (W.9-10.7, W.9-10.8, RI.9-10.2, RI.9-10.7)

Note his political awakening (SL.9-10.1, RI.9-10.1, RI.9-10.5)

Probe his early political activities (W.9-10.9b, SL.9-10.4, RI.9-10.2, RI.9-10.7)

Trace the political evolution of the African National Congress (W.9-10.9b, W.9-10.8, RI.9-10.1)

Note Alan Paton's attempts to help Mandela (SL.9-10.1, RI.9-10.1, RI.9-10.5)

Explore Mandela's years in Robben Island (W.9-10.9b, SL.9-10.4)

Examine his activities after his release (W.9-10.9b, RI.9-10.1, RI.9-10.3, RI.9-10.7)

Explore Mandela's leadership and vision (W.9-10.9b, RI.9-10.1, RI.9-10.3, RI.9-10.7, SL.9-10.4)

Lesson VIII: Nelson Mandela's Nobel Prize Acceptance Speech

Annotate Mandela's Nobel Prize Acceptance Speech for its main ideas (RI.9-10.1, RI.9-10.2, RI.9-10.3, RI.9-10.4, SL.9-10.1, L.9-10.4)

Discuss the lecture (SL.9-10.1, W.9-10.9b)

Explore the speech in the context of the history of South Africa (W.9-10.9b, SL.9-10.4)

Revisit the novel and the autobiography and discuss the vision of both authors in the context of Mandela's speech (RL.9-10.5, RL.9-10.6, RI.9-10.5, RI.9-10.6, SL.9-10.4, L.9-10.5)

Compose a three- to four-page essay in which you explore the relative strengths of the two genres, the novel (*Cry, the Beloved Country*) and the memoir (*Long Walk to Freedom*), in exploring the struggles of blacks in South Africa during apartheid (W.9-10.2, W.9-10.4, W.9-10.5, L.9-10.6)

Lesson VIII: Nelson Mandela's Nobel Prize Lecture

Objectives

Annotate Mandela's Nobel Prize Acceptance Speech for its main ideas (RI.9-10.1, RI.9-10.2, RI.9-10.3, RI.9-10.4, SL.9-10.1, L.9-10.4)

Discuss the speech (SL.9-10.1, W.9-10.9b)

Explore the speech in the context of the history of South Africa (W.9-10.9b, SL.9-10.4)

Revisit the novel and the autobiography and discuss the vision of both authors in the context of Mandela's speech (RL.9-10.5, RL.9-10.6, RI.9-10.5, RI.9-10.6, SL.9-10.4, L.9-10.5)

Compose a three- to four-page essay in which you explore the relative strengths of the two genres, the novel (*Cry, the Beloved Country*) and the memoir (*Long Walk to Freedom*), in exploring the struggles of blacks in South Africa during apartheid (W.9-10.2, W.9-10.4, W.9-10.5, L.9-10.6)

Required Materials

☐ Class set of *Cry, the Beloved Country* by Alan Paton

☐ Class set of *Long Walk to Freedom: The Autobiography of Nelson Mandela* by Nelson Mandela

☐ Class set of Nelson Mandela's Nobel Prize Acceptance Speech

Procedures

1. Lead-In:
   Silently read Mandela's Nobel Prize Acceptance Speech.

2. Step by Step:
   a. Annotate the speech for its main ideas. (Pay close attention to Mandela's depiction of the past and his vision for the future.)
   b. Discuss the speech.
   c. Recall details about the history of apartheid.
   d. Discuss *Cry, the Beloved Country* and *Long Walk to Freedom: The Autobiography of Nelson Mandela* in the context of Mandela's speech.

3. Closure:
   Introduce the students to the take-home essay.

Differentiation

Advanced

- Select student volunteers to read Mandela's Nobel Prize Acceptance Speech aloud; give the students an opportunity to practice reading with expression, recorded with a video camera, so they can evaluate and improve their performances.
- Encourage students to research other Nobel Prize winners. Compare and contrast them with Mandela, and perhaps challenge them to share their findings in a creative and engaging presentation.
- Allow students to create a web using an online program about apartheid. Encourage students to take this to an abstract level, although they must be able to justify their thinking based on examples from the text.

Struggling

- Allow students to listen to an audio recording of Mandela's Nobel Prize Acceptance Speech to support their understanding of the text.
- Allow students to create a Venn diagram on paper or online that compares experiences with apartheid.
- Work with a small group to identify collaboratively key passages from Mandela's Nobel Prize Acceptance Speech. Allow students to annotate or sketch (or use other nonlinguistic representations) to aid in understanding and memory of the passages. Have them share their findings, possibly using a document camera. If needed, be prepared to point out passages that show Mandela's depiction of the past and his vision for the future.
- Pair students to work collaboratively to explore and annotate the passages. Partners write their notes on a shared spreadsheet or on the class blog so that they can receive feedback from the teacher and use them as a reference for the take-home essay.
- Allow students to focus their contributions to the conversation on *Cry, the Beloved Country* or *Long Walk to Freedom: The Autobiography of Nelson Mandela* in the context of Mandela's speech. Perhaps have a small-group conversation with students and help point out elements to think about prior to class discussion.

Homework/Assessment

Compose a three- to four-page essay in which you explore the relative strengths of the two genres, the novel (*Cry, the Beloved Country*) and the memoir (*Long Walk to Freedom*), in exploring the struggles of blacks in South Africa during apartheid.

World Literature: Russia

The purpose of this twelve-week unit is twofold: to introduce students to some of the shorter masterpieces of nineteenth-century Russian literature and to explore the impact of twentieth-century historical events on Russian writers and their works.

ESSENTIAL QUESTION

? How is Russian literature both timeless and affected by historical events?

OVERVIEW

In the first part of this unit, students read short works by Pushkin, Gogol, Tolstoy, or Chekhov as an introduction to shared themes and literary devices. The class should read no more than three short works in four weeks, in order to devote adequate attention to each. At the end of the unit, teachers choose a novel to read as a seminal text, or opt for the short absurdist vignettes of Daniil Kharms. The literary reading in this part of the unit should be paired with historical readings. By the end of the unit, students begin to understand Russian literature from both a literary and a historical standpoint and will have a foundation for further reading and study.

Note: The tenth-grade World Literature Maps consist of four twelve-week units, each focusing on literature from a different part of the world. Select three out of the four units. As the middle unit will likely cross from one semester into another, it should be divided accordingly. Alternatively, teachers may choose to teach all four units by shortening each and selecting fewer works.

FOCUS STANDARDS

These Focus Standards have been selected for the unit from the Common Core State Standards.

RL.9–10.3: Analyze how complex characters (e.g., those with multiple or conflicting motivations) develop over the course of a text, interact with other characters, and advance the plot or develop the theme.

RL.9–10.5: Analyze how an author's choices concerning how to structure a text, order events within it (e.g., parallel plots), and manipulate time (e.g., pacing, flashbacks) create such effects as mystery, tension, or surprise.

RI.9–10.3: Analyze how the author unfolds an analysis or series of ideas or events, including the order in which the points are made, how they are introduced and developed, and the connections that are drawn between them.

RI.9–10.6: Determine an author's point of view or purpose in a text and analyze how an author uses rhetoric to advance that point of view or purpose.

RI.9–10.7: Analyze various accounts of a subject told in different mediums (e.g., a person's life story in both print and multimedia), determining which details are emphasized in each account.

W.9–10.1: Write arguments to support claims in an analysis of substantive topics or texts, using valid reasoning and relevant and sufficient evidence.

W.9–10.2: Write informative/explanatory texts to examine and convey complex ideas, concepts, and information clearly and accurately through the effective selection, organization, and analysis of content.

SL.9–10.3: Evaluate a speaker's point of view, reasoning, and use of evidence and rhetoric, identifying any fallacious reasoning or exaggerated or distorted evidence.

L.9–10.3: Apply knowledge of language to understand how language functions in different contexts, to make effective choices for meaning or style, and to comprehend more fully when reading or listening.

SUGGESTED STUDENT OBJECTIVES

- Read works of Russian literature both for their intrinsic qualities and for their relation to the historical context.
- Analyze the motives, qualities, and contradictions of a character in Russian literature (including the narrator).
- Describe the effect of the narrative structure, pacing, and tone in a work of Russian literature.
- Analyze the role of utopian ideology in select works of Russian literature.
- Consider the impact of the Bolshevik Revolution and Communist rule on twentieth-century Russian writers and literature.
- Offer insightful inferences regarding the themes of the text.
- Create a clear, original, specific thesis statement.
- Organize concrete evidence and/or supporting textual details to support a thesis statement.
- Use precise language, avoiding casual language and clichés.
- Write appropriate transitions to organize paragraphs.
- Apply new terminology to the texts.
- Analyze how historical events influence literature.
- Analyze how literary devices help convey theme.

SUGGESTED WORKS

(E) indicates a CCSS exemplar text; (EA) indicates a text from a writer with other works identified as exemplars.

LITERARY TEXTS

Note: Texts can be selected and combined in a number of ways. Teachers may substitute a story for another story by the same author, or they may substitute one author for another major author from the same period. The selections should combine well, and there should be a balance of nineteenth- and twentieth-century literature. Roughly four to five weeks should be devoted to nineteenth-century works, and two to four weeks to a pivotal text; roughly four to five weeks should be devoted to a twentieth-century work and historical readings.

Novels and Novellas
- *Notes from the Underground* (Fyodor Dostoevsky) (EA)
- *The Death of Ivan Ilyich* (Leo Tolstoy)
- *One Day in the Life of Ivan Denisovich* (Aleksandr Solzhenitsyn)
- *A Dead Man's Memoir* (Mikhail Bulgakov)

Short Stories
- "The Nose" (Nikolai Gogol) (E)
- "The Overcoat" (Nikolai Gogol) (EA)
- "The Tale of How Ivan Ivanovich Quarelled with Ivan Nikiforovich" (Nikolai Gogol) (EA)
- "Home" (Anton Chekhov) (E)
- "Ward No. 6" (Anton Chekhov) (EA)
- "Rothschild's Fiddle" (Anton Chekhov) (EA)
- "The Duel" (Anton Chekhov) (EA)
- "Sleepy" (Anton Chekhov) (EA)
- "The Head-Gardener's Story" (Anton Chekhov) (EA)
- "The Steppe" (Anton Chekhov) (EA)
- *Tales of the Late Ivan Petrovich Belkin* (Alexander Pushkin) (selections)
- *Today I Wrote Nothing: The Selected Works of Daniil Kharms* (Daniil Kharms) (selections)
- *Diary of a Madman and Other Stories* (Nikolai Gogol) (EA)

Poetry
- "The Twelve" (Aleksandr Blok)
- "To Urania" (Joseph Brodsky)

Drama
- *The Seagull* (Anton Chekhov) (EA)
- *The Inspector-General: A Comedy in Five Acts* (Nikolai Gogol) (EA)

INFORMATIONAL TEXTS
- *Literary St. Petersburg: A Guide to the City and Its Writers* (Elaine Blair) (selections)
- *Everyday Stalinism: Ordinary Life in Extraordinary Times: Soviet Russia in the 1930s* (Sheila Fitzpatrick) (Chapters One, Five, and Eight)
- *The Proud Tower: A Portrait of the World Before the War, 1890–1914* (Barbara Tuchman) (Chapter Two)
- *Russia and the Soviet Union: An Historical Introduction from the Kievan State to the Present* (John M. Thompson) (Chapters Nine through Twelve)
- *The Gulag Archipelago: An Experiment in Literary Investigation* (Aleksandr Solzhenitsyn) (excerpts)
- "Dostoyevsky's Metaphor of the 'Underground'" (Monroe C. Beardsley)

- *Nikolai Gogol* (Vladimir Nabokov) (Chapter One)
- "A Slap in the Face of Public Taste" (Velimir Khlebnikov, Aleksey Kruchenykh, and Vladimir Mayakovsky)
- *Poets with History and Poets Without History* (Marina Tsvetaeva)
- *My Pushkin* (Marina Tsvetaeva)
- *Night Wraps the Sky: Writings By and About Mayakovsky* (Vladimir Mayakovsky and Michael Almerayda, ed.) (selections)

ART, MUSIC, AND MEDIA

Art

- St. Basil's Cathedral (Moscow, Russia, 1555–1561)
- Wassily Kandinsky, *Moscow I* (1916)
- Marc Chagall, *I and the Village* (1911)

Music

- Dmitri Shostakovich, *The Nose* (1928)

SAMPLE ACTIVITIES AND ASSESSMENTS

For a full Scoring Rubric, see the Appendix.

Note: After reading and discussing a work or pairing of works as a class, students prepare for seminars and essays by reflecting individually, in pairs, and/or in small groups on a given question. In this way, students generate ideas. (Seminar and essay assignments include more than one question. Teachers may choose one or all of the questions to explore in the course of the seminar; students should choose one question for the essay.) Seminars should be held before students write essays so that they may explore their ideas thoroughly and refine their thinking before writing. Textual evidence should be used to support all arguments advanced in seminars and in essays. Page and word counts for essays are not provided here, but teachers should consider the suggestions regarding the use of evidence, for example, to determine the likely length of good essays.

1. COLLABORATION

Reflect on seminar questions, take notes on your responses, and note the page numbers of the textual evidence you will refer to in your seminar and/or essay answers. Share your notes with a partner for feedback and guidance. Have you interpreted the text correctly? Is your evidence convincing? This collaboration can be done in a journal or on a shared online document. (RL.9–10.1, SL.9–10.1)

2. SEMINAR AND INFORMATIVE/EXPLANATORY WRITING

How reliable is the narrator in the short story "The Nose"? What does the loss of the nose symbolize? Why does the author use the absurd in his writing? Use at least three pieces of textual evidence to support an original thesis statement. Your teacher may give you the opportunity to share your initial thoughts on the classroom blog in order to get feedback from your classmates. (RL.9–10.1, RL.9–10.4, SL.9–10.1, W.9–10.2, W.9–10.9)

3. SEMINAR AND INFORMATIVE/EXPLANATORY WRITING

How does the narrator in "The Overcoat" resemble and diverge from the protagonist? What is the importance of Akakii's name—how he was named, what his name means to the story, and how it plays out? What changes in Akakii's life when the tailor first informs him that he needs a "new" overcoat? The word *new* has a profound effect on him—why? Write an informative/explanatory essay that uses at least three pieces of textual evidence to support an original thesis statement answering one of these questions. Your teacher may give you the opportunity to share your initial thoughts on the classroom blog in order to get feedback from your classmates. (RL.9–10.1, SL.9–10.1, W.9–10.2, W.9–10.9)

4. SEMINAR AND INFORMATIVE/EXPLANATORY WRITING

Explore the spiritual and emotional changes of Ivan Ilyich in Tolstoy's *The Death of Ivan Ilyich* or of Dr. Ragin in Chekhov's "Ward No. 6." How and why does the main character change throughout the story? Write an informative/explanatory essay using three to six pieces of textual evidence to support an original thesis statement. Your teacher may give you the opportunity to share your initial thoughts on the classroom blog in order to get feedback from your classmates. (RL.9–10.1, RL.9–10.2, SL.9–10.1, W.9–10.2, W.9–10.9)

5. SEMINAR AND INFORMATIVE/EXPLANATORY WRITING

Why does Dostoevsky's "Underground Man" reject the idea of the Crystal Palace? Use textual evidence to support your response. Write an informative/explanatory essay using at least three textual details to support an original thesis statement. Your teacher may give you the opportunity to share your initial thoughts on the classroom blog in order to get feedback from your classmates. (SL.9–10.1, W.9–10.2, W.9–10.9, SL.9–10.3, L.9–10.3)

6. SEMINAR AND INFORMATIVE/EXPLANATORY WRITING

Discuss "A Slap in the Face of Public Taste" before and after learning the historical context. How do historical references affect your interpretation of the document? Refer to the literary and informational texts to support your response. Write an informative/explanatory essay using at least three textual details to support an original thesis. Your teacher may give you the opportunity to share your initial thoughts on the classroom blog in order to get feedback from your classmates. (RI.9–10.6, SL.9–10.1, W.9–10.2, W.9–10.9)

7. SEMINAR AND INFORMATIVE/EXPLANATORY WRITING

How does the Bolshevik Revolution help us understand Blok's poem "The Twelve" (or another work of early twentieth-century Russian literature)? Use evidence from informational texts, as well as the poem itself. Write an informative/explanatory essay using at least three pieces of textual evidence to support an original thesis. Your teacher may give you the opportunity to share your initial thoughts on the classroom blog in order to get feedback from your classmates. (RL.9–10.6, RI.9.10.3, SL.9–10.1, W.9–10.2, W.9–10.9)

8. INFORMATIVE/EXPLANATORY WRITING

This writing assignment follows the reading of *Notes from the Underground,* by Fyodor Dostoevsky (*optional:* and the reading of "Dostoyevsky's Metaphor of the 'Underground,'" by Monroe C. Beardsley). Compose an informative/explanatory essay in which you address the following questions: "Dostoyevsky laments the fate of the 'nineteenth century intellectual ... who has been affected by education and European civilization.' Beardsley argues that this man, Dostoevsky's Underground Man, has a 'need for absolute freedom.' How does the protagonist of *Notes* rebel? How does his condemnation of the 108,000 logarithms fit into his rebellion? How does he grapple with his need for freedom?" Your teacher may give you the opportunity to share your initial thoughts on the classroom blog in order to get feedback from your classmates. (RL.9–10.1, RL.9–10.2, RL.9–10.3, RL.9–10.6, W.9–10.2)

9. ORAL PRESENTATION

Conduct and present research on the life of one of the authors whose work you have read for this course. How did historical events affect the author's point of view? How does the author express his or her point of view through the use of a narrator? Cite at least three pieces of textual evidence to support an original thesis statement. Your teacher may ask you to record your presentation as a podcast for publication on the class web page. (SL.9–10.4)

10. ORAL PRESENTATION

Cite examples of narrative repetition or digression in one of the works you have read; comment on its significance in the story. Your teacher may ask you to record your presentation as a podcast for publication on the class web page. (RL9–10.5)

11. SPEECH

Recite a favorite passage from one of the stories in this unit. Include an introduction that states:

- From where it is excerpted
- Who wrote it
- Its literary significance

    Record your recitation using a video camera so you can evaluate your performance for accuracy. (RL.9–10.2, SL.9–10.4, SL.9–10.6)

12. RESEARCH AND INFORMATIVE/EXPLANATORY WRITING

Choose an important event in Russian history (e.g., the Bolshevik Revolution) and write an informative/explanatory essay in which you discuss its impact on a selection from Russian literature. Begin by defining a research question (and refining it as necessary as research is conducted). Determine and execute a strategy for locating primary and secondary sources that will enrich your understanding of the historical event in question. The paper should include the following sections:

- Summary of the historical event in question (i.e., causes, brief history, significant details, and effects)
- Key ideas (including passages) from the author's work that support the thesis about the impact of the historical event
- Reflective conclusion about the event and its short- and long-term effects on Russian literature

    The essay should reflect a synthesis of sources consulted, a balance of paraphrasing and quoting from sources, and proper citation of sources. (W.9–10.1, W.9–10.7, W.9–10.8, W.9–10.9, W.9–10.10)

13. VOCABULARY

While reading the texts in this unit, keep a record in your journal or on a shared spreadsheet of words with multiple connotations. List some possible synonyms for the word as you think the author intended it to be understood. (L.9–10.4, L.9–10.5)

14. ART/CLASS DISCUSSION

Examine the architecture of St. Basil's Cathedral. What do you see? How does the color, style, and opulence affect your perception of religion in Russia? How might you categorize this type of architecture? Is this distinctly Russian architecture, or do you see a hybridization of eastern and western European elements? (SL.10.1, SL.10.2)

15. ART/CLASS DISCUSSION

Look at two artists who were born in Russia and migrated to Western Europe: Kandinsky and Chagall. What do you see in their artworks? How does the fantastic interact with the figurative? Does this remind you of any of the literary works you are reading in this unit? Are these works abstract in a typical way, or in different ways? (SL.10.1, SL.10.2)

ADDITIONAL RESOURCES

- Friends & Partners—Linking U.S.-Russia Across the Internet
- REESWeb: The World Wide Web Virtual Library for Russian and Eastern European Studies (University Center for International Studies, University of Pittsburgh)

TERMINOLOGY

The absurd	Communism	Gulag	Repetition
Allusion	Digression	Irony	Stalinism
Antihero	Fantasy	Narrator reliability	Verse (syllabic, accentual, syllabic-accentual)
Bolshevik revolution	Fate	Paranormal	
Carnivalesque	Grotesque	Persona	

Grade Ten, Unit Four Sample Lesson Plan

Notes from the Underground by Fyodor Dostoevsky (Book I)

In this series of six lessons, students read *Notes from the Underground* by Fyodor Dostoevsky (Book I), and they:

Examine the historical background of Dostoevsky's writing
Explore Dostoevsky's critique of society (RL.10.1, RL.10.2, SL.10.1)
Investigate Dostoevsky's view of freedom and responsibility (RL.10.1, RL.10.2, SL.10.1)

Summary

Lesson I: Mouse-Man's Voice (I & II)

Analyze Mouse-Man—a sick man, a mouse man (RL.9-10.1, RL.9-10.2, RL.9-10.3)

Examine Mouse-Man's "descent into the mud" (RL.9-10.1, RL.9-10.2, RL.9-10.3)

Critique Mouse-Man's perspective of nineteenth-century intellectual man (RL.9-10.1, RL.9-10.2, RL.9-10.3, SL.9-10.1)

Lesson III: Mouse-Man's Critique of Laws of Nature (IV–VI)

(Using informational texts) contextualize Dostoevsky, Europe and the Enlightenment

Explore the pleasure in a toothache (RL.9-10.2, RL.9-10.3)

Examine the role that the laws of nature play in Mouse-Man's criticism of society (RL.9-10.2)

Lesson II: Spontaneous Man vs. Mouse-Man (II & III)

Explore Mouse-Man's claims about "types of" men (RL.9-10.1, RL.9-10.2, RL.9-10.3)

Examine the "stone wall" metaphor (RL.9-10.1, RL.9-10.2, RL.9-10.3)

Critique the role that the laws of nature play in Mouse-Man's view of society (RL.9-10.2, SL.9-10.1)

Lesson IV: 108,000 Logarithms (V–VII)

Consider Mouse-Man's techniques to discredit the laws of logic/nature (RL.9-10.1, RL.9-10.2, RL.9-10.3)

Examine Mouse-Man's understanding of independence/individuality (RL.9-10.1, RL.9-10.2, RL.9-10.3)

Lesson V: Reason and Desire (VIII–XI)

Investigate the tension Mouse-Man establishes between reason and desire (RL.9-10.1, RL.9-10.2, RL.9-10.3, W.9-10.3, W.9-10.1, SL.9-10.1a,b)

Explore Mouse-Man's notion of the inherent paradox of man (RL.9-10.2)

Challenge Mouse-Man's claims about truth and his motives for writing (SL.9-10.1)

Lesson VI: Responsibility of Man

Identify key ideas in Monroe C. Beardsley's passage below* (RL.9-10.1, RL.9-10.2)

Explore key passages from *Notes* that support Beardsley's assertion (RL.9-10.1, RL.9-10.2)

Investigate Dostoevsky's notion of freedom (RL.9-10.1, RL.9-10.2)

> To Dostoevsky morality is not summed up in intellectual knowledge of causal facts, and the most profound error of rationalism is this identification of the good with the true. It is one of the deepest intentions of his picture of the Underground to refute this thesis of rationalism through a study of human nature, which reveals to him the presence in man of a will which can deliberately choose against its "best interests," against the dictates of reason. There is in man a profound necessity to feel responsible for all actions to the full extent of their holiness sinfulness. (p. 288)

> From "Dostoevsky's Metaphor of the 'Underground,'" by Monroe C. Beardsley, *The Journal of the History of Ideas*, 1942

Lesson V: Reason and Desire (VIII–XI)

Objectives

Investigate the tension that Mouse-Man establishes between reason and desire (RL.9-10.1, RL.9-10.2, RL.9-10.3, W.9-10.1, SL.9-10.1a,b)

Explore Mouse Man's notion of the inherent paradox of man (RL.10.2)

Challenge Mouse-Man's claims about truth and his motives for writing (SL.10.1)

Required Materials

☐ *Notes from the Underground*, by Fyodor Dostoevsky

Procedures

1. Lead-In:

In pairs, review charts (for homework, students had to create a reason vs. desire chart — as shown in the sample here).

Reason	Desire
"Now, suppose they find a formula at the root of our wishes whims ..." →	"... man will then cease to feel desire" and will change into an "organ stop."

2. Step by Step:

a. Students compare quotations and add to their individual charts.

b. Guided discussion (based on charts prepared by students).

"... suppose ... they ... find a formula at the root of our wishes whims ..." → then "man will cease to feel desire" and will change into an "organ stop"

"For when desire merges with reason, then we will reason instead of desiring."

"I will admit that reason is a good thing." But?

But: "Desire ... is the manifestation of life itself ..."

"... it's still life and not a series of extractions of square roots." (108,000 logarithms)

Human nature is the opposite of reason.

"... a man can wish upon himself, in full awareness, something harmful, stupid, and even completely idiotic. He will do it in order to establish his right to wish for the most idiotic things and not to be obliged to have only sensible wishes."

"... it leaves us our most important, most treasured possession: our individuality."

c. Lead a discussion, asking the following questions:

What is the paradox Mouse-Man highlights about man?

What leads the reader to the conclusion that it is absolutely necessary to change man's desires?

→
→
→

the achieving versus the achieved (i.e., the thrill of the pursuit, the letdown of accomplishment ...)

suffering is an advantage to man ...

3. Closure:

Narrator's question leads closing discussion: "Then why have I written all this?"

"I want to test to see whether it is possible to be completely frank and unafraid of the whole truth."

Differentiation

Advanced

- Ask students to "translate" this reading into a more modern-day ("casual") language that makes the concept of tension between Reason and Desire easier to understand. Create an online cartoon, digital slide presentation, or movie that highlights key points.

Struggling

- Allow students to work with a partner, and type their responses into a shared spreadsheet that is pre-created for them (similar to the preceding sample chart).
- Give students note cards or stems of "reasons" and "desires" for them to sort into the appropriate columns for the prior day's homework.
- Meet with students in a small group prior to the end of class to talk through ideas for the homework paragraph.

Homework/Assessment
I. Writing Task

In a well-organized paragraph, discuss the tension between Reason and Desire as seen by Mouse-Man.

II. Writing Guidelines

- Clearly establish the topic of the paragraph and contextualize it
- Organize the sequence of ideas according to the purpose of the paragraph
- Cite the text using short quotations
- Use standard English form
- Avoid grammatical and mechanical errors
- Use present simple tense

* Reprinted by permission of the University of Pennsylvania Press from "Dostoyevsky's Metaphor of the 'Underground'" by Monroe C. Beardsley, *Journal of the History of Ideas*, Vol. 3, No. 3 (Jun., 1942), pp. 265–290.

GRADE 11

The ELA course for eleventh grade is devoted to a study of American literature from the colonial period to the late twentieth century. Because much of the early literature is nonfiction (diaries, letters, sermons, almanacs, speeches, and foundational documents), there are many opportunities to analyze historical and informational texts. Students come to see the fluid relationship between fiction and nonfiction: for instance, the literary tropes in Jonathan Edwards's "Sinners in the Hands of an Angry God," or the dual historical contexts of Arthur Miller's *The Crucible*. In seminars, students discuss questions such as "Does Anne Bradstreet's work typify or differ from the other Puritan literature that you have read?" and "How do Willy Loman and Tommy Wilhelm contend with being 'nobody'?" Throughout the year, students have opportunities to make connections with history, art, and other subjects. Essays range from the analytical to the creative: students might write a narrative essay in the style of Thoreau's *Walden* or compare the treatment of a given theme in works from different genres. Students build on their writing skills from previous years, integrating multiple sources and perspectives into their work, reading literary criticism, and writing longer and more complex essays. To build appreciation of the sounds and cadences of American literature, students continue to recite poems and speeches and refine their expressive delivery. By the end of the year, students have a foundation in American literature and are ready to branch out into European literature, which they study in twelfth grade.

Standards Checklist for Grade Eleven

Standard	Unit 1	Unit 2	Unit 3	Unit 4	Unit 5	Unit 6	Standard	Unit 1	Unit 2	Unit 3	Unit 4	Unit 5	Unit 6
Reading—Literature							3d						
1	A	A	A	A	FA	A	3e						
2	A		FA		A	A	4				A		F
3	A			F	A	A	5				F		
4	F	F	A		A	A	6			A	A	A	A
5			A		A	F	7		A				A
6				A	FA		8		A	A			A
7	A					FA	9	A	A	A	A		A
8 n/a							9a					A	A
9	FA		FA	A	A	A	9b		A				
10	A						10						
Reading—Informational Text							Speaking and Listening						
1	A	A	A		FA		1	FA	A	A	A	A	A
2	A	A	A		A	FA	1a						
3	A			F			1b						
4	A	A					1c						
5		FA	F				1d						
6	F						2	A	A	A	FA	A	A
7							3	A	A	A	A		F
8		F					4		FA	FA	A	A	A
9	A	FA		A			5		A		A	FA	A
10				A			6	A		A			A
Writing							Language						
1	A	FA		A	A		1		F			A	A
1a							1a	A					
1b							1b						
1c							2				F	A	A
1d							2a						
1e							2b						
2	FA	A	A	A	A	FA	3	F	A			A	A
2a							3a						
2b							4			FA			
2c							4a						
2d							4b						
2e							4c						
2f							4d						
3			FA				5	A				A	A
3a							5a						
3b							5b						
3c							6					F	F

F = Focus Standards; A = Activity/Assessment

The New World

This four-week unit, the first of six, allows students to experience the earliest American literature and note the contemporary endurance of some of its themes.

OVERVIEW

The first eleventh-grade unit focuses primarily on nonfiction prose—including sermons and diaries—and some poetry from seventeenth- and early eighteenth-century America. Students examine the works of some of the earliest settlers in various parts of the "New World." They consider the significance of the intersection of Native American, European, and African cultures. They explore whether conflicts were inevitable and how language and religion served as both barriers and as bridges. Students look for emerging themes in American literature, such as the "new Eden" and the "American Dream." Finally, works of art from the period are examined for their treatment of similar themes.

FOCUS STANDARDS

These Focus Standards have been selected for the unit from the Common Core State Standards.

RL.11–12.4: Determine the meaning of words and phrases as they are used in the text, including figurative and connotative meanings; analyze the impact of specific word choices on meaning and tone, including words with multiple meanings or language that is particularly fresh, engaging, or beautiful. (Include Shakespeare as well as other authors.)

RL.11–12.9: Demonstrate knowledge of eighteenth-, nineteenth-, and early twentieth-century foundational works of American literature, including how two or more texts from the same period treat similar themes or topics.

RI.11–12.6: Determine an author's point of view or purpose in a text in which the rhetoric is particularly effective, analyzing how style and content contribute to the power, persuasiveness, or beauty of the text.

W.11–12.2: Write informative/explanatory texts to examine and convey complex ideas, concepts, and information clearly and accurately through the effective selection, organization, and analysis of content.

SL.11–12.1: Write arguments to support claims in an analysis of substantive topics or texts, using valid reasoning and relevant and sufficient evidence.

L.11–12.3: Apply knowledge of language to understand how language functions in different contexts, to make effective choices for meaning or style, and to comprehend more fully when reading or listening.

SUGGESTED STUDENT OBJECTIVES

- Identify emerging themes in early American literature, such as a "new Eden," "salvation," and "cooperation and conflict."
- Compare and contrast the experiences of America's earliest settlers, as conveyed through primary source documents and literature of the Colonial period.
- Identify and explain elements of Puritan literature.
- Explain "preaching" as a type of formal speech and explain its role in the "First Great Awakening."
- Explain the role of religion in early American life.

SUGGESTED WORKS

(E) indicates a CCSS exemplar text; (EA) indicates a text from a writer with other works identified as exemplars.

LITERARY TEXTS

Poetry

- "On Being Brought from Africa to America" (Phillis Wheatley) (E)
- "An Hymn to the Evening" (Phillis Wheatley) (EA)
- "To His Excellency General Washington" (Phillis Wheatley) (EA)
- "To My Dear and Loving Husband" (Anne Bradstreet)
- "Upon the Burning of Our House" (Anne Bradstreet)
- "Upon a Spider Catching a Fly" (Edward Taylor)
- *An Almanack for the Year of Our Lord 1648* (Samuel Danforth) (selections)
- "The Day of Doom" (Michael Wigglesworth)
- "The Sot-Weed Factor" (Ebenezer Cook)

Drama

- *The Crucible* (Arthur Miller) (EA)

INFORMATIONAL TEXTS

- *Of Plymouth Plantation* (William Bradford) (excerpts)
- *The Bloody Tenent of Persecution, for Cause of Conscience* (Roger Williams) (excerpts)
- *A Key into the Language of America* (Roger Williams) (excerpts)
- *The Selling of Joseph: A Memorial* (Samuel Sewall)
- *The Trials of Phillis Wheatley: America's First Black Poet and Encounters with the Founding Fathers* (Henry Louis Gates Jr.) (excerpts)
- "The Negro Artist and the Racial Mountain" (Langston Hughes) (EA)

Autobiography

- *A Narrative of the Captivity and Restoration of Mrs. Mary Rowlandson* (Mary Rowlandson)
- *The Secret Diary of William Byrd of Westover, 1709–1712* (William Byrd) (excerpts)

Speeches

- "Sinners in the Hands of an Angry God" (July 8, 1741) (Jonathan Edwards)

ART, MUSIC, AND MEDIA

Art

- Charles Willson Peale, *Mrs. James Smith & Grandson* (1776)
- John Singleton Copley, *Mrs. George Watson* (1765)
- John Valentine Haidt, *Young Moravian Girl* (ca. 1755–1760)
- Joseph Wright (Wright of Derby), *Portrait of a Woman* (1770)

SAMPLE ACTIVITIES AND ASSESSMENTS

For a full Scoring Rubric, see the Appendix.

Note: After reading and discussing a work or pairing of works as a class, students prepare for seminars and essays by reflecting individually, in pairs, and/or in small groups on a given seminar or essay question. In this way, students generate ideas. (Seminar and essay assignments may include more than one question. Teachers may choose one or all of the questions to explore in the course of the seminar; students should choose one question for the essay.) Seminars should be held before students write essays so that they may explore their ideas thoroughly and refine their thinking before writing. Textual evidence should be used to support all arguments advanced in seminars and in all essays. Page and word counts for essays are not provided here, but teachers should consider the suggestions regarding the use of evidence, for example, to determine the likely length of good essays.

1. COLLABORATION

Reflect on seminar questions, take notes on your responses in your journal or on a shared spreadsheet, and note the page numbers of the textual evidence you will refer to in your seminar and/or essay answers. Share your notes with a partner for feedback and guidance. Have you interpreted the text correctly? Is your evidence convincing? (RL.11–12.1, RL.11–12.10, SL.11–12.1)

2. SEMINAR AND WRITING (ARGUMENT)

"Does Anne Bradstreet's work typify or differ from the other Puritan literature that you have read?" Write an argument in which you use at least three pieces of textual evidence to support your position. Your teacher may give you the opportunity to share your initial thoughts on the classroom blog in order to get feedback from your classmates. (RL.11–12.9, W.11–12.9, SL.11–12.1)

3. SEMINAR AND INFORMATIVE/EXPLANATORY WRITING

Select a passage from one of the poems and another from one of the informational texts that treat a similar theme (e.g., "On Being Brought from Africa to America" and *Of Plymouth Plantation*). How are the themes revealed in the different genres? What different techniques or literary devices do the authors use to convey theme? Write an informative/explanatory essay in which you use at least three pieces of textual evidence to support an original thesis statement. Your teacher may give you the opportunity to share your initial thoughts on the classroom blog in order to get feedback from your classmates. (RL.11–12.2, W.11–12.2, W.11–12.9, L.11–12.5)

4. SEMINAR AND WRITING (ARGUMENT)

Could some contemporary American approaches to religion be traced to Puritan origins? Why or why not? Write an argument in which you use at least three pieces of textual evidence to support your position. Your teacher may give you the opportunity to share your initial thoughts on the classroom blog in order to get feedback from your classmates. (RI.11–12.4, RI.11–12.9, W.11–12.2)

5. CLASSROOM ACTIVITY, SEMINAR, AND WRITING (ARGUMENT)

View a staged or film version of *The Crucible*. Then discuss this question: Is John Proctor a tragic figure? Why or why not? Compare him to other tragic figures studied in ninth grade, such as Oedipus Rex. Write an argument in which you use at least three pieces of textual evidence to support your position. Your teacher may give you the opportunity to share your initial thoughts on the classroom blog in order to get feedback from your classmates. (RL.11–12.3, RL.11–12.7)

6. SPEECH

Select a one- to two-minute passage from one of the texts and recite it from memory. Include an introduction that states:

- What the excerpt is from
- Who wrote it
- Why it exemplifies Puritan literature

Record your recitation using a video camera so you can evaluate your performance for accuracy. (RL.11–12.9, SL.11–12.6)

7. WRITING (ARGUMENT)

In his essay "The Trials of Phillis Wheatley" Henry Louis Gates Jr. discusses Wheatley's critics. He notes that her "trials" began when her white contemporaries doubted her ability to write. Today, Gates says, her "trials" continue. In the conclusion to his essay, Gates suggests that Wheatley's critics miss a crucial point: "The challenge isn't to read white, or read black; it is to read. If Phillis Wheatley stood for anything, it was the creed that culture was, could be, the equal possession of all humanity." Write an argument in which you agree or disagree with Gates; use evidence from Wheatley's work to support your position. Your teacher may give you the opportunity to share your initial thoughts on the classroom blog in order to get feedback from your classmates. (RL.11–12.1, RI.11–12.1, W.11–2.1)

8. WRITING (ARGUMENT)

After reading excerpts from "Sinners in the Hands of an Angry God," write an argument that explains why you think early settlers were persuaded by Edwards's sermon. Note evidence from the text to support your thesis. (RL.11–12.1, RL.11–12.2, W.11–12.1)

9. GRAMMAR AND USAGE

Examine one of the texts studied in this unit for usage (e.g., words or conventions) that differs from contemporary usage. Discuss with classmates online or in class whether and/or how the meanings of words and/or sentence structure has changed since that time. "Translate" instances of antiquated syntax into contemporary sentences; determine whether and/or how the meaning of the sentence is affected by the translation. (L.11–12.1a)

10. ART/CLASS DISCUSSION

Examine the artworks listed. What does each image show about "young America"? Examine the Copley painting in comparison to the Haidt. What can you learn about each of these women and their lives in America? How are the women different? Carefully examine the iconography present in each image. Compare the Peale, Copley, and Wright paintings. What can we learn about the new nation from the way these painters worked? Do you detect a European influence? What stylistic aspects or materials might American artists be borrowing from England, judging by the similarities between the Wright (English) and Copley or Peale (American) portraits? (SL.11–12.2, SL.11–12.3)

ADDITIONAL RESOURCES

- *Religion and The Founding of the American Republic* (Library of Congress) (RI.11–12.2, RI.11–12.3)
- *The First Great Awakening* (National Endowment for the Humanities) (RI.11–12.2, RI.11–12.3)
- *Africans in America (Part 1)* (PBS) (RL.11–12.1, RI.11–12.1, SL.11–12.1)

TERMINOLOGY

Allegory	Covenant of grace	Idealism	Parallelism
Apostrophe	Didactic poetry	Lyric poetry	Pragmatism
Conceit	The great awakening	Oxymoron	Sermon

Grade Eleven, Unit One Sample Lesson Plan

"On Being Brought from Africa to America" by Phillis Wheatley

In this series of four lessons, students read "On Being Brought from Africa to America" by Phillis Wheatley, as well as texts by Henry Louis Gates Jr. and Langston Hughes, and they:

> Evaluate the controversy over Wheatley's texts (RL.11-12.2, RI.11-12.2, W.11-12.2, W.11-12.1a,b,d; W.11-12.2a,b)
>
> Gather information relevant to Wheatley's "trials" (RL.11-12.1, RL.11-12.2, RI.11-12.1, RI.11-12.2)
>
> Debate the merits of each side of the dispute (RI.11-12.1, RI.11-12.2, SL.11-12.1b,c,d)

Summary

Lesson I: Meet Phillis Wheatley

Investigate the life of Phillis Wheatley (informational text) (RI.11-12.3)

Contextualize her works (informational text)

Evaluate the artistic merits of several of her texts (RL.11-12.1, RL.11-12.2, RL.11-12.3, RL.11-12.4, SL.11-12.1b,c)

Analyze Wheatley's complex message (RL.11-12.1, RL.11-12.2, RL.11-12.3, RL.11-12.4)

Lesson III: "The Negro Artist and the Racial Mountain"

Identify key ideas in Hughes's "The Negro Artist and the Racial Mountain" (RI.11-12.1, RI.11-12.2, RI.11-12.3, RI.11-12.6)

Revisit Wheatley's texts (RL.11-12.2)

Consider whether Wheatley fulfilled Hughes's challenge (RL.11-12.1, RI.11-12.2)

Challenge Hughes's perspective (RI.11-12.2, SL.11-12.1b, SL.11-12.1c)

Juxtapose Gates's and Hughes's views (RI.11-12.2, SL.11-12.1b,c,d)

Lesson II: Henry Louis Gates Jr. and *The Trials of Phillis Wheatley*

Identify key ideas in Gates's essay (RI.11-12.1, RI.11-12.2, RI.11-12.3)

Evaluate Gates's rhetorical moves (RI.11-12.5, RI.11-12.6)

Revisit Wheatley's texts (RL.11-12.2)

Consider the dilemma that Gates introduces (RL.11-12.2, RI.11-12.2, SL.11-12.1b,c,d)

Lesson IV: *The Trials of Phillis Wheatley*—A Debate

Gather information relevant to Wheatley's "trials" (RL.11-12.1, RL.11-12.2, RI.11-12.1, RI.11-12.2)

Evaluate the controversy over Wheatley's texts (RL.11-12.2, W.11-12.1a,b,d; W.11-12.2a,b)

Debate the merits of each side of the dispute (RI.11-12.1, RI.11-12.2, SL.11-12.1b,c,d)

Lesson IV: *The Trials of Phillis Wheatley*—A Debate

Objectives

Gather information relevant to Wheatley's "trials" (RL.11-12.1, RL.11-12.2, RI.11-12.1, RI.11-12.2)

Evaluate the controversy over Wheatley's texts (RL.11-12.2, RI.11-12.2, W.11-12.1a,b,d; W.11-12.2a,b)

Debate the merits of each side of the dispute (RI.11-12.1, RI.11-12.2, SL.11-12.1b,c,d)

Required Materials

- ☐ "On Being Brought from Africa to America," by Phillis Wheatley
- ☐ "An Hymn to the Evening," by Phillis Wheatley
- ☐ "To His Excellency General Washington," by Phillis Wheatley
- ☐ *The Trials of Phillis Wheatley*, by Henry Louis Gates Jr.
- ☐ "The Negro Artist and the Racial Mountain," by Langston Hughes

Procedures

1. Lead-In:

An introduction to the purpose of the debate over Wheatley's writings.

2. Step by Step:

a. Divide the class into two groups. Do not allow students to choose the side that they believe is correct. (An easy way to avoid dispute is to count the students in ones and twos, then all the ones become one side, while all the others are the other side.)

b. In groups, students:

   - Closely reread Wheatley's work
   - Analyze Gates and list his key ideas
   - Analyze Hughes and list his key ideas
   - Conduct further research on the dispute
   - Conduct internal debate and anticipate the other side's position

c. Each side produces a three-page document or digital presentation that presents and defends its views.

d. Each side summarizes its position.

e. Each side takes notes while listening.

f. Lead the debate following the reading of both papers.

3. Closure:

Provide the class with an assessment of the debate, pointing to key ideas in this ongoing dispute.

Differentiation

Advanced

- Encourage students to conduct research beyond the material provided.
- Ask students to share their findings with their groups and incorporate appropriate material into their presentations.
- Encourage students to find examples of strong debates, and create a "rubric" for what makes a strong debate. Share the rubric with all students, and point out these qualities during the debate.

Struggling

- Assist some of the students while they are working on step b. The class can collaboratively track key points using a shared spreadsheet. Or encourage students to use ReadWriteThink's "Literary Graffiti Interactive" to help them visualize and remember what they are reading about.
- Divide students into groups and act out/dramatize the key ideas by Wheatley, Gates, and Hughes (in order to reinforce them). These dramatizations can be recorded using a video camera for future reference.

Assessment/Homework
N/A

Grade 11 ▶ *Unit 2*

A New Nation

This six-week unit, the second of six, examines the writers and documents associated with the founding of the new American nation, as well as some of the poetry and other prose of the time.

ESSENTIAL QUESTION

Why was the founding of America unique?

OVERVIEW

Building on the themes explored in Unit One, students trace the movement toward revolution and the colonists' desire to establish a new government, noting the differences in opinions between federalists and anti-federalists and how their arguments were made. Students compare the radical purpose and tone of the Declaration of Independence to the measured and logical tone of the Preamble to the Constitution and the Bill of Rights. They analyze the expressions of conflict and/or cooperation between colonists and the British government, between colonists and Native Americans, and between colonists and slaves. They begin to recognize the emerging theme in American literature of "American exceptionalism." Works of visual art from the period will be examined for their treatment of similar themes.

Note: This unit in particular could be taught in collaboration with an American history teacher, given its emphasis on America's founding documents.

FOCUS STANDARDS

These Focus Standards have been selected for the unit from the Common Core State Standards.

RL.11–12.4: Determine the meaning of words and phrases as they are used in the text, including figurative and connotative meanings; analyze the impact of specific word choices on meaning and tone, including words with multiple meanings or language that is particularly fresh, engaging, or beautiful. (Include Shakespeare as well as other authors.)

RI.11–12.5: Analyze and evaluate the effectiveness of the structure an author uses in his or her exposition or argument, including whether the structure makes points clear, convincing, and engaging.

RI.11–12.8: Delineate and evaluate the reasoning in seminal U.S. texts, including the application of constitutional principles and use of legal reasoning (e.g., in U.S. Supreme Court majority opinions and dissents) and the premises, purposes, and arguments in works of public advocacy (e.g., The Federalist, presidential addresses).

RI.11–12.9: Analyze seventeenth-, eighteenth-, and nineteenth-century foundational U.S. documents of historical and literary significance (including The Declaration of Independence, the Preamble to the Constitution, the Bill of Rights, and Lincoln's Second Inaugural Address) for their themes, purposes, and rhetorical features.

W.11–12.1: Write arguments to support claims in an analysis of substantive topics or texts, using valid reasoning and relevant and sufficient evidence.

SL.11–12.4: Present information, findings, and supporting evidence, conveying a clear and distinct perspective, such that listeners can follow the line of reasoning, alternative or opposing perspectives are addressed, and the organization, development, substance, and style are appropriate to purpose, audience, and a range or formal and informal tasks.

L.11–12.1: Demonstrate command of the conventions of Standard English grammar and usage when writing or speaking.

SUGGESTED STUDENT OBJECTIVES

- Identify defining themes in American literature, such as "American exceptionalism."
- Identify and explain the historic and literary significance of America's founding documents.
- Analyze how tone is established in persuasive writing.
- Analyze the use of literary elements in persuasive writing.
- Compare and contrast points of view in arguments presented on related issues.
- Analyze the qualities of an effective argument (i.e., examine the truthfulness and validity of the argument, as well as its rhetorical devices).
- Apply knowledge of effective arguments when writing one of your own.

SUGGESTED WORKS

(E) indicates a CCSS exemplar text; (EA) indicates a text from a writer with other works identified as exemplars.

LITERARY TEXTS

Poetry
- "The Star-Spangled Banner" (Francis Scott Key)
- "The Wild Honeysuckle" (Philip Freneau)
- "The Indian Burying Ground" (Philip Freneau)

INFORMATIONAL TEXTS
- The Declaration of Independence (Thomas Jefferson) (E)
- Virginia Statute for Religious Freedom (Thomas Jefferson) (EA)
- Letter to John Adams (August 1, 1816) (Thomas Jefferson) (EA)
- Benjamin Banneker's Letter to Thomas Jefferson (August 19, 1791) (Benjamin Banneker)

- Thomas Jefferson's Letter to Benjamin Banneker (August 30, 1791) (Thomas Jefferson)
- Preamble to the Constitution and the Bill of Rights (E)
- "The Way to Wealth," *Poor Richard's Almanack* (Benjamin Franklin) (selections)
- *Common Sense* or *The Crisis* (Thomas Paine) (E)
- *Federalist* No. 1 (Alexander Hamilton) (E)
- *Federalist* No. 10 (James Madison)
- *The Complete Anti-Federalist* (Herbert J. Storing) (selections)
- *Letters from an American Farmer* (J. Hector St. John de Crèvecoeur) (selections)

Autobiography

- *The Autobiography of Benjamin Franklin* (Benjamin Franklin)
- *Equiano's Travels: The Interesting Narrative of the Life of Olaudah Equiano, or Gustavus Vassa, the African* (Olaudah Equiano)

Speeches

- Speech to the Virginia Convention (March 20, 1775) (Patrick Henry) (E)

ART, MUSIC, AND MEDIA

Art

- Emanuel Leutze, *Washington Crossing the Delaware* (1851)
- John Trumbull, *Declaration of Independence* (1819)
- John Copley, *Paul Revere* (ca. 1768)
- Thomas Pritchard Rossiter, *Washington and Lafayette at Mount Vernon* (1859)
- Gilbert Stuart, *James Monroe* (ca. 1820–1822)
- Gustavus Hesselius, *Lapowinsa* (1735)
- Auguste Couder, *Siège de Yorktown* (ca. 1836)

SAMPLE ACTIVITIES AND ASSESSMENTS

For a full Scoring Rubric, see the Appendix.

Note: After reading and discussing a work or pairing of works as a class, students prepare for seminars and essays by reflecting individually, in pairs, and/or in small groups on a given seminar or essay question. In this way, students generate ideas. (Seminar and essay assignments may include more than one question. Teachers may choose one or all of the questions to explore in the course of the seminar; students should choose one question for the essay.) Seminars should be held before students write essays so that they may explore their ideas thoroughly and refine their thinking before writing. Textual evidence should be used to support all arguments advanced in seminars and in all essays. Page and word counts for essays are not provided here, but teachers should consider the suggestions regarding the use of evidence, for example, to determine the likely length of good essays.

1. COLLABORATION

Reflect on seminar questions, take notes on your responses in your journal or on a shared spreadsheet, and note the page numbers of the textual evidence you will refer to in your seminar and/or essay answers. Share your notes with a partner for feedback and guidance. Have you interpreted the text correctly? Is your evidence convincing? (RL.11–12.1, SL.11–12.1)

2. WRITING (ARGUMENT)

Imagine that you are an early American colonist. Write a letter to a family member or friend persuading him or her to join your fight for American independence. Use at least three pieces of textual evidence to support your position. Your teacher may give you the opportunity to post your first draft on a shared spreadsheet and receive feedback from classmates before publication. (W.11–12.1, W.11–12.9b)

3. INFORMATIVE/EXPLANATORY WRITING

Write an essay in which you explain Madison's use of the term *faction* in *Federalist* No. 10. Use at least three pieces of textual evidence to support an original thesis statement. Your teacher may give you the opportunity to post your first draft on a shared spreadsheet and receive feedback from classmates before publication. (RI.11–12.4, W.11–12.2, W.11–12.9b)

4. SEMINAR AND WRITING (ARGUMENT)

Do the Declaration of Independence and the Constitution share similar tones? Why or why not? Use at least three pieces of textual evidence to support your argument. Your teacher may give you the opportunity to share your initial thoughts on the classroom blog in order to get feedback from your classmates. (RI.11–12.9, W.11–12.9b, SL.11–12.1)

5. RESEARCH AND INFORMATIVE/EXPLANATORY WRITING

Select one of the texts studied and write a research paper in which you trace the enduring significance of the work through contemporary American history. Cite at least three secondary sources to support an original thesis statement. The essay should reflect your reasoned judgment about the quality and reliability of sources consulted (i.e., why you emphasize some and not others), a balance of paraphrasing and quoting from sources, and proper citation of sources. Your teacher may give you the option of adding a multimedia component to your paper, either by creating a digital slide presentation to highlight key points, or a movie in which your paper becomes the narration. (RI.11–12.1, W.11–12.7, W.11–12.8, W.11–12.9, SL.11–12.5)

6. RESEARCH AND INFORMATIVE/EXPLANATORY WRITING

(This essay could be assigned in collaboration with an American history teacher.) Select one of the Founding Fathers and conduct independent research, defining and refining the research question independently. The final informative/explanatory essay should include the following sections:

- Biographical information
- Analysis of a document that the founder wrote, including its historical significance
- The Founder's unique contribution to the new nation
- The long-term importance of the Founder

The essay should reflect your reasoned judgment about the quality and reliability of sources consulted (i.e., why you emphasize some and not others), a balance of paraphrasing and quoting from sources, and proper citation of sources. Your teacher may give you the option of adding a multimedia component to your paper, either by creating a digital slide presentation to highlight key points, or a movie in which your paper becomes the narration. (RI.11–12.1, W.11–12.7, W.11–12.8, W.11–12.9, SL.11–12.5)

7. ORAL OR MIXED-MEDIA PRESENTATION

Students will prepare and give a formal summary (oral or mixed-media presentation) of the research paper, fielding questions from peers. (SL.11–12.3, SL.11–12.4)

8. GRAMMAR AND USAGE

Examine one of the founding documents for variety in sentence structure. (Teacher will select passages and highlight three sentences.) With guidance from your teacher, diagram the three highlighted sentences. Then rewrite each sentence in "contemporary" prose. (L.11–12.3)

9. ART/CLASS DISCUSSION

Examine the artworks listed. How did artists portray historical figures and events from the founding of America? Why might an artist choose to depict such events or figures? Examine each artwork for imagery detailing the founding of America and identify ways in which artists use history for inspiration. In addition, compare the Leutze and Trumbull paintings. How does the artist share each narrative with you? What visual clues lead you to discover what is happening in each scene? Why might these paintings inspire viewers during the time period as well as future viewers? (SL.11.2, SL.11.3)

ADDITIONAL RESOURCES

- *The Declaration of Independence: "An Expression of the American Mind"* (National Endowment for the Humanities) (RI.11–12.2, RI.11–12.5)
- *Jefferson vs. Franklin: Renaissance Men* (National Endowment for the Humanities) (RI.11–12.5)
- *Jefferson vs. Franklin: Revolutionary Philosophers* (National Endowment for the Humanities) (RI.11–12.1)
- *Africans in America (Part 2)* (PBS) (RL.11–12.1, RI.11–12.1, SL.11–12.2)

TERMINOLOGY

Anti-federalism	Heroic couplet	Separation of church
Aphorism	Maxim	and state
Deism	Natural law	
Federalism	Salvation	

Grade Eleven, Unit Two Sample Lesson Plan

The Declaration of Independence by Thomas Jefferson

In this series of five lessons, students read the Declaration of Independence by Thomas Jefferson, and they:

Conduct a close reading of the Declaration of Independence (RI.11–12.1, RI.11–12.2, RI.11–12.3, RI.11–12.4, RI.11–12.6, RI.11–12.9)

Explicate the Declaration of Independence (RI.11–12.1, RI.11–12.4, RI.11–12.9, W.11–12.4, SL.11–12.4, SL.11–12.6, L.11–12.6)

Conduct close reading of memorable historical documents (RI.11–12.1, RI.11–12.2, RI.11–12.3, RI.11–12.4, RI.11–12.6, RI.11–12.9)

Explicate the selected documents (RI.11–12.1, RI.11–12.4, RI.11–12.9, W.11–12.4, SL.11–12.4, SL.11–12.6, L.11–12.6)

Present the key ideas in the selected documents (RI.11–12.2, SL.11–12.4, L.11–12.6)

Explore the legacy of these documents (RI.11–12.8, RI.11–12.9, SL.11–12.1, SL.11–12.3)

Summary

Lesson I, II: The Declaration of Independence

Explore the historical context of the Declaration of Independence (RI.11–12.9, SL.11–12.1)

Conduct a close reading of the Declaration of Independence (RI.11–12.1, RI.11–12.2, RI.11–12.3, RI.11–12.4, RI.11–12.9)

Note the form of the Declaration of Independence (RI.11–12.5, SL.11–12.4, W.11–12.4)

Identify key ideas in the Declaration of Independence (RI.11–12.2, SL.11–12.4, L.11–12.6)

Explore the content of the Declaration of Independence (RI.11–12.8, RI.11–12.9, SL.11–12.1, SL.11–12.3)

Lesson III, IV: Key Historical Documents

Select a historical document from the list below:

"Give Me Liberty or Give Me Death," by Patrick Henry (1775)

First Inaugural Address of President George Washington (1789)

The First State of the Union Address of President George Washington (1790)

Inaugural Address of President John Adams (1797)

First Inaugural Address of President Thomas Jefferson (1801)

The Declaration of Causes of seceding states (select one of the states/1861)

Gettysburg Address, by President Abraham Lincoln (1863)

Conduct close reading (as illustrated in lessons I, II) of the document (RI.11–12.1, RI.11–12.2, RI.11–12.3, RI.11–12.4, RI.11–12.6, RI.11–12.9)

Identify main ideas in the document (RI.11–12.2, SL.11–12.1, W.11–12.4)

Analyze the form of the document (RI.11–12.5, SL.11–12.4, L.11–12.6)

Lesson V: The Legacy of Words

Share impressions of the selected text (RI.11-12.6, SL.11-12.4, SL.11-12.6, W.11-12.4)

Probe the historical significance of the nation's documents (RI.11-12.8, RI.11-12.9, SL.11-12.1, SL.11-12.3)

Lesson I, II: The Declaration of Independence

Objectives

Explore the historical context of the Declaration of Independence (RI.11-12.9, SL.11-12.1)

Conduct a close reading of the Declaration of Independence (RI.11-12.1, RI.11-12.2, RI.11-12.3, RI.11-12.4, RI.11-12.6, RI.11-12.9)

Note the form of the Declaration of Independence (RI.11-12.5, SL.11-12.4, W.11-12.4)

Identify key ideas in the Declaration of Independence (RI.11-12.2, SL.11-12.4, L.11-12.6)

Explore the content of the Declaration of Independence (RI.11-12.8, RI.11-12.9, SL.11-12.1, SL.11-12.3)

Required Materials

☐ Class set of the Declaration of Independence
☐ Access to the Internet

Procedures

1. Lead-In:

Students explore the historical background of the Declaration of Independence.

2. Step by Step:

a. Students share the Lead-In findings.

b. Students reread the Declaration of Independence. (For homework, students will already have read the Declaration of Independence.) While they reread, the students identify its four sections:

- The introduction (paragraphs I & II)
- The "injuries and usurpations" caused by the King
- The conclusion
- The signatures

c. In pairs, or small groups, the students annotate the Declaration of Independence for the content of the first three sections. Here is an example:

> *When in the Course of human events, it becomes necessary for one people to dissolve the*

> *political bands* [The purpose of the document is stated at the very beginning.] *which have connected them with another, and to assume among the*

> *powers of the earth, the separate and equal station to which the <u>Laws of Nature</u>* [The words evoke the "Laws of Nature," and "Nature's God."] *and of*

> *Nature's God entitle them, a decent respect to the opinions of <u>mankind requires that they</u>*

> *should declare the causes which impel them to the separation* [The "causes" will be detailed].

> *[Note that the first paragraph is a single sentence.]*

3. Closure:
Lead a class discussion of the findings.

Differentiation

Advanced

- Select student volunteers to read sections of the Declaration of Independence aloud; give the students an opportunity to practice reading with expression, recorded with a video camera, so they can evaluate their performances and improve upon them. Create a collaborative reading and post on the class web page.
- Encourage students to write a poem or other creative interpretation of the Declaration of Independence that summarizes the key points.

Struggling

- Pre-assess (all) students for their knowledge of the Declaration of Independence. Consider pre-teaching key ideas to students on the day prior (for example, giving them the handout of the lecture to read).

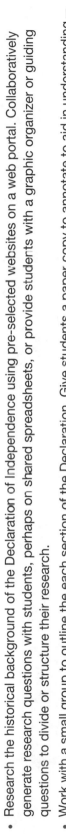

- Research the historical background of the Declaration of Independence using pre-selected websites on a web portal. Collaboratively generate research questions with students, perhaps on shared spreadsheets, or provide students with a graphic organizer or guiding questions to divide or structure their research.

- Work with a small group to outline the each section of the Declaration. Give students a paper copy to annotate to aid in understanding — possibly as a group using a document camera. Alternatively, give students an electronic copy in a text document to annotate, similar to the example above.

Homework/Assessment

N/A

American Romanticism

This six-week unit, the third of six, focuses on the emerging movement of American romanticism in the early nineteenth century and the period leading up to the Civil War.

OVERVIEW

Students explore America's first prolific period of literature by examining works from Cooper and Irving to Hawthorne, Melville, Poe, Whitman, Emerson, and Thoreau. The prominent theme of manifest destiny during this period in American literature may be introduced by reading John O'Sullivan's essay "Annexation." Students will wrestle with how the romantics perceived individualism and how this focus on individualism relates to other themes in American literature. Students will explore transcendentalism as an aspect of American romanticism and compare the romantics with the transcendentalists. Teachers are encouraged to select one novel and a variety of the other poetry and prose in order to give students maximum exposure to the various works of the period.

FOCUS STANDARDS

These Focus Standards have been selected for the unit from the Common Core State Standards.

RL.11–12.2: Determine two or more themes or central ideas of a text and analyze their development over the course of the text, including how they interact and build on one another to produce a complex account; provide an objective summary of the text.

RL.11–12.9: Demonstrate knowledge of eighteenth-, nineteenth-, and early twentieth-century foundational works of American literature, including how two or more texts from the same period treat similar themes or topics.

RI.11–12.5: Analyze and evaluate the effectiveness of the structure an author uses in his or her exposition or argument, including whether the structure makes points clear, convincing, and engaging.

W.11–12.3: Write narratives to develop real or imagined experiences or events using effective technique, well-chosen details, and well-structured event sequences.

SL.11–12.4: Present information, findings, and supporting evidence, conveying a clear and distinct perspective, such that listeners can follow the line of reasoning, alternative or opposing perspectives are addressed, and the organization, development, substance, and style are appropriate to purpose, audience, and a range or formal and informal tasks.

L.11–12.4: Determine or clarify the meaning of unknown and multiple-meaning words and phrases based on grades 11–12 reading and content, choosing flexibly from a range of strategies.

SUGGESTED STUDENT OBJECTIVES

- Define the major characteristics of American romanticism (e.g., use of symbols, myth, and the "fantastic"; veneration of nature; celebration of the "self"; and isolationism).
- Define transcendentalism as an aspect of American romanticism and explain how the two differ.
- Trace characterization techniques in American romantic novels.
- Analyze the structure and effectiveness of arguments in transcendentalist essays studied.

SUGGESTED WORKS

(E) indicates a CCSS exemplar text; (EA) indicates a text from a writer with other works identified as exemplars.

LITERARY TEXTS
Novels
- *The Scarlet Letter* (Nathaniel Hawthorne) (E)
- *The Pioneers* (James Fenimore Cooper)
- *Moby-Dick* (Herman Melville) (EA)
- *Uncle Tom's Cabin* (Harriet Beecher Stowe)

Short Stories
- "Billy Budd" (Herman Melville) (E)
- "The Fall of the House of Usher" (Edgar Allan Poe) (EA)
- "The Piazza" (Herman Melville) (EA)
- "The Legend of Sleepy Hollow" (Washington Irving)
- "Rip Van Winkle" (Washington Irving)
- "Rappaccini's Daughter" (Nathaniel Hawthorne) (EA)
- "The Minister's Black Veil" (Nathaniel Hawthorne) (EA)
- "Young Goodman Brown" (Nathaniel Hawthorne) (EA)

Poetry
- "The Old Oaken Bucket" (Samuel Woodworth)
- "The Raven" (Edgar Allan Poe) (E) (This is a CCSS exemplar text for grades 9–10.)
- "Annabel Lee" (Edgar Allan Poe) (EA)
- "Song of Myself" (Walt Whitman) (E)
- "I Hear America Singing" (Walt Whitman) (EA)

- "When Lilacs Last in the Dooryard Bloom'd" (Walt Whitman) (EA)
- "A Bird came down the Walk" (Emily Dickinson) (EA)
- "This is my letter to the World" (Emily Dickinson) (EA)
- "Because I could not stop for Death" (Emily Dickinson) (E)

INFORMATIONAL TEXTS

- *Walden; or, Life in the Woods* (Henry David Thoreau) (E)

Essays

- "Self-Reliance" (Ralph Waldo Emerson) (EA)
- "Society and Solitude" (Ralph Waldo Emerson) (E)
- "Civil Disobedience" (Henry David Thoreau) (EA)
- "Annexation" (John O'Sullivan) (*United States Magazine and Democratic Review, 17*, No. 1, 1845)
- "Anne Hutchinson: Brief Life of Harvard's 'Midwife': 1595–1643" (Peter J. Gomes)

Speeches

- "Address to William Henry Harrison" (1810) (Shawnee Chief Tecumseh)

ART, MUSIC, AND MEDIA

Art

- Frederic Church, *Niagara* (1857)
- George Inness, *The Lackawanna Valley* (1855)
- Asher Durand, *Kindred Spirits* (1849)
- Albert Bierstadt, *Looking Down Yosemite Valley* (1865)
- Thomas Cole, *Romantic Landscape with Ruined Tower* (1832–1836)

SAMPLE ACTIVITIES AND ASSESSMENTS

For a full Scoring Rubric, see the Appendix.

Note: After reading and discussing a work or pairing of works as a class, students prepare for seminars and essays by reflecting individually, in pairs, and/or in small groups on a given seminar or essay question. In this way, students generate ideas. (Seminar and essay assignments may include more than one question. Teachers may choose one or all of the questions to explore in the course of the seminar; students should choose one question for the essay.) Seminars should be held before students write essays so that they may explore their ideas thoroughly and refine their thinking before writing. Textual evidence should be used to support all arguments advanced in seminars and in all essays. Page and word counts for essays are not provided here, but teachers should consider the suggestions regarding the use of evidence, for example, to determine the likely length of good essays.

1. COLLABORATION

Reflect on seminar questions, take notes on your responses in your journal or on a shared spreadsheet, and note the page numbers of the textual evidence you will refer to in your seminar and/or essay answers. Share your notes with a partner for feedback and guidance. Have you interpreted the text correctly? Is your evidence convincing? (RL.11–12.1, SL.11–12.1)

2. NARRATIVE WRITING

Write your own narrative essay in the style of *Walden*. Your teacher may give you the opportunity to post your first draft on a shared spreadsheet and receive feedback from classmates before publication. (W.11–12.3, W.11–12.9)

3. SEMINAR AND WRITING (ARGUMENT)

Agree or disagree with this Emerson quotation: "What is popularly called Transcendentalism among us, is Idealism; Idealism as it appears in 1842." Use at least three pieces of textual evidence to support your opinion. Your teacher may give you the opportunity to share your initial thoughts on the classroom blog in order to get feedback from your classmates. (RI.11–12.2, SL.11–12.6, W.11–12.9)

4. SEMINAR AND WRITING (ARGUMENT)

Select one of the short stories and explain why you think it is a good example of American romanticism. Use at least three pieces of textual evidence to support your position. Your teacher may give you the opportunity to share your initial thoughts on the classroom blog in order to get feedback from your classmates. (RL.11–12.1, RL.11–12.9, W.11–12.2, SL.11–12.1)

5. INFORMATIVE/EXPLANATORY WRITING

(This writing assignment would follow the reading of biographical information about Anne Hutchinson—such as the Gomes essay—and *The Scarlet Letter* by Nathaniel Hawthorne.) In Chapter One of *The Scarlet Letter,* the author describes a rosebush that "had sprung up under the footsteps of the sainted Anne Hutchinson." In the closing chapter of the novel, the narrator observes that Hester "assured them … of her firm belief that, at some higher period, when the world should have grown ripe for it, in heaven's own time, a new truth would be revealed, in order to establish the whole relation between man and woman on a surer ground of mutual happiness." Write an argument in response to the following question: Why does Hawthorne choose an intellectual rebel, Anne Hutchinson, to frame the story of Hester Prynne? Cite evidence from the texts to support your thesis; include citations from Hutchinson's own work, if possible. Your teacher may give you the opportunity to share your initial thoughts on the classroom blog in order to get feedback from your classmates. (RL.11–12.1. RL.11–12.2, RL.11–12.5, RI.11–12.1, RI.11–12.2, W.11–12.2, W.11–12.8)

6. ORAL COMMENTARY

Students will be given a passage they have not seen before from one of the other works by Hawthorne or Melville (teacher's choice) and asked to provide a ten-minute commentary on two of the following questions:

- What is the primary significance of this passage?
- Identify the poetic techniques used in this poem (or extract from a poem). Relate them to the content.
- Which poetic techniques in this poem or extract are typical of the writer?
- What are the effects of the dominant images used in this work?
- What do you think the important themes in this work are?

Record your commentary using a video camera so you can evaluate how well you answered the questions. (RL.11–12.1, SL.11–12.4, SL.11–12.6)

7. LANGUAGE/VOCABULARY

Keep track of new words (or different uses of words that you know) in the works read in this unit. Use the dictionary to confirm the words' definitions and parts of speech. Note their etymology and whether or how the author used the word differently than it is used today. In your journal—or on a shared spreadsheet completed with others—write new sentences of your own using each new word encountered. (L.11–12.4, W.11–12.4, W.11–12.6)

8. ART/CLASS DISCUSSION

After reading literary examples of American romanticism, examine the paintings featured. Why do you believe these are romantic paintings? What visual aspects do the artists employ to interact with the viewer? How do they use the formal principles of art and design? View Thomas Cole's work *Romantic Landscape with Ruined Tower*. What has Cole done to create a "romantic landscape"? Continue viewing the other works of art as comparisons. After viewing all of these paintings, what do you think are the characteristics of a romantic work of art? Brainstorm a list of the visual aspects of romantic painting. (SL.11.2, SL.11.3)

ADDITIONAL RESOURCES

- *Walt Whitman's Notebooks and Poetry: The Sweep of the Universe* (National Endowment for the Humanities) (RL.11–12.4)
- *The American Renaissance and Transcendentalism* (PBS) (RL.11–12.9)
- *Africans in America (Part 3)* (PBS) (RL.11–12.1, RI.11–12.1, SL.11–12.1)
- *The Life of Anne Hutchinson* (RL.11–12.1, RI.11–12.1)

TERMINOLOGY

Alliteration	Individualism	Noble savage	Transcendentalism
Anaphora	Lyric poetry	Paradox	Verbal irony
Assonance	Manifest destiny	Romanticism	
Consonance	Metonymy	Synecdoche	

Grade Eleven, Unit Three Sample Lesson Plan

The Scarlet Letter by Nathaniel Hawthorne

In this series of seven lessons, students read *The Scarlet Letter* by Nathaniel Hawthorne, and they:

- Investigate Nathaniel Hawthorne's background (RI.11-12.1, RI.11-12.2, SL.11-12.4)
- Explore the complex character of Hester Prynne (RL.11-12.3, RL.11-12.9, SL.11-12.4)
- Note the ambiguity of the Scarlet Letter (RL.11-12.4, RL.11-12.6, L.11-12.4)
- Examine the role that Anne Hutchinson's story plays in exploring the emerging themes of the novel (RL.11-12.2, RL.11-12.3, RL.11-12.9, SL.11-12.4)
- Consider Hawthorne's message in the final pages of the novel (RL.11-12.5, RL.11-12.6, RL.11-12.9, SL.11-12.4)

Summary

Lessons I, II: Nathaniel Hawthorne, The Custom House, a Prison Door and Anne Hutchinson	Lessons III, IV: Pearl as "the Emblem and Product of Sin"
Meet Hawthorne's family/historical background (informational text) (RL.11-12.1, RL.11-12.2)	Examine the function of Chapter 3 (RL.11-12.1, RL.11-12.5, SL.11-12.4)
Explore the narrative voice(s) of the novel (RL.11-12.3, RL.11-12.5)	Revisit and critique the nature of Hester's punishment (RL.11-12.2)
Identify the narrator's motives for writing *The Scarlet Letter* (RL.11-12.9)	Re-examine the social function of the scarlet letter (RL.11-12.2, L.11-12.4, SL.11-12.6)
Examine the prison door (RL.11-12.1, RL.11-12.3, L.11-12.4, SL.11-12.6)	Juxtapose Hester's and Chillingworth's relationship with the "race of man" (RL.11-12.1, RL.11-12.3, RL.11-12.5, L.11-12.4)
Consider the depiction of the rosebush and the role that Anne Hutchinson may play in the novel (RL.11-12.2, RL.11-12.3, RL.11-12.1, SL.11-12.4)	Explore the narrator's characterization of Pearl (RL.11-12.1, SL.11-12.4)
Meet Hester Prynne (RL.11-12.1, RL.11-12.2, RL.11-12.5)	Analyze the relationship between Hester and Pearl (RL.11-12.1, SL.11-12.4)
Explore the nature of Hester Prynne's punishment (RL.11-12.2, SL.11-12.4)	

Lessons V, VI: Silence and Broken Silence in *The Scarlet Letter*?

Analyze Dimmesdales's/Chillingworth's "masks" and "silence" (RL.11–12.1)

Explore the dramatic impact of Chapter 12 (RL.11–12.3, RL.11–12.5, SL.11–12.4)

Explore Hester, Pearl, and the "enigma" of the scarlet letter (RL.11–12.3, L.11–12.4, SL.11–12.1)

Examine Hester's declaration that, "It lies not in the pleasure of the magistrates to take off the badge" (p. 112) (RL.11–12.1, L.11–12.4)

Juxtapose the two market scenes (Chapters 2 and 23) (RL.11–12.1, RL.11–12.2)

Explore the ambiguity of the "office" of the scarlet letter (RL.11–12.2, L.11–12.4, SL.11–12.1)

Lesson VII: Has the Scarlet Letter Done Its Office?

Investigate Hester's return "of her own free will" (RL.11–12.3, SL.11–12.1, SL.11–12.4)

Consider Hester's challenge to the Puritan society (RL.11–12.3, SL.11–12.1, SL.11–12.4)

Revisit the role of Anne Hutchinson in the context of the novel (SL.11–12.1, SL.11–12.4)

Ponder Hawthorne's intent when the narrator observes that Hester "assured them … of her firm belief that, at some higher period, when the world should have grown ripe for it, in heaven's own time, a new truth would be revealed, in order to establish the whole relation between man and woman on a surer ground of mutual happiness." (RL.11–12.3, SL.11–12.1, SL.11–12.4, L.11–12.6)

Lessons I, II: Nathaniel Hawthorne, the Custom House, a Prison Door, and Anne Hutchinson

Objectives

Meet Hawthorne's family/historical background (informational text) (RL.11–12.1, RL.11–12.2)

Explore the narrative voice(s) of the novel (RL.11–12.3, RL.11–12.5)

Identify the narrator's motives for writing *The Scarlet Letter* (RL.11–12.9)

Examine the prison door (RL.11–12.1, RL.11–12.3, L.11–12.4, SL.11–12.6)

Consider the depiction of the rosebush and the role that Anne Hutchinson may play in the novel (RL.11–12.2, RL.11–12.3, RI.11–12.1, SL.11–12.4)

Meet Hester Prynne (RL.11–12.1, RL.11–12.2, RL.11–12.5)

Explore the nature of Hester Prynne's punishment (RL.11–12.2, SL.11–12.4)

Required Materials

☐ Class set of *The Scarlet Letter* by Nathaniel Hawthorne

☐ Class set of "Anne Hutchinson: Brief Life of Harvard's 'Midwife': 1595–1643" by the Reverend Peter J. Gomes (*Harvard Magazine*, Nov–Dec 2002)

Procedures

1. Lead-In:

Meet Nathaniel Hawthorne. Choose the type of activity here: Hand out a brief biography of Hawthorne, rely on assigned homework, or conduct in-class research.

2. Step by Step:

a. Introduce the students to the frame of the novel (select passages that are necessary for understanding the background and the frame).

"The Custom House": the narrator is surveyor of the Custom House.

He tells us about himself; note the similarities to Hawthorne's life.

One day a discovery: Surveyor Pue and his account of events one hundred years earlier (and he is one hundred years before the narrator).

How is the story explained to the reader? From where does this story emanate?

Custom House, documents and scarlet letter found in the storage room, Puritan past, Pue's ghost, narrator's imagination.

The narrator: motives for writing *The Scarlet Letter.*

Charged with writing the story by Pue's ghost.

Redemption for ancestor's sins?

The framed narrative gives the fiction that follows the feeling that it is based on truth.

The Scarlet Letter is a work of fiction that has its own reality.

b. Chapter One: The Prison Door and the Rosebush

Class will read (aloud) and discuss Chapter One.

Note the title of the chapter.

Closely examine the description of door and the "virgin soil."

In contrast, study the wild rosebush.

c. Anne Hutchinson

Read the handout silently.

Annotate for the main ideas.

Conduct a class discussion.

d. Meet Hester Prynne in Chapter Two. Discuss how Hester's entrance is set up. Following are some of the details that students should pay attention to:

Criticism of Hester by other women

The contrast between the black shadow and the sunshine

Hester's body language as she is led by the town beadle; she rejects him of her own "free will"

The representation of Puritanical law, the male power system

The baby in Hester's arms conjures Mary/virgin image "revealed" to the crowd

Hester clasps baby

Artistry of the scarlet letter "A" is rich

3. Closure:
A summary of early impressions of Hester Prynne will be useful here.

Differentiation

Advanced

- Encourage students to research Hawthorne and prepare a biographical summary of his life for classmates. Students should also research what inspired Hawthorne to write *The Scarlet Letter* and perhaps present this information as digital slides or an online poster.

- Give students an opportunity to evaluate and bookmark the most helpful websites about Hawthorne. Collect the websites on a web portal.

- Develop a character summary for Anne Hutchinson and/or Hester Prynne in a similar manner to the one that was done for Hawthorne. This can be done in written or multimedia format.

- Students should be working at the evaluation and synthesis level.

Struggling

- Ask students to research Hawthorne using pre-selected websites on a web portal (selected by classmates, above) or using an easier article/website. Provide students with a graphic organizer or guiding questions to structure their research of Hawthorne.

- Make Chapter One available as an audio recording so students can follow along as they listen.

- Give students an outline to annotate or sketch (or use nonlinguistic representations) to aid in understanding and recall of Chapter One, especially of their first impressions of the characters. Perhaps have students complete a T-chart for each character, noting their first impressions and what words in the text give them these impressions. Ask students to revisit these impressions later in the text and compare their first impressions with the character's development.

- Encourage students to use a graphic organizer to collect their thoughts, perhaps using the Character Traits Interactive Chart available from ReadWriteThink. Students can also collaborate to create their own template that all students can access, perhaps on the classroom blog or on shared online documents, and receive individual teacher feedback.

Homework

Reread Chapters Three through Eight. Using sticky notes, continue to identify key passages that reveal Hester Prynne's character and her interaction with the people around her.

"Anne Hutchinson: Brief Life of Harvard's 'Midwife': 1595–1643"
by Peter G. Gomes

On June 2, 1922, the Commonwealth of Massachusetts received from the Anne Hutchinson Memorial Association and the State Federation of Women's Clubs a bronze statue of Anne Hutchinson. The inscription read in part:

> *In Memory of Anne Marbury Hutchinson*
> *Courageous Exponent of Civil Liberty*
> *and Religious Toleration*

It might have added that Mrs. Hutchinson was the mother of New England's first and most serious theological schism (traditionally known as the Antinomian Controversy); that in debate she bested the best of the Massachusetts Bay Colony's male preachers, theologians, and magistrates; and that as a result of her heresy, the colony determined to provide for the education of a new generation of ministers and theologians who would secure New England's civil and theological peace against future seditious Mrs. Hutchinson "when our present ministers shall lie in the dust," as the inscription on the Johnston Gate puts it. Thus, Anne Hutchinson was midwife to what would become Harvard College.

The colony's first generation of clergy, described by C. Conrad Wright as "a speaking aristocracy in the face of a silent democracy," included John Cotton, the charismatic minister of St. Botolph's in Boston, England, who moved with many of his parishioners to the new Boston in New England. Hutchinson, a minister's child, was among his most devoted admirers and determined to follow him. She chafed under the constraints of the Anglican Church and yearned for the soul liberty she imagined would flourish in the Puritan commonwealth, where she and her merchant husband, William, arrived in 1634.

Two public talents commended her to the new community. She was an able midwife to the women producing the first generation of New Englanders, and — theologically literate — she provided useful Bible-study classes for women and later for men.

At first she simply invited a few women in to discuss Mr. Cotton's sermons. But as her reputation for scriptural interpretation grew, so did the gatherings, which often included the young governor, Sir Henry Vane. Many saw her as a welcome antidote to the clerical establishment: an admirer noted, "I'll bring you to a woman who preaches better gospel than any of your black-coats who have been at the university, a woman of another kind of spirit who has had many revelations of things to come . . . . I had rather such a one who speaks from the mere notion of the Spirit without any study at all than any of your learned scholars."

Soon, however, Hutchinson moved from commentary to criticism. Lacking the authority of the magistracy or the clergy, she claimed the authority of the Spirit and an inner light. At her trial, in response to the charge that she had traduced the laws of church and state, she replied, "As I understand it, laws, commands, rules, and edicts are for those who have not the light which makes plain the pathway." This audacious claim proved the beginning of the end of her time in Massachusetts.

In 1637, her friend Henry Vane lost the governorship to John Winthrop, who considered her a threat to the order of his "city set on a hill," describing her meetings as a "thing not tolerable nor comely in the sight of God, nor fitting for your sex." She was accused of breaking the Fifth Commandment, which requires honoring one's parents, by refusing to defer to the magistrates, her fathers in the colony, and to the clergy, her fathers in the church. The transcript of her trial shows her to have been deft in theological and legal sparring, intellectually superior to her accusers, and a woman of conscience who yielded to no authority.

Having been found guilty in her civil trial, she was placed under house arrest to await ecclesiastical trial. In 1638, the final blows were delivered. A sentence of banishment was never in doubt. Her former mentor, John Cotton, fearing for his own credibility, described her weekly Sunday meeting as a "promiscuous and filthie coming together of men and women without Distinction of Relation of Marriage" and continued, "Your opinions frett like a Gangrene and spread like a Leprosie, and will eate out the very Bowells of Religion."

With her family and 60 followers, Hutchinson was banished into the more tolerant wilds of Rhode Island; she is counted among the founders of Portsmouth. After her husband's death, in 1642, she took her youngest children and removed to New York where, a year later, she and all but one child were slaughtered in an Indian raid.

Eleanor Roosevelt claimed Mrs. Hutchinson as the first of America's foremothers; others see her as the "courageous exponent of civil liberty and religious toleration" of the Boston monument. Contemporary readers might see her as a woman who declined to stay in the place assigned her by society. At Harvard we may seek her memorial in vain, but without her it is difficult to do justice to the motivating impulse of our foundation. Inadvertent midwife to a college founded in part to protect posterity from her errors, Anne Marbury Hutchinson, ironically, would be more at home at Harvard today than any of her critics.

The Reverend Peter J. Gomes, B.D. '68, is Plummer professor of Christian morals and Pusey minister in the Memorial Church.

A Troubled Young Nation

This eight-week unit, the fourth of six, examines the literature of the late nineteenth century in America. Students explore the themes related to the evolving young nation, such as the challenges of westward expansion, slavery, the changing role of women, regionalism, the displacement of Native Americans, the growth of cities, and immigration.

ESSENTIAL QUESTION

? What is an American?

OVERVIEW

The range and depth of potential topics covered in this substantial unit can be tailored to suit various classroom populations or teacher preference. Building on the previous unit, in which individualism figures as a prominent theme in American romanticism and transcendentalism, this unit explores the expanding idea of the American individual and the related idea of the pursuit of liberty in various forms. Teachers are encouraged to have students read *The Adventures of Huckleberry Finn*, a classic American novel that deals with issues of racism and slavery and raises important questions about what America promises—and to whom. Beyond *The Adventures of Huckleberry Finn*, teachers can select from among the other novels listed or ask different students to read different novels, so that the variety of the novels' compelling themes may be shared and discussed as a class (e.g., via presentations and seminars). Teachers are encouraged to sample heavily from the informational texts, many of which are critical to understanding the era of the Civil War and the struggle to fulfill America's promise.

FOCUS STANDARDS

These Focus Standards have been selected for the unit from the Common Core State Standards.

RL.11–12.3: Analyze the impact of the author's choices regarding how to develop and relate elements of a story or drama (e.g., where a story is set, how the action is ordered, how the characters are introduced and developed).

RI.11–12.3: Analyze a complex set of ideas or sequence of events and explain how specific individuals, ideas, or events interact and develop over the course of the text.

W.11–12.5: Develop and strengthen writing as needed by planning, revising, editing, rewriting, or trying a new approach, focusing on addressing what is most significant for a specific purpose and audience. (Editing for conventions should demonstrate command of Language standards 1–3 up to and including grades 11–12 on page 54 of the Common Core State Standards.)

SL.11–12.2: Integrate multiple sources of information presented in diverse formats and media (e.g., visually, quantitatively, orally) in order to make informed decisions and solve problems, evaluating the credibility and accuracy of each source and noting any discrepancies among the data.

L.11–12.2: Demonstrate command of the conventions of Standard English capitalization, punctuation, and spelling when writing.

SUGGESTED STUDENT OBJECTIVES

- Determine and analyze the development of the theme or themes in American literature of the nineteenth century (e.g., freedom, the American dream, racism, regionalism, survival, "individual vs. society," and "civilized society" vs. the wilderness).
- Compare the treatment of related themes in different genres (e.g., *The Adventures of Huckleberry Finn* and *Narrative of the Life of Frederick Douglass, an American Slave*).
- Explain how fictional characters in late nineteenth-century America express the challenges facing America at the time, citing textual evidence from both fiction and nonfiction to make the case.

SUGGESTED WORKS

(E) indicates a CCSS exemplar text; (EA) indicates a text from a writer with other works identified as exemplars.

LITERARY TEXTS
Novels
- *The Adventures of Huckleberry Finn* (Mark Twain) (EA)
- *The Awakening* (Kate Chopin)
- *Ethan Frome* (Edith Wharton)
- *Daisy Miller* (Henry James)
- *The Call of the Wild* (Jack London)
- *Sister Carrie* (Theodore Dreiser)
- *My Ántonia* (Willa Cather)
- *The Autobiography of an Ex-Coloured Man* (James Weldon Johnson)

Folk Tales
- "Plantation Proverbs" (*Uncle Remus*)

Short Stories
- "The Celebrated Jumping Frog of Calaveras County" (Mark Twain) (EA)
- "What Stumped the Bluejays" (Mark Twain) (EA)

- "Roman Fever" (Edith Wharton)
- "The Story of an Hour" (Kate Chopin)
- "The Yellow Wallpaper" (Charlotte Perkins Gilman)

INFORMATIONAL TEXTS

- Letter to Albert G. Hodges (Abraham Lincoln) (EA)
- Declaration of Sentiments, Seneca Falls Convention (1848)
- "The Higher Education of Women," from *A Voice from the South* (Anna Julia Cooper)

Autobiography

- *Narrative of the Life of Frederick Douglass, an American Slave, Written by Himself* (Frederick Douglass) (EA) (excerpts)
- *Up From Slavery: An Autobiography* (Booker T. Washington)
- *The Narrative of Sojourner Truth* (Sojourner Truth and Olive Gilbert)
- *Twenty Years at Hull House* (Jane Addams) (selections)

Speeches

- "Gettysburg Address" (Abraham Lincoln) (E)
- "A House Divided" (Abraham Lincoln) (EA)
- "Ain't I a Woman?" (Sojourner Truth) (May 29, 1851)
- "I will fight no more forever" (Chief Joseph the Younger of the Nez Perce Nation) (October 5, 1877)

Essays

- "Why I Wrote 'The Yellow Wallpaper'" (Charlotte Perkins Gilman)
- "'The Yellow Wallpaper' and Women's Discourse" (Karen Ford)
- "'I Had Barbara': Women's Ties and Wharton's 'Roman Fever'" (Rachel Bowlby)

ART, MUSIC, AND MEDIA
Art

- Winslow Homer, *A Visit from the Old Mistress* (1876)

Spirituals

- "Go Down, Moses" (Traditional)
- "Swing Low, Sweet Chariot" (Traditional)
- "I Thank God I'm Free at Last" (Traditional)
- "Lift Every Voice and Sing" (James Weldon Johnson) (E)
- "All God's Children Had Wings" (Traditional)
- "Promises of Freedom" (Traditional)

Film

- Ed Bell and Thomas Lennon, dir., *Unchained Memories* (2003)

SAMPLE ACTIVITIES AND ASSESSMENTS

For a full Scoring Rubric, see the Appendix.

Note: After reading and discussing a work or pairing of works as a class, students prepare for seminars and essays by reflecting individually, in pairs, and/or in small groups on a given seminar or essay question. In this way, students generate ideas. (Seminar and essay assignments may include more than one question. Teachers may choose one or all of the questions to explore in the course of the seminar; students should choose one question for the essay.) Seminars should be held before students write essays so that they may explore their ideas thoroughly and refine their thinking before writing. Textual evidence should be used to support all arguments advanced in seminars and in all essays. Page and word counts for essays are not provided here, but teachers should consider the suggestions regarding the use of evidence, for example, to determine the likely length of good essays.

1. COLLABORATION

Reflect on seminar questions, take notes on your responses in your journal or on a shared spreadsheet, and note the page numbers of the textual evidence you will refer to in your seminar and/or essay answers. Share your notes with a partner for feedback and guidance. Have you interpreted the text correctly? Is your evidence convincing? (RL.11–12.1, SL.11–12.1)

2. SEMINAR AND WRITING (ARGUMENT)

Write an argument in which you agree or disagree with the following statement, offering at least three pieces of evidence from the texts to support your position: Women in nineteenth-century America could not really be free. Your teacher may give you the opportunity to share your initial thoughts on the classroom blog in order to get feedback from your classmates. (RL.11–12.1, W.11–12.1)

3. SEMINAR AND INFORMATIVE/EXPLANATORY WRITING

Choose two women from among the works studied and compare and contrast their life experiences, noting the ways in which they either exemplified or were an exception to the times in which they lived. Use at least three pieces of evidence from the texts to support an original thesis statement. Your teacher may give you the opportunity to share your initial thoughts on the classroom blog in order to get feedback from your classmates. (RL.11–12.1, RI.11–12.10, W.11–12.1, W.11–12.9)

4. SEMINAR AND WRITING (ARGUMENT)

Does Huckleberry Finn embody the values inherent in the American Dream? Write an argument in which you use at least three pieces of evidence to support an original thesis statement. Your teacher may give you the opportunity to share your initial thoughts on the classroom blog in order to get feedback from your classmates. (RL.11–12.9, SL.11–12.1, W.11–12.9)

5. SEMINAR AND INFORMATIVE/EXPLANATORY WRITING

How does Mark Twain address the issue of slavery in *The Adventures of Huckleberry Finn*? Use at least three pieces of textual evidence to support an original thesis statement. Your teacher may give you the opportunity to share your initial thoughts on the classroom blog in order to get feedback from your classmates. (RL.11–12.6, W.11–12.2, W.11–12.9)

6. INFORMATIVE/EXPLANATORY WRITING

Edith Wharton, Charlotte Perkins Gilman, and Kate Chopin are often referred to as feminist authors. Their protagonists are usually women, and their conflicts are frequently with men. Read two of the following stories: "Roman Fever" by Edith Wharton, "The Yellow Wallpaper" by Charlotte Perkins

Gilman, and "The Story of an Hour" by Kate Chopin. Then, write an informative/explanatory essay in which you explore how the positioning of the women protagonists in the stories exposes the authors' views of women in society. (*Extension:* For further literary analysis upon which students may draw, they can read "'The Yellow Wallpaper' and Women's Discourse" by Karen Ford and/or "'I Had Barbara': Women's Ties and Wharton's 'Roman Fever'" by Rachel Bowlby.) (RL.11-12.1, RL.11–12.2, RL.11–12.3, RI.11–12.1, RI.11–12.2, RI.11–12.3, W.11–12.2)

7. SPEECH

Recite the Gettysburg Address from memory. Include an introduction that discusses why the excerpt exemplifies America's core conflicts and its finest values. Record your recitation using a video camera so you can evaluate your performance. (RI.11–12.9, SL.11–12.3)

8. MIXED-MEDIA PRESENTATION

Create a mixed-media presentation that summarizes one of the novels you've read and presents questions that you think the novel raises about its uniquely American themes. Prepare the presentation for posting on the class web page for this unit. (RL.11–12.1, W.11–12.6, SL.11–12.5)

9. GRAMMAR AND USAGE

Examine a page from one of the stories in this unit (selected by the teacher) and highlight the prepositional phrases; identify what they modify and determine whether they are adjectival or adverbial. (L.11–12.1)

10. ART/CLASS DISCUSSION

Focus on the Homer painting. Without knowing any background information on the time period or setting of this work, discuss the following questions with classmates: What do you think might be going on in this scene? Who are these women? Notice each person's dress and body position. What do these details suggest about their relationships? Note that the painting is sectioned. But where is the division: between the white woman and the black family, or at the painting's center, to the left of the central figure? How does noticing this division add to our understanding of the relationships in the painting? What do you think each character might be thinking or feeling? Why do you think Homer created such a complex composition to depict what at first appears to be a simple interaction? Now learn some background information about the painting. Did you come up with "correct" assumptions? Is there a "right" answer to analyzing this work of art? (SL.11–12.1, SL.11–12.2, SL.11–12.4, SL.11–12.5)

ADDITIONAL RESOURCES

- *Personal or Social Tragedy? A Close Reading of Edith Wharton's Ethan Frome* (National Endowment for the Humanities) (RL.11–12.1, RI.11–12.2)
- *After the American Revolution: Free African Americans in the North* (National Endowment for the Humanities) (RL.11–12.6)
- *Critical Ways of Seeing* The Adventures of Huckleberry Finn *in Context* (National Endowment for the Humanities) (RL.11–12.6)

- *The New Americans* (PBS) (RI.11–12.7)
- *Charlotte Perkins Gilman's "The Yellow Wallpaper": Writing Women* (National Endowment for the Humanities) (RL.11–12.1, RI.11–12.2)
- *Melting Pot: American Fiction of Immigration* (PBS)
- *Africans in America (Part 4)* (PBS) (RL.11–12.1, RI.11–12.1, SL.11–12.1)

TERMINOLOGY

Abolition	Autobiography	"Melting pot"	Realism
American Dream	Biography	Mood	Regionalism
Assimilation	Determinism	Naturalism	Satire

Grade Eleven, Unit Four Sample Lesson Plan

"The Yellow Wallpaper" and *"Why I Wrote 'The Yellow Wallpaper'"* by Charlotte Perkins Gilman

"The Story of an Hour" by Kate Chopin

"Roman Fever" by Edith Wharton

"'The Yellow Wallpaper' and Women's Discourse" by Karen Ford

"'I Had Barbara': Women's Ties and Wharton's 'Roman Fever'" by Rachel Bowlby

In this series of eight lessons, students read "The Yellow Wallpaper" by Charlotte Perkins Gilman, "The Story of an Hour" by Kate Chopin, "Roman Fever" by Edith Wharton, "Why I Wrote 'The Yellow Wallpaper'" by Charlotte Perkins Gilman, "'The Yellow Wallpaper' and Women's Discourse" by Karen Ford, and "'I Had Barbara': Women's Ties and Wharton's 'Roman Fever'" by Rachel Bowlby, and they:

Examine the forms of the three stories (RL.11-12.2, RL.11-12.5, RI.11-12.1, SL.11-12.1)

Note the relationships between form and content (RL.11-12.3, SL.11-12.4)

Explore the relationships between the female protagonists and the male antagonists (RL.11-12.3, RL.11-12.4, SL.11-12.1)

Integrate literary criticism into the analysis of the stories (RL.11-12.9, RI.11-12.1, W.11-12.2, W.11-12.9, L.11-12.6)

Summary

Lesson I: "The Yellow Wallpaper"

Outline the plot of the story (RL.11-12.2)

Annotate the story for its narrative technique (RL.11-12.1, RL.11-12.3, RL.11-12.4)

Examine the literary devices that the author uses (SL.11-12.4, RL.11-12.5, L.11-12.5)

Explore the voice of the narrator (RL.11-12.3, SL.11-12.1, SL.11-12.4)

Lesson II: "The Yellow Wallpaper"

Examine the form of the story (RL.11-12.2, RL.11-12.5, SL.11-12.1)

Explore the voice of the narrator (RL.11-12.3, SL.11-12.1, SL.11-12.4)

Explore (closely) the ending of the story (RL.11-12.5, SL.11-12.1, SL.11-12.4)

Investigate the relationship between the form and the content of the story (RL.11-12.3, SL.11-12.1)

Probe the relationship between the protagonist and the male in her life (RL.11-12.3, RL.11-12.4, SL.11-12.1)

Note Charlotte Perkins Gilman's rationale for writing the story (RI.11-12.1, SL.11-12.4)

Lesson III: "'The Yellow Wallpaper' and Women's Discourse"	Lesson IV: "The Story of an Hour"
Conduct a close reading of Ford's essay (RI.11-12.1, RI.11-12.3, RI.11-12.3)	Outline the plot of the story (RL.11-12.2)
Identify key ideas (RI.11-12.3, SL.11-12.4)	Examine the use of foreshadowing (SL.11-12.4, RL.11-12.4, RL.11-12.5, L.11-12.5)
Investigate the complexity of meanings that Ford's perspective Contributes to the reading of the story (RL.11-12.6, SL.11-12.1)	Explore the use of irony (SL.11-12.1, RL.11-12.5, RL.11-12.4, L.11-12.5)
Note the use of academic discourse (RL.11-12.1, SL.11-12.1, L.11-12.5)	Note the appearances of male characters in the story (RL.11-12.1, SL.11-12.1, L.11-12.5)
Lessons V: "Roman Fever"	**Lesson VI: "Roman Fever"**
Map the characters in the story (RL.11-12.1)	Annotate (second reading) for usage of foreshadowing in the story (SL.11-12.1, RL.11-12.5, RL.11-12.4, L.11-12.5)
Outline the plot of the story (RL.11-12.2)	Trace the way that foreshadowing impacts the rising tensions in the story (SL.11-12.4, RL.11-12.5, RL.11-12.6, L.11-12.5)
Probe the role of men in the story (RL.11-12.3, SL.11-12.1)	Examine the ironic ending of the story (SL.11-12.4, RL.11-12.5)
Lesson VII: "'I Had Barbara': Women's Ties and Wharton's 'Roman Fever'"	**Lesson VIII: Forms and Meanings**
Outline Bowlby's essay (RL.11-12.2)	Recall the form of "'I Had Barbara': Women's Ties and Wharton's 'Roman Fever'" (SL.11-12.1)
Explore Bowlby's key ideas (RL.11-12.2, SL.11-12.1, SL.11-12.4)	Revisit the forms of "The Yellow Wallpaper," "The Story of an Hour," and "Roman Fever" (RL.11-12.1, RL.11-12.3, SL.11-12.4)
Analyze the form of Bowlby's essay (RL.11-12.5, SL.11-12.1)	Examine the ways that the forms of the three stories expose a dichotomy between men and women (RL.11-12.9, W.11-12.9, L.11-12.6)
Problematize Bowlby's thesis RL.11-12.2, RL.11-12.5, SL.11-12.3	Investigate connections between forms and meanings (RL.11-12.9, W.11-12.2, SL.11-12.6)

Lesson VIII: Forms and Meanings

Objectives

Recall the form of "'I Had Barbara': Women's Ties and Wharton's 'Roman Fever'" (SL.11-12.1)

Revisit the forms of "The Yellow Wallpaper," "The Story of an Hour," and "Roman Fever" (RL.11-12.1, RL.11-12.3, SL.11-12.4)

Examine the ways that the forms of the three stories expose a dichotomy between men and women (RL.11-12.9, W.11-12.9, L.11-12.6)

Investigate connections between forms and meanings (RL.11-12.9, W.11-12.2, SL.11-12.6)

Required Materials

- ☐ Class set of "The Story of an Hour" by Kate Chopin
- ☐ Class set of "Roman Fever" by Edith Wharton
- ☐ Class set of "Why I Wrote 'The Yellow Wallpaper'" by Charlotte Perkins Gilman
- ☐ Class set of "'The Yellow Wallpaper' and Women's Discourse" by Karen Ford
- ☐ Class set of "'I Had Barbara': Women's Ties and Wharton's 'Roman Fever'" by Rachel Bowlby
- ☐ Class set of relationship between form and content (sample is below)

Procedures

1. Lead-In:

Lead a class discussion in which the students recall the form of the essay, "'I Had Barbara': Women's Ties and Wharton's 'Roman Fever.'" Elicit discussion about the following:

Her thesis seems concealed.

She uses foreshadowing.

Her ideas unfold, leading to the "punch line," "I had Barbara."

In its form, the essay is therefore similar to the story "Roman Fever," in which "I had Barbara" provides the final ironic twist of the story.

2. Step by Step:

a. In groups, students work to complete the chart below; a few examples are provided.

	Literary Devices/Form	The Relationships Between the Protagonists and Male Characters	Thematic Connections Between Form and Content
"The Yellow Wallpaper"	The story is in diary form. The narrator tells her own story.	She is not in control of the situation (it seems). Her husband decides what her situation is.	She is not in control of her life, but the diary — a first-person narrative — gives her a voice.
"The Story of an Hour"	Foreshadowing and irony frame the story. The ending is foreshadowed at the begi ning.	Male characters are introduced at the beginning and at the end.	The form of the story suggests that she is trapped.
"Roman Fever"	There is an extensive use of foreshadowing leading up to the final irony.	Wharton deliberately excludes all male characters.	"I had Barbara" — the statement that provides the final ironic twist in the story — excludes the father.

b. Students discuss their findings and continue to work or their charts.

3. Closure:

Introduce the students to the take-home assessment (below).

Differentiation

Advanced

- Allow students to choose another short story by a female author to compare and contrast with the ones listed above. Add an extra row to the chart for these comparisons.
- Students should be working at the evaluation and synthesis level, possibly adding an extra column to the chart on a challenging area or question to answer across the texts.
- Collect and create an annotated booklist of female authors. This list should include authors not chosen; justify the reasons why they were not placed on the "recommended" list.

Struggling

- Consider pre-teaching key ideas to students for the Lead-In at the end of the prior day (for example, giving them the handout of the lecture to read), so that they are prepared to participate in the discussion.
- Have key ideas from the graphic organizer (above) pre-printed on index cards or paper. Students read the ideas and sort them into the appropriate boxes.
- Assign groups one story to analyze, rather than doing multiple comparisons. Allow students to reread the short story, or allow them to listen to a pre-recorded version.
- Give students additional time, as needed, to complete this essay, creating one paragraph each evening and reviewing and revising it with a partner and/or teacher the following day. Alternatively, encourage students to communicate and collaborate with each other online, such as on the classroom blog or shared online documents, or provide students with a graphic organizer with which to draft their papers.

Homework/Assessment

I. Writing Prompt

Edith Wharton, Charlotte Perkins Gilman, and Kate Chopin are often referred to as "feminist" authors. Their protagonists are usually women and their conflicts are frequently with men.

II. Writing Task

Select two of the three stories and compose a four- to five-page essay in response to the following question: How do the stories' forms reveal the authors' views of women in society?

III. Writing Guidelines

Your final paper will:

- Provide a **narrow, focused** thesis statement
- Contain **an analysis — not a summary —** of the idea that you choose to discuss
- Present a thorough analysis, using fully-developed, coherent paragraphs
- Cite both the stories and the critical essays
- Insightfully organize the sequence of ideas according to the purpose of the essay
- Be carefully and deliberately developed
- Demonstrate a mastery of organizational skills (topic sentences, transitions, order of ideas, etc.)
- Use Standard English grammar
- Avoid all grammar and usage errors
- Use simple present tense
- Include a title — be original!

Grade 11 ▶ *Unit 5*

Emerging Modernism

This six-week unit, the fifth of six, addresses early twentieth-century American literature, including writers of the Lost Generation and the Harlem Renaissance.

ESSENTIAL QUESTION

? How did modernization result in isolation and disillusionment in the early American twentieth century?

OVERVIEW

The unit traces the emergence of American modernism, including literature from World War I, and tracks the literature of "disillusionment" that followed the war. Students explore Robert Frost's vision of nature as modernist rather than transcendentalist in its perspective. They identify the alienation of the modern man and the tensions that are embedded in the modernist works of F. Scott Fitzgerald and Ernest Hemingway. The works of Countee Cullen, Langston Hughes, and Zora Neale Hurston illustrate the breadth of the Harlem Renaissance literary movement. Informational and critical texts enrich the students' analysis of the literary works.

FOCUS STANDARDS

These Focus Standards have been selected for the unit from the Common Core State Standards.

RL.11–12.1: Cite strong and thorough textual evidence to support analysis of what the text says explicitly as well as inferences drawn from the text, including determining where the text leaves matters uncertain.

RL.11–12.6: Determine an author's point of view or purpose in a text in which the rhetoric is particularly effective, analyzing how style and content contribute to the power, persuasiveness, or beauty of the text.

RI.11–12.1: Cite strong and thorough textual evidence to support analysis of what the text says explicitly as well as inferences drawn from the text, including determining where the text leaves matters uncertain.

W.11–12.4: Produce clear and coherent writing in which the development, organization, and style are appropriate to task, purpose, and audience. (Grade-specific expectations for writing types are defined in standards 1–3 above.)

SL.11–12.5: Make strategic use of digital media (e.g., textual, graphical, audio, visual, and interactive elements) in presentations to enhance understanding of findings, reasoning, and evidence and to add interest.

L.11–12.6: Acquire and use accurately general academic and domain-specific words and phrases, sufficient for reading, writing, speaking, and listening at the college and career readiness level; demonstrate independence in gathering vocabulary knowledge when considering a word or phrase important to comprehension or expression.

SUGGESTED STUDENT OBJECTIVES

- Define and explain the origins of the Harlem Renaissance.
- Explore the relationship between historical events and literature as they emerge in the works of Harlem Renaissance poets and authors.
- Define and explain the Lost Generation, noting experimental aspects of some works.
- Note the relationship between themes in early twentieth-century American literature and nineteenth-century American thought.
- Identify modernist ideas (using the informational texts).
- Analyze the relationship between modernist style and content.
- Examine evidence of the alienation of "modern man."

SUGGESTED WORKS

(E) indicates a CCSS exemplar text; (EA) indicates a text from a writer with other works identified as exemplars.

LITERARY TEXTS
Novels
- *Their Eyes Were Watching God* (Zora Neale Hurston) (E)
- *The Great Gatsby* (F. Scott Fitzgerald) (E)
- *As I Lay Dying* (William Faulkner) (E)
- *A Farewell to Arms* (Ernest Hemingway) (E)
- *The Pearl* (John Steinbeck) (EA)
- *Of Mice and Men* (John Steinbeck) (EA)
- *Winesburg, Ohio* (Sherwood Anderson) (selections)

Short Stories
- "A Rose for Emily" (William Faulkner) (EA)
- "Hills Like White Elephants" (Ernest Hemingway) (EA)
- "The Snows of Kilimanjaro" (Ernest Hemingway) (EA)
- "A Clean, Well-Lighted Place" (Ernest Hemingway) (EA)

Poetry
- "Yet Do I Marvel" (Countee Cullen) (E) (This is a CCSS exemplar text for grades 9 and 10.)
- "Tableau" (Countee Cullen) (EA)
- "The Road Not Taken" (Robert Frost) (E) (This is a CCSS exemplar text for grades 6 through 8.)

- "The Death of the Hired Man" (Robert Frost) (EA)
- "Birches" (Robert Frost) (EA)
- "The Love Song of J. Alfred Prufrock" (T. S. Eliot) (E)
- "Richard Cory" (E. A. Robinson)
- "The House on the Hill" (E. A. Robinson)
- "The Negro Speaks of Rivers" (Langston Hughes) (EA)
- "Mother to Son" (Langston Hughes) (EA)
- "Harlem" (Langston Hughes) (EA)
- "Conscientious Objector" (Edna St. Vincent Millay) (EA)
- "Grass" (Carl Sandburg) (EA)
- "Poetry" (Marianne Moore)
- *The Pisan Cantos* (Ezra Pound) (selections)
- "Domination of Black" (Wallace Stevens)
- "A High-Toned Old Christian Woman" (Wallace Stevens)
- "In the Dordogne" (John Peale Bishop)
- "The Silent Slain" (Archibald MacLeish)

Drama

- *The Piano Lesson* (August Wilson)

INFORMATIONAL TEXTS

Speeches

- *Black Elk Speaks* (Black Elk, as told through John G. Ncihardt) (selections)
- "The Solitude of Self" (February 20, 1892) (Elizabeth Cady Stanton)
- "The Spirit of Liberty" speech at "I Am an American Day" (Learned Hand, 1944) (EA)

Essays

- "If Black English Isn't a Language, Then Tell Me, What Is?" (James Baldwin)
- "Towards a Definition of American Modernism" (Daniel Joseph Singal, *American Quarterly*, 39, Spring 1987, 7–26)
- "*The Great Gatsby* and the Twenties" (Ronald Berman)
- "*A Farewell to Arms*: The Impact of Irony and the Irrational" (Fred H. Marcus) (excerpts)

ART, MUSIC, AND MEDIA

Art

- Marsden Hartley, *Mount Katahdin, Maine* (1939–1940)
- Georgia O'Keeffe, *Ram's Head, Blue Morning Glory* (1938)
- Alfred Stieglitz, *From the Back Window, 291* (1915)
- Jacob Lawrence, *War Series: The Letter* (1946)
- Charles Sheeler, *Criss-Crossed Conveyors, River Rouge Plant, Ford Motor Company* (1927)
- Stuart Davis, *Owh! In San Pao* (1951)
- Charles Demuth, *My Egypt* (1927)
- Arthur Dove, *Goat* (1934)
- Imogen Cunningham, *Calla* (1929)

SAMPLE ACTIVITIES AND ASSESSMENTS

For a full Scoring Rubric, see the Appendix.

Note: After reading and discussing a work or pairing of works as a class, students prepare for seminars and essays by reflecting individually, in pairs, and/or in small groups on a given seminar or essay question. In this way, students generate ideas. (Seminar and essay assignments may include more than one question. Teachers may choose one or all of the questions to explore in the course of the seminar; students should choose one question for the essay.) Seminars should be held before students write essays so that they may explore their ideas thoroughly and refine their thinking before writing. Textual evidence should be used to support all arguments advanced in seminars and in all essays. Page and word counts for essays are not provided, but teachers should consider the suggestions regarding the use of evidence, for example, to determine the likely length of good essays.

1. COLLABORATION

Reflect on seminar questions, take notes on your responses in your journal or on a shared spreadsheet, and note the page numbers of the textual evidence you will refer to in your seminar and/or essay answers. Share your notes with a partner for feedback and guidance. Have you interpreted the text correctly? Is your evidence convincing? (RL.11–12.1, SL.11–12.1)

2. SEMINAR AND WRITING (INFORMATIVE/EXPLANATORY)

What are the effects of the shifting point of view on the reader's understanding of events in *As I Lay Dying*? Why do you think Faulkner chose to tell the story from different points of view? Use at least three pieces of textual evidence to support your position. Your teacher may give you the opportunity to share your initial thoughts on the classroom blog in order to get feedback from your classmates. (RL.11–12.3, RL.11–12.5, W.11–12.2, W.11–12.9a, L.11–12.5)

3. SEMINAR AND WRITING (ARGUMENT)

After reading "The Love Song of J. Alfred Prufrock" and *The Great Gatsby,* decide whether you agree or disagree with the following statement: Prufrock and Gatsby have similar characters. Use at least three pieces of textual evidence to support your position. Your teacher may give you the opportunity to share your initial thoughts on the classroom blog in order to get feedback from your classmates. (RL.11–12.1, RL.11–12.5, SL.11–12.4, W.11–12.9a)

4. SEMINAR AND WRITING (INFORMATIVE/EXPLANATORY)

After reading James Baldwin's essay, "If Black English Isn't a Language, Then Tell Me, What Is?" and Zora Neale Hurston's *Their Eyes Were Watching God*, discuss the pivotal role that dialect plays in *Their Eyes Were Watching God*. Use at least three pieces of textual evidence to support an original thesis. Your teacher may give you the opportunity to share your initial thoughts on the classroom blog in order to get feedback from your classmates. (RL.11–12.1, RL.11–12.4, RL.11–12.6, RL.11–12.9, SL.11–12.4, W.11–12.9a, L.11–12.3)

5. INFORMATIVE/EXPLANATORY WRITING

In "Towards a Definition of American Modernism," Daniel Joseph Singal notes that novelists like F. Scott Fitzgerald and Ernest Hemingway (among other American writers) "chronicled the disintegration of modern society and culture, but [their] primary concern ... was somehow 'to make the world re-cohere'" (p. 20). Write an informative/explanatory essay in which you consider Singal's words as you examine Fitzgerald's or Hemingway's social-political critique of the modern world. You may discuss one or both authors. You must cite evidence from the novels to support your thesis. You must also cite "Towards a Definition of American Modernism" by Singal. (RL.11–12.1, RL.11–12.2, RL.11–12.3, RL.11–12.5, RI.11–12.1, RI.11–12.2, W.11–12.2)

6. WRITING

Conduct a close reading of Langston Hughes's "The Negro Speaks of Rivers," "Mother to Son," and "Harlem," identifying Hughes's use of metaphors to depict ideas. After reading the poems, compose your own poem in response to Hughes's ideas and vision. Use a metaphor that depicts your perception of Hughes (e.g., "Hughes, a fearless lion / roaring whispers of distant memories"). (RL.11–12.10, W.11–12.3d)

7. SEMINAR AND WRITING (ARGUMENT)

How do the poems of this unit—especially by Eliot, Frost, and Pound—grapple with hope and despair? By the end of the poems selected, does hope or despair triumph? Organize textual evidence to support your position. (RL.11–12.2, SL.11–12.4, W.11–12.1)

8. MULTIMEDIA PRESENTATION

Make a formal multimedia presentation in which you define and discuss the Lost Generation in American literary history. Cite at least three sources. Prepare the presentation for posting on the class web page for this unit. (RL.11–12.9, W.11–12.6, SL.11–12.5)

9. ORAL PRESENTATION OR WRITING (ARGUMENT)

Discuss what you think Learned Hand meant when he said of Americans, "For this reason we have some right to consider ourselves a picked group, a group of those who had the courage to break from the past and brave the dangers and the loneliness of a strange land." Cite examples from works read in this unit and describe how the characters exhibit this quality. Record your recitation using a video camera so you can evaluate how well you discussed Hand's quotation. (*Note:* This quotation could also be used as a prompt for argument, asking students to agree or disagree with Hand and requiring at least three pieces of evidence to support the position.) (RL.11–12.9, SL.11–2.4, L.11–12.5)

10. GRAMMAR AND MECHANICS

Read the draft of a classmate's essay and highlight all the independent and dependent clauses; make sure they are punctuated correctly. (L.11–12.1, L.11–12.2)

11. ART/CLASS DISCUSSION

Examine and discuss the paintings listed. Do you see modernism emerging in these works? Can you make any fruitful comparisons with the way modernism emerges in the works you are reading? What new stylistic developments do you see in the paintings? What do we mean when we talk about modernists creating "art for art's sake"? For instance, compare the Hartley, Dove, and Demuth paintings. To what extent do you think these painters were interested in painting a mountain (Hartley), a goat (Dove), and silos (Demuth) versus experimenting with the possibilities of paint, space, and line? What role do you think fine art photography (see the Stieglitz image) might have played in the transition of painting away from a primary focus on depiction? (SL.11–12.1, SL.11–12.2, SL.11–12.4, SL.11–12.5)

ADDITIONAL RESOURCES

- *Faulkner's* As I Lay Dying: *Form of a Funeral* (National Endowment for the Humanities) (RL.11–12.3, RL.11–12.5)
- *Introduction to Modernist Poetry* (National Endowment for the Humanities) (RL.11–12.4)

TERMINOLOGY

Alienation	Flashback	Industrialization	Stream of consciousness
American modernism	Foreshadowing	Interior monologue	
Dialect	"Great migration"	The Lost Generation	Villanelle
Disillusionment	Harlem Renaissance	Motif	

Grade Eleven, Unit Five Sample Lesson Plan

The Great Gatsby by F. Scott Fitzgerald

In this series of seven lessons, students read *The Great Gatsby* by F. Scott Fitzgerald, and they:

- Identify key ideas of modernism (RI.11–12.1, RI.11–12.2, SL.11–12.1, SL.11–12.4)
- Explore *The Great Gatsby* in the context of modernism (RL.11–12.1, RL.11–12.2, SL.11–12.1, L.11–12.6)
- Assess Fitzgerald's novel in the context of modernist ideas (W.11–12.1, SL.11–12.4)

Summary

Lesson I: American Modernism

Articulate the difference (and relationship) between modernism and modernization (informational text) (RI.11–12.2, SL.11–12.1)

Identify the characteristics of Victorianism (informational text) (RI.11–12.2, RI.11–12.10, SL.11–12.1)

Establish the relationship between Victorianism and the rise of modernism (informational text) (RI.11–12.2, SL.11–12.4, L.11–12.6)

Lessons II, III: The Landscape of *Gatsby*

Explore the purpose of the introduction (paragraphs one and two) (RL.11–12.1, RL.11–12.2, SL.11–12.1)

Expose the presence of modernist tension in Chapter I (RL.11–12.1, RL.11–12.2, SL.11–12.4)

Examine the characters in the novel (RL.11–12.1, RL.11–12.6, SL.11–12.1, L.11–12.5)

- Relationships
- Characteristics
- In setting
- Narrator's attitude

Explore the use of symbolism in the novel (RL.11–12.1, RL.11–12.2, RL.11–12.3, SL.11–12.1, L.11–12.5)

Discuss applicable literary terms on the handout distributed (RL.11–12.6, SL.11–12.1, L.11–12.6)

Lessons IV, V: The Tragedy of Gatsby

Reconstruct the presentation of Gatsby (RL.11-12.1, RL.11-12.2, RL.11-12.3, SL.11-12.4)

Revisit the network of relationships and tensions among the characters (RL.11-12.1, RL.11-12.2, RL.11-12.3, L.11-12.5)

Link Gatsby's presentation to modernism — specifically to Impressionism and Cubism (RL.11-12.2, SL.11-12.4, L.11-12.4)

Consider Nick's observation that Gatsby had "an extraordinary gift of hope, and a romantic readiness …" (RL.11-12.2. SL.11-12.1)

Lesson VI: Gatsby in the Jazz Age

Consider the idea that "These characters are more than the sum of their own experiences: they constitute America itself as it moves into the Jazz Age. There is a larger story which swirls around them, and its meaning is suggested by Fitzgerald's unused title for the novel: *Under the Red, White, and Blue*." (Ronald Berman) (RL.11-12.2, SL.11-12.1, L.11-12.5)

Lesson VII: Preparing to Assess *The Great Gatsby*, a Modernist Novel

Critically examine the prompt (SL.11-12.1, SL.11-12.4)

Develop analytical questions (SL.11-12.1, SL.11-12.4)

Revisit text and select quotations (RL.11-12.1, RL.11-12.2, L-11.12.5)

Identify thesis (response to the questions) (RL.11-12.2)

Outline textual support of thesis (RL.11-12.1, RL.11-12.2)

Compose a critical analysis of the assigned topic (W.11-12.1)

Lesson VII: Preparing to Assess *The Great Gatsby*, a Modernist Novel

Objectives

Critically examine the prompt (SL.11-12.1, SL.11-12.4)

Develop analytical questions (SL.11-12.1, SL.11-12.4)

Revisit text and select quotations (RL.11-12.1, RL.11-12.2, L-11.12.5)

Identify thesis (response to the questions) (RL.11-12.2)

Outline textual support of thesis (RL.11-12.1, RL.11-12.2)

Compose a critical analysis of the assigned topic (W.11-12.1)

Required Materials

- ☐ Class set of *The Great Gatsby* by F. Scott Fitzgerald
- ☐ Students' notes
- ☐ Assessment handout (below)

Procedures

1. Lead-In:

Distribute the assessment handout (below) and allow students to read it.

2. Step by Step:
   a. Discuss the assignment.
   b. Place students in groups and ask them to develop writing prompts; the questions should emerge from previous class discussions. For example:
      - How does Tom Buchanan's role as a foil expose tensions in the novel?
      - Is Gatsby a romantic hero trapped in a modern world?
   c. Direct students to move into individual work. They will refine their own questions and return to the novel to consider the answers.
   d. Students write thesis statements that answer their questions.

3. Closure:

Remind the students of the specific writing guidelines.

Differentiation

Advanced

- Students select key quotations from the text to illustrate their understanding of Fitzgerald's commentary. Encourage them to create a movie or multimedia presentation that makes the thesis come alive visually, as well as in writing. Alternatively, ask students to write a poem or other creative presentation to accompany the essay.
- Students create a class newspaper or website for the essays when they are complete.
- Encourage students to research F. Scott Fitzgerald and prepare a biography of his life. Students should also research what inspired Fitzgerald to write *The Great Gatsby*, and perhaps present this information as a online poster or podcast. Students should select a modern-day "Fitzgerald" and justify why they chose him/her as a comparison.

Struggling

- Discuss the meaning of the writing task with a small group of students. Students will generate a list of questions together. Questions will be more concrete than abstract, referring students back to the text to generate ideas. If needed, be prepared with questions to prompt student thinking (i.e., "Where are some places in the book where you find Gatsby commenting about society?"). If additional prompting is needed, select quotations, including page numbers where they are found in the text, and ask students to discuss the commentary made about society based on the quotations.

- Use some of the scaffolding strategies for teaching *The Great Gatsby* suggested online at ReadWriteThink's "The Great Gatsby in the Classroom: Searching for the American Dream."

- Give students the opportunity to talk through the homework with a partner before doing it individually at home. Allow students to communicate and collaborate with each other online, perhaps on the classroom blog. Alternatively, encourage them to use a graphic organizer, in print or on a shared spreadsheet, or online support (e.g., ReadWriteThink's "Persuasion Map").

Homework/Assessment

Write an essay on *The Great Gatsby* by F. Scott Fitzgerald.

I. Writing Task

In his essay "Towards a Definition of American Modernism," Daniel Joseph Singal notes that novelists such as F. Scott Fitzgerald and Ernest Hemingway (among other American writers) "chronicled the disintegration of modern society and culture, but [their] primary concern, Bradbury rightly observes, was somehow 'to make the world re-cohere'" (p. 20). Consider Singal's words as you answer the following prompt:

How does F. Scott Fitzgerald's *The Great Gatsby* provide a critique of the modern world?

II. Writing Guidelines

Your final paper will:

- Provide a **narrow, focused** thesis statement that responds to the prompt
- Contain **an analysis – not a summary –** of the idea that you choose to discuss
- Demonstrate originality of ideas
- Be carefully and deliberately developed
- Demonstrate a mastery of organizational skills (topic sentences, transitions, order of ideas, etc.)
- Balance the use of primary sources with your own analysis (cite the text to support ideas)
- Use Standard English grammar
- Use simple present tense
- Include a title – be original!

Challenges and Successes of the Twentieth Century

This six-week unit, the last of six, concludes the exploration of the American experience by addressing literary and nonfiction texts that reflect the challenges and successes of America in the latter half of the twentieth century.

ESSENTIAL QUESTION

? Does twentieth-century American literature represent a fulfillment of America's promise, as discussed in Unit Four?

OVERVIEW

The unit traces the flourishing of the American short story and the development of the novel and dramas since World War II. The unit includes a few titles from the twenty-first century as well. Students will read masters of the southern short story—writers such as Eudora Welty and Flannery O'Connor. The unit also explores works by Richard Wright and Ralph Ellison, whose texts expose tensions within the emerging African American literary tradition. The 1960s are rich with both informational and literary works mirroring profound cultural shifts in the American landscape. This unit also emphasizes how a changing political landscape, exemplified in the words of leaders such as John Fitzgerald Kennedy and Ronald Reagan, shaped the world in which we live.

FOCUS STANDARDS

These Focus Standards have been selected for the unit from the Common Core State Standards.

RL.11–12.5: Analyze how an author's choices concerning how to structure specific parts of a text (e.g., the choice of where to begin or end a story, the choice to provide a comedic or tragic resolution) contribute to its overall structure and meaning as well as its aesthetic impact.

RL.11–12.7: Analyze multiple interpretations of a story, drama, or poem (e.g., recorded or live production of a play or recorded novel or poetry), evaluating how each version interprets the source text. (Include at least one play by Shakespeare and one play by an American dramatist.)

RI.11–12.2: Determine two or more central ideas of a text and analyze their development over the course of the text, including how they interact and build on one another to provide a complex analysis; provide an objective summary of the text.

W.11–12.2: Write informative/explanatory texts to examine and convey complex ideas, concepts, and information clearly and accurately through the effective selection, organization, and analysis of content.

SL.11–12.3: Evaluate a speaker's point of view, reasoning, and use of evidence and rhetoric, assessing the stance, premises, links among ideas, word choice, points of emphasis, and tone used.

L.11–12.5: Demonstrate understanding of figurative language, word relationships, and nuances in word meanings.

SUGGESTED STUDENT OBJECTIVES

- Analyze the development of the short story in post–World War II America.
- Trace the development of the Southern Gothic tradition in American literature.
- Distinguish between the two distinct views within the African American literary tradition as represented by Richard Wright and Ralph Ellison.
- Explore the nature of African American literature during the Civil Rights movement following World War II.
- Recognize the emergence of dynamic views represented in literary texts by first- and second-generation Americans.
- Explain how the Beat Generation challenged traditional forms and subjects in literature.
- Identify multiple postmodernist approaches to critical analyses of literature.
- Note the influence that postmodernism has had on the "common reader."

SUGGESTED WORKS

(E) indicates a CCSS exemplar text; (EA) indicates a text from a writer with other works identified as exemplars.

LITERARY TEXTS

Novels

- *Love Medicine* (Louise Erdrich) (EA)
- *Song of Solomon* (Toni Morrison) (EA)
- *The Joy Luck Club* (Amy Tan) (EA)
- *Invisible Man* (Ralph Ellison)
- *Native Son* (Richard Wright)
- *Seize the Day* (Saul Bellow)
- *The Catcher in the Rye* (J. D. Salinger)
- *Cat's Cradle* (Kurt Vonnegut)
- *Into the Wild* (Jon Krakauer)
- *All the Pretty Horses* or *The Road* (Cormac McCarthy)

Short Stories
- "The Man Who Was Almos' a Man" (Richard Wright) (EA)
- "Petrified Man" (Eudora Welty)
- "A Good Man is Hard to Find" (Flannery O'Connor)
- "The Swimmer" (John Cheever)
- "A Small, Good Thing" (Raymond Carver)
- "Flying Home" (Ralph Ellison)
- "A & P" (John Updike)
- "Where Are You Going, Where Have You Been?" (Joyce Carol Oates)

Drama
- *Death of a Salesman* (Arthur Miller) (E)
- *A Streetcar Named Desire* (Tennessee Williams) (EA)

Poetry
- "Sestina" (Elizabeth Bishop) (E)
- "The Fish" (Elizabeth Bishop) (EA)
- "One Art" (Elizabeth Bishop) (EA)
- "America" (Allen Ginsberg)
- "Love Calls Us to the Things of This World" (Richard Wilbur)
- "Skunk Hour" (Robert Lowell)
- "Memories of West Street and Lepke" (Robert Lowell)
- "July in Washington" (Robert Lowell)
- "The Black Swan" (James Merrill)
- "The Octopus" (James Merrill)
- "Days of 1964" (James Merrill)
- "The Tartar Swept" (August Kleinzahler)
- "Happiness" or "The Current" (Raymond Carver)
- "The Visitor" (Carolyn Forche)
- "My Friends" (W. S. Merwin)
- "Tulips" (Sylvia Plath)
- "Advice to a Prophet" (Richard Wilbur)

INFORMATIONAL TEXTS
- *The Feminine Mystique* (Betty Friedan)

Speeches
- "Address to the Broadcasting Industry" (1961) (Newton Minow)
- Inaugural Address (January 20, 1961) (John F. Kennedy)
- Brandenburg Gate Address (June 12, 1987) (Ronald Reagan)

Essays

- "On Being an American" (H. L. Mencken)
- "Seeing" or other essays from *Pilgrim at Tinker Creek* (Annie Dillard)
- "Letter from a Birmingham Jail" (Martin Luther King Jr.)
- "Remembering Richard Wright" (Ralph Ellison)
- "The Content of His Character" (Shelby Steele)

Biography/Autobiography

- *Patton: A Biography* (Alan Axelrod) (excerpts)
- *The Autobiography of Malcolm X: As Told to Alex Haley* (Malcolm X) (excerpts)

ART, MUSIC, AND MEDIA

Art

- Willem de Kooning, *Excavation* (1950)
- Barnett Newman, *Concord* (1949)
- Jackson Pollock, *Number 28, 1950* (1950)
- Mark Rothko, *Untitled* (1964)
- Franz Kline, *Untitled* (1957)
- Robert Motherwell, *Elegy to the Spanish Republic, 70* (1961)
- David Smith, *Pillar of Sundays* (1945)
- Mark di Suvero, *Are Years What? (For Marianne Moore)* (1967)
- Louise Bourgeois, *Red Fragmented Figure* (1953)

Architecture

- Farnsworth House, Plano, Illinois (1951)
- Seagram Building, New York City, New York (1957)

Music and Lyrics

- "This Land is Your Land" (Woody Guthrie)
- "Where Have All the Flowers Gone?" (Pete Seeger)
- "Blowin' in the Wind" (Bob Dylan)

Film

- Elia Kazan, dir., *A Streetcar Named Desire* (1951)
- Glenn Jordan, dir., *A Streetcar Named Desire* (1995)

Media

- *Omnibus: A Streetcar Named Desire* (television episode, 1955)

SAMPLE ACTIVITIES AND ASSESSMENTS

For a full Scoring Rubric, see the Appendix.

Note: After reading and discussing a work or pairing of works as a class, students prepare for seminars and essays by reflecting individually, in pairs, and/or in small groups on a given seminar or essay question. In this way, students generate ideas. (Seminar and essay assignments include more than one question. Teachers may choose one or all of the questions to explore in the course of the seminar; students should choose one question for the essay.) Seminars should be held before students write essays so that they may explore their ideas thoroughly and refine their thinking before writing. Textual evidence should be used to support all arguments advanced in seminars and in essays. Page and word counts for essays are not provided here, but teachers should consider the suggestions regarding the use of evidence, for example, to determine the likely length of good essays.

1. COLLABORATION

Reflect on seminar questions, take notes on your responses in your journal or on a shared spreadsheet, and note the page numbers of the textual evidence you will refer to in your seminar and/or essay answers. Share your notes with a partner for feedback and guidance. Have you interpreted the text correctly? Is your evidence convincing? (RL.11–12.1, SL.11–12.1)

2. SEMINAR AND INFORMATIVE/EXPLANATORY WRITING

Discuss the characterization techniques authors use to create Huckleberry Finn, Jay Gatsby, and/or John Grady Cole. How are they similar? How are they different? Are some more effective than others? Why? Use at least three pieces of evidence to support an original thesis statement. Your teacher may give you the opportunity to share your initial thoughts on the classroom blog in order to get feedback from your classmates. (RL.11–12.3, W.11–12.2, SL.11–12.1, L.11–12.5)

3. SEMINAR AND WRITING (ARGUMENT)

Compare a scene from the 1951 film of *A Streetcar Named Desire* with the same scene in the 1995 film or a stage performance. Do you think the film or stage production is faithful to the author's intent? Why or why not? Cite at least three pieces of evidence to support an original thesis statement. Your teacher may give you the opportunity to share your initial thoughts on the classroom blog in order to get feedback from your classmates. (RL.11–12.7, W.11–12.2, SL.12.1)

4. SEMINAR AND INFORMATIVE/EXPLANATORY WRITING

How do Willy Loman and Tommy Wilhelm contend with being "nobody"? Cite at least three pieces of evidence from *Death of a Salesman* to support an original thesis statement. Your teacher may give you the opportunity to share your initial thoughts on the classroom blog in order to get feedback from your classmates. (RL.11–12.9, W.11–12.2, SL.11–12.1, W.11–12.9a)

5. INFORMATIVE/EXPLANATORY WRITING

In his essay "The Content of His Character," Shelby Steele observes that authors Richard Wright and Ralph Ellison, both African Americans, hold vastly different political visions of America. The protagonists of "The Man Who Was Almos' a Man" by Richard Wright and "Flying Home" by Ralph Ellison reflect this philosophical divide. In an informative/explanatory essay, discuss how the authors' opposing visions of America's promise emerge in two stories. (RL.11–12.1, RL.11–12.2, RL.11–12.3, RI.11–12.2, W.11–12.2)

6. ORAL PRESENTATION

Play recordings of two of the poets reading their work. Make a presentation to the class about how their reading influences the listener's interpretation of the poem (e.g., tone, inflection, pitch, emphasis, and pauses). Record your presentation with a video camera so you can evaluate your performance. (RL.11–12.4, W.11–12.6, SL.11–12.4, SL.11–12.5, SL.11–12.6)

7. RESEARCH PAPER

Write a research paper in which you trace the influence of World War II on American literature. Cite at least three pieces of textual evidence and three secondary sources to support an original thesis statement. The essay should reflect your reasoned judgment about the quality and reliability of sources consulted (i.e., why you emphasize some sources and not others), a balance of paraphrasing and quoting from sources, and proper citation of sources. Your teacher may give you the opportunity to share and refine your initial research questions on the classroom blog in order to get feedback from your classmates. (RL.11–12.1, W.11–12.7, W.11–12.8, W.11–12.9)

8. ORAL COMMENTARY

Students will be given an unfamiliar passage from a contemporary novel, poem, or short story and asked to provide a ten-minute commentary on two of the following questions:

- What are the effects of the dominant images used in this extract?
- Identify the literary or poetic techniques used in this work. Relate them to the content.
- What do you think the important themes in this extract are?

    Record your presentation with a video camera so you can evaluate your performance. (RL.11–12.1, RL.11–12.4, SL.11–12.4)

9. GRAMMAR

Examine a one- to two-page excerpt (selected by the teacher) from *All The Pretty Horses*. Insert punctuation where you think convention would demand it. Explain in a brief essay why you think McCarthy has omitted standard punctuation in some places in his novel. (L.11–12.2, L.11–12.3)

10. ART/CLASS DISCUSSION

The paintings listed are all signal examples of abstract expressionist art. What do you see in each image? Consider these paintings in comparison to romantic painting, discussed in Unit Three, and the early modernist works in Unit Five. Why do you believe the abstract expressionists took such a grand leap away from figurative art (i.e., creating a representational image)? What words come to mind when you see these images? Many of these works are large-scale paintings. Can you appreciate the monumental scale of these works without being in front of them? Do you need to view this image in person to be affected—by the colors, textures, and shapes used? What happens to an image when it is reproduced? (RL.11–12.9, SL.11–12.1, SL.11–12.4)

11. ART/CLASS DISCUSSION

View the two works of architecture, one residential and one commercial. The same architect, Ludwig Mies van der Rohe, designed these buildings. How do they compare? Do you see similar elements in both of them? What is different? How is each building site-specific (i.e., reacting specifically to the place where it resides)? Compare this duo to the di Suvero and Bourgeois sculptures. How might you compare them—or can we even compare them? Does the comparison suggest that artists and architects sometimes work on similar ideas? (SL.11–12.1, SL.11–12.2, SL.11–12.4, SL.11–12.5)

ADDITIONAL RESOURCES

- *Flannery O'Connor's "A Good Man is Hard to Find": Who's the Real Misfit?* (National Endowment for the Humanities) (RL.11–12.9)
- Exploring *A Streetcar Named Desire* (ArtsEdge, The Kennedy Center) (RL.11–12.3)
- *Every Punctuation Mark Matters: A Mini-lesson on Semicolons* (ReadWriteThink) (RI.11–12.9, L.11–12.2, W.11–12.5)

TERMINOLOGY

Beatniks	Minimalism	Parody	Postmodernism
The Beat Generation	Nonlinear narratives	Pastiche	

Grade Eleven, Unit Six Sample Lesson Plan

"The Man Who Was Almos' a Man" by Richard Wright

"Flying Home" by Ralph Ellison

"Remembering Richard Wright" by Ralph Ellison

"The Content of His Character" by Shelby Steele

In this series of seven lessons, students read "The Man Who Was Almos' a Man" by Richard Wright and "Flying Home" by Ralph Ellison, and they:

Examine the plight of the protagonists of the two short stories (RL.11-12.1, RL.11-12.1, RL.11-12.2, RL.11-12.3, SL.11-12.1, L.11-12.4)

Probe the different political stances that the protagonists represent (RL.11-12.1, RL.11-12.1, RL.11-12.2, SL.11-12.1, L.11-12.6)

Explore the complex relationship between writing and author's political views (RL.11-12. 1, SL.11-12.1, SL.11-12.1, SL.11-12.3, W.11-12.1)

Summary

Lesson I: A Narrator's Voice in "The Man Who Was Almos' a Man"

Explore the complexity of narration in "The Man Who Was Almos' a Man" (RL.11-12.1, RL.11-12.4, RL.11-12.5, SL.11-12.1)

Examine the use of vernacular ("Black English") in the story (RL.11-12.1, RL.11-12.4, RL.11-12.5, SL.11-12.4)

Identify the third-person narrator's point of view (RL.11-12.1, RL.11-12.4, RL.11-12.5, SL.11-12.1)

Lesson II: Dave's Choices

Identify Dave's point of view (RL.11-12.1, RL.11-12.6, SL.11-12.1)

Note the role that society plays in Dave's life (SL.11-12.1)

Explore the tensions among Dave's thoughts, his oral expressions, and his actions (RL.11-12.1, RL.11-12.6, SL.11-12.1)

(From the narrator's point of view) critique Dave's choices (RL.11-12.2, SL.11-12.4)

Lesson III: Varying Representations of Todd's Plight in "Flying Home"

Identify the shifts in the narrative voices (RL.11-12.1, RL.11-12.4, RL.11-12.5, SL.11-12.4)

Determine the purpose of the girl's letter (RL.11-12.5, SL.11-12.4)

Examine the role of Jefferson's story (RL.11-12.5, SL.11-12.4)

Explore Todd's character (RL.11-12.1. SL.11-12.1)

Lesson IV: "Flying Home": Todd's Ambitions

Trace and qualify the recurring symbolism of birds (RL.11-12.1, RL.11-12.6, L.11-12.5)

Trace and qualify the recurring symbolism of flying (RL.11-12.1, RL.11-12.6, L.11-12.5)

Explore the meaning of the final image in the story, "glow like a bird of flaming gold" (RL.11-12.2, RL.11-12.6, L.11-12.5)

Problematize Todd's struggle (RL.11-12.2, SL.11-12.1)

Lesson V: Dave's Flight vs. Todd's Flight

Juxtapose Dave's and Todd's flights (SL.11-12.1)

Source of embarrassment

Definition of manhood

Concept of flight

Fear of what?

Notion of freedom?

Relationships to whites

Motives for actions (RL.11-12.1, RL.11-12.2)

Determine authors' intent (RL.11-12.2)

Critique authors' intent (RL.11-12.2, SL.11-12.4)

Lesson VI, VII: Wright Versus Ellison: Writing and Politics

Identify key ideas in "Remembering Richard Wright," by Ralph Ellison (RI.11-12.1, SL.11-12.1)

Examine Ellison's critique of Wright (RI.11-12.1, SL.11-12.1)

Identify key ideas in "The Content of His Character" by Shelby Steele (RI.11-12.1, W.11-12.1, SL.11-12.1)

Examine and critique the political views expressed (RI.11-12.2, W.11-12.1, SL.11-12.4)

Explore the validity of assuming an author's intent (W.11-12.1, SL.11-12.1)

Note the gap between Wright's and Ellison's view of America's promise (W.11-12.1a,b,d, SL.11-12.1)

Lessons VI, VII: Wright Versus Ellison: Writing and Politics

Objectives

Identify key ideas in "Remembering Richard Wright," by Ralph Ellison (RI.11-12.1, , SL.11-12.1)

Examine Ellison's critique of Wright (RI.11-12.2, SL.11-12.4)

Identify key ideas in "The Content of His Character" by Shelby Steele (RI.11-12.1, W.11-12.1, SL.11-12.1)

Examine and critique the political views expressed (RI.11-12.2, W.11-12.1, SL.11-12.4)

Explore the validity of assuming an author's intent (W.11-12.1, SL.11-12.1)

Note the gap between Wright's and Ellison's view of America's promise (W.11-12.1a,b,d, SL.11-12.1)

Required Materials

☐ Class set of "The Man Who Was Almos' a Man" by Richard Wright

☐ Class set of "Flying Home" by Ralph Ellison

☐ Class set of "Remembering Richard Wright" by Ralph Ellison

☐ Class set of "The Content of His Character" by Shelby Steele

Procedures

1. Lead-In:
   Students will review the notes they have taken while reading "Remembering Richard Wright" by Ralph Ellison (previous lesson's homework).

2. Step by Step:
   a. Lead a discussion of Ellison's essay. Students will identify autobiographical information (where the two authors came from):
      - It is important to note the fact that Wright inspired and mentored Ellison.
      - Students should realize the shift in the essay when Ellison says: "But there I must turn critic . . ."
      - Ellison's specific criticism of Wright's failure needs to be closely studied.
   b. Students will review the notes they have taken while reading "The Content of His Character" by Shelby Steele (previous lesson's homework). Students will identify all of the following elements:
      - Steele's definition of "protest writing"
      - Steele's critique of "protest writing"
      - Steele's critical view of Wright's vision
      - Steele's praise of Ellison's vision
   c. Lead a discussion of the two stories and the two essays using the following question: Can we assume an author's political or social intent?

3. Closure:
   Lead a closing discussion about Wright's and Ellison's opposing visions of America; offer a summary of the views and the disputes expressed.

Differentiation

Advanced

- Divide students into two groups. One group researches Richard Wright, and the other researches Ralph Ellison. Ask students to prepare a biography of the author's life for classmates. Students should also research what inspired Ellison and Wright to write their pieces, and perhaps present this information as an online poster, podcast, or posting on the classroom blog.

- Students should be working at the evaluation and synthesis level.
- Allow students to help classmates edit their work for transitions, grammar, and use of present tense (in other words, the conventions, but not the ideas).

Struggling

- Read/reread the pertinent sections of text to students, or allow them to listen to a pre-recorded version.
- Give students an outline or graphic organizer to annotate or sketch (or use other nonlinguistic representations) to aid in understanding and memory of the comparison between Ellison's and Steele's work. Perhaps have students complete a T-chart noting social or political intent. Alternatively, the notes could be color-coded to differentiate the motivation.
- Provide students with a Venn diagram, written or online, where they can outline Wright's and Ellison's views of America, including citations from the texts.
- Give students the opportunity to talk through the homework with a partner before doing it individually at home. Allow students to communicate and collaborate with each other online, perhaps on the classroom blog. Alternatively, encourage them to use a graphic organizer, in print or on a shared online document, or online support.

Homework/Assessment
Reading Writers' Politics
I. Writing Task

Richard Wright and Ralph Ellison are both African American authors. In his essay titled "The Content of His Character," Shelby Steele argues that Wright and Ellison hold vastly different political visions of America. The protagonists of "The Man Who Was Almos' a Man," by Richard Wright, and "Flying Home," by Ralph Ellison, reflect this philosophical divide. Craft an informative/explanatory essay in which you discuss how the authors' opposing visions emerge in the two stories.

II. Writing Guidelines

Your essay will:

- Provide a **narrow, focused** thesis statement
- Contain **an analysis — not a summary** — of the idea that you choose to discuss
- Demonstrate originality of ideas
- Be carefully and deliberately developed
- Demonstrate a mastery of organizational skills (topic sentences, transitions, order of ideas, etc.)
- Cite the texts to support the analysis
- Use Standard English grammar
- Use simple present tense
- Include a title — be original!

GRADE 12

Upon entering twelfth grade, students have read and discussed literary classics across the major genres and have studied world literature and American literature. Now they focus on European literature from the Middle Ages to the present: from Chaucer's *Canterbury Tales* and Dante's *Inferno* to twentieth-century works such as Ionesco's *Rhinoceros* and Kafka's *Metamorphosis*. Units are arranged chronologically, so that students may see how earlier works influence later works and how forms and ideas have evolved over time. Students consider prominent themes for each time period: for instance, the tension between reason and emotion in seventeenth-century literature, and questions of the relationship between art and nature in the literature of the eighteenth and early nineteenth century. It is important to read poems in their original language, so most of the poetry studied this year is in English. Through immersion in the poetry of Shakespeare, Donne, Milton, Blake, Wordsworth, Byron, Auden, and others, students develop an ear for English metrical forms and learn to recite poems expressively from memory. In their essays and discussions, students may relate a work to its historical circumstances, trace a symbol through a work or works, or consider a moral or philosophical question. Writing assignments include essays and research papers. By the end of twelfth grade, students have become familiar with some of the major works and ideas of European literature, have honed their skills of literary analysis, and have learned to write a research paper.

Standards Checklist for Grade Twelve

Standard	Unit 1	Unit 2	Unit 3	Unit 4	Unit 5	Unit 6	Standard	Unit 1	Unit 2	Unit 3	Unit 4	Unit 5	Unit 6
Reading—Literature							3d						
1	A	A	FA	A	A	A	3e						
2	A	A	A	FA	A	A	4			F			
3	A			FA	FA	F	5			FA		F	A
4		FA		A	F	A	6						
5	FA			A			7	A	A	A	FA	FA	FA
6	A	F		A		F	8	A	A		FA	FA	FA
7			FA				9						
8 n/a							9a						
9							9b						
10			A			F	10						
Reading—Informational Text							Speaking and Listening						
1		FA	A		A	A	1	A	A	A	A	A	FA
2	FA	F	A		FA	A	1a						
3			F				1b						
4			F				1c						
5	A			F		F	1d						
6			F				2	A	A	FA	A	A	A
7							3	A	A	A	A	A	A
8							4	FA	FA	A	A	FA	A
9							5	A	A	A	A	A	A
10							6			A	A		
Writing							Language						
1	FA			A	A	A	1			F			
1a							1a						
1b							1b						
1c							2			F			
1d							2a						
1e							2b						
2	A	F		A			3	A					
2a							3a	F					
2b							4		F				
2c							4a						
2d							4b						
2e							4c						
2f							4d						
3				F			5					F	
3a							5a						
3b							5b						
3c							6						FA

F = Focus Standards; A = Activity/Assessment

Grade 12 ▶ *Unit 1*

European Literature: Middle Ages

In this six-week unit, students explore the tension between humans and the divine in the literature of the Middle Ages.

OVERVIEW

Although the Middle Ages often is characterized as a period of darkness, the literature and art of the time typically suggest a more complex picture. Through a combination of close reading and exposure to an array of texts, students observe how satire reveals some of the contradictions and divergences within medieval literature and draw connections between literary form and philosophy. In addition, they consider how certain traits of medieval literature can also be found in the art of the period: for instance, how characters have symbolic meaning both in literature and in iconography. Students write essays in which they analyze a work closely, compare two works, or trace an idea or theme through the works they have read.

FOCUS STANDARDS

These Focus Standards have been selected for the unit from the Common Core State Standards.

RL.11–12.5: Analyze how an author's choices concerning how to structure specific parts of a text (e.g., the choice of where to begin or end a story, the choice to provide a comedic or tragic resolution) contribute to its overall structure and meaning as well as its aesthetic impact.

RI.11–12.2: Determine two or more central ideas of a text and analyze their development over the course of the text, including how they interact and build on one another to provide a complex analysis; provide an objective summary of the text.

W.11–12.1: Write arguments to support claims in an analysis of substantive topics or texts, using valid reasoning and relevant and sufficient evidence.

SL.11–12.4: Present information, findings, and supporting evidence, conveying a clear and distinct perspective, such that listeners can follow the line of reasoning, alternative or opposing perspectives are addressed, and the organization, development, substance, and style are appropriate to purpose, audience, and a range or formal and informal tasks.

L.11–12.3(a): Apply knowledge of language to understand how language functions in different contexts, to make effective choices for meaning or style, and to comprehend more fully when reading or listening.

SUGGESTED STUDENT OBJECTIVES

- Analyze how medieval literature exhibits many tendencies rather than a single set of characteristics.
- Note the literary elements (e.g., allegory, farce, satire, and foil) in medieval literary works and identify characteristics of medieval literary forms.
- Explain how literary elements contribute to meaning and author intention.
- Note glimpses of the Renaissance in certain works of medieval literature and art.
- Explain how medieval literary and artistic forms reflect the writers' and artists' philosophical views.
- Examine the literary, social, and religious satire in Chaucer's *Canterbury Tales*.
- Explain the role of the framed narrative in Chaucer's *Canterbury Tales*, Dante's *Inferno*, and other works.
- Compare works of medieval literature and art, particularly their depiction of character and their focus on the otherworldly.

SUGGESTED WORKS

(E) indicates a CCSS exemplar text; (EA) indicates a text from a writer with other works identified as exemplars.

LITERARY TEXTS
Novella

- *The Decameron* (continued in Unit Two) (Giovanni Boccaccio)

Drama

- *The Summoning of Everyman* (Anonymous)
- *Farce of Master Pierre Pathelin* (Anonymous)

Poetry

- The General Prologue in *The Canterbury Tales* (Geoffrey Chaucer) (E)
- "The Wife of Bath's Tale" in *The Canterbury Tales* (Geoffrey Chaucer) (E)
- "The Knight's Tale" in *The Canterbury Tales* (Geoffrey Chaucer) (E)
- "The Monk's Tale" in *The Canterbury Tales* (Geoffrey Chaucer) (E)
- "The Pardoner's Tale" in *The Canterbury Tales* (Geoffrey Chaucer) (E)
- "The Nun's Priest's Tale" in *The Canterbury Tales* (Geoffrey Chaucer) (E)
- *Sir Gawain and the Green Knight* (Anonymous)
- *Inferno* (Cantos I–XI, XXXI–XXXIV) (Dante Alighieri)
- "When the leaf sings" (Arnaut Daniel)
- "The bitter air" (Arnaut Daniel)
- "I see scarlet, green, blue, white, yellow" (Arnaut Daniel)

- "The Ruin" in *The Exeter Book* (Anonymous)
- "The Wanderer" in *The Exeter Book* (Anonymous)
- "Lord Randall" (Anonymous)
- "Dance of Death" ("Danza de la Muerte") (Anonymous)

INFORMATIONAL TEXTS

- *Confessions* (Book XI) (Saint Augustine)
- *The One and the Many in the Canterbury Tales* (Traugott Lawler)
- *Medieval Images, Icons, and Illustrated English Literary Texts: From Ruthwell Cross to the Ellesmere Chaucer* (Maidie Hilmo)
- *St. Thomas Aquinas* (G. K. Chesterton)
- *The History of the Medieval World: From the Conversion of Constantine to the First Crusade* (Susan Wise Bauer)

ART, MUSIC, AND MEDIA

Art

- Cimabue, *Maestà* (1280)
- Giotto, Arena (Scrovegni) Chapel frescos, Padua (after 1305): *Joachim Among the Shepards, Meeting at the Golden Gate, Raising of Lazarus, Jonah Swallowed Up by the Whale*
- Duccio, *Maestà* (1308–1311)
- Masaccio, *The Tribute Money*, Brancacci Chapel, Florence (ca. 1420)
- Lorenzo Ghiberti, *Gates of Paradise* (1425–1452)

SAMPLE ACTIVITIES AND ASSESSMENTS

For a full Scoring Rubric, see the Appendix.

Note: After reading and discussing a work or pairing of works as a class, students prepare for seminars and essays by reflecting individually, in pairs, and/or in small groups on a given seminar or essay question. In this way, students generate ideas. (Seminar and essay assignments include more than one question. Teachers may choose one or all of the questions to explore in the course of the seminar; students should choose one question for the essay.) Seminars should be held before students write essays so that they may explore their ideas thoroughly and refine their thinking before writing. Textual evidence should be used to support all arguments advanced in seminars and in all essays. Page and word counts for essays are not provided here, but teachers should consider the suggestions regarding the use of evidence, for example, to determine the likely length of good essays.

1. COLLABORATION

Reflect on seminar questions, take notes on your responses, and note the page numbers of the textual evidence you will refer to in your seminar and/or essay answers. Share your notes with a partner for feedback and guidance. Have you interpreted the text correctly? Is your evidence convincing? (RL.11–12.1, SL.11–12.1)

2. SEMINAR AND INFORMATIVE/EXPLANATORY WRITING

Compare and contrast *Sir Gawain and the Green Knight* and "The Knight's Tale." What are the qualities of the ideal knight? Do they differ at all? Use textual evidence from both texts to support an original, concise thesis. (RL.11–12.1, RL.11–12.3, SL.11–12.1, SL.11–12.4, W.11–12.2)

3. SEMINAR AND INFORMATIVE/EXPLANATORY WRITING

Choose one of the *Canterbury Tales*. Explain how the main character shows his or her personality through narration. How do fabliaux reveal the point of view of the character? Use textual evidence to support an original, concise thesis statement. (RL.11–12.5, RI.11–12.2, SL.11–12.1, SL.11–12.4, W.11–12.2)

4. SEMINAR AND INFORMATIVE/EXPLANATORY WRITING

Compare "The Monk's Tale" in *The Canterbury Tales* with Dante's story of Ugolino in Cantos XXXII through XXXIII of *Inferno*, paying special attention to depiction of character. Use at least one critical source. Use textual evidence to support an original, concise thesis statement. (RL.11–12.3, SL.11–12.1, SL.11–12.4, W.11–12.2, W.11–12.7, L.11–12.3)

5. SEMINAR AND WRITING (ARGUMENT)

Is the Wife of Bath from *The Canterbury Tales* a feminist? Use textual evidence to support your position. (RL.11–12.1, RL.11–12.3, SL.11–12.1, SL.11–12.4, W.11–12.2)

6. SEMINAR AND INFORMATIVE/EXPLANATORY WRITING

Discuss "The Pardoner's Tale" as a satire. What exactly is being literally described versus being satirized? Why does Chaucer use satire? Is Chaucer satirizing human nature or the Church as an establishment? Use textual evidence to support an original, concise thesis statement. (RL.11–12.1, RL.11–12.3, RL.11–12.5, SL.11–12.1, SL.11–12.4, W.11–12.2)

7. INFORMATIVE/EXPLANATORY WRITING

Draw parallels between representations of character in a medieval play and in medieval icons. Compare and contrast their similarities and differences. Are they more alike or different? Use concrete evidence from both texts to support an original, concise thesis statement. (RL.11–12.1, RL.11–12.3, W.11–12.2)

8. SEMINAR AND WRITING (ARGUMENT)

Explain how Saint Augustine attempts to resolve a paradox in Book XI of *Confessions*. Is his resolution convincing? Why or why not? (RI.11–12.5, W.11–12.1, SL.11–12.1, SL.11–12.3)

9. SEMINAR AND WRITING (ARGUMENT)

Read Book XI of Saint Augustine's *Confessions*. Agree or disagree with Augustine's idea: "Evil stems not from God but from a perversion of human will." Use textual evidence to support an original, concise thesis statement. (RI.11–12.5, W.11–12.1, SL.11–12.1, SL.11–12.3)

10. SPEECH

Select one of the poems from this unit and recite it from memory. Include an introduction that states:

- What the excerpt is from
- Who wrote it
- Why it exemplifies the medieval period (SL.11–12.4)

11. SEMINAR AND WRITING (ARGUMENT)

"To what degree does medieval literature regard human existence as secondary to the divine?" Use textual evidence from one of the texts read in this unit to support an original, concise thesis statement. (RL.11–12.2, W.11–12.1, SL.11–12.1, SL.11–12.3)

12. SEMINAR AND WRITING (ARGUMENT)

Read Dante's *Inferno*. How does the allegory reveal the values of the Middle Ages? What sins are punished most severely and why? Do you agree with the hierarchical circles of hell that Dante creates? Use textual evidence to support an original, concise thesis statement. (RL.11–12.1, RL.11–12.3, RL.11–12.5, RL.11–12.6, SL.11–12.1, SL.11–12.4, W.11–12.2)

13. RESEARCH PAPER (ARGUMENT)

Does the term *Dark Ages* accurately describe the Middle Ages? Use primary and secondary sources from this unit or outside of the unit to support an original, concise thesis statement to answer the question. Cite at least three sources. The essay should reflect your reasoned judgment about the quality and reliability of sources consulted (i.e., why you emphasize some and not others), a balance of paraphrasing and quoting from sources, original thinking, the anticipation and addressing of questions or counterclaims, and the proper citation of sources. Your teacher may give you the opportunity to share and refine your initial research questions on the classroom blog in order to get feedback from your classmates. (RL.11–12.1, W.11–12.1, W.11–12.7, W.11–12.8)

14. RESEARCH PAPER (INFORMATIVE/EXPLANATORY)

Answer the essential question: "How did medieval man distinguish between the earthly and the divine?" Use primary and secondary sources from this unit or outside of the unit to support an original thesis statement to answer the question. Cite at least three sources. The essay should reflect your reasoned judgment about the quality and reliability of sources consulted (i.e., why you emphasize some and not others), a balance of paraphrasing and quoting from sources, original thinking, the anticipation and addressing of questions or counterclaims, and the proper citation of sources. Your teacher may give you the opportunity to share and refine your initial research questions on the classroom blog in order to get feedback from your classmates. (RL.11–12.1, W.11–12.1, W.11–12.7, W.11–12.8)

15. ART/CLASS DISCUSSION

Compare earlier images from the medieval period to later ones. For instance, compare Giotto's Arena Chapel frescos with Masaccio's at the Brancacci Chapel. How do we see depictions of man change? Do religious figures begin to take on earthly characteristics as the Middle Ages wane? What changes do you observe in the various depictions of Jesus, both as a child and as an adult (consider comparing both *Maestà* images)? (SL.11–12.1, SL.11–12.2, SL.11–12.3, SL.11–12.4, SL.11–12.5)

ADDITIONAL RESOURCES

- *Danteworlds* (The University of Texas at Austin) (RL.11–12.1, SL.11–12.3)
- *Digital Dante* (Institute for Learning Technologies, Columbia University)
- *Chaucer's Wife of Bath* (National Endowment for the Humanities) (RL.11–12.3)
- *Canterbury Tales Project* (ITSEE, University of Birmingham)

TERMINOLOGY

Allegory

Anonymity

Caesura

"Dance of death"

Epic

Fabliaux

Farce

Foil

Framed narrative

Hyperbole

Icon (religious art)

Miracle, mystery, and morality plays

Perspective (art and literature)

Symbol

Grade Twelve, Unit One Sample Lesson Plan

The Divine Comedy by Dante Alighieri

<u>*"Tragedy or Romance? A Reading of the Paolo and Francesca Episode in Dante's Inferno" by Renato Poggioli*</u>

In this series of five lessons, students read excerpts from *The Divine Comedy* by Dante Alighieri and "Tragedy or Romance? A Reading of the Paolo and Francesca Episode in Dante's *Inferno*" by Renato Poggioli*, and they:

    Gather information about Dante Alighieri (RI.11–12.1, RI.11–12.2, RI.11–12.7, W.11–12.7)

    Explore the form of *The Divine Comedy* (RI.11–12.2, RL.11–12.5, RL.11–12.1, SL.11–12.1)

    Perform a close reading of Cantos I and V (RL.11–12.1, RL.11–12.2, RL.11–12.4, RL.11–12.5, RL.11–12.9, SL.11–12.1, L.11–12.5)

    Explicate a section of Canto V (RL.11–12.1, RL.11–12.2, RL.11–12.2, RL.11–12.9, SL.11–12.4, W.11–12.9, L.11–12.4)

Summary

Lesson I: Dante Alighieri

Conduct online/library research about Dante's

    Life

    Philosophical perspective

    Influences

    Works

    (W.11–12.7, RI.11–12.1, RI.11–12.2, RI.11–12.7)

Document results of research (W.11–12.4, W.11–12.7)

Share results of research (SL.11–12.1, SL.11–12.4)

Lesson II: *The Divine Comedy*—Canto I

Note the form of *The Divine Comedy* (RL.11–12.5, RL.11–12.1, SL.11–12.1)

Identify the speaker of the poem (RL.11–12.3, SL.11–12.4)

Probe the Christian tradition of the afterlife (through Dante's *Inferno, Purgatory,* and *Paradise*) (RI.11–12.2, RL.11–12.9, SL.11–12.1)

Explore the role of the three beasts (RI.11–12.2, RL.11–12.1, SL.11–12.1)

Explore the role of the poet Virgil (RI.11–12.2, RL.11–12.1, SL.11–12.1)

<table>
<tr><td>

Lessons III, IV: Canto V—Paolo and Francesca

Explore Dante's depiction of the second circle of Hell (RL.11-12.1, RL.11-12.2, RL.11-12.4, RL.11-12.9, SL.11-12.1, L.11-12.5)

Examine the impact of the storm (SL.11-12.4, RL.11-12.1, RL.11-12.5)

Analyze the use of bird imagery (SL.11-12.1, RL.11-12.4, L.11-12.5)

Examine the tension between pathos/pity and God's justice (SL.11-12.4, RL.11-12.1, RL.11-12.9, L.11-12.5)

Explore the role of the sinners as a prelude to the appearance of Paolo and Francesca (RL.11-12.1, RL.11-12.3, RL.11-12.9, SL.11-12.1)

Examine Dante's invitation to Paolo and Francesca (RL.11-12.3, SL.11-12.4, L.11-12.5)

Explore Francesca's depiction of their love (RL.11-12.1, RL.11-12.3, RL.11-12.9, SL.11-12.1, L.11-12.4)

Examine the tension between temptation and sin (RL.11-12.2, RL.11-12.9, SL.11-12.1, L.11-12.5)

Expose the tension between Love and God's order (RL.11-12.2, RL.11-12.9, SL.11-12.1, L.11-12.5)

</td><td>

Lesson V: Explicating Poetry

Identify key components of explication (SL.11-12.4, W.11-12.4)

Explicate any three-stanza sections from Canto V in Dante's *The Divine Comedy* (W.11-12.9, RL.11-12.1, RL.11-12.2, RL.11-12.9, L.11-12.4)

Address specifically one of the following:

Bird imagery

The description of the storm

Francesca welcomes the visitors

Francesca's description of their love

(RL.11-12.1, RL.11-12.4, L.11-12.5)

Pay close attention to the poet's use of poetic devices, such as:

Metaphors

Imagery

Symbolism

Contrast (light and sound)

(RL.11-12.5, L.11-12.5, SL.11-12.1)

</td></tr>
</table>

Lessons III, IV: Canto V—Paolo and Francesca

Objectives

Explore Dante's depiction of the second circle of Hell (RL.11-12.1, RL.11-12.2, RL.11-12.4, RL.11-12.9, SL.11-12.1, L.11-12.5)

Examine the impact of the storm (SL.11-12.1, RL.11-12.4, RL.11-12.1, RL.11-12.5)

Analyze the use of bird imagery (SL.11-12.4, RL.11-12.1, RL.11-12.9, L.11-12.5)

Examine the tension between pathos/pity and God's justice (SL.11-12.3, SL.11-12.4, L.11-12.5)

Explore the role of the sinners as a prelude to the appearance of Paolo and Francesca (RL.11-12.1, RL.11-12.3, RL.11-12.9, SL.11-12.1)

Examine Dante's invitation to Paolo and Francesca (RL.11-12.3, SL.11-12.4, L.11-12.5)

Explore Francesca's depiction of their love (RL.11-12.1, RL.11-12.3, RL.11-12.9, SL.11-12.1, L.11-12.4)

Examine the tension between temptation and sin (RL.11-12.2, RL.11-12.9, SL.11-12.4, L.11-12.5)

Expose the tension between Love and God's order (RL.11-12.2, RL.11-12.9, SL.11-12.4, L.11-12.5)

Required Materials

☐ Class set of Canto V of *The Divine Comedy* by Dante Alighieri

☐ Class set of "Tragedy or Romance? A Reading of the Paolo and Francesca Episode in Dante's *Inferno*" by Renato Poggioli, *Publications of the Modern Language Association of America*, Vol. 72, No. 3 (June 1957): 313–358 (found in JSTOR)

Procedures

1. Lead-In:

Read Canto V silently.

2. Step by Step:

With guidance, the students conduct a close reading of Canto V. (A series of excerpts from Renato Poggioli's essay are included in the steps below. Teachers should determine how best to use the excerpts to assist in the close reading and the discussion of the text.)

a. The Second Circle

Dante classified sins punished in descending order.

Second circle—"carnal sinners."

There is a divine order.

Poggioli (read the excerpts below) points to the "tensions" between the suffering that the traveler witnesses and divine order.

Dante classified the sins punished in the Inferno in descending order, going from transgressions caused by the abuse of our normal instincts down to the graver violations involving perfidy and malice, which both deface the nobility of the human soul and sever us from our fellow men. So, even before crossing the passage from the first to the second circle, we know that there we shall find damned souls worthy still of tears of pity. The damned of the second circle, carnal sinners, are men and women who have subjected their nobler impulses to the animal urges of the flesh. Foremost in the ranks of these stand Paolo and Francesca. (Poggioli, 313)

One could say that the entire Paolo and Francesca story is based on a continuous tension between the ethos of contemplation and the pathos of experience. The artistic achievement lies in the fact that the poem reconciles within itself Dante the witness of the wretched misery of man, and Dante the beholder of the awful majesty of God. (Poggioli, 313–314)

b. The Storm

Minos assigns sinners a place in hell based on their sins.

Dante and Virgil enter an area where "All light is mute" but it is full of sound (lines 28–30).

Absence of light—"silence."

It is not a natural storm and it evokes tension.

The storm sweeps the "ravaged spirits" (line 32).

Lines 40–41 provide further description of the storm; it never ends, and there is not "ease from pain or hope of rest."

Dante described the sinners' cries, laments, and groans — *but* he stops.

The reader realizes Dante's suffering.

We are reminded that the sinners are there because of their sins (line 35). Think of the divine order to which Poggioli draws our attention.

c. The Birds

Dante moves from the description of the storm to the people. Dante and the poet are now looking at the sinners.

The climatic conditions, winter, and the darkness of the second circle are present and connected.

Dante uses imagery of birds repeatedly (wings, flocks, cranes).

The souls forever hover in the air like birds.

The word *crowded* (line 38) indicates that there are many of them.

The sinners are pushed and pulled by the wind. They are powerless.

> Like the preceding bird simile, also, the crane image has a dynamic function besides the metaphorical one: it helps us to visualize the positions successively taken by the crowd of sinners, and to localize them in space and time. From the comparison with the starlings we learned that at the moment the shades were moving toward Dante and Virgil in frontal formation: from the new comparison we learn that after a long wide turn the wind is now driving them in such a way that the two travelers, still standing motionless, see the troop through a longitudinal perspective, rather than a transverse one. (Poggioli, 318)

Poggioli points to the parallel between the "singing of the cranes" and the "lamenting of the sinners"; he notes that there is a harmony between the trope and the object. Like the bird earlier, here "the crane image has a dynamic function besides the metaphorical one: it helps us to visualize the positions successively taken by the crowd of sinners, and to localize them in space and time." (Poggioli, 318)

d. The Sinners

Dante and Virgil can now see some of the figures and Dante asks, "who are these people?"

Virgil points to several sinners. We meet them before we meet Paolo and Francesca.

The sinners are not described in detail here, though it is important for the students to realize that they set up the next scene.

Dante tells us that he sees a thousand souls (line 59).

Poggioli says that the poetic license here (so many) is to provide us with the "immensity of their numbers." (Poggioli, 321)

Poggioli also argues that the unknown amount of time spent in the second circle, learning about the sinners, implies that Dante has a particular interest in the subject. When he first notices the figures, he asks for facts; he wants to know who they are.

The pity is so intense that he almost faints (he does faint after Francesca's tale).

> Dante's statement that his guide identified for him 'more than a thousand' (più di mille) souls is but a verbal exaggeration or poetic license, through which he conveys a sense of the immensity of their numbers, considering that most of them must have remained unrecognized and nameless. The vastness of the figure stated by Dante, as well as the unknown total quantity it implies, will also suggest the unusual amount of time spent by the pilgrim in getting acquainted with the souls of the second circle, thus betraying the peculiar intensity of his interest. (Poggioli, 321)

e. The Paolo and Francesca Part Begins

Dante calls to Paulo and Francesca.

When Dante recovers from his moments of weakness he tells Virgil that he wants to speak to "those two two who move along together" (line 65). Poggioli notes the fact that unlike the other sinners who were on their own, these two are together.

Virgil tells Dante to approach them "In the name of love," and they will respond (line 68).

Dante invites them warmly "O wearied souls!" but does not mention love. A few lines later, though (line 78), he says it was a "loving call" that was strong and had a "powerful compulsion."

Dante then hopes that "Another" (God) will not prevent them.

f. The Dove Image

Dante uses the third bird image, a pair of doves, to depict the movement of the lovers toward Dante and Virgil.

The doves "glide" (line 73), they do not "fly."

"steady," with "raised wings" (line 73).

Poggioli also notes that what Dante sees is a "miracle" since God grants his wish (line 71).

It is a reminder that their will is no longer free.

Poggioli speaks of the reciprocal relationship between the poet's tender call and the lovers' desire to go where the heart is, "sweetness of their nest" (line 74). He also notes that there is no conflict here with God's will.

> It is clear that God has granted Dante's wish, that he has allowed the two sinners to heed his friendly and tender call. For this very reason the action of Paolo and Francesca is described as the almost unconscious effect of a sympathetic and reciprocal attraction, as the operation of an "elective affinity," rather than as the unilateral decision of their will, which is no longer free. (Poggioli, 325)

g. Francesca's Greetings

Francesca (we figure out that it is her, but Dante does not make it specific) talks to the visitors (probably directly to Dante) (lines 79–81).

Her words indicate that the visitors came specifically to see them: "who stained / The world with blood."

Francesca thanks the visitors for their "compassion" but adds that she (they) cannot pray because of their situation — they are in Hell. Unlike Dante, however, whose reference to God was vague ("Another" line 71), Francesca's reference is to "heaven's King" (line 81) and "Him" (line 83).

In the next stanza (lines 85–88) Francesca "gracefully" grants (as befitting a lady of her social status) the two visitors permission to "speak and hear" (line 86). But in reality she is the only one who speaks. (Poggioli, 328)

h. Francesca's Story

In lines 89–96, Francesca describes the love between her and Paolo.

In the first stanza there is an action of love that "seizes" him (Paolo) and then the consequence that her body was "torn away from" her.

In the next stanza Francesca describes that their love, even in Hell, remains.

In the last stanza Francesca says that "Love" gave them death but that her husband would go to Caina — a deep level of Hell.

Note that "Love" is always in capital letters.

i. "Interlude"

The next section is a pause between Francesca's two speeches.

Since Dante tells us that he "lowered [h]is head" we know that up until that point he was looking at Francesca. We also know that he is silent until Virgil interrupts him asking him what he thinks.

When Dante responds, his first word "Alas" reflects the depth of his emotions. Notice that the word is separated from what follows, an indication that Dante emphasizes this exclamation.

We know that when he speaks next, Dante still looks down and he considers the actions that led the lovers to their current situation.

He then looks up toward the lovers, but addresses Francesca.

j. Back to Francesca's Story

Francesca resumes by stating that "No sadness ...joy" (lines 107–109). She remembers times of joy.

She says to Dante that she will tell him their story, but that she will "weep" (line 112) while she tells.

Francesca tells her story; one day, she and Paolo were reading the story of Lancelot and Guinevere (make sure the students know who they were) (lines 112–114). They were sitting alone and suspected nothing.

The passage that they read depicts Guinevere's kiss; "*the longed for smile*" is the metaphor for her lips.

But this parallel between the two couples stops when she brings the scene back to them and to Paolo, who is by her side and would never leave her. It is no longer an abstract "Love" — they are in Hell.

Dante mentions the crying Paolo and, out of compassion, he (Dante) collapses.

Dante's collapse is a reminder of the tension between sympathy for the sinners and the divine order.

3. Closure:
Explain the homework.

Differentiation

Advanced

- Select student volunteers to read sections of *The Divine Comedy* aloud; give the students an opportunity to practice reading with expression, recorded with a video camera, so they can evaluate and improve their performances.

- Have students create a modern-day interpretation of Canto V. They must be able to justify how the modern version stays true to the original while also changing style. Perhaps challenge them to create a movie to present their interpretation.
- Have students choose an additional theme, device, technique, or other aspect of the reading to explicate. This can be in addition to one, but not both, of the requirements below. Have students post their work on the classroom blog for group or individual teacher comment.

Struggling:

- Allow students to listen to select sections of *The Divine Comedy* to support their understanding of the text.
- Pre-teach students the concepts found in the Poggioli article, so that they will be better prepared to participate in class discussion.
- Work with a small group to outline Canto V. Give students a paper copy to annotate or sketch (or use other nonlinguistic representations) to aid in understanding and memory, possibly as a group using a document camera. Alternatively, give students an electronic document to annotate. Allow students to share their notes on a shared online document or the classroom blog so that all students can benefit from each other's learning in class discussion.
- Begin to outline the homework with students in small groups before sending it home for individual completion. Perhaps provide students with a reference chart of poetic devices.

Homework/Assessment

Explicate any three-stanza sections from Canto V of Dante Alighieri's *The Divine Comedy*. Specifically address **one** of the following:

- Bird imagery
- The description of the storm
- Francesca welcomes the visitors
- Francesca's description of their love

Pay close attention to the poet's use of poetic devices, such as:

- Metaphors
- Imagery
- Symbolism
- Contrast (light and sound)

* Reprinted by permission of the Modern Language Association of America from: "'Tragedy or Romance? A Reading of the Paolo and Francesca Episode in Dante's Inferno,'" Renato Poggioli, Publications of the Modern Language Association of America, Vol. 72, No. 3 (June 1957), pp. 331–358.

Grade 12 ▶ *Unit 2*

European Literature: Renaissance and Reformation

This six-week unit introduces students to the literature of the Renaissance and Reformation, exploring its continuity with and departure from the literature of the Middle Ages.

ESSENTIAL QUESTION

? How does Renaissance literature break with and build on the literature of the Middle Ages?

OVERVIEW

Students consider Renaissance writers' interest in ancient Greek and Latin literature and myth; their preoccupation with human concerns and life on earth; their aesthetic principles of harmony, balance, and divine proportion; and exceptions to all of these. This leads to a discussion of how literary forms themselves reflect religious, philosophical, and aesthetic principles. As students compare the works of the Renaissance with those of the Middle Ages, they will recognize the overlap and continuity of these periods. In addition, they consider how the outstanding works of the era transcend their time and continue to inspire readers and writers. The English Renaissance of the seventeenth century includes additional works by William Shakespeare. In their essays, students may analyze the ideas, principles, and form of a literary work; discuss how a work bears attributes of both the Middle Ages and the Renaissance; discuss convergences of Renaissance literature and arts; or pursue a related topic of interest.

FOCUS STANDARDS

These Focus Standards have been selected for the unit from the Common Core State Standards.

RL.11–12.4: Determine the meaning of words and phrases as they are used in the text, including figurative and connotative meanings; analyze the impact of specific word choices on meaning and tone, including words with multiple meanings or language that is particularly fresh, engaging, or beautiful. (Include Shakespeare as well as other authors.)

RL.11–12.6: Analyze a case in which grasping point of view requires distinguishing what is directly stated in a text from what is really meant (e.g., satire, sarcasm, irony, or understatement).

RI.11–12.1: Cite strong and thorough textual evidence to support analysis of what the text says explicitly as well as inferences drawn from the text, including determining where the text leaves matters uncertain.

RI.11–12.2: Determine two or more central ideas of a text and analyze their development over the course of the text, including how they interact and build on one another to provide a complex analysis; provide an objective summary of the text.

W.11–12.2: Write informative/explanatory texts to examine and convey complex ideas, concepts, and information clearly and accurately through the effective selection, organization, and analysis of content.

SL.11–12.4: Present information, findings, and supporting evidence, conveying a clear and distinct perspective, such that listeners can follow the line of reasoning, alternative or opposing perspectives are addressed, and the organization, development, substance, and style are appropriate to purpose, audience, and a range or formal and informal tasks.

L.11–12.4: Determine or clarify the meaning of unknown and multiple-meaning words and phrases based on grades 11–12 reading and content, choosing flexibly from a range of strategies.

SUGGESTED STUDENT OBJECTIVES

- Read novels, literary nonfiction, stories, plays, and poetry from the Renaissance era, observing the continuity from the Middle Ages as well as the departures.
- Identify and investigate allusions to classical literature in Renaissance texts.
- Explain how a concept such as symmetry or divine proportion is expressed both in literature and in art.
- Analyze Renaissance conceptions of beauty and their literary manifestations.
- Describe how Renaissance writers took interest in human life and the individual person.
- Analyze the playful, satirical, irreverent aspects of Renaissance literature—in particular, the writing of Rabelais, Boccaccio, and Shakespeare.
- Explain how literary forms and devices reflect the author's philosophical, aesthetic, or religious views.
- Write an essay in which they (a) compare a literary work with a work of art; (b) compare a Renaissance work with a medieval work; or (c) relate a literary work to a philosophical work.

SUGGESTED WORKS

(E) indicates a CCSS exemplar text; (EA) indicates a text from a writer with other works identified as exemplars.

Note: More works have been listed than can be covered; teachers are encouraged to select from the list so that students may analyze certain works closely while gaining a broad sense of the era. It is possible, for instance, to focus entirely on Rabelais or Boccaccio, with only a few additional short works for contrast; to consider a philosophical work in relation to a literary work; to focus on the idea of divine proportion as expressed in literature, art, and mathematics; or to consider a variety of Renaissance works. The unit should include close readings so that students may observe how Renaissance forms emerge in both literature and art and reflect religious, philosophical, and aesthetic views.

LITERARY TEXTS

Novels

- *The Life of Gargantua and the Heroic Deeds of Pantagruel* (Books 1 and 2) (François Rabelais)
- *The Decameron* (continued from Unit One) (Giovanni Boccaccio)

Drama

- *The Jewish Women (Les Juifves)* (Robert Garnier)
- *Nine Carnival Plays* (Hans Sachs)
- *Henry IV, Part I* (William Shakespeare)
- *The Tragedy of Macbeth* (William Shakespeare)
- *Richard III* (William Shakespeare)

Poetry

- *Dark Night of the Soul* (Saint John of the Cross) (excerpts)
- "The Nightingale of Wittenberg" (Hans Sachs)
- *The Faerie Queene* (Edmund Spenser) (excerpts)
- Sonnets 29, 30, 40, 116, 128, 130, 143, and 146 (William Shakespeare)
- "The Passionate Shepherd to His Love" (Christopher Marlowe)
- "The Nymph's Reply to the Shepherd" (Sir Walter Raleigh)

INFORMATIONAL TEXTS

- *Rabelais and His World* (Mikhail Bakhtin)
- *The Prince* (Niccolo Machiavelli) (excerpts)

Essays

- "Of Cannibals" (Michel de Montaigne)
- *On the Divine Proportion (De divina proportione)* (illustrations only) (Luca Pacioli)
- *Lives of the Most Excellent Painters, Sculptors, and Architects* (Giorgio Vasari)
- "On Introducing Shakespeare: Richard III" (Charles A. Pennel)

ART, MUSIC, AND MEDIA

Art

- Sandro Botticelli, *Primavera* (1482)
- Leonardo da Vinci, *Vitruvian Man* (1487)
- Leonardo da Vinci, *Mona Lisa* (1503–1506)
- Michelangelo, *David* (1505)
- Leonardo da Vinci, *The Virgin and Child with St. Anne* (1508)
- Michelangelo, Sistine Chapel, ceiling (1508–1512)
- Raphael, *The Niccolini-Cowper Madonna* (1508)
- Jacopo da Pontormo, *Deposition from the Cross (Entombment)* (1525–1528)
- Michelangelo, *The Last Judgment*, Sistine Chapel altar wall (1536–1541)

- Michelangelo Merisi da Caravaggio, *The Entombment of Christ* (1602–1603)
- Giovanni Lorenzo Bernini, *Ecstasy of Saint Teresa* (1647–1652)

SAMPLE ACTIVITIES AND ASSESSMENTS

For a full Scoring Rubric, see the Appendix.

Note: After reading and discussing a work or pairing of works as a class, students prepare for seminars and essays by reflecting individually, in pairs, and/or in small groups on a given seminar or essay question. In this way, students generate ideas. (Seminar and essay assignments include more than one question. Teachers may choose one or all of the questions to explore in the course of the seminar; students should choose one question for the essay.) Seminars should be held before students write essays so that they may explore their ideas thoroughly and refine their thinking before writing. Textual evidence should be used to support all arguments advanced in seminars and in all essays. Page and word counts for essays are not provided here, but teachers should consider the suggestions regarding the use of evidence, for example, to determine the likely length of good essays.

1. COLLABORATION

Reflect on seminar questions, take notes on your responses, and note the page numbers of the textual evidence you will refer to in your seminar and/or essay answers. Share your notes with a partner for feedback and guidance. Have you interpreted the text correctly? Is your evidence convincing? (RL.11–12.1, SL.11–12.1)

2. SEMINAR AND INFORMATIVE/EXPLANATORY WRITING

Read *Macbeth*. How does the play illustrate the demise of the Great Chain of Being? What does the play say about the divine right of kings? What does it reveal about fate and free will? Use textual evidence from the play to support your response in an original, concise thesis statement. (RL.11–12.1, RI.11–12.1)

3. SEMINAR AND WRITING (ARGUMENT)

After reading *Macbeth* and excerpts from *The Prince* by Machiavelli, answer one of the following questions. How do Machiavelli's principles apply to the play? What is Shakespeare saying about Machiavelli's approach to attaining and maintaining political power? Consider the quotation, "It is better to be feared than to be loved." Is this true for Macbeth? Use textual evidence from both texts to support your position. (RL.11–12.1, RI.11–12.1)

4. SEMINAR AND INFORMATIVE/EXPLANATORY WRITING

Read *Henry IV, Part I*. How does Falstaff reflect the new ideas of the Renaissance regarding chivalry and honor? How does the play illustrate the demise of the Great Chain of Being? What does the play say about the divine right of kings? Use textual evidence from the play to support your response in an original, concise thesis statement. (RL.11–12.1, RI.11–12.1)

5. SEMINAR AND INFORMATIVE/EXPLANATORY WRITING

Relate Pacioli's *On the Divine Proportion* to a Shakespeare sonnet. In what ways is the sonnet an expression of divine proportion (or not)? Cite specific evidence from both texts to support an original, concise thesis statement. (RL.11–12.1, RI.11–12.1)

6. SEMINAR AND INFORMATIVE/EXPLANATORY WRITING

Compare one of the satirical stories of *The Canterbury Tales* (from Unit One) with one of the stories from Boccaccio's *The Decameron*. What does the satire reveal about the author's intention and message? Use textual evidence to support an original, concise thesis. (RL.11–12.2)

7. SEMINAR AND INFORMATIVE/EXPLANATORY WRITING

Show how one of the plays from this unit departs from the medieval conceptions of drama. Use specific textual evidence to support an original, concise thesis statement. (RL.11–12.1, RI.11–12.1)

8. SPEECH

Select a poem from this unit and recite it from memory. Include an introduction that states:

- Who wrote the poem
- Its form, meter, rhyme scheme, and key literary elements
- An aspect of the poem that comes through after multiple readings (RL.11–12.4)

9. SEMINAR AND INFORMATIVE/EXPLANATORY WRITING

Using literary works as textual evidence, do **one** of the following: (a) compare two Renaissance literary works, with attention to symmetry and form; (b) compare a Renaissance literary work with a medieval literary work, with attention to depiction of character; or (c) relate a literary work to a philosophical work. Include at least one critical source and one reference to a literary work to support an original, concise thesis statement. (RL.11–12.4, W.11–12.7)

10. RESEARCH PAPER

Using texts from this unit as well as additional sources, explain how literature from the Renaissance breaks with or builds on ideas derived from the Middle Ages. Cite specific textual evidence to support an original, concise thesis statement to answer the essential question. The essay should reflect your reasoned judgment about the quality and reliability of sources consulted (i.e., why you emphasize some and not others), a balance of paraphrasing and quoting from sources, original thinking, the anticipation and addressing of questions or counterclaims, and the proper citation of sources. Your teacher may give you the opportunity to share and refine your initial research questions on the classroom blog in order to get feedback from your classmates. (RL.11–12.4, W.11–12.7, W.11–12.8)

11. ART/CLASS DISCUSSION

View Michelangelo's *Last Judgment*, da Vinci's *Virgin and Child*, Pontormo's *Deposition*, and Bernini's *Ecstasy of Saint Teresa*. What range of emotions is evident in these works of art? What imagery or symbols do the artists use to convey these emotions? What painting or sculpting techniques are used to heighten the effect? Which work do you respond to the most and why? (SL.11–12.1, SL.11–12.2, SL.11–12.3, SL.11–12.4, SL.11–12.5)

12. ART/CLASS DISCUSSION

Examine and discuss the following artworks: Michelangelo's *David*, Raphael's *Madonna*, and da Vinci's *Mona Lisa* and *Vitruvian Man*. How has each artist worked to depict human beauty? What elements of beauty do they highlight? What is idealized? Are there any aspects that are realistic? Do you believe these portrayals are beautiful? Why or why not? (SL.11–12.1, SL.11–12.2, SL.11–12.3, SL.11–12.4, SL.11–12.5)

ADDITIONAL RESOURCES

- *The English Renaissance in Context* (ERIC) (University of Pennsylvania Library) (RL.11–12.1, RL.11–12.2)
- *The Forest of Rhetoric* (Brigham Young University) (RL.11–12.4)
- *Literary Resources—Renaissance* (Rutgers University)

TERMINOLOGY

Allusion	Divine right of kings	The Great Chain of Being	Idyll
Classicism	Eclogue		Ode
Divine proportion (golden ratio, golden mean)	Epistle	Humanism	Satire
	Fate	Iambic pentameter	Sonnet
	Free will	Iambic tetrameter	Symmetry

Grade Twelve, Unit Two Sample Lesson Plan

Richard III by William Shakespeare

"On Introducing Shakespeare: Richard III" by Charles A. Pennel

In this series of six lessons, students read *Richard III* by William Shakespeare and "On Introducing Shakespeare: *Richard III*" by Charles A. Pennel, and they:

Investigate the historical context of *Richard III* (RI.11-12.1, RI.11-12.2, SL.11-12.4)

Study the antagonists of Richard III (RL.11-12.1, RL.11-12.3)

Note the importance of Richard's soliloquies (RL.11-12.1, RL.11-12.3, SL.11-12.4)

Analyze the use of irony in the play (RL.11-12.6, RL.11-12.4)

Examine the dramatic structure of *Richard III* (RL.11-12.1, RI.11-12.1, RI.11-12.2)

Explore the fall of Richard III and the politics of evil (RL.11-12.2, SL.11-12.1, SL.11-12.1d, SL.11-12.4)

Summary

Lesson I: Historical Context of *Richard III*

Identify key facts about the War of the Roses (teacher-selected informational text) (RI.11-12.1, RI.11-12.1, SL.11-12.4)

Examine the family tree of Richard III (teacher-selected informational text) (RI.11-12.1, SL.11-12.1)

Identify the members of House of York and the House of Lancaster (teacher-selected informational text) (RI.11-12.1, SL.11-12.4)

Chronicle Richard's moves (RI.11-12.1, RI.11-12.2, SL.11-12.4)

Lesson II: Richard III and the World Around Him

Examine the roles of secondary characters in establishing Richard's character (RL.11-12.1, RL.11-12.3, SL.11-12.1, L.11-12.6)

Cite the characteristics that are attributed to Richard (SL.11-12.4)

Explore the tensions between Richard and the characters around him (RL.11-12.1, RL.11-12.6, SL.11-12.1, SL.11-12.4)

Juxtapose Richard's desires with the cruel intent of external forces (RL.11-12.5, SL.11-12.1, L.11-12.6)

Lesson III: Soliloquies and Dramatic Ironies

Revisit Richard's soliloquies and asides (RL.11-12.1, L.11-12.4)

Examine the role of Richard's numerous soliloquies and asides (RL.11-12.3, SL.11-12.1)

Note the use of irony throughout the play (RL.11-12.6, L.11-12.5)

Note the tension between what is said and what the audience knows (RLa11-12.6, SL.11-12.4)

Lesson IV: The Fall of Richard III

Chronicle Richard's moves leading to his fall (SL.11-12.1)

Juxtapose the fall of the "classic tragic hero" with Richard's (SL.11-12.1, L.11-12.6)

Examine the vision behind Richmond's closing words (SL.11-12.1)

Lesson V: Dramatic Structure of *Ricahard III*

Explore Pennel's ideas in "On Introducing Shakespeare: *Richard III*" (informational/critical text) (RL.11-12.1, RI.11-12.2, SL.11-12.1, SL.11-12.4)

Identify Pennel's analytical style (RI.11-12.1, RI.11-12.2, SL.11-12.4)

Apply Pennel's ideas to the rest of *Richard III* (RL.11-12.1, RI.11-12.1, SL.11-12.4)

Identify and critically explore the dramatic structure of *Richard III* (RL.11-12.5, W.11-12.1a,c, W.11-12.2a,b, W.11-12.4)

Lesson VI: The Meaning of the Politics of Evil in *Richard III*

Examine the complexity of evil in *Richard III* (RL.11-12.2, SL.11-12.1)

Problematize Shakespeare's vision

Apply Shakespeare's enduring ideas to other historical situations (SL.11-12.1d)

Argue Shakespeare's relevance (SL.11-12.1d)

Lesson V: Dramatic Structure of *Richard III*

Objectives

Explore Pennel's ideas (informational/critical text) (RI.11-12.1, RI.11-12.2, SL.11-12.1, SL.11-12.4)

Identify Pennel's analytical style (RI.11-12.1, RI.11-12.2, SL.11-12.4)

Apply Pennel's ideas to the rest of *Richard III* (RL.11-12.1, RI.11-12.1, SL.11-12.4)

Identify and critically explore the dramatic structure of *Richard III* (RL.11-12.5, W.11-12.1a,c, W.11-12.2a,b, W.11-12.4)

Required Materials

☐ Class set of *Richard III* by William Shakespeare

☐ Class set of "On Introducing Shakespeare: *Richard III*" by Charles A. Pennel, *College English*, Vol. 26, No. 8 (May, 1965): 643–645 (found in JSTOR)

Procedures

1. Lead-In:

Students read and annotate "On Introducing Shakespeare: *Richard III*" by Charles A. Pennel. They specifically note Pennel's analysis of Act I.

2. Step by Step:

a. In groups, students discuss Pennel's analytical technique.

- In their discussion, students will cite specific examples from Pennel's text.
- They will pay close attention to his analytical style. For example, Pennel points out that, "The soliloquy in which Richard announces his general plans concludes with his specific plot against Clarence: enter Clarence."
- Remind the students that while Pennel offers a brief contextual summary (Richard announces his plans), his comment is, in fact, analytical; he highlights the timing of Clarence's entry.

b. In groups, students apply Pennel's technique and ideas to the assigned acts from *Richard III*. (Since each act has several scenes, assist in assigning sections to the participants in each of the groups.)

c. Using specific prompts, guide the groups to share their analyses of each of the remaining four acts. The purpose of the discussion is to explore the dramatic structure of the play.

3. Closure:

Introduce the homework assignment.

Differentiation

Advanced

- Select student volunteers to practice reading sections aloud prior to this lesson. The students should practice reading as Shakespeare intended it, recorded with a video camera, so they can evaluate and improve their performances. As an extension, students can read sections with a variety of dramatic interpretations and choose the most unique one to present to other advanced students. Students should evaluate the different interpretations and discuss how they work to enhance or detract from the work. These readings may be recorded with a video camera to share with other students, as time permits.
- Encourage students to create a modern-day interpretation of selected acts from *Richard III*, or find examples/references to the play in contemporary literature, movies, and online. They must be able to justify how the modern version/references stay true to the original, while also changing style. Perhaps challenge students to create a movie presentation of their modern-day interpretation.
- Encourage students to write their essay about two to three dramatic techniques, and make comparisons and contrasts among them. Allow them to use an online organizer if needed.

Struggling

- Read/reread selected acts or Pennel's article to students, and allow them to listen to a pre-recorded version.
- Be prepared with a list of guiding questions to support students in their application of Pennel's techniques to their assigned acts. Students can mark their *Richard III* text with sticky notes prior to class discussion.

- Create a chart of dramatic techniques and examples, on a shared spreadsheet or a worksheet, so all students can add and refer to it. Include two examples from *Richard III*, including page numbers for reference.
- Give students the opportunity to talk through the homework with a partner before doing it individually at home. Allow students to communicate and collaborate with each other online, such as on the classroom blog. Alternatively, encourage them to use an online essay organizer.

Homework/Assessment

Reread the excerpt from Charles A. Pennel's essay, "On Introducing Shakespeare: *Richard III*." Pay close attention to the second column, in which Pennel explores Shakespeare's dramatic technique. Revisit your class notes. Then, in a well-organized paragraph, discuss the dramatic technique of the act that you have been assigned. You **must** follow Pennel's format.

Writing Guidelines

- Clearly establish the **topic** of the paragraph and **contextualize** it.
- Organize the sequence of ideas according to the purpose (your topic sentence) of the paragraph.
- Present clear, thorough support of your topic sentence.
- Cite the text using short ("shoelace") quotations.
- Avoid grammatical and mechanical errors.
- **Use simple present tense.**

Grade 12 ▶ *Unit 3*

European Literature: Seventeenth Century

In this six-week unit, students explore literary works of the seventeenth century, with particular attention to questions of human reason and emotion.

ESSENTIAL QUESTION

? How did seventeenth-century writers regard the relationship between reason and emotion?

OVERVIEW

Students gain understanding of the early Enlightenment and its conception of reason. They see another side of the thought and literature of this period: an emphasis on human emotion, irrationality, and paradox. They consider how certain works express tension or conflict between emotion and reason while others present reason and emotion as complementary and interdependent. They write a critical essay exploring an aspect of the conflict between reason and emotion. Alternatively, teachers might choose to culminate the unit with a research paper that answers the essential question.

FOCUS STANDARDS

These Focus Standards have been selected for the unit from the Common Core State Standards.

RL.11–12.1: Cite strong and thorough textual evidence to support analysis of what the text says explicitly as well as inferences drawn from the text, including determining where the text leaves matters uncertain.

RL.11–12.7: Analyze multiple interpretations of a story, drama, or poem (e.g., recorded or live production of a play or recorded novel or poetry), evaluating how each version interprets the source text. (Include at least one play by Shakespeare and one play by an American dramatist.)

RI.11–12.3: Analyze a complex set of ideas or sequence of events and explain how specific individuals, ideas, or events interact and develop over the course of the text.

RI.11–12.4: Determine the meaning of words and phrases as they are used in a text, including figurative, connotative, and technical meanings; analyze how an author uses and refines the meaning of a key term or terms over the course of a text (e.g., how Madison defines "faction" in *Federalist* No. 10).

RI.11–12.6: Determine an author's point of view or purpose in a text in which the rhetoric is particularly effective, analyzing how style and content contribute to the power, persuasiveness, or beauty of the text.

W.11–12.4: Produce clear and coherent writing in which the development, organization, and style are appropriate to task, purpose, and audience. (Grade-specific expectations for writing types are defined in standards 1–3 above.)

W.11–12.5: Develop and strengthen writing as needed by planning, revising, editing, rewriting, or trying a new approach, focusing on addressing what is most significant for a specific purpose and audience. (Editing for conventions should demonstrate command of Language standards 1–3 up to and including grades 11–12 on page 54 of the Common Core State Standards.)

SL.11–12.2: Integrate multiple sources of information presented in diverse formats and media (e.g., visually, quantitatively, orally) in order to make informed decisions and solve problems, evaluating the credibility and accuracy of each source and noting any discrepancies among the data.

L.11–12.1(a,b): Demonstrate command of the conventions of Standard English grammar and usage when writing or speaking.

SUGGESTED STUDENT OBJECTIVES

- Read literary and philosophical works from the seventeenth century, with particular attention to questions of reason and emotion.
- Explain the idea of reading literature as a quest—for truth, for beauty, and for understanding.
- Analyze two philosophical works of the seventeenth century for their treatment of an idea related to human reason.
- Write literary and philosophical analyses with a focus on clarity and precision of expression.
- Conduct research, online and in libraries, on a particular seventeenth-century author, work, or idea.
- Analyze the relationship between reason and emotion as illustrated in literature of the seventeenth century.
- Explain the use of satire as a technique to reveal authorial intent.

SUGGESTED WORKS

(E) indicates a CCSS exemplar text; (EA) indicates a text from a writer with other works identified as exemplars.

LITERARY TEXTS

Note: Because of the number and length of works included in this unit, teachers may want to organize it around two major works, one fiction (or dramatic or poetic) and one nonfiction, with other works supplementing these selections. At a minimum, students should read one full literary work, a substantial excerpt from a philosophical or scientific work, and several shorter works of fiction and poetry.

Novels

- *Don Quixote* (Miguel de Cervantes) (E) (selections)
- *The Pilgrim's Progress* (John Bunyan)

Drama
- *Hamlet* (William Shakespeare)
- *King Lear* (William Shakespeare) (E)
- *The Merchant of Venice* (William Shakespeare) (E)
- *The Alchemist* (Ben Jonson)
- *The Miser* (Jean-Baptiste Molière) (EA)

Poetry
- "The Flea" (John Donne) (E)
- "Song: Goe, and catche a falling starre" (John Donne) (E)
- "Holy Sonnet 10" (John Donne) (E)
- "To His Coy Mistress" (Andrew Marvell)
- "To the Virgins, to Make Much of Time" (Robert Herrick)
- "To Daffodils" (Robert Herrick)
- "Love III" (George Herbert)
- "The Apparition" (John Donne)

INFORMATIONAL TEXTS
- *Leviathan* (Thomas Hobbes) (excerpts)
- *Novum Organum* (Francis Bacon) (excerpts)
- *An Essay Concerning Human Understanding* (John Locke)
- "Explicating Donne: 'The Apparition' and 'The Flea'" (Laurence Perrine)

ART, MUSIC, AND MEDIA
Art
- Peter Paul Rubens, *The Debarkation at Marseilles* (1622–1625)
- Nicolas Poussin, *Et in Arcadia Ego* (ca. 1630s)
- Rembrandt van Rijn, *The Nightwatch* (1642)
- Johannes Vermeer, *Girl with a Pearl Earring* (1665)

Film
- Grigori Kozintsev and Iosif Saphiro, dir., *Hamlet* (1964)
- Laurence Olivier, dir., *Hamlet* (1948)
- Arthur Hiller, dir., *Man of La Mancha* (1972)
- Dale Wasserman, *Man of La Mancha* (the musical) (1966)

SAMPLE ACTIVITIES AND ASSESSMENTS

For a full Scoring Rubric, see the Appendix.

Note: After reading and discussing a work or pairing of works as a class, students prepare for seminars and essays by reflecting individually, in pairs, and/or in small groups on a given seminar or essay question. In this way, students generate ideas. (Seminar and essay assignments include more than one question. Teachers may choose one or all of the questions to explore in the course of the seminar;

students should choose one question for the essay.) Seminars should be held before students write essays so that they may explore their ideas thoroughly and refine their thinking before writing. Textual evidence should be used to support all arguments advanced in seminars and in all essays. Page and word counts for essays are not provided here, but teachers should consider the suggestions regarding the use of evidence, for example, to determine the likely length of good essays.

1. COLLABORATION

Reflect on seminar questions, take notes on your responses, and note the page numbers of the textual evidence you will refer to in your seminar and/or essay answers. Share your notes with a partner for feedback and guidance. Have you interpreted the text correctly? Is your evidence convincing? (RL.11–12.1, SL.11–12.1)

2. SEMINAR AND WRITING (INFORMATIVE/EXPLANATORY AND ARGUMENT)

Analyze "The Flea" by addressing one of the following questions: (1) Why is it considered metaphysical poetry? (I/E); (2) How does it use irony to convey its message? (I/E); (3) Is it a poem of logic or of emotion? (A). Use textual evidence to discuss and write an original, concise thesis statement to support your position (#3). (W.11–12.5, W.11–12.7)

3. SEMINAR AND INFORMATIVE/EXPLANATORY WRITING

Read *The Pilgrim's Progress*. Consider the text as an allegory. What themes do the characters represent? How do these characters work together to create an allegory? What does the allegory reveal about Bunyan's point of view on religious ideas of the seventeenth century? Use textual evidence from the novel to support an original, concise thesis statement. (W.11–12.5, W.11–12.7)

4. SEMINAR AND INFORMATIVE/EXPLANATORY WRITING

Read *The Alchemist*. How does the plot reveal satire? What values of this time period are being mocked? How does the author use satire to reveal his point of view? Use textual evidence from the play to support an original, concise thesis statement. (W.11–12.5, W.11–12.7)

5. SEMINAR AND INFORMATIVE/EXPLANATORY WRITING

Read *The Miser*. How does the plot reveal satire? What values of this time period are being mocked? How does the satire reveal Molière's point of view? Use textual evidence from the play to support an original, concise thesis statement. (W.11–12.5, W.11–12.7)

6. SEMINAR AND INFORMATIVE/EXPLANATORY WRITING

Analyze Donne's "Holy Sonnet 10." Is the speaker of the poem pious or irreverent with regard to the Church's teachings? How does the use of personification convey the poem's message? Why is the poem considered metaphysical? Cite specific textual evidence from the poem to support an original, concise thesis statement. (W.11–12.5, W.11–12.7)

7. SEMINAR AND WRITING (ARGUMENT)

Read Donne's "Song: Goe, and catche a falling starre." Is the point of view a cynical one? Or is its point of view realistic? Does it build upon religious views or does it depart from the Church's teachings? How does emotion affect the logic of the speaker? Use textual evidence to support your position. (W.11–12.5, W.11–12.7)

8. SEMINAR AND INFORMATIVE/EXPLANATORY WRITING

Compare and contrast Donne's "Song: Goe, and catche a falling starre" to Marvell's "To His Coy Mistress." How do emotion and logic affect the speaker's point of view in each poem? How does gender affect the author's attitudes? Use textual evidence to support an original, concise thesis statement. (W.11–12.5, W.11–12.7)

9. SEMINAR AND WRITING (ARGUMENT)

Read *Hamlet*. With special consideration to his soliloquies, is Prince Hamlet influenced by his sense of logic or sense of emotion? Use specific textual evidence to support your position. (W.11–12.5, W.11–12.7)

10. SEMINAR AND INFORMATIVE/EXPLANATORY WRITING

Read *King Lear*. In the beginning of the play, is King Lear motivated by his sense of reason or by emotion? By the end of the play, how has King Lear resolved his emotional needs with his rational thought? Consider the same question for Edmund, Edgar, Regan, Goneril and/or Cordelia. Use textual evidence to support an original, concise thesis statement. (W.11–12.5, W.11–12.7)

11. SEMINAR AND WRITING (ARGUMENT)

Read excerpts of the *Leviathan*. Agree or disagree with Hobbes's assessment of human nature. Defend your opinion with specific textual evidence that supports an original, concise thesis statement. (W.11–12.1, W.11–12.5, W.11–12.7)

12. SEMINAR AND INFORMATIVE/EXPLANATORY WRITING

Read excerpts from *Don Quixote* and/or watch the film version of *Man of La Mancha*. Compare Don Quixote's outlook on life with that of another character, such as the priest. Use textual evidence citing either the novel or the film to support an original, concise thesis statement. (RL.11–12.1, W.11–12.5, W.11–12.7)

13. SEMINAR AND INFORMATIVE/EXPLANATORY WRITING

Analyze "To Daffodils," "To the Virgins, to Make Much of Time," and "To His Coy Mistress." Compare the message and intention of each. Do these poems appeal to human emotion or human logic to convey their ideas? Use textual evidence from two or more poems to write a comparative essay. Be sure your thesis is specific, concise, and original. (W.11–12.5, W.11–12.7, SL.11–12.1, SL.11–12.2)

14. SPEECH

Select a poem or excerpt from a longer poem and recite it from memory. Include an introduction that states:

- What the excerpt is from
- Who wrote it
- What kind of poetry it exemplifies and why (SL.11–12.6)

15. RESEARCH PAPER

Using multiple texts from this unit and additional sources, discuss how writers of the seventeenth century regard the relationship between reason and emotion. Include an original, concise thesis statement that directly answers the essential question. The essay should reflect your reasoned judgment about the quality and reliability of sources consulted (i.e., why you emphasize some and not others), a balance of paraphrasing and quoting from sources, original thinking, the anticipation and addressing of questions or counterclaims, and the proper citation of sources. Your teacher may give you the opportunity to share and refine your initial research questions on the classroom blog in order to get feedback from your classmates. (RL.11–12.1, RL.11–12.2, RI.11–12.1, RI.11–12.2, W.11–12.7)

16. ART/CLASS DISCUSSION

As scholars and philosophers moved into an age of reason and rationality, why do you think there was still a push for romanticized, opulent imagery, labeled as baroque art? View the painting by Rubens, which is a part of a series of twenty-one paintings. What is emphasized in this work of art: color, the senses, movement? View the Rubens and Poussin in comparison to the Dutch works by Rembrandt and Vermeer. These Dutch artists were said to be working in a Golden Age. What aspects of the Dutch art are similar to the French and Flemish works? What influence do you think location has on artistic style? (SL.11–12.1, SL.11–12.2, SL.11–12.3, SL.11–12.4, SL.11–12.5)

ADDITIONAL RESOURCES

- *Exploring Don Quixote* (ArtsEdge, The Kennedy Center) (RL.11–12.1, RL.11–12.10)
- *Hamlet and the Elizabethan Revenge Ethic in Text and Film* (National Endowment for the Humanities) (RL.11–12.1, RL.11–12.7, RL.11–12.10)

TERMINOLOGY

Aesthetics	Conceit	Fate	Personification
Allegory	Dissent	Free will	Rationalism
Allusion	Doubt	"In medias res"	Satire
Argumentation	Dramatic irony	Inductive reasoning	Tragic flaw
Authorial intent	Enlightenment	Metaphysical poetry	
Blank verse	Ethics	Paradox	

Grade Twelve, Unit Three Sample Lesson Plan

"The Apparition" by John Donne

"The Flea" by John Donne

"Explicating Donne: 'The Apparition' and 'The Flea'" by Laurence Perrine

In this series of four lessons, students read "The Apparition" and "The Flea" by John Donne and "Explicating Donne: 'The Apparition' and 'The Flea'" by Laurence Perrine, and they:

Identify key characteristics of the metaphysical poets (RI.11-12.2, RL.11-12.3, RL.11-12.9)

Meet John Donne (RI.11-12.2)

Read and explicate "The Apparition" and "The Flea," by John Donne (RL.11-12.1, RL.11-12.2, RL.11-12.5, RL.11-12.9)

Explore the method of explication in "Explicating Donne: 'The Apparition' and 'The Flea'" by Laurence Perrine (RL.11-12.1, RL.11-12.3, RL.11-12.5, SL.11-12.1)

Explicate a poem (by Donne) of their choice (W.11-12.2, RL.11-12.1, RL.11-12.2, RL.11-12.5)

Summary

Lesson I: The Metaphysical Poets

Explore the historical/social context of the metaphysical poets (RL.11-12.9, RI.11-12.2, SL.11-12.1)

Identify key poets in the metaphysical tradition (RL.11-12.9, RL.11-12.1, SL.11-12.4)

Meet John Donne (RI.11-12.2)

Lesson II: "The Apparition"

Read and reread "The Apparition" (RL.11-12.2, RL.11-12.9)

Annotate "The Apparition" for the speaker's central reason for writing the poem (RL.11-12.9, W.11-12.2, SL.11-12.4, L.11-12.3)

Explore the theme of "The Apparition" (RL.11-12.2, SL.11-12.1, L.11-12.5)

<table>
<tr><td>

Lesson III: "The Flea"

Read and reread "The Flea" (RL.11-12.2, RL.11-12.9)

Annotate "The Flea" for the speaker's central reason for writing the poem (RL.11-12.9, W.11-12.2, SL.11-12.4, L.11-12.3)

Explore the theme of "The Flea" (RL.11-12.2, SL.11-12.1)

</td><td>

Lesson IV: The Art of Explicating Poetry

Outline "Explicating Donne: 'The Apparition' and 'The Flea'" by Laurence Perrine (RL.11-12.2, RL.11-12.1, RL.11-12.9)

Explore Perrine's method of explication in "Explicating Donne: 'The Apparition and 'The Flea'" (RL.11-12.1, RL.11-12.3, RL.11-12.5, SL.11-12.1)

Identify key ideas explored by Perrine (RL.11-12.2, RL.11-12.3, SL.11-12.4, L.11-12.3)

Analyze Perrine's perspective (RL.11-12.1, SL.11-12.1, L.11-12.6)

Apply (independently) Perrine's method of explication (RL.11-12.9, W.11-12.2)

</td></tr>
</table>

Lesson IV: The Art of Explicating Poetry

Objectives

Outline "Explicating Donne: 'The Apparition' and 'The Flea'" by Laurence Perrine (RL.11-12.2, RL.11-12.1, RL.11-12.9)

Explore Perrine's method of explication in "Explicating Donne: 'The Apparition' and 'The Flea'" (RL.11-12.1, RL.11-12.3, RL.11-12.5, SL.11-12.1)

Identify key ideas explored by Perrine (RL.11-12.2, RL.11-12.3, SL.11-12.4, L.11-12.3)

Analyze Perrine's perspective (RL.11-12.1, SL.11-12.1, L.11-12.6)

Apply (independently) Perrine's method of explication (RL.11-12.9, W.11-12.2)

Required Materials

☐ Class set of "The Flea" by John Donne

☐ Class set of "The Apparition" by John Donne

☐ Class set of "Explicating Donne: 'The Apparition' and 'The Flea'" by Laurence Perrine

Procedures

1. Lead-In:

Assign selected paragraphs; students will then read assigned passages.

2. Step by Step:
   a. In small groups (three or four students), students will:
      - Identify topic sentence(s) in the assigned passages
      - Identify supporting details
      - Discuss the main ideas
      - Prepare to share with the class
   b. Students (the whole class) will:
      - Share their findings
      - Discuss Perrine's methodology
      - Analyze Perrine's perspective

3. Closure:
   Introduce the writing assignment.

Differentiation

Advanced

- Encourage students to create a modern-day interpretation of the poem. They must be able to justify how the modern version stays true to the original while also changing style. Perhaps challenge them to create a movie to engage their classmates.
- Prior to this lesson, select a student volunteer to read the poem for classmates or create an audio-recording of the poem. Give the student an opportunity to practice reading dramatically, recorded with a video camera, so he/she can evaluate and improve his/her performance.
- Encourage students to create notes on a shared spreadsheet (in a T-chart) that can be shared with all classmates following the discussion. This information can be used to help students with the writing assignment.

Struggling

- Read the passage to students, or allow them to listen to a pre-recorded version.
- Give students a handout of the poem they can write on, possibly even with sketches (or nonlinguistic representations) to help aid memory and understanding. Students should highlight the topic sentence in one color and the supporting details in another. Highlighting can be done on the paper copy; if given an electronic version, they can use highlighter tools.
- Work with a small group to help them prepare the presentation (discussed in step b) for the class. Perhaps provide a graphic organizer to help them structure their presentation.
- Work with students to get them started on the homework prior to doing it alone at home.

Homework/Assessment
Following a close analytical reading of "'The Apparition'' and "The Flea'' by John Donne, and "Explicating Donne: 'The Apparition' and 'The Flea''" by Laurence Perrine, students will select a poem of their choice (written by John Donne) and explicate it following the model of Perrine.

European Literature: Eighteenth and Early Nineteenth Century

In this four-week unit, students will read fiction, drama, poetry, biography, and autobiography from the eighteenth and early nineteenth centuries, paying particular attention to the relationship between man and nature.

ESSENTIAL QUESTION

? What role does nature play in eighteenth- and early nineteenth-century literature?

OVERVIEW

Observing themes related to nature as well as "natural" forms and language, students consider whether nature appears as a force of good or a menace. Observing narrative digressions, idiosyncrasies, exaggerations, and biases, they consider human, unpredictable, and idiosyncratic aspects of storytelling. They have the opportunity to practice some of these narrative techniques in their own fiction and nonfiction writing. Students also explore some of the philosophical ideas in the literary texts—questions of free will, fate, human conflict, and loss. In seminar discussions, students consider a philosophical question in relation to a particular text. Students write short essays and also develop an essay or topic from an earlier unit, refining the thesis and consulting additional sources. These essays can be used to inform and inspire longer research papers at the end of the unit that answer the essential question. By the end of this unit, students will have an appreciation for some of the tendencies of early romanticism and will recognize that this era, like all others, is filled with exceptions, contradictions, and subtleties.

FOCUS STANDARDS

These Focus Standards have been selected for the unit from the Common Core State Standards.

RL.11–12.2: Determine two or more themes or central ideas of a text and analyze their development over the course of the text, including how they interact and build on one another to produce a complex account; provide an objective summary of the text.

RL.11–12.3: Analyze the impact of the author's choices regarding how to develop and relate elements of a story or drama (e.g., where a story is set, how the action is ordered, how the characters are introduced and developed).

RI.11–12.5: Analyze and evaluate the effectiveness of the structure an author uses in his or her exposition or argument, including whether the structure makes points clear, convincing, and engaging.

W.11–12.3: Write narratives to develop real or imagined experiences or events using effective technique, well-chosen details, and well-structured event sequences.

W.11–12.7: Conduct short as well as more sustained research projects to answer a question (including a self-generated question) or solve a problem; narrow or broaden the inquiry when appropriate; synthesize multiple sources on the subject, demonstrating understanding of the subject under investigation.

W.11–12.8: Gather relevant information from multiple authoritative print and digital sources, using advanced searches effectively; assess the strengths and limitations of each source in terms of the task, purpose, and audience; integrate information into the text selectively to maintain the flow of ideas, avoiding plagiarism and overreliance on any one source and following a standard format for citation.

L.11–12.2(a,b): Demonstrate command of the conventions of Standard English capitalization, punctuation, and spelling when writing.

SUGGESTED STUDENT OBJECTIVES

- Read fiction, drama, poetry, biography, and autobiography from the eighteenth and early nineteenth centuries.
- Consider the relationship between art and nature in these works.
- Observe narrative digressions, idiosyncrasies, exaggerations, and biases.
- Consider the dual role of the narrator as a character and as a storyteller.
- Consider the role of the supernatural in the literary works read in this unit.
- Write a story in which they practice some of the narrative devices they have observed in this unit.
- Explore and analyze some of the philosophical ideas in the literary texts—questions of free will, fate, human conflict, and loss.
- Consider the difference between natural and forced language, as explained by Wordsworth.
- Consider both the common tendencies of works of this period and the contradictions, exceptions, and outliers.
- Participate in a seminar discussion in which a philosophical question is explored in relation to a specific text.

SUGGESTED WORKS

(E) indicates a CCSS exemplar text; (EA) indicates a text from a writer with other works identified as exemplars.

    Note: For this shorter unit, teachers may want to choose one novel, several short stories or a play, and poetry.

LITERARY TEXTS

Novels

- *Robinson Crusoe* (Daniel Defoe)
- *Gulliver's Travels* (Jonathan Swift)

- *The Vicar of Wakefield* (Oliver Goldsmith)
- *Emma* (Jane Austen)
- *The Sufferings of Young Werther* (Johann Wolfgang von Goethe)
- *The Surprising Adventures of Baron Munchhausen* (Rudolf Erich Raspe)

Short Story

- "Micromégas" (Voltaire)

Poetry

- "Auguries of Innocence" and *Songs of Innocence and of Experience* (selected poems) (William Blake) (EA)
- "Ode on Indolence" and "Ode on a Grecian Urn" (John Keats) (excerpts)
- *In Memoriam A.H.H.* (Alfred, Lord Tennyson)
- "The Deserted Village" (Oliver Goldsmith)
- "Tintern Abbey," "London, 1802," "The World is Too Much with Us," "Ode: Intimations of Immortality" (William Wordsworth) (excerpts)

INFORMATIONAL TEXTS

- *The Diary of Samuel Pepys* (Samuel Pepys)
- *The Life of Samuel Johnson* (James Boswell)
- "Preface to *Lyrical Ballads*" (William Wordsworth)

ART, MUSIC, AND MEDIA

Art

- John Singleton Copley, *Watson and the Shark* (1778)
- Frederic Edwin Church, *Morning in the Tropics* (1877)
- John Constable, *Seascape Study with Rain Cloud* (1827)
- Théodore Géricault, *The Raft of the Medusa* (1818–1819)
- Jean Honoré-Fragonard, *The Progress of Love: The Pursuit* (1771–1773)
- Henry Fuseli, *The Nightmare* (1781)
- William Blake, *The Lovers' Whirlwind* (1824–1827)

SAMPLE ACTIVITIES AND ASSESSMENTS

For a full Scoring Rubric, see the Appendix.

Note: After reading and discussing a work or pairing of works as a class, students prepare for seminars and essays by reflecting individually, in pairs, and/or in small groups on a given seminar or essay question. In this way, students generate ideas. (Seminar and essay assignments include more than one question. Teachers may choose one or all of the questions to explore in the course of the seminar; students should choose one question for the essay.) Seminars should be held before students write essays so that they may explore their ideas thoroughly and refine their thinking before writing. Textual evidence should be used to support all arguments advanced in seminars and in essays. Page and word counts for essays are not provided here, but teachers should consider the suggestions regarding the use of evidence, for example, to determine the likely length of good essays.

1. COLLABORATION

Reflect on seminar questions, take notes on your responses, and note the page numbers of the textual evidence you will refer to in your seminar and/or essay answers. Share your notes with a partner for feedback and guidance. Have you interpreted the text correctly? Is your evidence convincing? (RL.11–12.1, SL.11–12.1)

2. SEMINAR AND INFORMATIVE/EXPLANATORY WRITING

Read selected poems from Blake's *Songs of Innocence and Experience*. Consider biblical allusion to explain the relationship between Innocence and Paradise. How is Experience a metaphor for the Fall of Man? Use textual evidence from the poems selected to create an original, concise thesis statement. (RL.11–12.1, RL.11–12.4, W.11–12.2, SL.11–12.1, SL.11–12.6)

3. SEMINAR AND INFORMATIVE/EXPLANATORY WRITING

How does Tennyson's *In Memoriam A.H.H.* use nature to express metaphorically human feelings and emotions? What point of view is Tennyson revealing? Use textual evidence from the poem to support an original, concise thesis statement. (RL.11–12.1, RL.11–12.4, W.11–12.2, SL.11–12.1, SL.11–12.6)

4. SEMINAR AND WRITING (ARGUMENT)

Explicate "Ode on Indolence." Agree or disagree with Keats: "This (Indolence) is the only happiness; and is a rare instance of advantage in the body overpowering the Mind." Use textual evidence to support your position. (RL.11–12.1, RL.11–12.4, W.11–12.1, SL.11–12.1, SL.11–12.6)

5. SEMINAR AND WRITING (ARGUMENT)

Does *Robinson Crusoe* reveal Defoe's point of view on imperialism or colonization? Why or why not? Alternatively, you may consider what *Robinson Crusoe* suggests about the author's view of human nature. Is this a reflection of the period in which it was written, or do you think Defoe's view represents a departure from the established beliefs of his day? Use textual evidence to support your position. (RL.11–12.1, RL.11–12.5, W.11–12.2, SL.11–12.1, SL.11–12.6)

6. SEMINAR AND INFORMATIVE/EXPLANATORY WRITING

Compare and contrast the themes found in *Gulliver's Travels* and "Micromégas." Do the texts share similar messages? Do they use satire in the same way? How does Swift's allegory compare to Voltaire's science fiction? Use evidence from both texts and organize in a comparative essay. Include an original, concise thesis statement. (RL.11–12.1, RL.11–12.3, RL.11–12.6, W.11–12.2, SL.11–12.1, SL.11–12.6)

7. SEMINAR AND INFORMATIVE/EXPLANATORY WRITING

Compare the science fiction elements in Voltaire's "Micromégas" and one of the tall tales in *The Surprising Adventures of Baron Munchhausen*. How does the science fiction genre enable the authors to express their ideas? Use textual evidence from both texts to support an original, concise thesis statement. (RL.11–12.3, W.11–12.2, SL.11–12.1, SL.11–12.6)

8. SEMINAR AND INFORMATIVE/EXPLANATORY WRITING

What point of view is revealed by Swift's allegory in *Gulliver's Travels*? How does his allegory satirize human behavior and human history? Are Swift's views reflective of the beliefs of his day? Use textual evidence to support an original, concise thesis statement. (RL.11–12.1, RL.11–12.3, RL.11–12.6, W.11–12.2, SL.11–12.1, SL.11–12.6)

9. SEMINAR AND WRITING (ARGUMENT)

Read *The Vicar of Wakefield*. Is it a sentimental and idealistic novel? Or is it a cynical satire? Use textual evidence to support your position. (RL.11–12.1, RL.11–12.3, RL.11–12.6, W.11–12.2, SL.11–12.1, SL.11–12.6)

10. SEMINAR AND INFORMATIVE/EXPLANATORY WRITING

Read the poems "London, 1802" and "The Deserted Village." What values and concerns do they share? Cite specific evidence from both texts to support an original, concise thesis statement. (RL.11–12.1, RL.11–12.4, W.11–12.2, SL.11–12.1, SL.11–12.6)

11. SPEECH

Recite one of the poems in this unit from memory. Include an introduction that discusses how the poem relates to the natural world. (SL.11–12.6)

12. RESEARCH PAPER

Using specific evidence from various sources studied in this unit, write a research paper that answers the essential question: What role does nature play in eighteenth- and early nineteenth-century literature? Include an original, concise thesis statement to answer this essential question. (RL.11–12.1, RL.11–12.2, W.11–12.7, W.11–12.8)

13. ART/CLASS DISCUSSION

Examine and discuss the artworks listed. Begin by viewing the Church, Copley, and Constable paintings. How did artists of this period frame the relationship between man and nature? Where does man belong in these images—or does he even belong? Now compare the Géricault and the Fragonard. What do you see in these images? Which painting do you believe would be more "typical" of the period? Which looks more romantic in style to you, and why? Do you believe these images were painted for "art's sake," or for a larger social purpose? (SL.11–12.1, SL.11–12.2, SL.11–12.3, SL.11–12.4, SL.11–12.5)

ADDITIONAL RESOURCES

- *William Blake's Notebook* (Online Gallery: Turning the Pages) (British Library)

TERMINOLOGY

Allegory	Elegy	Pastoral	Tall tale
Allusion	Grotesque	Satire	Unreliable narrator
Assonance	Metaphor	Science fiction	
Defamiliarization	Moral imperative	Sturm und drang	
Digression	Narrative devices	Supernatural	

Grade Twelve, Unit Four Sample Lesson Plan

Songs of Innocence and of Experience by William Blake

In this series of five lessons, students read *Songs of Innocence and of Experience* by William Blake, and they:

- Explore the life of William Blake (W.11-12.7, RI.11-12.1, RI.11-12.2, RI.11-12.7, W.11-12.8, SL.11-12.1, SL.11-12.2)
- Examine the historical tradition of illuminated writing (W.11-12.7, RI.11-12.7, SL.11-12.1, SL.11-12.2)
- Explore the romantics' view of the world (W.11-12.7, RI.11-12.1, RI.11-12.2, RI.11-12.3, SL.11-12.1, L.11-12.5)
- Analyze selected poems from *Songs of Innocence and of Experience* (RL.11-12.1, RL.11-12.2, RL.11-12.3, RL.11-12.5, RL.11-12.7, SL.11-12.4, L.11-12.5)
- Study the drawings of William Blake (SL.11-12.4)

Summary

Lesson I: William Blake—An Introduction

Conduct research about:

- The life of William Blake
- The historical tradition of illuminated writing
- The romantics' view of the world (W.11-12.7)

Explore Blake's concept of "mind-forg'd manacles" (SL.11-12.4)

Lesson II: Songs of Innocence

- Explore the content of "Introduction" (RL.11-12.1, RL.11-12.2, SL.11-12.1)
- Identify the speaker of the poem (RL.11-12.1, SL.11-12.1)
- Identify the speaker's audience (RL.11-12.3, RL.11-12.5, SL.11-12.1)
- Examine the illustration of "Introduction" (SL.11-12.1)
- Discuss the impact of the illustration on the reading of the poem (SL.11-12.4, RL.11-12.2, RL.11-12.7)
- Conduct a close reading of "The Shepherd" (RL.11-12.1, RL.11-12.2, RL.11-12.3, RL.11-12.4, L.11-12.5, SL.11-12.6)
- Analyze the pastoral setting of the poem (SL.11-12.1, RL.11-12.3)
- Explore the relationships that the poem depicts (SL.11-12.4, RL.11-12.1, RL.11-12.3, RL.11-12.5)
- Examine the illustration of "The Shepherd" (SL.11-12.1)
- Discuss the impact of the illustration on the reading of the poem (SL.11-12.4, RL.11-12.2, RL.11-12.7)

Lesson III: Songs of Experience

- Annotate "Introduction" to *Songs of Experience* for the speaker's call (RL.11-12.9, W.11-12.2, SL.11-12.4, L.11-12.3)
- Examine Blake's depiction of man's situation (SL.11-12.1, RL.11-12.1, RL.11-12.6)
- Examine the illustration of *Songs of Experience* (SL.11-12.1)
- Discuss the impact of the illustration on the reading of the poem (SL.11-12.4, RL.11-12.2, RL.11-12.7)
- Explore "Earth' Answer" (SL.11-12.1, RL.11-12.6, L.11-12.5)
- Analyze Earth's condition (SL.11-12.4, RL.11-12.6, L.11-12.5)
- Note the use of questions (SL.11-12.1, RL.11-12.1)
- Examine the illustration of "Earth's Answer" (SL.11-12.1)
- Discuss the impact of the illustration on the reading of the poem (SL.11-12.4, RL.11-12.2, RL.11-12.7)
- Explore the romantic ideas that the poem represents (SL.11-12.4, RL.11-12.1)

Lesson IV: Songs of Innocence and of Experience

- Juxtapose "Introduction" to *Songs of Innocence* with "Introduction" to *Songs of Experience* (SL.11-12.1, RL.11-12.9, L.11-12.5)
- Revisit Blake's concept of "mind-forg'd manacles" in the Context of the four poems (SL.11-12.4, RL.11-12.1, RL.11-12.2)
- Select two poems to study independently (one each from *Songs of Innocence and of Experience*) (SL.11-12.1)
- Follow the format of the previous two lessons
- Explore the selected poems' content (SL.11-12.1, RL.11-12.6, L.11-12.5)
- Identify romantic themes in the poems (SL.11-12.4, RL.11-12.1)
- Examine the illustrations of the poems (SL.11-12.1)
- Discuss the impact of the illustrations on the reading of the poems (SL.11-12.4, RL.11-12.2, RL.11-12.7)

Lesson V: Songs of Innocence and of Experience

- Share impressions of the poems (SL.11-12.4, RL.11-12.3, RL.11-12.5, RL.11-12.9)
- Explore the romantic themes in the poems (SL.11-12.4, RL.11-12.1, RL.11-12.2)
- Explore the thematic tensions in the paired poems (SL.11-12.4, RL.11-12.2)
- Evaluate the contribution of the drawings to the reading of the poem (SL.11-12.4)
- Assign the take-home assessment: Compose a four- to five-page essay in which you analyze two poems (one from *Songs of Innocence* and one from *Songs of Experience*) in the context of romanticism (W.11-12.2, W.11-12.4)

Lesson III: Songs of Experience

Objectives

Annotate "Introduction" to *Songs of Experience* for the speaker's call (RL.11-12.9, W.11-12.2, SL.11-12.2, SL.11-12.4, L.11-12.3)

Examine Blake's depiction of man's situation (SL.11-12.1, RL.11-12.1, RL.11-12.6)

Examine the illustration of *Songs of Experience* SL.11-12.1

Discuss the impact of the illustration on the reading of the poem (SL.11-12.4, RL.11-12.2, RL.11-12.7)

Explore "Earth's Answer" (SL.11-12.1, RL.11-12.1, RL.11-12.6, L.11-12.5)

Analyze Earth's condition (SL.11-12.4, RL.11-12.6, L.11-12.5)

Note the use of questions (SL.11-12.1, RL.11-12.1)

Examine the illustration of "Earth's Answer" (SL.11-12.1)

Discuss the impact of the illustration on the reading of the poem (SL.11-12.4, RL.11-12.2, RL.11-12.7)

Explore the romantic ideas that the poem represents (SL.11-12.4, RL.11-12.1)

Required Materials

☐ Class set of *Songs of Innocence and of Experience* by William Blake (The Oxford University Press edition is recommended since it has both the poems and the illustrations.)

☐ Interactive whiteboard

Procedures

1. Lead-In:
Read "Introduction" to *Songs of Experience.*

2. Step by Step:
   a. Annotate the poem for its speaker's call.
   b. A discussion of the students' findings follows. Here are a few examples (a partial list) of the ideas that are likely to emerge.
      • The first sentence is a command (exclamation mark) to "Hear."
      • The "Bard" hears the "Holy Word."
      • The speaker depicts a situation. He speaks of a "lapsed Soul."
      • He describes a "fallen light."
      • But his call suggests that his audience, man, has the power to "return."
      • The third stanza points to a transformation from "Night" to "morn."
      • The third stanza begins with the same charge: "To turn away no more."
   c. Project the illustration of the poem "Introduction" onto an interactive whiteboard or a screen.
      • Direct students to discuss the details of the illustration.
      • Offer prompts to further the discussion:
         – How does the illustration impact the reading of the poem?
         – Does it add to its interpretation or perhaps to its mood?

d. Students transition to the second poem, "Earth's Answer." They read the poem and annotate it for words that depict Earth's situation. Following are a few examples:

- " . . . darkness dread & drear"
- "Stony dread"
- " . . . grey despair"
- Earth is "prison'd"
- The last stanza seems to be a response to the command of the Bard: "Break this heavy chain."

e. Students view the illustration for "Earth's Answer" and discuss its details and how it impacts their reading of the poem.

f. Help the students recall the ideas of the romantics. Then ask the students to discuss the relationship between man and nature as it appears in both poems.

3. Closure:

Student volunteers read the two poems of the lesson aloud.

Differentiation

Advanced

- Select student volunteers to read poems aloud; give the students an opportunity to practice reading with expression, recorded with a video camera, so they can evaluate and improve their performances.

- Encourage students research William Blake and prepare a biography of him for classmates. Students should also research what inspired Blake to write *Songs of Innocence and of Experience* and perhaps present this information as an online poster or podcast.

- Have students create a modern-day interpretation of select poems from *Songs of Innocence and of Experience*. They must be able to justify how the modern version stays true to the original, while also changing style. Perhaps challenge them to create a movie or use an online presentation tool to present their interpretation.

Struggling

- After reading the poems twice, allow students to listen to the poems from *Songs of Innocence and of Experience* to support their understanding of the text.

- Work with a small group to annotate poems from this lesson. Give students a paper copy to annotate or sketch (or use other nonlinguistic representations) to aid in understanding and memory, possibly as a group using a document camera. Alternatively, give students an electronic copy to annotate. Allow students to share their notes on shared online documents or the classroom blog so that all students can benefit from each other's learning in class discussion.

- Encourage students to create their own visual interpretations of poems, as Blake did.

Homework/Assessment

N/A

European Literature: Nineteenth Century

In this eight-week unit, students will observe common tendencies, contradictions, outliers, and subtleties of nineteenth-century romantic literature, including the Victorian, gothic, and Edwardian periods.

ESSENTIAL QUESTION

? How do romantic and Victorian literature embody the tension between art for art's sake and art as a response to social and cultural conflict?

OVERVIEW

In this unit, students explore both form and meaning in literary works and consider historical context. Through close readings of selected texts, students examine how subtle narrative and stylistic details contribute to the meaning of the whole. They consider how certain poems of this unit can be simultaneously intimate and reflective of a larger civilization. Moral conflicts and subtle psychological portrayals of characters are other areas of focus; students consider how novels of the nineteenth century develop character and how their conflicts are both universal and bound by culture. In their essays, students will continue to strive for precision and clarity, paying close attention to the nuances of words.

FOCUS STANDARDS

These Focus Standards have been selected for the unit from the Common Core State Standards.

RL.11–12.3: Analyze the impact of the author's choices regarding how to develop and relate elements of a story or drama (e.g., where a story is set, how the action is ordered, how the characters are introduced and developed).

RL.11–12.4: Determine the meaning of words and phrases as they are used in the text, including figurative and connotative meanings; analyze the impact of specific word choices on meaning and tone, including words with multiple meanings or language that is particularly fresh, engaging, or beautiful. (Include Shakespeare as well as other authors.)

RI.11–12.2: Determine two or more central ideas of a text and analyze their development over the course of the text, including how they interact and build on one another to provide a complex analysis; provide an objective summary of the text.

W.11–12.5: Develop and strengthen writing as needed by planning, revising, editing, rewriting, or trying a new approach, focusing on addressing what is most significant for a specific purpose and audience. (Editing for conventions should demonstrate command of Language standards 1–3 up to and including grades 11–12 on page 54 of the Common Core State Standards.)

W.11–12.7: Conduct short as well as more sustained research projects to answer a question (including a self-generated question) or solve a problem; narrow or broaden the inquiry when appropriate; synthesize multiple sources on the subject, demonstrating understanding of the subject under investigation.

W.11–12.8: Gather relevant information from multiple authoritative print and digital sources, using advanced searches effectively; assess the strengths and limitations of each source in terms of the task, purpose, and audience; integrate information into the text selectively to maintain the flow of ideas, avoiding plagiarism and over-reliance on any one source and following a standard format for citation.

SL.11–12.4: Present information, findings, and supporting evidence, conveying a clear and distinct perspective, such that listeners can follow the line of reasoning, alternative or opposing perspectives are addressed, and the organization, development, substance, and style are appropriate to purpose, audience, and a range or formal and informal tasks.

L.11–12.5(a,b): Demonstrate understanding of figurative language, word relationships, and nuances in word meanings.

SUGGESTED STUDENT OBJECTIVES

- Explain the tension between art for art's sake and art as a response to social and cultural conflict, as expressed in the works of this unit.
- Closely analyze a key passage from a novel and comment on how it illuminates the work as whole.
- Contrast two works by a single author.
- Observe common tendencies, contradictions, outliers, and subtleties of the romantic and Victorian periods in literature.
- Contrast the moral conflicts of characters in two works of this unit.
- Consider how the poetry of this period reflects both on the human psyche and on the state of civilization.
- Analyze how the forms of the poems in this unit contribute to their meanings.
- Explain how the works of this period show signs of early modernism.
- Identify elements of romanticism and gothic romanticism in works of literature.

SUGGESTED WORKS

(E) indicates a CCSS exemplar text; (EA) indicates a text from a writer with other works identified as exemplars.

   Note: This is a longer unit. Teachers may want to select one novel, one play, one long poem, and several short poems. Alternatively, teachers might choose to include two plays instead of a novel, or two long poems instead of a play. The selections of the unit should show a range of literary imagination and contrasting attitudes toward the role of literature in society.

LITERARY TEXTS

Novels

- *The Red and the Black* (Stendhal)
- *The Hunchback of Notre Dame* (Victor Hugo)
- *The Three Musketeers* and *The Count of Monte Cristo* (Alexandre Dumas)
- *Twenty Thousand Leagues Under the Sea* (Jules Verne)
- *The Time Machine* (H. G. Wells)
- *Heart of Darkness* (Joseph Conrad)
- *A Passage to India* (E. M. Forster)
- *Sense and Sensibility* (Jane Austen)
- *Jane Eyre* (Charlotte Brontë) (E)
- *Wuthering Heights* (Emily Brontë)
- *A Christmas Carol* (Charles Dickens)
- *Frankenstein* (Mary Shelley)
- *Dracula* (Bram Stoker)
- *The Picture of Dorian Gray* (Oscar Wilde)

Children's Literature

- *Peter and Wendy* (J. M. Barrie)
- *Alice's Adventures in Wonderland* (Lewis Carroll)
- *The Jungle Book* (Rudyard Kipling)

Drama

- *A Doll's House* (Henrik Ibsen) (E)
- *The Sunken Bell* (Gerhart Hauptmann)
- *The Importance of Being Earnest* (Oscar Wilde) (E)

Poetry

- *The Flowers of Evil* (Charles Baudelaire) (selections)
- *Childe Harold's Pilgrimage* (George Gordon, Lord Byron)
- *The Ballad of Reading Gaol* (Oscar Wilde) (EA)
- "Dover Beach" (Matthew Arnold)
- "Goblin Market" (Christina Rossetti) (EA)
- "Spring and Fall" (Gerard Manley Hopkins)
- Sonnet 43 (Elizabeth Barrett Browning)
- "Love Among the Ruins" (Robert Browning)
- "The Raven" (Edgar Allan Poe)
- "Annabel Lee" (Edgar Allan Poe)
- *The Rime of the Ancient Mariner* (Samuel Taylor Coleridge)

INFORMATIONAL TEXTS

- *Culture and Anarchy* (Matthew Arnold) (excerpts)
- *Faust* (Johann Wolfgang von Goethe) (excerpts, e.g., the opening)
- *Reveries of a Solitary Walker* (Jean-Jacques Rousseau) (excerpts)
- *The Origin of Species* (Charles Darwin) (excerpts)
- *Hard Times* (Charles Dickens) (excerpts)
- *The Decay of Lying* (Oscar Wilde) (EA)
- *Tallis's History and Description of the Crystal Palace, and the Exhibition of the World's Industry in 1851* (John Tallis)

ART, MUSIC, AND MEDIA

Art

- James McNeill Whistler, *Mother of Pearl and Silver: The Andalusian* (1888–1900)
- James McNeill Whistler, *Symphony in White, No.1: The White Girl* (1862)
- James McNeill Whistler, *Arrangement in Gray and Black: The Artist's Mother* (1871)
- James McNeill Whistler, *Symphony in Flesh Colour and Pink: Portrait of Mrs. Frances Leyland* (1871–1874)

SAMPLE ACTIVITIES AND ASSESSMENTS

For a full Scoring Rubric, see the Appendix.

Note: After reading and discussing a work or pairing of works as a class, students prepare for seminars and essays by reflecting individually, in pairs, and/or in small groups on a given seminar or essay question. In this way, students generate ideas. (Seminar and essay assignments include more than one question. Teachers may choose one or all of the questions to explore in the course of the seminar; students should choose one question for the essay.) Seminars should be held before students write essays so that they may explore their ideas thoroughly and refine their thinking before writing. Textual evidence should be used to support all arguments advanced in seminars and in essays. Page and word counts for essays are not provided here, but teachers should consider the suggestions regarding the use of evidence, for example, to determine the likely length of good essays.

1. COLLABORATION

Reflect on seminar questions, take notes on your responses, and note the page numbers of the textual evidence you will refer to in your seminar and/or essay answers. Share your notes with a partner for feedback and guidance. Have you interpreted the text correctly? Is your evidence convincing? (RL.11–12.1, SL.11–12.1)

2. SEMINAR AND INFORMATIVE/EXPLANATORY WRITING

Compare the moral conflict of Julien Sorel in *The Red and the Black* and Nora Helmer in *A Doll's House*. What are their similarities and differences? Organize textual evidence to support an original, concise thesis statement. (RI.11–12.2, RL.11–12.3, W.11–12.1)

3. SEMINAR AND INFORMATIVE/EXPLANATORY WRITING

Analyze an author's view of art (and literature) as expressed in a work from this unit. Organize textual evidence to support an original, concise thesis statement. (RI.11–12.2, W.11–12.1)

4. SEMINAR AND INFORMATIVE/EXPLANATORY WRITING

Closely analyze a key passage from a novel and comment on how setting illuminates the themes of the work as a whole. How do the aesthetics of setting create larger meaning? Consider Notre Dame Cathedral in *The Hunchback of Notre Dame*, the red room in *Jane Eyre*, or the castle in *Dracula*. Organize textual evidence to support an original, concise thesis statement. (RI.11–12.2, SL.11–12.4, W.11–12.1)

5. SEMINAR AND WRITING (ARGUMENT)

According to Charles Darwin: "Of all the differences between man and the lower animal, man's sense of moral conscience is by far the most important." Do you agree with Darwin? Consider *Heart of Darkness*. Does this novel support or challenge Darwin's idea? Organize textual evidence to support your position. (RI.11–12.2, SL.11–12.4, W.11–12.1)

6. SEMINAR AND WRITING (ARGUMENT)

Some people believe Victorians "invented" childhood through art and literature. Is childhood a product of nature and science, or is it socially engineered? What qualities of childhood are illustrated by the children's classics *Peter and Wendy* or *Alice's Adventures in Wonderland*? What social conventions are these texts responding to? What literary devices are used to respond to the adult world of the Victorian era? Organize textual evidence to support your position. (RI.11–12.2, SL.11–12.4, W.11–12.1)

7. SEMINAR AND INFORMATIVE/EXPLANATORY WRITING

Consider *The Jungle Book* as an allegorical tale. What lessons do the laws of the jungle teach the reader? How does the text demonstrate romanticism through science? Organize textual evidence to support an original, concise thesis statement. (RI.11–12.2, SL.11–12.4, W.11–12.1)

8. SEMINAR AND WRITING (ARGUMENT)

How do the poems of this unit—especially those by Arnold, Baudelaire, Hopkins, Wilde, and Robert Browning—grapple with hope and despair? By the end of the poems selected, does hope or despair triumph? How do these poems compare with American poems written at the same time? (See Grade Eleven, Unit Five.) Organize textual evidence to support your position. (RL.11–12.2, SL.11–12.4, W.11–12.1)

9. SEMINAR AND WRITING (ARGUMENT)

Is it helpful or misleading to define literature in terms of trends and movements such as romanticism? Organize textual evidence to support your position. (W.11–12.1, SL.11–12.4)

10. SEMINAR AND INFORMATIVE/EXPLANATORY WRITING

Trace the distinction between logic and emotion in *Sense and Sensibility*. How does this text demonstrate itself as a romantic novel? Compare or contrast its depiction of class and gender hierarchies to another text in this unit. Organize textual evidence to support an original, concise thesis statement. (RL.11–12.2, SL.11–12.4, W.11–12.1)

11. SEMINAR AND WRITING (ARGUMENT)

Consider *The Three Musketeers* or *Twenty Thousand Leagues Under the Sea* as adventure novels. Do these texts serve the reader as a means of entertainment? Or are they meant to illustrate a social statement and moral message? Organize textual evidence to support your position. (RI.11–12.2, W.11–12.1)

12. SEMINAR AND WRITING (ARGUMENT)

Consider the horror novels *Dracula* and/or *Frankenstein*. Are these texts written for the sake of entertaining us with horror and heightening our senses? Or is social commentary weaved into the stories? Organize textual evidence to support your position. (RI.11–12.2, W.11–12.1)

13. SEMINAR AND INFORMATIVE/EXPLANATORY WRITING

Charlotte Brontë once said, "Conventionality is not morality." How is this statement illustrated in her novel *Jane Eyre*? Consider the text as a gothic novel. How do its gothic characteristics help convey its themes? Organize textual evidence to support an original, concise thesis statement. (RI.11–12.2, SL.11–12.4, W.11–12.1)

14. SEMINAR AND WRITING (ARGUMENT)

In *Wuthering Heights*, Catherine has to choose between nature and culture. Explain how this is illustrated in the text. Is this a moral choice? Organize textual evidence to support your position. (RI.11–12.2, SL.11–12.4, W.11–12.1)

15. SEMINAR AND WRITING (ARGUMENT)

Compare and contrast in a balanced argument *Wuthering Heights* or *Jane Eyre* with *Frankenstein* or *Dracula*. All are considered gothic novels. What characteristics make them gothic? Does the gothic motif serve as a source of entertainment, or does it help illustrate social commentary? Organize textual evidence to support your position. (RI.11–12.2, SL.11–12.4, W.11–12.1)

16. SEMINAR AND INFORMATIVE/EXPLANATORY WRITING

H. G. Wells called himself a socialist. How does *The Time Machine* illustrate socialist values? Does this text maintain the tradition of the Victorian novel? How? Organize textual evidence to support an original, concise thesis statement. (RI.11–12.2, SL.11–12.4, W.11–12.1)

17. SEMINAR AND WRITING (ARGUMENT)

Ibsen's *A Doll's House* is considered by some to be the first feminist play. Do you agree or disagree with this designation? What do we mean when we call a piece of literature feminist? Do we make such a judgment according to today's standards or according to the standards in the day the text was written? You may refer to other texts to illustrate your point. Organize textual evidence to support your position. (RI.11–12.2, SL.11–12.4, W.11–12.1)

18. SPEECH

Memorize and recite a poem from this unit (or a two-minute passage from a long poem). Include an introduction that discusses how the poem's structure and form contributes to its meaning. (RI.11–12.2, SL.11–12.4, W.11–12.1)

19. RESEARCH PAPER

Use specific evidence from various sources studied in this unit and/or additional sources to write a research paper that answers the following question: How does the literature of the romantic and Victorian eras show tension between art for art's sake (where art includes literature) and art as a response to social and cultural conflict? Include an original, concise thesis statement to answer this essential question. The essay should reflect your reasoned judgment about the quality and reliability of sources consulted (i.e., why you emphasize some and not others), a balance of paraphrasing and quoting from sources, original thinking, the anticipation and addressing of questions or counterclaims, and the proper citation of sources. Your teacher may give you the opportunity to share and refine your initial research questions on the classroom blog in order to get feedback from your classmates. (RL.11–12.1, RI.11–12.1, W.11–12.7, W.11–12.8)

20. ART/CLASS DISCUSSION

Examine the four paintings by James McNeill Whistler. As you have done throughout this unit, describe with partners the small details and specific elements you can see in each painting. What do you find when you closely examine each painting? What has Whistler done to capture your attention? What draws you into the painting: the color, mood, line, texture, or light? How might these artworks show signs of early modernism? Are these paintings "art for art's sake"? Why or why not? (SL.11–12.1, SL.11–12.2, SL.11–12.3, SL.11–12.4, SL.11–12.5)

ADDITIONAL RESOURCES

- *Introducing Jane Eyre: An Unlikely Victorian Heroine* (National Endowment for the Humanities) (RL.11–12.1, RL.11–12.2)

TERMINOLOGY

Antihero	Feminism	Horror	Sprung rhythm
Adventure	Foreshadowing	Narrator	Symbol
Caste systems	Framed narrative	Romanticism	Victorian
Decadence	Gender	Scientific rationalism	Worldview
Edwardian	Gothic	Social satire	

Grade Twelve, Unit Five Sample Lesson Plan

Wuthering Heights by Emily Brontë

In this series of nine lessons, students read *Wuthering Heights* by Emily Brontë, and they:

Conduct an analytical study of the novel (RL.11–12.1, RL.11–12.2, RL.11.12–3, RL.11–12.4, RL.11–12.10, SL.11–12.1, SL.11–12.4, L.11–12.4)

Note the structure of the novel (RL.11–12.5, RL.11–12.1, RL.11–12.3, SL.11–12.1, L.11–12.3)

Explore the relationships among its characters (RI.11–12.3, RL.11–12.5, RL.11–12.1, SL.11–12.1)

Analyze Heathcliff's and Catherine's love (RL.11–12.1, RL.11–12.2, RL.11–12.9, SL.11–12.4, L.11–12.6)

Summary

Lesson I: *Wuthering Heights*, Form and Narrators

Examine the frame of the novel (RL.11–12.5, RL.11–12.1, RL.11–12.9, SL.11–12.4)

Examine the Earnshaw and Linton family trees (RL.11–12.3, SL.11–12.4, L.11–12.5)

Identify the two main settings of the novel, Wuthering Heights and Thrushcross Grange (RL.11–12.3, RL.11–12.1, SL.11–12.4)

Identify the novel's narrators (RL.11–12.3, SL.11–12.4)

Explore Lockwood's early impression of Wuthering Heights (RI.11–12.2, RL.11–12.6, RL.11–12.1, SL.11–12.1)

Note the mystery that emerges in Chapter III (RL.11–12.5, RL.11–12.1, SL.11–12.1)

Lesson II: Nelly's Story Begins

Explore Heathcliff's origins (RI.11–12.1, RL.11–12.4, SL.11–12.1)

Revisit Chapter IV and identify passages where Mrs. Dean discusses her involvement in the novel's events (RL.11–12.3, SL.11–12.4)

Analyze Nelly's accounts of Catherine (RL.11–12.6, RL.11–12.4, SL.11–12.4)

Note the early relationship between Heathcliff and Catherine (Chapters V and VI) (RL.11–12.1, RL.11–12.2, RL.11–12.9, SL.11–12.4, L.11–12.6)

Lesson III: Catherine, the Lintons, and Heathcliff

Closely analyze the events of Chapter VII (RL.11–12.3, RL.11–12.6, SL.11–12.4, L.11–12.6)

Trace Hindley's attitude towards Heathcliff (RL.11–12.1, SL.11–12.1)

Examine Heathcliff's appeal to Nelly to "make [him] decent" (RL.11–12.2, RL.11–12.9, SL.11–12.4, L.11–12.5)

Explore the change in Catherine (RI.11–12.2, RL.11–12.5, RL.11–12.1, SL.11–12.1, L.11–12.4)

Note Heathcliff's statement that he will "pay Hindley back" (RL.11–12.1, RL.11–12.6, SL.11–12.1)

Analyze the significance of Chapter VII in establishing Nelly's narration (RL.11–12.3, RL.11–12.5, L.11–12.4)

Lesson V: Relationships

Note the change in Heathcliff when he returns (RL.11–12.3, RL.11–12.1, SL.11–12.1)

Analyze Catherine's response to his return (SL.11–12.4, FL.11–12.1, RL.11–12.3)

Examine the growing tension between Catherine and Isabella (RL.11–12.2, RI.11–12.9, SL.11–12.4, L.11–12.5)

Explore Heathcliff's contempt of Edgar (RI.11–12.2, RL.11–12.6, RL.11–12.1, SL.11–12.1)

Begin to explore Catherine's deteriorating physical and mental state (RI.11–12.2, RL.11–12.5, RL.11–12.1, SL.11–12.1)

Lesson IV: Catherine's and Heathcliff's Love

Examine Catherine's decision to marry Edgar Linton (RL.11–12.2, RL.11–12.3, SL.11–12.4)

Revisit Nelly's role as narrator (RL.11–12.3, SL.11–12.1)

Analyze the implication of Catherine's statement: "I *am* Heathcliff" (RL.11–12.1, RL.11–12.6, SL.11–12.4, L.11–12.4)

Note the reason for Heathcliff's departure (RL.11–12.3, RL.11–12.1, SL.11–12.1)

Analyze the significance of Chapter IX in establishing the nature of Heathcliff's and Catherine's love (RL.11–12.2, RL.11–12.4, RL.11–12.5, L.11–12.3)

Lesson VI: Catherine's Death

Continue to explore Catherine's deteriorating physical and mental state (RI.11–12.2, RL.11–12.5, RL.11–12.1, SL.11–12.1)

Analyze the purpose of Isabella's letter (RL.11–12.6, RL.11–12.3, L.11–12.3)

Revisit Heathcliff's contempt for Edgar (Chapter XIV) (RI.11–12.2, RL.11–12.6, RL.11–12.1, SL.11–12.1)

Analyze Heathcliff's words, "I *cannot* live without my life! I cannot live without my soul!" in the context of Catherine's death (SL.11–12.4, RL.11–12.1, RL.11–12.3, L.11–12.3)

Lessons VII, VIII: The Second Generation

Map the characters of the two families (Earnshaw and Linton) (RL.11–12.3, RL.11–12.1, W.11–12.4, L.11–12.3)

Investigate the parallels between the two generations (RL.11–12.2, RL.11.12–3, RL.11–12.6, SL.11–12.4)

Critique Brontë's use of Heathcliff's character as the instrument responsible for creating the parallel structure of the two generations (SL.11–12.4, RL.11–12.1)

Analyze the thematic purpose of the second generation (RL.11–12.1, RL.11–12.2, RL.11.12–3, RL.11–12.6, SL.11–12.4, L.11–12.6)

Probe the conclusion of the novel (RL.11–12.4, RL.11–12.5, L.11–12.3, SL.11–12.1)

Lesson IX: A Love Revisited

Reexamine Catherine's choices (SL.11–12.4, RL.11–12.1, RL.11–12.3, L.11–12.5)

Revisit Heathcliff's motives (SL.11–12.4, RL.11–12.1, RL.11–12.3, L.11–12.5)

Retrace the love between Heathcliff and Catherine (RL.11–12.3, RL.11–12.9, SL.11–12.4)

Select passages that provide insight into their love (RL.11–12.1, SL.11–12.4)

In essay form, examine the ways that the second generation provides a greater insight into Heathcliff's and Catherine's love (W.11–12.2, W.11–12.4, W.11–12.9a, L.11–12.1, L.11–12.2, L.11–12.6)

Lesson IV: Catherine's and Heathcliff's Love

Objectives

Examine Catherine's decision to marry Edgar Linton (RL.11–12.2, RL.11–12.3, SL.11–12.4)

Revisit Nelly's role as narrator (RL.11–12.3, SL.11–12.1)

Analyze the implication of Catherine's statement: "I *am* Heathcliff" (RL.11–12.1, RL.11–12.6, SL.11–12.4, L.11–12.4)

Note the reason for Heathcliff's departure (RL.11–12.3, RL.11–12.1, SL.11–12.1)

Analyze the significance of Chapter IX in establishing the nature of Heathcliff's and Catherine's love (RL.11–12.2, RL.11–12.4, RL.11–12.5, L.11–12.3)

Required Materials

☐ Class set of *Wuthering Heights* by Emily Brontë

Procedures

1. Lead-In:
Students quietly reread Chapter IX.

2. Step by Step:
   a. Students, in small groups, identify key passages for discussion. (The lesson's objectives should serve as a guide.)
   b. Based on the findings in previous activity, students conduct a class discussion. Below are some important passages and prompts:

Heathcliff's action saves Hareton's life.

   — *Why is this incident important?*

Catherine and Nelly discuss Catherine's decision to marry Edgar.

—*Nelly, the story's narrator, is also an active character in the novel. How does she describe Catherine's decision? What are the possible implications of her point of view?*

Catherine tells Nelly that Heathcliff is "more [herself] than [she] is."

—*Why is Catherine's "speech" important?*

Later in the same chapter Catherine says, "I *am* Heathcliff."

—*What does Heathcliff hear? And what does he miss?*

Discuss the connection between Catherine's emotional turmoil and the storm.

3. Closure:

The lesson concludes with the class exploring the nature of Heathcliff's and Catherine's love.

Differentiation

Advanced

- Select student volunteers to read key passages of *Wuthering Heights* aloud; give the students an opportunity to practice reading with expression, recorded with a video camera, so they can evaluate and improve their performances.
- Have students create a modern-day interpretation of a key passage, such as one that addresses the relationship between Heathcliff and Catherine. Students must be able to justify how the modern version stays true to the original, while also changing style. Perhaps challenge them to create a movie or use an online presentation tool to present their interpretation.
- Have students choose an additional piece of literature with which to compare character interaction and tensions. For example, they might select *Jane Eyre* by Charlotte Brontë.
- Encourage students to create notes on online spreadsheets (in a T-chart) that can be shared with all classmates following discussion. This information can be used to help students with the writing assignment.

Struggling

- After reading select passages twice, allow students to listen to select passages of *Wuthering Heights* to support their understanding of the text.
- Work with a small group to identify key passages from *Wuthering Heights*. Allow students to annotate or sketch (or use nonlinguistic representations) to aid in understanding and memory on sticky notes, possibly as a group using a document camera. Allow students to share their notes on shared online documents or the classroom blog so that all students can benefit from each other's learning in class discussion.
- Provide students with a graphic organizer (such as ReadWriteThink's Story Map, Literary Elements Mapping, or Compare and Contrast Map) to use to analyze the tensions among Heathcliff, Catherine, Edgar, and Isabella. Alternatively, give students the opportunity to communicate and collaborate with each other online about the homework, such as on the classroom blog.

Homework/Assessment

Prepare to discuss Heathcliff's return and the growing tensions among Heathcliff, Catherine, Edgar, and Isabella.

European Literature: Twentieth Century

Using Auden's term "Age of Anxiety" as a focal idea, students consider both the breakdown and affirmation of meaning in twentieth-century literature in this final six-week unit.

ESSENTIAL QUESTION

? Why might the twentieth century be regarded as the Age of Anxiety?

OVERVIEW

Through the close reading of "dystopian" works such as *Pygmalion, 1984,* and *Rhinoceros,* students consider the problems inherent in fashioning a perfect society or perfect individual. At the same time, they also consider how authors of the twentieth century affirm the possibility of beauty and meaning—for instance, in T. S. Eliot's *Four Quartets,* Federico García Lorca's *Poem of the Deep Song,* or Thomas Hardy's "The Darkling Thrush." To gain a deeper appreciation of the role of beauty in twentieth-century literature, they appraise connections between poetry and music: for instance, the relation of Eliot's *Four Quartets* to a Beethoven quartet, and the relation of Lorca's poetry to the rhythms of flamenco music. Examining how authors rework classical stories and themes (e.g., in Anouilh's *Antigone* or Camus' *Caligula*), students ponder how historical context affects an enduring story or theme. Students complete research papers in which they consult literary criticism and historical materials. They engage in discussions resembling college seminars, where they pursue focused questions in depth over the course of one or two class sessions. At the close of the unit, students have the opportunity to research the literature they have read over the course of the year and the concepts they have studied.

FOCUS STANDARDS

These Focus Standards have been selected for the unit from the Common Core State Standards.

RL.11–12.3: Analyze the impact of the author's choices regarding how to develop and relate elements of a story or drama (e.g., where a story is set, how the action is ordered, how the characters are introduced and developed).

RL.11–12.6: Analyze a case in which grasping point of view requires distinguishing what is directly stated in a text from what is really meant (e.g., satire, sarcasm, irony, or understatement).

RL.11–12.10: By the end of grade 12, read and comprehend literature, including stories, dramas, and poems, at the high end of the grades 11–CCR text complexity band independently and proficiently.

RI.11–12.5: Analyze and evaluate the effectiveness of the structure an author uses in his or her exposition or argument, including whether the structure makes points clear, convincing, and engaging.

W.11–12.7: Conduct short as well as more sustained research projects to answer a question (including a self-generated question) or solve a problem; narrow or broaden the inquiry when appropriate; synthesize multiple sources on the subject, demonstrating understanding of the subject under investigation.

W.11–12.8: Gather relevant information from multiple authoritative print and digital sources, using advanced searches effectively; assess the strengths and limitations of each source in terms of the task, purpose, and audience; integrate information into the text selectively to maintain the flow of ideas, avoiding plagiarism and overreliance on any one source and following a standard format for citation.

SL.11–12.1: Initiate and participate effectively in a range of collaborative discussions (one-on-one, in groups, and teacher-led) with diverse partners on grades 11–12 topics, texts, and issues, building on others' ideas and expressing their own clearly and persuasively.

L.11–12.6: Acquire and use accurately general academic and domain-specific words and phrases, sufficient for reading, writing, speaking, and listening at the college and career readiness level; demonstrate independence in gathering vocabulary knowledge when considering a word or phrase important to comprehension or expression.

SUGGESTED STUDENT OBJECTIVES

- Read works of the twentieth century, focusing on the earlier decades.
- Consider aspects of modernism (such as anxiety) in their historical context.
- Explain both the breakdown and affirmation of form and meaning in modernist literature.
- Analyze dystopian literature, considering the problems inherent in fashioning a perfect person or society.
- Explain how poems in this unit reflect on poetry itself and its possibilities.
- Examine the implications of modern versions of classical works.
- Identify and explain the musical allusions and their meanings in twentieth-century poetical works in seminars.
- Pursue focused questions in depth over the course of one or two class sessions.
- Explain absurdist and existential philosophy as it applies to literature and theatre.

SUGGESTED WORKS

(E) indicates a CCSS exemplar text; (EA) indicates a text from a writer with other works identified as exemplars.

Note: Teachers may make the literary selections in a number of ways. They may select works across the genres, or they may focus on a particular genre. The selections should address the ideas of anxiety and beauty in some manner and should offer contrasting responses to the tension and crises of the twentieth century.

LITERARY TEXTS

Novels

- *The Mayor of Casterbridge* (Thomas Hardy)
- *Pan: From Lieutenant Thomas Glahn's Papers* (Knut Hamsun)
- *Steppenwolf* (Hermann Hesse)
- *Briefing for a Descent into Hell* (Doris Lessing)
- *1984* (George Orwell)
- *Brave New World* (Aldous Huxley)
- *All Quiet on the Western Front* (Erich Maria Remarque)
- *The Metamorphosis* (Franz Kafka) (E)

Drama

- *Antigone* (Jean Anouilh)
- *Mother Courage and Her Children* (Bertolt Brecht)
- *Caligula* (Albert Camus)
- *Pygmalion* (George Bernard Shaw)
- *Rhinoceros* (Eugene Ionesco) (E)
- *Waiting for Godot* (Samuel Beckett)
- *King Lear* (William Shakespeare)
- *Hamlet* (William Shakespeare)

Poetry

- "The Darkling Thrush" (Thomas Hardy)
- "Archaic Torso of Apollo" (Rainer Maria Rilke)
- "The Second Coming" (William Butler Yeats)
- *Poem of the Deep Song* (Federico García Lorca) (selections)
- *Four Quartets* (T. S. Eliot) (EA)
- *The Wasteland* (T. S. Eliot) (EA)
- "Conversation with a Stone" (Wislawa Szymborska)
- "Suicide in the Trenches" (Siegfried Sassoon)
- "Counter-Attack" (Siegfried Sassoon)
- "The Old Huntsman" (Siegfried Sassoon)
- "Dreamers" (Siegfried Sassoon)
- "The Daffodil Murderer" (Siegfried Sassoon)
- *The Age of Anxiety: A Baroque Eclogue* (W. H. Auden) (EA)

INFORMATIONAL TEXTS

- *Thus Spoke Zarathustra* (Friedrich Wilhelm Nietzsche)
- *Letters to a Young Poet* (Rainer Maria Rilke)
- *The Courage to Be* (Paul Tillich) (excerpts)
- *The Ego and the Id* (Sigmund Freud) (excerpts)

Speech

- "Their Finest Hour" (House of Commons, June 18, 1940) (Winston Churchill) (EA)

Essays

- "Crisis of the Mind" (Paul Valéry)
- "The Fallacy of Success" (G. K. Chesterton) (E)

ART, MUSIC, AND MEDIA

Art

- Pablo Picasso, *Reading at a Table* (1934)
- Henri Matisse, *Blue Nude* (1952)
- Georges Braque, *Candlestick and Playing Cards on a Table* (1910)
- Joan Miró, *The Potato* (1928)
- Kurt Schwitters, *Untitled (Oval Construction)* (1925)
- Piet Mondrian, *Composition No. III* (1921, repainted 1925)

Music

- Ludwig van Beethoven, String Quartet No. 15 in A Minor, Op. 132 (1825)
- Flamenco guitar music (e.g., Carlos Montoya, Paco Peña)

SAMPLE ACTIVITIES AND ASSESSMENTS

For a full Scoring Rubric, see the Appendix.

Note: After reading and discussing a work or pairing of works as a class, students prepare for seminars and essays by reflecting individually, in pairs, and/or in small groups on a given seminar or essay question. In this way, students generate ideas. (Seminar and essay assignments include more than one question. Teachers may choose one or all of the questions to explore in the course of the seminar; students should choose one question for the essay.) Seminars should be held before students write essays so that they may explore their ideas thoroughly and refine their thinking before writing. Textual evidence should be used to support all arguments advanced in seminars and in all essays. Page and word counts for essays are not provided here, but teachers should consider the suggestions regarding the use of evidence, for example, to determine the likely length of good essays.

1. COLLABORATION

Reflect on seminar questions, take notes on your responses, and note the page numbers of the textual evidence you will refer to in your seminar and/or essay answers. Share your notes with a partner for feedback and guidance. Have you interpreted the text correctly? Is your evidence convincing? (RL.11–12.1, SL.11–12.1)

2. SEMINAR AND INFORMATIVE/EXPLANATORY WRITING

How does Auden's "September 1, 1939" (in *The Age of Anxiety*) shed light on the works studied in this unit? Write an essay that uses specific textual evidence to support an original, concise thesis statement. (RL.11–12.4, SL.11–12.4, W.11–12.5, W.11–12.7, W.11–12.8, L.11–12.6)

3. SEMINAR AND INFORMATIVE/EXPLANATORY WRITING

How did Sassoon's war-era poetry contribute to the shaping of existentialism as a philosophy? Write an essay that uses specific textual evidence to support an original, concise thesis statement. (RL.11–12.4, SL.11–12.4, W.11–12.5, W.11–12.7, W.11–12.8, L.11–12.6)

4. SEMINAR AND INFORMATIVE/EXPLANATORY WRITING

How do *All Quiet on the Western Front* and Sassoon's war poems influence and contribute to the existential movement? Write an essay that uses specific textual evidence to support an original, concise thesis statement. (RL.11–12.4, SL.11–12.4, W.11–12.5, W.11–12.7, W.11–12.8, L.11–12.6)

5. SEMINAR AND INFORMATIVE/EXPLANATORY WRITING

Compare Anouilh's *Antigone* with Sophocles's *Antigone* (which students read in ninth grade). Cite at least two sources of outside literary criticism. Write an essay that uses specific textual evidence to support an original, concise thesis statement. (RL.11–12.4, SL.11–12.4, W.11–12.5, W.11–12.7, W.11–12.8, L.11–12.6)

6. SEMINAR AND WRITING (ARGUMENT)

Was Orwell's classic novel *1984* prophetic? Consider the rise, fall, and endurance in the twentieth century of political regimes that restrict personal freedoms. Write an essay that uses specific textual evidence to support your position. (RL.11–12.4, SL.11–12.4, W.11–12.5, W.11–12.7, W.11–12.8, L.11–12.6)

7. SEMINAR AND INFORMATIVE/EXPLANATORY WRITING

Compare the outcasts in two dystopian works in this unit, *1984* and *Brave New World*. How are their struggles different? How are they similar? Write an essay that uses specific textual evidence to support an original, concise thesis statement. (RL.11–12.4, SL.11–12.4, W.11–12.5, W.11–12.7, W.11–12.8, L.11–12.6)

8. SEMINAR AND INFORMATIVE/EXPLANATORY WRITING

What social values are discarded in the dystopian works *1984* and/or *Brave New World*? Write an essay that uses specific textual evidence to support an original, concise thesis statement. (RL.11–12.4, SL.11–12.4, W.11–12.5, W.11–12.7, W.11–12.8, L.11–12.6)

9. SEMINAR AND INFORMATIVE/EXPLANATORY WRITING

Hesse is a master of blending fantasy and reality. He claims his novel *Steppenwolf* has been "violently misunderstood." Consider it as an existential novel. Why could it easily be misunderstood? Write an essay that uses specific textual evidence to support an original, concise thesis statement. (RL.11–12.4, SL.11–12.4, W.11–12.5, W.11–12.7, W.11–12.8, L.11–12.6)

10. SEMINAR AND INFORMATIVE/EXPLANATORY WRITING

Relate the loss of hope and despair to one of the dystopian novels in this unit to Hardy's poem "The Darkling Thrush." From where does this hopelessness derive in both texts? Write an essay that uses specific textual evidence to support an original, concise thesis statement. (RL.11–12.4, SL.11–12.4, W.11–12.5, W.11–12.7, W.11–12.8, L.11–12.6)

11. SEMINAR AND INFORMATIVE/EXPLANATORY WRITING

Consider *Mother Courage and Her Children* as an allegorical, moral tale where war is depicted as a business. What moral is presented by the story? Write an essay that uses specific textual evidence to support an original, concise thesis statement. (RL.11–12.4, SL.11–12.4, W.11–12.5, W.11–12.7, W.11–12.8, L.11–12.6)

12. SEMINAR AND INFORMATIVE/EXPLANATORY WRITING

How is Gregor Samsa's transformation in *The Metamorphosis* a metaphor for the existential experience? Write an essay that uses specific textual evidence to support an original, concise thesis statement. (RL.11–12.4, SL.11–12.4, W.11–12.5, W.11–12.7, W.11–12.8, L.11–12.6)

13. SEMINAR AND INFORMATIVE/EXPLANATORY WRITING

Examine how the author reworks classical stories and themes in Anouilh's *Antigone* and/or Camus's *Caligula*. Consider how historical context affects an enduring story or theme. Write an essay that uses specific textual evidence to support an original, concise thesis statement. (RL.11–12.2, SL.11–12.1, W.11–12.5, L.11–12.6)

14. SEMINAR AND INFORMATIVE/EXPLANATORY WRITING

Consider musical allusions and their contribution to the meaning of twentieth-century poetical works using Eliot's *Four Quartets* and/or Lorca's *Poem of the Deep Song*. What musical characteristics highlight the themes in the poetry? Write an essay that uses specific textual evidence to support an original, concise thesis statement. (RL.11–12.4, SL.11–12.4, W.11–12.5, W.11–12.7, W.11–12.8, L.11–12.6)

15. SEMINAR AND WRITING (ARGUMENT)

Paying close attention to the storm scenes and the role of the fool in *King Lear*, how could the play be regarded as an existential work? Write an essay that uses specific textual evidence to support your position. (RL.11–12.4, SL.11–12.4, W.11–12.5, W.11–12.7, W.11–12.8, L.11–12.6)

16. SEMINAR AND WRITING (ARGUMENT)

Paying close attention to Hamlet's soliloquies, how can *Hamlet* be regarded as a work of existentialism? How does it apply to Auden's concept of anxiety? Write an essay that uses specific textual evidence to support your position. (RL.11–12.4, SL.11–12.4, W.11–12.5, W.11–12.7, W.11–12.8, L.11–12.6)

17. SEMINAR AND WRITING (ARGUMENT)

"The Second Coming" is an allegorical poem that describes the state of Europe after World War I. How do the metaphors in the poem convey meaning? Does the poem reveal an existential world view? Why or why not? Write an essay that uses specific textual evidence to support your position. (RL.11–12.4, SL.11–12.4, W.11–12.5, W.11–12.7, W.11–12.8, L.11–12.6)

18. SEMINAR AND INFORMATIVE/EXPLANATORY WRITING

Compare and contrast how both *The Mayor of Casterbridge* and *Pygmalion* are concerned with fashioning the perfect individual. How do these texts conform to Auden's Age of Anxiety? Write an essay that uses specific textual evidence to support an original, concise thesis statement. (RL.11–12.4, SL.11–12.4, W.11–12.5, W.11–12.7, W.11–12.8, L.11–12.6)

19. SPEECH

Memorize and recite a one- to two-minute passage from one of the texts. Include an introduction that discusses one of the following issues:

- How the passage deals with the question of meaning and meaninglessness
- How the passage comments, directly or indirectly, on historical events (SL.11–12.4)

20. RESEARCH PAPER

Using texts from this unit or additional outside sources, write a research paper that answers the essential question: Why (in literature) might the twentieth century be regarded as the Age of Anxiety? Use textual evidence to support an original thesis statement designed to answer this question. The paper should reflect your reasoned judgment about the quality and reliability of sources consulted (i.e., why you emphasize some and not others), a balance of paraphrasing and quoting from sources, original thinking, the anticipation and addressing of questions or counterclaims, and the proper citation of sources. Your teacher may give you the opportunity to share and refine your initial research questions on the classroom blog in order to get feedback from your classmates. (RL.11–12.1, RL.11–12.2, RI.11–12.1, RI.11–12.2, W.11–12.7, W.11–12.8)

21. ART/CLASS DISCUSSION

Examine the Picasso, Matisse, Mondrian, and Miró images. Do these works of art have anything in common? Do they depict anything you recognize? Do you think they were made for a particular buyer, a patron, or just because the painters wanted to make them? How might you categorize each work, besides "abstract"? How has the artist evolved by the twentieth century to be an untethered individual? Can you see how these artists might be driven by their own artistic tendencies or desires? What are these paintings "about"? (SL.11–12.1, SL.11–12.2, SL.11–12.3, SL.11–12.4, SL.11–12.5)

ADDITIONAL RESOURCES

- *Dystopias: Definition and Characteristics* (ReadWriteThink)

TERMINOLOGY

Absurd	Existentialism	Neologism	Totalitarianism
Affirmation	Free verse	Postmodernism	Understatement
Anxiety	Modernism	Rhetorical device	
Dystopia	Negation	Satire	

Grade Twelve, Unit Six Sample Lesson Plan

Metamorphosis by Franz Kafka

In this series of six lessons, students read *Metamorphosis* by Franz Kafka, and they:

Examine Kafka's novella as a modernist text

Consider aspects of modernism (such as anxiety) in their historical context

Note the wider significance and implications of Gregor's metamorphosis (RL.12.1, RL.12.2, SL.12.1a, SL.12.1d)

Explore the plight of Gregor Samsa — a modern man (RL.12.1, RL.12.2, RL.12.3, SL.12.1a, SL.12.1d)

Summary

Lesson I: Franz Kafka and Modernism

Meet Franz Kafka (biographical information)

Revisit modernist concepts (informational text)

Focus on alienation of modern man

Lesson II: Gregor Samsa's Physical Transformation

Map out events in Part One of the novella (RL.12.5)

Identify passages that illustrate Gregor's state of mind (RL.12.1)

Explore Gregor's remaining humanity (RL.12.1, RL.12.2, SL.12.1a,d)

Lesson III: Growing Alienation of Gregor Samsa

Trace Gregor's continuing transition from a human to a beetle (in Part Two) (RL.12.5)

Juxtapose Gregor's human qualities with his insect features (RL.12.1, RL.12.3, SL.12.1a,d)

(Continue to) explore the bigger picture behind Gregor's persisting humanity (RL.12.1, RL.12.2, RL.12.3, SL.12.1a,d)

Lesson IV: Gregor's Death

Trace the events leading to Gregor's death (RL.5)

Detail Grete's (Gregor's sister) antagonistic attitude toward her brother (in Parts Two and Three) (RL.12.1, RL.12.5, SL.12.1a,d)

Consider why Gregor dies (RL.12.1, RL.12.2, SL.12.1a,d)

Lesson V: Why Does Gregor Samsa Turn into a Beetle?

Characterize Gregor's relationship with his family (RL.12.1)

Explore Gregor's view of his life (RL.12.1)

Investigate Kafka's depiction of Gregor's stubborn humanity (RL.12.1, SL.12.1a,d)

Lesson VI: The Greater Significance and Implications of Gregor's Metamorphosis

Apply Franz Kafka's words: "Anything that has real and lasting value is always a gift from within" to Gregor's inevitable transformation (RL.12.1, RL.12.2, RL.12.3, SL.12.1a,d)

Identify the wider issues of existence and individuality that Kafka explores in *Metamorphosis* (RL.12.1, RL.12.2, SL.12.1a,d)

Examine Kafka's text within the context of modernist and existentialist traditions

Lesson III: Growing Alienation of Gregor Samsa

Objectives

Trace Gregor's continuing transition from a human to a beetle (in Part Two) (RL.5)

Juxtapose Gregor's human qualities with his insect features (RL.12.1, RL.12.3, SL.12.1a,d)

(Continue to) explore the bigger picture behind Gregor's persisting humanity (RL.12.1, RL.12.2, RL.12.3, SL.12.1a,d)

Required Materials

☐ Copies of Part Two of *Metamorphosis*

Procedures

1. Lead-In:

In small groups, students share their annotations (for homework, students read Part Two of *Metamorphosis* and annotate the text for Gregor's continuing transition).

2. Step by Step:

a. Students map out Gregor's continuing transition from human to beetle. Recommended assigned pages: 21–22, 23–25, 26–28, 29–31, 32–34, 35–37, 38–39

b. Discuss findings. Below are samples of what students should look for:

p. 21: does not like the milk

p. 24: change in diet, including rotten food

p. 25: his family discusses his eating habit in third person

p. 25: cannot communicate with his family (but he understands what they say)

p. 26: the maid, scared of Gregor, leaves

p. 29: losing eyesight

p. 30: immobile

p. 31: hanging from the ceiling

p. 32: learning to control his "new" body

p. 33: on the verge of forgetting his mother's voice

p. 34: under the couch

p. 35: prefers the empty room

p. 36: his mother's reaction indicates what he looks like

p. 37: crawls over everything

p. 39: Gregor cannot escape his father's attack

c. Students consider the second objective of the lesson. At the same time that Gregor physically turns into a beetle, he is still human. Find these passages and notice how they juxtapose his human attributes and physical condition. The purpose of this prompt is to lead the students to appreciate Gregor's humanity:

He is proud that he supports his family.

He has plans for the future.

He thinks of his family fondly and tries to avoid hurting them.

He does not mean to scare his mother.

He tries to get out of the way.

He understands all that they say.

They behave as if he is no longer human, when in fact he is.

His feelings are hurt.

3. Closure:

In a concluding class discussion, encourage students to consider the bigger picture here. Why is Gregor so human while his family acts in such an inhuman fashion?

Differentiation

Advanced

- Encourage students to create a digital slide presentation or a movie that shows the juxtaposition of Gregor's physical metamorphosis and human characteristics.

- Challenge students to develop a visual representation to accompany their (homework) paragraph, using ReadWriteThink's "Literary Grafitti Interactive" or by generating a word cloud online.

- During the lesson, allow students to collaborate on a shared online document, explaining connections to other literature read or discussed.

- For the assessment below, students will write two paragraphs. Their challenge is to develop a single topic in two related paragraphs.

Struggling

- During the Lead-In activities, students are given the opportunity to catch up with their annotations. An extensive selection of notes will assure their productive participation in step b.
- Collaboratively create a concept map or an online word cloud of synonyms for the words *metamorphosis* and *juxtaposition* to assist in student understanding.

Homework/Assessment
I. Writing Task

In a well-organized paragraph, discuss Gregor's lingering humanity.

II. Writing Guidelines

- Clearly establish the topic of the paragraph and contextualize it
- Insightfully organize the sequence of ideas according to the purpose of the paragraph
- Present a clear and thorough explication of the passage
- Cite the text using short quotations
- Use Standard English form
- Avoid grammatical and mechanical errors
- Use present simple tense

APPENDIX: SCORING RUBRIC*

	4	3	2	1
Speaking	Speaks clearly and articulately Uses sophisticated and appropriate language Effectively uses tone and emotion Uses an appropriately loud voice Makes effective eye contact with the group	Speaks clearly and articulately Uses a loud voice Makes eye contact with the group	Comment is unclear; may be vague, rambling, or insufficiently explained Volume is too low Words are mumbled Language is inappropriate and/or too colloquial Does not make eye contact with the group	Comment is so unclear as to make it incomprehensible Comment is irrelevant and/or inappropriate to the discussion Language is inappropriate and/or offensive
Arguing from Evidence	Every argument is grounded in relevant texts and/or historical or literary references Evidence from outside the text is detailed, specific, and relevant Makes direct references to specific passages from the text Closely reads the text to make an in-depth and original analysis	Arguments are based in relevant texts and/or historical and literary references Evidence from outside the text is specific and relevant	Arguments have little basis in relevant texts and/or historical and literary references Evidence from outside the text is unspecific, and/or irrelevant Textual evidence used does not support the argument being made and/or is insufficiently or incorrectly explained	Provides no relevant and/or appropriate evidence to support argument
Preparation	All important sections of the text are annotated Annotation shows full understanding of the text Annotation includes sophisticated connections, comments, and/or questions	All important sections of the text are annotated Shows a grasp of key concepts in the text	Some sections are not annotated Does not understand key ideas in the text	Little to no annotation
Leadership	Effectively moves conversation forward by summarizing student ideas, linking student ideas, questioning student ideas, and/or clarifying student ideas Listens closely and reflects upon what others have said Brings out a key idea missed by the group May bring up a relevant idea or question that radically alters the direction of the discussion	Moves conversation forward by summarizing student ideas, linking student ideas, questioning student ideas, and/or clarifying student ideas Listens to others and reflects upon their ideas	Does not effectively move conversation forward Comments do not connect to the ideas previously discussed Does not actively listen and/or take notes	Takes no responsibility for the seminar May not speak at all, or comment may reflect a lack of interest or respect for the group Body language shows disinterest during seminar Comes to seminar unprepared and/or late

*This rubric represents the collective work of teachers at the Brooklyn Latin School over the course of five years. It is intended to be a dynamic document—one that will evolve in response to teacher input.

ABOUT COMMON CORE

Common Core is a nonprofit 501(c)3 organization formed in 2007 to advocate for a content-rich liberal arts education for all students in America's K–12 schools. We believe that a student who graduates from high school without an understanding of culture, the arts, history, literature, civics, and language has been left behind. To improve education in America, we promote programs, policies, and initiatives at the local, state, and federal levels that provide students with challenging, rigorous instruction in the full range of liberal arts and sciences. We also undertake research and projects, such as the Common Core Curriculum Mapping Project, which aim to provide educators with tools that will help students to become strong readers and learners. Go to www.commoncore.org for more information. Despite the coincidence of name, Common Core and the Common Core State Standards are not affiliated.

Common Core has been led by Lynne Munson, as president and executive director, since its founding. From 2001 to 2005, Munson was deputy chairman of the National Endowment for the Humanities. In that post, Munson conceived of and designed Picturing America. The most successful public humanities project in NEH history, Picturing America put more than 75,000 sets of fine art images and teaching guides into libraries, K–12 classrooms, and Head Start centers. From 1993 to 2001, Munson was a research fellow at the American Enterprise Institute, where she wrote *Exhibitionism: Art in an Era of Intolerance*. Munson has written on contemporary cultural and educational issues for numerous national publications, including the *New York Times, The Wall Street Journal, USA Today, Educational Leadership,* and *American Educator*. She has appeared on CNN, FoxNews, CNBC, C-SPAN, and NPR.

Joy Hakim, author, *A History of the US* and *The Story of Science*

Bill Honig, president, Consortium on Reading Excellence (CORE); former California superintendent of public instruction

Carol Jago, director, California Reading and Literature Project at UCLA; former president, National Council of Teachers of English (NCTE)

Juan Rangel, chief executive officer, United Neighborhood Organization (UNO)

ACKNOWLEDGMENTS

Common Core and I, personally, have many people to thank for their support of and contribution to this mapping project. The Bill & Melinda Gates Foundation's support of these Maps was central to their creation. Jamie McKee and Melissa Chabran deserve our deepest thanks. Dane Linn from the National Governors Association encouraged this project all along. David Coleman and Sue Pimentel of the Common Core State Standards ELA writing team have become wonderful colleagues in the course of this work. Our expert advisors—David Driscoll, Toni Cortese, and Russ Whitehurst—provided crucial guidance. And Checker Finn, Pat Riccards, and Andy Rotherham each offered well-timed counsel that was always on target. Wiley's Kate Bradford is an engaged and enthusiastic editor.

We are tremendously thankful to the American Federation of Teachers members, Milken educators, National Alliance of Black School Educators representatives, and the many other teachers and administrators who reviewed our Maps with care, thoroughness, and honesty. I am grateful for the wise guidance and unwavering encouragement of Common Core's trustees. Extra thanks to trustees Pat Forgione, Jason Griffiths, and Carol Jago, who each played a key role in this work. I'm grateful to research assistant Stephanie Porowski, her predecessor James Elias, as well as interns Meagan Estep and Denise Wilkins, each of whose investigatory skills is surpassed only by their ability to keep track of the nearly 200 documents that comprise these Maps. Thanks to Ed Alton for converting our Maps into a navigable—and now interactive—digital feast. And to Shannon Last, Laura Bornfreund, and Kathleen Porter-Magee for perfecting our every last word. Diana Senechal, Melissa Mejias, and Leslie Skelton each made important contributions to our high school Maps. Many thanks to Jack Horak, Ed Spinella, Christine Miller, Donald Holland, and particularly to Stephen Griffith, for keeping our increasingly complex affairs in order.

We've made many new friends as a result of this work as calls and e-mails have poured in from nearly every state. Very special thanks to Buddy Auman and Teresa Chance of the Northwest Arkansas Educational Cooperative, who have helped us to see our Maps in action. Julie Duffield from WestEd introduced us to twenty-first-century outreach. Donna Perrigo, Karen Delbridge, Linda Diamond, Joe Pizzo, Julie Joslin, and Laura Bednar have helped to spread word of our Maps in Arizona, Wyoming, California, New Jersey, North Carolina, and Arkansas. Many others from those states—and from New York, Florida, Ohio, Pennsylvania, and Utah, in particular—deserve our gratitude.

Lastly, the teachers who wrote the Maps deserve the utmost thanks. Each of our lead writers brought deep dedication, along with years of experience, to the project: Sheila Byrd Carmichael, our project coordinator and lead writer of the high school Maps, is an expert on education standards and former leader of the American Diploma Project; Ruthie Stern, who, in addition to her work on the high school Maps, led the writing of the seventy-six sample lesson plans, is a longtime New York City Public Schools teacher and a professor at Columbia Teachers College; Lorraine Griffith, lead writer for the elementary grades, is a fifth-grade teacher in Asheville, North Carolina, coauthor of numerous books on reading, and a Common Core trustee; Cyndi Wells, lead writer for the middle grades, is a teacher and fine arts facilitator in Charlottesville, Virginia, and our project's jack-of-all-trades; and Louisa Moats, author of our pacing guide for reading foundations, is a writer of the CCSS in reading and a true leader in her field. These women stuck with this project as it grew, wonderfully, beyond what any of us originally had imagined. They did all of this despite the challenges of the school schedules, motherhood, book deadlines, family vacations, and much else. It was an honor for me to have the opportunity to work alongside these teachers as they drew on their wealth of knowledge and experience to forge what we hope are tools that their peers nationwide will enjoy.

Lynne Munson
President and Executive Director, Common Core
Washington, D.C.
September 2011

INDEX OF SUGGESTED WORKS

This index lists the creators and titles of works included in the Maps. To search for other information (for example, ideas, places, events) please go to the online version of the Maps at http://commoncore.org/maps/ and use the search function.

A

"A & P" (Updike), 175

Achebe, Chinua, *Things Fall Apart*, 97, 100–101

Addams, Jane, *Twenty Years at Hull House*, 153

"Address at the March on Washington" (King), 59, 60

"Address to the Broadcasting Industry" (1961) [Minow], 175

"Address to William Henry Harrison" (1810) [Tecumseh], 141

The Adventures of Huckleberry Finn (Twain), 152, 154

"Advice to a Prophet" (Wilbur), 175

The Aeneid (Virgil), 47, 48, 49, 50

After Dark (Murakami), 83

Against All Hope: A Memoir of Life in Castro's Gulag (Valladares), 72

The Age of Anxiety: A Baroque Eclogue (Auden), 245, 246, 248

Agosin, Marjorie, *Gabriela Mistral: A Reader*, 71

"Ain't I a Woman?" (May 29, 1851) [Truth], 153

Air (2010) [Shonibare], 99, 101–102

Akutagawa, Ryunosuke
"In a Bamboo Grove," 85
Rashomon and Other Stories, 83, 87

The Alchemist (Jonson), 213, 214

Alice's Adventures in Wonderland (Carroll), 233, 235

"All God's Children Had Wings" (Traditional), 153

All the Pretty Horses (McCarthy), 174, 178

All Quiet on the Western Front (Remarque), 14, 245, 247

Allbery, Debra, "Walking Distance," 25

Allen, Frederick Lewis, *Only Yesterday*, 14

Allende, Isabel
The House of the Spirits, 71, 72–73
The Stories of Eva Luna, 71, 72–73

An Almanack for the Year of Our Lord 1648 (Danforth), 122

Almereyda, Michael, *Night Wraps the Sky: Writings By and About Mayakovsky*, 110

Alvarez, Julia, "Homecoming," 24

"America from the Great Depression to World War II: Photographs from the FSA-OWI, 1935–1945" (Library of Congress), 15

"America" (Ginsberg), 175

American Quarterly, "Towards a Definition of American Modernism" (Singal), 165

Amichai, Yehuda
Open Closed Open: Poems, 98
The World Is a Room and Other Stories, 98

The Analects (Confucius), 84, 86

Anderson, Sherwood, *Winesburg, Ohio*, 164

"Annabel Lee" (Poe), 233

"Anne Hutchinson: Brief Life of Harvard's 'Midwife': 1595–1643 (Gomes), 141, 142, 148–149

"Annexation" (O'Sullivan), 141

Anouilh, Jean, *Antigone*, 245, 247, 248

"The Answer Is No" (Mahfouz), 98

Antigone (Anouilh), 245, 247, 248

Antigone (Sophocles), 37, 38, 39, 41–46, 247

"The Apparition" (Donne), 217–219

Arabian Nights, 98

"Archaic Torso of Apollo" (Rilke), 245

Are Years What? (For Marianne Moore) [1967] (Suvero), 176, 178

Aristotle, *Poetics*, 37, 38, 48, 52, 54–56

Arnold, Matthew
Culture and Anarchy, 234
"Dover Beach," 233, 235

Arrangement in Gray and Black: The Artist's Mother (1871) [Whistler], 234, 237

As I Lay Dying (Faulkner), 164, 166

Asturias, Miguel Angel, 74, 76–79

Aswany, Alaa Al, "The Kitchen Boy," 4

Attar of Nishapur, *The Conference of the Birds: A Sufi Allegory*, 98

Auden, W. H., *The Age of Anxiety: A Baroque Eclogue*, 245, 246, 248

"Auguries of Innocence" (Blake), 223

Augustine, Saint, *Confessions* (Book XI), 189, 190

Austen, Jane
Emma, 223
Sense and Sensibility, 233, 235

The Autobiography of an Ex-Coloured Man (Johnson), 152

The Autobiography of Benjamin Franklin (Franklin), 131

The Autobiography of Malcolm X: As Told to Alex Haley (Malcolm X), 176

"Avant-Garde and Kitsch" (Greenberg), 59

The Awakening (Chopin), 152

Axelrod, Alan, *Patton: A Biography*, 176

Azuela, Mariano, *The Underdogs: A Novel of the Mexican Revolution*, 71

B

Ba, Mariama, *So Long a Letter*, 97
Bacon, Francis
    Novum Organum, 213
    Self-Portrait (1973), 59
Bakhtin, Mikhail, *Rabelais and His World*, 203
Baldwin, James
    "If Black English Isn't a Language, Then Tell Me, What Is?," 165, 166
    Notes of a Native Son, 58
The Ballad of Reading Gaol (Wilde), 233, 235
Balthus, *Le roi des chats (The king of cats)* [1935], 59
Banneker, Benjamin, Benjamin Banneker's Letter to Thomas Jefferson (August 19, 1791), 130
Barks, Coleman, *The Illuminated Rumi*, 98
Barney, Tina, *Marina's Room* (1987), 5
Barrie, J. M., *Peter and Wendy*, 233, 235
Baudelaire, Charles, *The Flowers of Evil*, 233, 235
Bauer, Susan Wise, *The History of the Medieval World: From the Conversion of Constantine to the First Crusade*, 189
Beardsley, Monroe C., "Dostoyevsky's Metaphor of the 'Underground'," 109, 111
"Because I could not stop for Death" (Dickinson), 141
Beckett, Samuel, *Waiting for Godot*, 245
Beethoven, Ludwig van, String Quartet No. 15 in A Minor, Op. 132 (1825), 246
Beirut Blues (Shaykh), 97
Bell, Ed, *Unchained Memories* (2003), 153
Bellow, Saul, *Seize the Day*, 174
Benjamin Banneker's Letter to Thomas Jefferson (August 19, 1791) [Banneker], 130

Benner, Susan E.
    "Complex Feelings about Borges" *The Noé Jitrik Reader: Selected Essays on Latin American Literature*, 72
    The Noé Jitrik Reader: Selected Essays on Latin American Literature, 72
Berman, Ronald, "*The Great Gatsby* and the Twenties," 165
Bernini, Giovanni Lorenzo, *Ecstasy of Saint Teresa* (1647– 1652), 204, 205
Bierstadt, Albert, *Looking Down Yosemite Valley* (1865), 141
"Billy Budd" (Melville), 140
"Birches" (Frost), 165, 167
Bird Pendant (Costa Rica, first century BCE to first century CE), 72, 75
"A Bird came down the Walk" (Dickinson), 141
The Birth of Venus (1486) [Botticelli], 25, 26
Bishop, Elizabeth
    "The Fish," 175
    "One Art," 175
    "Sestina," 175
Bishop, John Peale, "In the Dordogne," 165
"The bitter air" (Daniel), 188
Black Boy (Wright), 14
Black Elk, *Black Elk Speaks*, 165
Black Elk Speaks (Black Elk), 165
Black, James, "The Visual Artistry of *Romeo and Juliet*," 38, 39–40
"The Black Cat" (Poe), 4
"The Black Swan" (Merrill), 175
Blair, Elaine, *Literary St. Petersburg: A Guide to the City and Its Writers*, 109
Blake, William
    "Auguries of Innocence," 223
    The Lovers' Whirlwind (1824– 1827), 223
    Songs of Innocence and of Experience, 223, 224, 226–229
Blok, Aleksandr, "The Twelve," 109, 111

The Bloody Tenent of Persecution, for Cause of Conscience (Williams), 122
"Blowin' in the Wind" (Dylan), 176
Blue Nude (1952) [Matisse], 246, 249
Boccaccio, Giovanni, *The Decameron*, 188, 203, 205
Bogin, Magda, *The House of the Spirits*, 71, 72–73
"Bogland" (Heaney), 25, 28
"The Bonnie Lass o'Fyvie" ("Peggy-O"), 5
"Book of Twilight" (Neruda), 71
The Book of Lamentations (Castellanos), 71
Borges, Jorge Luis
    "The Garden of Forking Paths," 71, 72–73
    "The Secret Miracle," 71, 72–73
Boswell, James, *The Life of Samuel Johnson*, 223
Botticelli, Sandro
    The Birth of Venus (1486), 25, 26
    Primavera (1482), 203
Bourgeois, Louise, *Red Fragmented Figure* (1953), 176, 178
Bowlby, Rachel, "'I Had Barbara': Women's Ties and Wharton's 'Roman Fever'," 153, 155, 157–161
Box with lid (Indian, late sixteenth century), 84
Bradford, William, *Of Plymouth Plantation*, 122, 123
Bradstreet, Anne
    "To My Dear and Loving Husband," 122, 123
    "Upon the Burning of Our House," 122, 123
Brandenburg Gate Address (June 12, 1987) [Reagan], 59, 175
Braque, Georges, *Candlestick and Playing Cards on a Table* (1910), 246
Brave New World (Huxley), 245, 247
Brecht, Bertolt, *Mother Courage and Her Children*, 245, 247
Briefing for a Descent into Hell (Lessing), 245
Brodsky, Joseph, "To Urania," 109

Brontë, Charlotte, *Jane Eyre*, 233, 235, 236

Brontë, Emily, *Wuthering Heights*, 233, 236, 238–241

Brooklyn Bridge (1981) [Burns, dir], 5

Brother, Can You Spare a Dime? The Great Depression of 1929–1933 (Meltzer), 14

Browning, Elizabeth Barrett, Sonnet 43, 233

Browning, Robert, "Love Among the Ruins," 233, 235

Bulgakov, Mikhail, *A Dead Man's Memoir*, 109

Bunyan, John, *The Pilgrim's Progress*, 212, 214

Burkina Faso, hawk mask (no date), 99

Burns, Ken, *Brooklyn Bridge* (1981), 5

The Butterfly's Burden (Darwish), 98

Bynner, Witter, *The Jade Mountain: A Chinese Anthology, Being Three Hundred Poems of the T'ang Dynasty, 618–906*, 83

Byrd, William, *The Secret Diary of William Byrd of Westover, 1709–1712*, 123

Byron, Lord George Gordon, *Childe Harold's Pilgrimage*, 233

C

Caligula (Camus), 245, 248

Calla (1929) [Cunningham], 165

The Call of the Wild (London), 152

Campbell, Joseph, *The Hero with a Thousand Faces*, 49

"Campo di Fiori" (Milosz), 24

Camus, Albert, *Caligula*, 245, 248

Candlestick and Playing Cards on a Table (1910) [Braque], 246

The Canterbury Tales (Chaucer), 188, 190, 205

Caravaggio, Michelangelo Merisi da
   The Death of the Virgin (1604–1606), 38, 39
   The Entombment of Christ (1602–1603), 204

Carpentier, Alejo, "Journey Back to the Source," 71

Carroll, Andrew, *Operation Homecoming: Iraq, Afghanistan,* and the Home Front in the Words of U.S. Troops and Their Families, 49

Carroll, Lewis, *Alice's Adventures in Wonderland*, 233, 235

Carver, Raymond
   "A Small, Good Thing," 175
   "The Current," 175
   "Happiness," 175

"The Cask of Amontillado" (Poe), 4, 6

Castellanos, Rosario, *The Book of Lamentations*, 71

The Catcher in the Rye (Salinger), 174

Cather, Willa, *My Antonia*, 152

Cat's Cradle (Vonnegut), 174

"The Celebrated Jumping Frog of Calaveras County" (Twain), 152

Cervantes, Miguel de, *Don Quixote*, 212, 215

Chagall, Marc, *I and the Village* (1911), 110, 113

Chartres Cathedral (1193–1250), 25

Chaucer, Geoffrey
   The Canterbury Tales, 188, 190, 205
   "The General Prologue" (*The Canterbury Tales*), 188
   "The Knight's Tale" (*The Canterbury Tales*), 188, 189
   "The Monk's Tale" (*The Canterbury Tales*), 188, 190
   "The Nun's Priest's Tale" (*The Canterbury Tales*), 188
   "The Pardoner's Tale" (*The Canterbury Tales*), 188, 190
   "The Wife of Bath's Tale" (*The Canterbury Tales*), 188

Cheever, John, "The Swimmer," 175

Chekhov, Anton
   "The Duel," 109
   "The Head-Gardener's Story," 109
   "Home," 109
   "Rothschild's Fiddle," 109
   The Seagull, 109
   "Sleepy," 109
   "The Steppe," 109
   "Ward No. 6," 109, 111

Chesterton, G. K.
   "The Fallacy of Success," 246
   St. Thomas Aquinas, 189

Chief Joseph the Younger of the Nez Perce Nation, "I will fight no more forever" (October 5, 1877), 153

Ch'ien, T'ao
   "Substance, Shadow, and Spirit," 83, 86

Childe Harold's Pilgrimage (Byron), 233

A Childhood: The Biography of a Place (Crews), 58

Chinese Poems of the Tang and Sung Dynasties: Read by Lo Kung-Yuan in Northern Chinese, Peking Dialect (Folkways Records, 1963), 84, 86

Chopin, Kate
   The Awakening, 152
   "The Story of An Hour," 153, 154–155, 157–161

"Chosen" (2001) [Lee, dir], 5

Christensen, Thomas, *Like Water for Chocolate*, 71, 72–73

A Christmas Carol (Dickens), 233

"Chronicle of a Death Foretold" (García Márquez), 71

Church, Frederic Edwin
   Morning in the Tropics (1877), 223, 225
   Niagara (1857), 141

Churchill, Winston
   "Sinews of Peace Address," 59
   "Their Finest Hour" (House of Commons, June 18, 1940), 246

Cimabue, *Maestà* (1280), 189

"Civil Disobedience" (Thoreau), 141

"A Clean, Well-Lighted Place" (Hemingway), 164

"Clothesline Saga" (Dylan), 5

Coetzee, J. M., *Waiting for the Barbarians or Life and Times of Michael K*, 97

Cole, Thomas, *Romantic Landscape with Ruined Tower* (1832–1836), 141, 143

Coleridge, Samuel Taylor, *The Rime of the Ancient Mariner*, 233

The Collector of Treasures and Other Botswana Village Tales (Head), 97

The Color Purple (Walker), 14, 16

The Columbia Companion to Modern East Asian Literature (Mostow), 84

Common Sense (Paine), 131

The Complete Anti-Federalist (Storing), 131

"Complex Feelings about Borges" (*The Noé Jitrik Reader: Selected Essays on Latin American Literature*) [Jitrik and Benner], 72

Composition No. III (1921, repainted 1925) [Mondrian], 246, 249

Concord (1949) [Newman], 176

The Conference of the Birds: A Sufi Allegory (Farīd al Dīn Attār or Attar of Nishapur)**, 98

Confessions (Book XI) [Saint Augustine], 189, 190

Confucius, *The Analects*, 84, 86

Connell, Richard, "The Most Dangerous Game," 4

Conrad, Joseph, *Heart of Darkness*, 233, 235

"Conscientious Objector" (Millay), 165

Constable, John, *Seascape Study with Rain Cloud* (1827), 223, 225

"The Content of His Character" (Steele), 176, 177, 181–183

"Conversation with a Stone" (Szymborska), 245

Cook, Ebenezer, "The Sot-Weed Factor," 122

Cooper, Anna Julia, "The Higher Education of Women" (*A Voice from the South*), 153

Cooper, James Fenimore, *The Pioneers*, 140

Copley, John Singleton
  Mrs. George Watson (1765), 123, 125
  Paul Revere (ca. 1768), 131
  Watson and the Shark (1778), 223, 225

Cortázar, Julio
  "End of the Game," 71
  "Letter to a Young Lady in Paris," 71

Couder, Auguste, *Siège de Yorktown* (ca. 1836), 131

"Counter-Attack" (Sassoon), 245, 247

The Count of Monte Cristo (Dumas), 233

The Courage to Be (Tillich), 245

Courbet, Gustave, *The Desperate Man* (self-portrait) [1843], 59, 61

The Creation of Adam, Sistine Chapel (1482) [Michelangelo], 5

"Crediting Poetry," The Nobel Prize Acceptance Speech, (1995) [Heaney], 25

Crews, Harry E., *A Childhood: The Biography of a Place*, 58

"Crisis of the Mind" (Valéry), 246

The Crisis (Paine), 131

Criss-Crossed Conveyors, River Rouge Plant, Ford Motor Company (1927) [Sheeler], 165

The Crucible (Miller), 122, 124

Cry, the Beloved Country (Paton), 97, 100, 103–105

Cullen, Countee
  "Saturday's Child," 24
  "Tableau," 164
  "Yet Do I Marvel," 164

Culture and Anarchy (Arnold), 234

Cunningham, Imogen, *Calla* (1929), 165

"The Current" (Carver), 175

Curse of the Golden Flower (2006) [Yimou, dir], 84

D

"The Daffodil Murderer" (Sassoon), 245, 247

Daisy Miller (James), 152

"Dance of Death" ("Danza de la Muerte") [Anonymous], 189

Danforth, Samuel, *An Almanack for the Year of Our Lord, 1648*, 122

Daniel, Arnaut
  "The bitter air," 188
  "I see scarlet, green, blue, white, yellow," 188
  "When the leaf sings," 188

Dante Alighieri
  The Divine Comedy, 193–199
  Inferno (Cantos I-XI, XXXI-XXXIV), 188, 190, 191

Dark Night of the Soul (Saint John of the Cross), 203

"The Darkling Thrush" (Hardy), 25, 245, 247

Darwin, Charles, *The Origin of Species*, 234, 235

Darwish, Mahmoud, *The Butterfly's Burden*, 98

David (1504) [Michelangelo], 25, 26, 203, 205–206

Davis, Stuart, *Owh! In San Pao* (1951), 165

"Days of 1964" (Merrill), 175

"The Day of Doom" (Wigglesworth), 122

A Dead Man's Memoir (Bulgakov), 109

The Death of Ivan Ilyich (Tolstoy), 109, 111

Death and the King's Horseman: A Play (Soyinka), 98

Death of a Salesman (Miller), 175, 177

"The Death of the Hired Man" (Frost), 165, 167

The Death of the Virgin (1604–1606) [Caravaggio], 38, 39

The Debarkation at Marseilles (1622–1625) [Rubens], 213, 216

The Decameron (Boccaccio), 188, 203, 205

DeCarava, Roy, *Untitled* (1950), 5

The Decay of Lying (Wilde), 234

Declaration of Independence (1819) [Trumbull], 131, 133

Declaration of Sentiments, Seneca Falls Convention (1848), 153

The Declaration of Independence (Jefferson), 130, 132, 134–137

Defoe, Daniel, *Robinson Crusoe*, 222, 224

Deity Figure (Honduras, third to sixth century), 72, 75

Demuth, Charles, *My Egypt* (1927), 165, 167

Deposition from the Cross (Entombment) [1525–1528] (Pontormo), 203, 205

Desai, Anita, *In Custody*, 83

"The Deserted Village" (Goldsmith), 223, 225

The Desperate Man (self-portrait) [1843] (Courbet), 59, 61

"The Devious Narrator of 'The Odyssey'" (Richardson), 49

Diary of a Madman and Other Stories (Gogol), 109

The Diary of Samuel Pepys (Pepys), 223

Dickens, Charles
  A Christmas Carol, 233
  Hard Times, 234

Dickinson, Emily
  "Because I could not stop for Death," 141
  "A Bird came down the Walk," 141
  "This is my letter to the World," 141
  "We Grow Accustomed to the Dark," 24, 29, 30, 31–34

Dido and Aeneas (1689) [Purcell], 49

"Digging" (Heaney), 25, 28

Dillard, Annie
  Pilgrim at Tinker Creek, 176
  "Seeing," 176

Dīn Attār, Farīd al (or Attar of Nishapur), *The Conference of the Birds: A Sufi Allegory,* 98

Dinesen, Isak, *Out of Africa,* 98

Dirks, Nicholas B., *The Scandal of Empire: India and the Creation of Imperial Britain,* 84, 85

Dish, Turkey (second half of the sixteenth century), 99

The Divine Comedy (Dante Alighieri), 193–199

A Doll's House (Ibsen), 233, 234, 236

"Domination of Black" (Stevens), 165

Don Quixote (Cervantes), 212, 215

Donne, John
  "The Apparition," 217–219
  "The Flea," 213, 214, 217–219
  "Holy Sonnet 10," 213, 214
  "Song: Goe, and catche a falling starre," 213, 214, 215

Dostoevsky, Fyodor, *Notes from the Underground,* 109, 111, 114–117

"Dostoyevsky's Metaphor of the 'Underground'" (Beardsley), 109, 111

Douglass, Frederick
  "Learning to Read and Write," 58

Narrative of the Life of Frederick Douglass, an American Slave, Written by Himself, 153

Dove, Arthur, *Goat* (1934), 165, 167

"Dover Beach" (Arnold), 233, 235

Dracula (Stoker), 233, 235, 236

"Dream Variations" (Hughes), 24

"Dreamers" (Sassoon), 245, 247

Dreiser, Theodore, *Sister Carrie,* 152

Drinking Coffee Elsewhere: Stories (Packer), 4

Drinking Vessel (Peru, late fifteenth to early sixteenth century), 72

Duccio, *Maestà* (1308–1311), 189

"The Duel" (Chekhov), 109

Dumas, Alexandre
  The Count of Monte Cristo, 233
  The Three Musketeers, 233, 235

Durand, Asher, *Kindred Spirits* (1849), 141

Dürer, Albrecht, *Self-Portrait at the age of 13 (1484),* 59

Dylan, Bob
  "Blowin' in the Wind," 176
  "Clothesline Saga," 5

E

Eagle or Sun? (Paz), 72

Earth (2010) [Shonibare], 99, 101–102

Ecstasy of Saint Teresa (1647–1652) [Bernini], 204, 205

Edwards, Jonathan, "Sinners in the Hands of an Angry God" (July 8, 1741), 123, 124

The Ego and the Id (Freud), 245

Elegy to the Spanish Republic, 70 (1961) [Motherwell], 176

"Elegy Written in A Country Churchyard" (Gray), 25

Elgar, Edward, "Variations on an Original Theme ('Enigma')," 5

Eliot, T. S.
  Four Quartets, 245, 248
  "The Love Song of J. Alfred Prufrock," 165, 166, 167
  The Wasteland, 245

Ellison, Ralph
  "Flying Home," 175, 177, 180–183
  Invisible Man, 174
  "Remembering Richard Wright," 176, 181–183

Emecheta, Buchi, *The Joys of Motherhood,* 97, 100

Emerson, Ralph Waldo
  "Self-Reliance," 141
  "Society and Solitude," 141

Emma (Austen), 223

"End of the Game" (Cortázar), 71

"Endymion" (Keats), 48

The Entombment of Christ (1602–1603) [Caravaggio], 204

The Epic of Gilgamesh (ancient poem from Mesopotamia), 98

Equiano, Olaudah, *Equiano's Travels: The Interesting Narrative of the Life of Olaudah Equiano, or Gustavus Vassa, the African,* 131

Equiano's Travels: The Interesting Narrative of the Life of Olaudah Equiano, or Gustavus Vassa, the African (Equiano), 131

Erdrich, Louise, *Love Medicine,* 174

Esquivel, Laura, *Like Water for Chocolate,* 71, 72–73

An Essay Concerning Human Understanding (Locke), 213

Et in Arcadia Ego (ca. 1630s) [Poussin], 213, 216

Ethan Frome (Wharton), 152

Ethics of the Aristocrats and Other Satirical Works (Zakani), 98, 99

Everyday Stalinism: Ordinary Life in Extraordinary Times: Soviet Russia in the 1930s (Fitzpatrick), 109

"Everyday Use" (Walker), 4

Excavation (1950) [de Kooning], 176

The Exeter Book (Anonymous), 189

"Explicating Donne: 'The Apparition' and 'The Flea'" (Perrine), 217–219

F

The Faerie Queene (Spenser), 203

"The Fallacy of Success" (Chesterton), 246

"The Fall of the House of Usher" (Poe), 140

Family (Jin), 82

Farce of Master Pierre Pathelin (Anonymous), 188

"*A Farewell to Arms*: The Impact of Irony and the Irrational" (Marcus), 165

A Farewell to Arms (Hemingway), 164, 166–167

Farnsworth House, Plano, Illinois (1951), 176, 178

Farrington, Anthony, *Trading Places: The East India Company and Asia, 1600–1834,* 84, 85

Faulkner in the University: Class Conferences at the University of Virginia 1957–1958 (Faulkner and Gwynn, ed.), 25

Faulkner, William
    As I Lay Dying, 164, 166
    Faulkner in the University: Class Conferences at the University of Virginia 1957–1958, 25
    Nobel Prize Acceptance Speech (1949), 59, 60
    "A Rose for Emily," 164

Faust (Goethe), 234

Federalist No. 1 (Hamilton), 131

Federalist No. 10 (Madison), 131, 132

The Feminine Mystique (Friedan), 175

Fire (2010) [Shonibare], 99, 101–102

First Inaugural Speech, March 4, 1933 (Roosevelt), 14

"The Fish" (Bishop), 175

Fitzgerald, F. Scott, *The Great Gatsby,* 164, 166–167, 169–172

Fitzpatrick, Sheila, *Everyday Stalinism: Ordinary Life in Extraordinary Times: Soviet Russia in the 1930s,* 109

Flamenco guitar music
    Carlos Montoya, 246
    Paco Péna, 246

"The Flea" (Donne), 213, 214, 217–219

The Flowers of Evil (Baudelaire), 233, 235

"Flying Home" (Ellison), 175, 177, 180–183

Folio from The Ramayana of Valmiki: Ram a Shatters the Trident of the Demon Viradha (India, 1597–1605), 49

Folkways Records, *Chinese Poems of the Tang and Sung Dynasties: Read by Lo Kung-Yuan in Northern Chinese, Peking Dialect* (1963), 84, 86

Forche, Carolyn, "The Visitor," 175

Ford, Karen, "'The Yellow Wallpaper' and Women's Discourse," 153, 155, 157–161

Forster, E. M., *A Passage to India,* 233

Foster, Fred, "Me and Bobby McGee," 5

Four Mandala Vajravali Thangka (Tibetan, ca. 1430), 84

Four Quartets (Eliot), 245, 248

"A Four Hundred Year Old Woman" (Mukherjee), 58

Frankenstein (Shelley), 233, 236

Franklin, Benjamin
    The Autobiography of Benjamin Franklin, 131
    "The Way to Wealth," *Poor Richard's Almanack,* 131

Frederick C. Robie House (1909) [Wright], 25

Freneau, Philip
    "The Indian Burying Ground," 130
    "The Wild Honeysuckle," 130

Freud, Sigmund, *The Ego and the Id,* 245

Friedan, Betty, *The Feminine Mystique,* 175

From the Back Window, 291 (1915) [Stieglitz], 165

From a Khamsa of Nizamia (1539–1543) [Muhammad], 5

Frost, Robert
    "Birches," 165, 167
    "The Death of the Hired Man," 165, 167
    "Mending Wall," 24, 27, 28, 29, 30
    "The Road Not Taken," 164, 167

Fu, Shen, *Six Records of a Floating Life,* 84

Fuentes, Carlos, *The Old Gringo,* 71

Fugard, Athol, *"Master Harold" . . . and the Boys,* 98

Fuseli, Henry, *The Nightmare* (1781), 223

G

Gabriela Mistral: A Reader (Mistral and Giachetti, Agosin, ed.), 71

Garciá Lorca, Federico, *Poem of the Deep Song,* 245, 248

García Márquez, Gabriel
    "Chronicle of a Death Foretold," 71
    "The Handsomest Drowned Man in the World," 77
    "No One Writes to the Colonel," 71
    One Hundred Years of Solitude, 71, 73
    "The Sea of Lost Time," 71
    "The Solitude of Latin America," Nobel Prize Acceptance Speech, (1982), 72, 73

The Garden of Forking Paths" (Borges), 71, 72–73

Garnier, Robert, *The Jewish Women* (Les Juifves), 203

Gaspar, Kelley Victor, "Going to War," 49

Gates, Henry Louis, Jr., *The Trials of Phillis Wheatley: America's First Black Poet and Encounters with the Founding Fathers,* 122, 124, 126–128

Gates of Paradise (1425–1452) [Ghiberti], 189

The General Prologue *(The Canterbury Tales)* [Chaucer], 188

The General Retires and Other Stories (Thiep), 83, 87

Gentileschi, Artemisia
    Judith and Her Maidservant with the Head of Holofernes (1625), 38
    Self-Portrait as the Allegory of Painting (1638–1639), 59

Géricault, Théodore, *The Raft of the Medusa* (1818–1819), 223, 225

"Gettysburg Address" (Lincoln), 58, 60, 62–64, 153, 155

Ghiberti, Lorenzo, *Gates of Paradise* (1425–1452), 189

Giachetti, Maria, *Gabriela Mistral: A Reader,* 71

"The Gift" (Lee), 24

"The Gift of the Magi" (O. Henry), 4, 8–11

Gilbert, Olive, *The Narrative of Sojourner Truth,* 153

Gilman, Charlotte Perkins
  "Why I Wrote 'The Yellow
    Wallpaper'," 153, 157–161
  "The Yellow Wallpaper," 153,
    154–155, 157–161
Ginsberg, Allen, "America," 175
Giotto
  Arena (Scrovegni) Chapel frescos,
    Padua (after 1305), 189, 191
  Joachim Among the Shepards,
    Arena (Scrovegni) Chapel
    frescos, Padua (after 1305),
    189, 191
  Jonah Swallowed Up by the Whale,
    Arena (Scrovegni) Chapel
    frescos, Padua (after 1305),
    189, 191
  Meeting at the Golden Gate, Arena
    (Scrovegni) Chapel frescos,
    Padua (after 1305), 189, 191
  Raising of Lazarus, Arena
    (Scrovegni) Chapel frescos,
    Padua (after 1305), 189, 191
Giovanni, Nikki, "Love Is," 24
Girl with a Pearl Earring (1665)
  [Vermeer], 213, 216
"Go Down, Moses" (Traditional), 153
Goat (1934) [Dove], 165, 167
"Goblin Market" (Rossetti), 233
The God of Small Things (Roy), 83
Goethe, Johann Wolfgang von
  Faust, 234
  The Sufferings of Young Werther,
    223
Gogh, Vincent van
  Self-Portrait (1889), 59
  The Starry Night (1889), 25, 26
Gogol, Nikoali
  *Diary of a Madman and Other
    Stories*, 109
  *The Inspector-General: A Comedy
    in Five Acts*, 109
  "The Nose," 109
  "The Overcoat," 109, 110–111
  "The Tale of How Ivan Ivanovich
    Quarelled with Ivan
    Nikiforovich," 109
Gogol, Nikolai, "The Overcoat," 4
"Going to War" (Gaspar), 49
The Golden Craft (Tagore), 83

Goldsmith, Oliver
  "The Deserted Village," 223, 225
  The Vicar of Wakefield, 223, 225
The Gold of Troy (Payne), 48
Gomes, Peter J., "Anne Hutchinson:
  Brief Life of Harvard's 'Midwife':
  1595–1643," 141, 142, 148–150
"A Good Man is Hard to Find"
  (O'Connor), 175
*Goodbye Darkness: A Memoir of the
  Pacific War* (Manchester), 47, 49
Gordimer, Nadine, *Living in Hope and
  History: Notes From Our Century*,
  98, 100
"Grass" (Sandburg), 165
Gray, Thomas, "Elegy Written in A
  Country Churchyard," 25
The Great Gatsby (Fitzgerald), 164,
  166–167, 169–172
"*The Great Gatsby* and the Twenties"
  (Berman), 165
Green, Michael, *The Illuminated Rumi*,
  98
Greenberg, Clement, "Avant-Garde
  and Kitsch," 59
Greene, Graham, "The Lost
  Childhood," 59
*The Gulag Archipelago: An Experiment
  in Literary Investigation*
  (Solzhenitsyn), 109
Gulliver's Travels (Swift), 222, 224
Guthrie, Woody, "This Land is Your
  Land," 176
Gwynn, Frederick L., *Faulkner in the
  University: Class Conferences at
  the University of Virginia*,
  1957–1958, 25

H

Ha Jin, *Under The Red Flag*, 83
"'I Had Barbara': Women's Ties and
  Wharton's 'Roman Fever'"
  (Bowlby), 153, 155, 157–161
Haidt, John Valentine, *Young Moravian
  Girl* (ca. 1755–1760), 123, 125
Hamilton, Alexander, *Federalist* No. 1,
  131
Hamilton, Edith, *Mythology*, 48
Hamlet (1948) [Olivier, dir], 213
Hamlet (1964) [Kozintsev and Saphiro,
  dir], 213

Hamlet (Shakespeare), 213, 215, 245,
  248
Hamsun, Knut, *Pan: From Lieutenant
  Thomas Glahn's Papers*, 245
Han Clothing (pre-seventeenth
  century), 84
"The Handsomest Drowned Man in the
  World" (García Márquez), 77
Hang-Hu, Kiang, *The Jade Mountain: A
  Chinese Anthology, Being Three
  Hundred Poems of the T'ang
  Dynasty*, 618–906, 83
"Happiness" (Carver), 175
Hard Times (Dickens), 234
Hardy, Thomas
  "The Darkling Thrush," 25, 245,
    247
  The Mayor of Casterbridge, 245,
    248
"Harlem" (Hughes), 165, 167
Hartley, Marsden, *Mount Katahdin,
  Maine* (1939–1940), 165, 167
Hauptmann, Gerhart, *The Sunken Bell*,
  233
Hawthorne, Nathaniel
  "The Minister's Black Veil," 4,
    140
  "Rappaccini's Daughter," 140
  The Scarlet Letter, 140, 142,
    144–148
  "Young Goodman Brown," 140
Head, Bessie, *The Collector of Treasures
  and Other Botswana Village Tales*,
  97
"The Head-Gardener's Story"
  (Chekhov), 109
Heaney, Seamus
  "Bogland," 25, 28
  "Crediting Poetry," the Nobel
    Prize Acceptance Speech
    (1995), 25
  "Digging," 25, 28
  "The Underground," 25, 27, 28
Heart of Darkness (Conrad), 233, 235
Hemingway, Ernest
  "A Clean, Well-Lighted Place,"
    164
  A Farewell to Arms, 164, 166–167
  "Hills Like White Elephants," 164
  "The Snows of Kilimanjoro," 164

Henry IV, Part I (Shakespeare), 203, 204

Henry, Patrick, Speech to the Virginia Convention (March 20, 1775), 131

Herbert, George, "Love III," 213

The Hero with a Thousand Faces (Campbell), 49

Herrick, Robert
    "To Daffodils," 213, 215
    "To the Virgins, to Make Much of Time," 213, 215

Hesse, Hermann, *Steppenwolf*, 245, 247

Hesselius, Gustavus, *Lapowinsa* (1735), 131

"A High-Toned Old Christian Woman" (Stevens), 165

"The Higher Education of Women" (*A Voice from the South*) [Cooper], 153

Hiller, Arthur, *Man of La Mancha* (1972), 213, 215

"Hills Like White Elephants" (Hemingway), 164

Hilmo, Maidie, *Medieval Images, icons, and Illustrated English Literary Texts: From Ruthwell Cross to the Ellesmere Chaucer*, 189

Hiroshige, Ando, *One Hundred Views of Edo* (1856), 84

Historical Dictionary of Modern Japanese Literature and Theater (Miller), 84

The History of the Medieval World: From the Conversion of Constantine to the First Crusade (Bauer), 189

The History of Mexico: The Ancient Indian World (1929–1935) [Rivera], 72, 75

Hobbes, Thomas, *Leviathan*, 213, 215

Hoff, Bengamin, *The Tao of Pooh and the Te of Piglet*, 84, 86

"Holy Sonnet 10" (Donne), 213, 214

"Home" (Chekhov), 109

"Homecoming" (Alvarez), 24

Homer, *The Odyssey*, 47, 48, 49, 50, 52–56

Homer, Winslow, *A Visit from the Old Mistress* (1876), 153, 155

Honoré-Fragonard, Jean, *The Progress of Love: The Pursuit* (1771–1773), 223

Honwana, Luis Bernardo, *We Killed Mangy-Dog and Other Mozambique Stories*, 97

Hopkins, Gerard Manley, "Spring and Fall," 233, 235

"A House Divided" (Lincoln), 153

"The House on the Hill" (Robinson), 165

The House of the Spirits (Allende and Bogin), 71, 72–73

"How Much Land Does a Man Need?" (Tolstoy), 4

Hughes, Langston
    "Dream Variations," 24
    "Harlem," 165, 167
    "In Time of Silver Rain," 24
    "Mother to Son," 165, 167
    "The Negro Artist and the Racial Mountain," 122, 126–128
    "The Negro Speaks of Rivers," 165, 167

Hugo, Victor, *The Hunchback of Notre Dame*, 233, 235

The Hunchback of Notre Dame (Hugo), 233, 235

Hurst, James, "The Scarlet Ibis," 3, 4

Hurston, Zora Neale, *Their Eyes Were Watching God*, 164, 166

Huxley, Aldous, *Brave New World*, 245, 247

"An Hymn to the Evening" (Wheatley), 122

I

"I Ask My Mother to Sing" (Lee), 24

"I Hear America Singing" (Whitman), 140

"I see scarlet, green, blue, white, yellow" (Daniel), 188

"I Thank God I'm Free at Last" (Traditional), 153

I and the Village (1911) [Chagall], 110, 113

"I Wandered Lonely as a Cloud" (Wordsworth), 25

"I will fight no more forever" (Chief Joseph the Younger of the Nez Perce Nation) [October 5, 1877], 153

Ibsen, Henrik, *A Doll's House*, 233, 234, 236

"If Black English Isn't a Language, Then Tell Me, What Is?" (Baldwin), 165, 166

The Illuminated Rumi (Rumi, Green, and Barks), 98

The Importance of Being Earnest (Wilde), 233

The Imposter: A Play for Demagogues (Usigli and Layera), 71

"In a Bamboo Grove" (Akutagawa), 85

In Custody (Desai), 83

"In the Dordogne" (Bishop), 165

In Memoriam A.H. H. (Tennyson), 223, 224

"In Search of Our Mothers' Gardens" (Walker), 14, 16, 58

"In Trackless Woods" (Wilbur), 25

Inaugural Address (January 20, 1961) [Kennedy], 175

"The Indian Burying Ground" (Freneau), 130

Inferno (Cantos I-XI, XXXI-XXXIV) [Dante], 188, 190, 191

Inness, George, *The Lackawanna Valley* (1855), 141

The Inspector-General: A Comedy in Five Acts (Gogol), 109

Into the Wild (Krakauer), 174

Invisible Man (Ellison), 174

Ionesco, Eugene, *Rhinoceros*, 245

Iran, antique Kurdish rug, 99

Irving, Washington
    "The Legend of Sleepy Hollow," 140
    "Rip Van Winkle," 140

The I Ching (Zhi), 84

Ivory Coast, leopard stool (twentieth century), 99

J

The Jade Mountain: A Chinese Anthology, Being Three Hundred Poems of the T'ang Dynasty 618–906 (Hang-Hu and Bynner), 83

James, Henry, *Daisy Miller*, 152

James Monroe (ca. 1820–1822) [Stuart], 131

Jane Eyre (Brontë), 233, 235, 236

Jefferson, Thomas
 The Declaration of Independence, 130, 132, 134–137
 Letter to Benjamin Banneker (August 30, 1791), 131
 Letter to John Adams (August 1, 1816), 130
 Virginia Statute for Religious Freedom, 130

The Jewish Women (Les Juifves) [Garnier], 203

Jin, Pa, *Family*, 82

Jitrik, Noé, "Complex Feelings about Borges" (*The Noé Jitrik Reader: Selected Essays on Latin American Literature*), 72

Joachim Among the Shepards, Arena (Scrovegni) Chapel frescos, Padua (after 1305) [Giotto], 189, 191

John of the Cross, Saint, *Dark Night of the Soul*, 203

Johnson, James Weldon
 The Autobiography of an Ex-Coloured Man, 152
 "Lift Every Voice and Sing," 153

Jonah Swallowed Up by the Whale, Arena (Scrovegni) Chapel frescos, Padua (after 1305) [Giotto], 189, 191

Jonson, Ben, *The Alchemist*, 213, 214

Jordan, Glenn, *A Streetcar Named Desire* (television episode, 1955), 176, 177

"Journey Back to the Source" (Carpentier), 71

The Joys of Motherhood (Emecheta), 97, 100

The Joy Luck Club (Tan), 174

Judith and Her Maidservant with the Head of Holofernes (1625) [Gentileschi], 38

"July in Washington" (Lowell), 175

The Jungle Book (Kipling), 233, 235

K

Kafka, Franz, *The Metamorphosis*, 245, 248, 250–253

Kandinsky, Wassily, *Moscow I* (1916), 110, 113

Kazan, Elia, *A Streetcar Named Desire* (1951), 176, 177

Keats, John
 "Endymion," 48
 "Ode on a Grecian Urn," 24, 26, 29, 30, 31, 223
 "Ode on Indolence," 223, 224

Kennedy, John F., Inaugural Address (January 20, 1961), 175

Key, Francis Scott, "The Star-Spangled Banner," 130

A Key into the Language of America (Williams), 122

Kharms, Daniil, *Today I Wrote Nothing: The Selected Works of Daniil Kharms*, 109

Khlebnikov, Velimir, "A Slap in the Face of Public Taste," 110, 111

The Killer Angels (Shaara), 14

Kimono with carp, water lilies, and morning glories (1876), 84

Kindred Spirits (1849) [Durand], 141

King Baabu (Soyinka), 98, 99

King James Bible, Psalm 96, 24

King Lear (Shakespeare), 213, 215, 245, 248

King, Martin Luther, Jr.
 "Address at the March on Washington," 59, 60
 "Letter from a Birmingham Jail," 59, 176

Kingston, Maxine Hong, *The Woman Warrior: Memoirs of a Girlhood Among Ghosts*, 58

Kipling, Rudyard, *The Jungle Book*, 233, 235

"The Kitchen Boy" (Aswany), 4

Kleinzahler, August, "The Tartar Swept," 175

Kline, Franz, *Untitled* (1957), 176

"The Knight's Tale" (*The Canterbury Tales*) [Chaucer], 188, 189

Kooning, Willem de, Excavation (1950), 176

Kozintsev, Grigori, *Hamlet* (1964), 213

Krakauer, Jon, *Into the Wild*, 174

Kristofferson, Kris, "Me and Bobby McGee," 5

Kruchenykh, Aleksey, "A Slap in the Face of Public Taste," 110, 111

Kurdish rug (Iran), 99

Kurosawa, Akira, *Rashomon* (1950), 84, 85

L

The Lackawanna Valley (1855) [Inness], 141

"The Lady of Shalott" (Tennyson), 25

LaFantasie, Glenn, "Lincoln and the Gettysburg Awakening," 59, 63–65

Lange, Dorothea, 15, 16

Lapowinsa (1735) [Hesselius], 131

The Last Judgment, Sistine Chapel altar wall (1536–1541) [Michelangelo], 203, 205

Lawler, Traugott, *The One and the Many in the Canterbury Tales*, 189

Lawrence, Jacob
 On The Way (1990), 5
 Self-Portrait (1977), 59, 60
 War Series: The Letter (1946), 165

Layera, Ramon, The Imposter: A Play for Demagogues, 71

Le roi des chats (The king of cats) [1935] (Balthus), 59

"Lear, Tolstoy, and The Fool" (Orwell), 59

Learned Hand, "The Spirit of Liberty" speech at "I Am an American Day" (1944), 165, 167

"Learning to Read and Write" (Douglass), 58

Lee, Ang, "Chosen" (2001), 5

Lee, Harper, *To Kill a Mockingbird*, 13, 14, 15–16, 18–21

Lee, Li-Young
 "I Ask My Mother to Sing," 24
 "The Gift," 24

"The Legend of Sleepy Hollow" (Irving), 140

"A Lemon" (Neruda), 24

Lennon, Thomas, *Unchained Memories* (2003), 153

Leonardo da Vinci
 Mona Lisa (1503–1506), 25, 26, 203, 205–206
 Possible Self-Portrait of Leonardo da Vinci (ca. 1513), 59

Leonardo da Vinci (*continued*)
　　The Virgin and Child with St. Anne (1508), 203, 205
　　Vitruvian Man (1487), 203, 205–206
Lessing, Doris
　　Briefing for a Descent into Hell, 245
　　Martha Quest, 97
"Letter from a Birmingham Jail" (King), 59, 176
"Letter to Albert G. Hodges" (Lincoln), 62–63, 153
Letter to John Adams (August 1, 1816) [Jefferson], 130
"Letter to a Young Lady in Paris" (Cortázar), 71
Letters from an American Farmer (St. John de Crèvecoeur), 131
Letters to a Young Poet (Rilke), 245
Leutze, Emanuel, *Washington Crossing the Delaware* (1851), 5, 131, 133
Leviathan (Hobbes), 213, 215
Li Bai, "A Song of Ch'ang-kan," 83
"Li Bai, "A Hero among Poets, in the Visual, Dramatic, and Literary Arts of China" (Liscomb), 84, 90
Li Bai (Li Po), "A Song of Ch'ang," 87, 89, 91–93
Life on the Mississippi (Twain), 58
The Life of Gargantua and the Heroic Deeds of Pantagruel (Books 1 and 2) [Rabelais], 203
The Life of Samuel Johnson (Boswell), 223
"Lift Every Voice and Sing" (Johnson), 153
Like Water for Chocolate (Esquivel and Christensen, trans.), 71, 72–73
Lincoln, Abraham
　　"Gettysburg Address," 58, 60, 62–64,153, 155
　　"A House Divided," 153
　　"Letter to Albert G. Hodges," 62–63, 153
　　"Second Inaugural Address," 58, 62–63
"Lincoln and the Gettysburg Awakening" (LaFantasie), 59, 63–65

The Lion and the Jewel, 100–101
Liscomb, Kathlyn, Maurean, "Li Bai, A Hero among Poets, in the Visual, Dramatic, and Literary Arts of China," 84, 90
Literary St. Petersburg: A Guide to the City and Its Writers (Blair), 109
Lives of the Most Excellent Painters, Sculptors, and Architects (Vasari), 203
Living in Hope and History: Notes From Our Century (Gordimer), 98, 100
Locke, John, *An Essay Concerning Human Understanding*, 213
"London, 1802" (Wordsworth), 223, 225
London, Jack, *The Call of the Wild*, 152
Long Walk to Freedom: The Autobiography of Nelson Mandela (Mandela), 98, 100, 103–105
Longfellow, Henry Wadsworth
　　"The Sound of the Sea," 25
　　"The Song of Hiawatha," 47, 48
Looking Down Yosemite Valley (1865) [Bierstadt], 141
"Lord Randall" (Anonymous), 24, 189
"Lost in Translation" (Merrill), 86
"The Lost Childhood" (Greene), 59
"The Lotos-Eaters" (Tennyson), 47, 48
"Love Among the Ruins" (Browning), 233, 235
"Love Calls Us to the Things of This World" (Wilbur), 175
"Love III" (Herbert), 213
"Love Is" (Giovanni), 24
Love Medicine (Erdrich), 174
The Lovers' Whirlwind (1824–1827) [Blake], 223
"The Love Song of J. Alfred Prufrock" (Eliot), 165, 166, 167
Lowell, Robert
　　"July in Washington," 175
　　"Memories of West Street and Lepke," 175
　　"Skunk Hour," 175
Lucia, Saint, 74

M

Ma Lin, wall scroll (1246), 84
McCarthy, Cormac

All the Pretty Horses, 174, 178
The Road, 174
McElheny, Kenneth L., *Points of View: An Anthology of Short Stories*, 4
Machiavelli, Niccolo, *The Prince*, 203, 204
MacLeish, Archibald, "The Silent Slain," 165
Madison, James, *Federalist* No. 10, 131, 132
Madonna (Raphael), 205–206
Maestà
　　Cimabue (1280), 189
　　Duccio (1308– 1311), 189
Mahfouz, Naguib
　　"The Answer Is No," 98
　　The Thief and the Dogs, 97
Malcolm X, *The Autobiography of Malcolm X: As Told to Alex Haley*, 176
Man of La Mancha (1966) [Wasserman], 213
Man of La Mancha (1972) [Hiller, dir], 213
Manchester, William, *Goodbye Darkness: A Memoir of the Pacific War*, 47, 49
Mandela, Nelson
　　Long Walk to Freedom: The Autobiography of Nelson Mandela, 98, 100, 103–105
　　Nobel Prize Acceptance Speech (1993), 98, 103–105
"The Man Who Was Almos' a Man" (Wright), 175, 177, 180–183
Marcus, Fred H., "A Farewell to Arms: The Impact of Irony and the Irrational," 165
Marina's Room (1987) [Barney], 5
Markandaya, Kamala, *Nectar in a Sieve*, 83, 85
Marlowe, Christopher, "The Passionate Shepherd to His Love," 203
Márquez, Gabriel García, 76–79
Martha Quest (Lessing), 97
Marvell, Andrew, "To His Coy Mistress," 213, 215
Masaccio, *The Tribute Money*, Brancacci Chapel, Florence (ca. 1420), 189, 191

Mask for the Okuyi Society, Gabon (late nineteenth century), 99

Masked Figure Pendant (Colombia, tenth to sixteenth century), 72, 75

"Master Harold" . . . and the Boys (Fugard), 98

Matisse, Henri, Blue Nude (1952), 246, 249

Matthíasdóttir, Louisa, Self Portrait with Dark Coat, 59, 61

Mayakovsky, Vladimir
Night Wraps the Sky: Writings By and About Mayakovsky, 110
"A Slap in the Face of Public Taste," 110, 111

The Mayor of Casterbridge (Hardy), 245, 248

"Me and Bobby McGee" (Kristofferson and Foster), 5

Medieval Images, Icons, and Illustrated English Literary Texts: From Ruthwell Cross to the Ellesmere Chaucer (Hilmo), 189

Meeting at the Golden Gate, Arena (Scrovegni) Chapel frescos, Padua (after 1305) [Giotto], 189, 191

Meltzer, Milton, Brother, Can You Spare a Dime? The Great Depression of, 1929–1933, 14

Melville, Herman
"Billy Budd," 140
Moby-Dick, 140
"The Piazza," 140

"Memories of West Street and Lepke" (Lowell), 175

Mencken, H. L., "On Being an American," 176

"Mending Wall" (Frost), 24, 27, 28, 29, 30

The Merchant of Venice (Shakespeare), 213

Merrill, James
"The Black Swan," 175
"Days of 1964," 175
"Lost in Translation," 86
"The Octopus," 175

Merwin, W. S.
"My Friends," 175
Twenty Love Poems and a Song of Despair, 71

The Metamorphosis (Kafka), 245, 248, 250–253

Meyer, Doris, The Testimony of Contemporary Latin American Authors, 72

Michaels, Anne, "Phantom Limbs," 24

Michelangelo
The Creation of Adam, Sistine Chapel (c. 1511), 5
David (1504), 25, 26, 203, 205–206
The Last Judgment, Sistine Chapel altar wall (1536–1541), 203, 205
Sistine Chapel, ceiling (1508–1512), 203

"Micromégas" (Voltaire), 223, 224

Midnight's Children (Rushdie), 83, 85, 87

Mies van der Rohe, Ludwig, 178

Millay, Edna St. Vincent, "Conscientious Objector," 165

Miller, Arthur
The Crucible, 123, 124
Death of a Salesman, 175, 177

Miller, J. Scott, Historical Dictionary of Modern Japanese Literature and Theater, 84

Milosz, Czeslaw, "Campo di Fiori," 24

"The Minister's Black Veil" (Hawthorne), 4, 140

Minow, Newton, "Address to the Broadcasting Industry" (1961), 175

Miró, Joan, The Potato (1928), 246, 249

The Miser (Molière), 213, 214

Mishima, Yukio, The Sound of Waves, 83

Mistral, Gabriela, 74, 76–79
Gabriela Mistral: A Reader, 71

Moby-Dick (Melville), 140

Moffett, James, Points of View: An Anthology of Short Stories, 4

Molière, Jean-Baptiste, The Miser, 213, 214

Mona Lisa (1503–1506) [Leonardo da Vinci], 25, 26, 203, 205–206

Mondrian, Piet, Composition No. III (1921, repainted 1925), 246, 249

"The Monk's Tale" (The Canterbury Tales) [Chaucer], 188, 190

Montaigne, Michel de, "Of Cannibals," 203

Montoya, Carlos, Flamenco guitar music, 246

Moon-shaped flask with birds (1723–1725), 84

Moore, Marianne, "Poetry," 25, 165

"Morning Glory" (Nye), 25

Morning in the Tropics (1877) [Church], 223, 225

Morrison, Toni, Song of Solomon, 174

Moscow I (1916) [Kandinsky], 110, 113

Mostow, Joshua, The Columbia Companion to Modern East Asian Literature, 84

"The Most Dangerous Game" (Connell), 4

Mother Courage and Her Children (Brecht), 245, 248

Mother of Pearl and Silver: The Andalusian (1888–1900) [Whistler], 234, 237

"Mother to Son" (Hughes), 165, 167

Motherwell, Robert, Elegy to the Spanish Republic, 70 (1961), 176

Mount Katahdin, Maine (1939–1940) [Hartley], 165, 167

Mrs. George Watson (1765) [Copley], 123, 125

Mrs. James Smith & Grandson (1776) [Peale], 123, 125

Mtwa, Percy, Woza Albert!, 98

Muhammad, Sultan, From a Khamsa of Nizamia (1539–1543), 5

Mukherjee, Bharati, "A Four Hundred Year Old Woman," 58

Mulligan, Robert, To Kill a Mockingbird (film), 15

Murakami, Haruki
After Dark, 83
Norwegian Wood, 83

Murals at Bonampak (Mayan, ca. 580 to 800 CE), 72

Murals from Teotihuacan (Tetitla, ca. 100 BCE to 250 CE), 72

My Antonia (Cather), 152

My Egypt (1927) [Demuth], 165, 167

"My Friends" (Merwin), 175

My Name is Red (Pamuk), 97

My Pushkin (Tsvetaeva), 110
Mythology (Hamilton), 48

N

Nabokov, Vladimir, *Nikolai Gogol*, 110
Naipaul, V. S., 74, 76–79
Narrative of the Life of Frederick Douglass, an American Slave, Written by Himself (Douglass), 153
A Narrative of the Captivity and Restoration of Mrs. Mary Rowlandson (Rowlandson), 123
The Narrative of Sojourner Truth (Truth and Gilbert), 153
Native Son (Wright), 174
Nectar in a Sieve (Markandaya), 83, 85
"The Negro Artist and the Racial Mountain" (Hughes), 122, 126–128
"The Negro Speaks of Rivers" (Hughes), 165, 167
Neihardt, John G., *Black Elk Speaks*, 165
Neruda, Pablo, 74, 76–79
  "Book of Twilight," 71
  "A Lemon," 24
  Twenty Love Poems and a Song of Despair, 71
Neshat, Shirin
  Soliloquy Series (Figure in Front of Steps) (1999), 99
  Untitled (1999), 99, 102
Newman, Barnett, *Concord* (1949), 176
Ngema, Mbongeni, *Woza Albert!*, 98
Ngũgĩ wa Thiong'o, *The River Between*, 97
Niagara (1857) [Church], 141
The Niccolini-Cowper Madonna (1508) [Raphael], 203
Nietzsche, Friedrich Wilhelm, *Thus Spoke Zarathustra*, 245
Nigeria, House of the Head Shrine: Equestrian, Yoruba (nineteenth to twentieth century), 99
Night Wraps the Sky: Writings By and About Mayakovsky (Mayakovsky and Almerayda, ed.), 110
"The Nightingale of Wittenberg" (Sachs), 203
The Nightmare (1781) [Fuseli], 223

The Nightwatch (1642) [Rembrandt Van Rijn], 213, 216
Nikolai Gogol (Nabokov), 110
Nine Carnival Plays (Sachs), 203
1984 (Orwell), 245, 247
No Direction Home (2005) [Scorsese, dir], 5
"No One Writes to the Colonel" (García Márquez), 71
Nobel Prize Acceptance Speech
  William Faulkner (1949), 59, 60
  Gabriel García Márquez (1982), 72, 73
  Seamus Heaney (1995), 25
  Nelson Mandela (1993), 98, 103–105
Norwegian Wood (Murakami), 83
"The Nose" (Gogol), 109
The Nose (Shostakovich), 110
Notes from the Underground (Dostoevsky), 109, 111, 114–117
Notes of a Native Son (Baldwin), 58
Novum Organum (Bacon), 213
Number 28, 1950 (1950) [Pollock], 176
"The Nun's Priest's Tale" (*The Canterbury Tales*) [Chaucer], 188
Nye, Naomi Shihab, "Morning Glory," 25
"The Nymph's Reply to the Shepherd" (Raleigh), 203

O

O. Henry, "The Gift of the Magi," 4, 8–11
"O mio babbino caro" (*Gianni Schicchi*, 1918) [Puccini], 25
Oates, Joyce Carol, "Where Are You Going, Where Have You Been?," 175
O'Connor, Flannery, "A Good Man is Hard to Find," 175
"The Octopus" (Merrill), 175
"Ode: Intimations of Immortality" (Wordsworth), 223
"Ode on a Grecian Urn" (Keats), 24, 26, 29, 30, 31, 223
"Ode on Indolence" (Keats), 223, 224
Odysseus in America: Combat Trauma and the Trials of Homecoming (Shay), 48

The Odyssey (Homer), 47, 48, 49, 50, 52–56
Oedipus the King (Sophocles), 37, 38, 39
"Of Cannibals" (Montaigne), 203
Of Mice and Men (Steinbeck), 14, 164
Of Plymouth Plantation (Bradford), 122, 123
O'Keeffe, Georgia, *Ram's Head, Blue Morning Glory* (1938), 165
The Old Gringo (Fuentes and Peden), 71
"The Old Huntsman" (Sassoon), 245, 247
"The Old Oaken Bucket" (Woodworth), 140
Olivier, Laurence, *Hamlet* (1948), 213
Omnibus: A Streetcar Named Desire (television episode, 1955), 176
"On Being an American" (Mencken), 176
"On Being Brought from Africa to America" (Wheatley), 122, 123, 126–128
On the Divine Proportion (De divina proportione) [Pacioli], 203, 204
"On a Gate-tower at Yuzhou" (Zi'ang), 83
"On Introducing Shakespeare: Richard III" (Pennel), 203, 207–210
On The Way (1990) [Lawrence], 5
Ondaatje, Michael, *Running in the Family*, 58
"One Art" (Bishop), 175
One Day in the Life of Ivan Denisovich (Solzhenitsyn), 109
One Hundred Views of Edo (1856) [Hiroshige], 84
One Hundred Years of Solitude (García Márquez), 71, 73
One Thousand and One Nights or Arabian Nights, 98
One Writer's Beginnings (Welty), 58
The 100 Most Influential Books Ever Written: The History of Thought from Ancient Times to Today (Seymour-Smith), 59
The One and the Many in the Canterbury Tales (Lawler), 189
Only Yesterday (Allen), 14
Open Closed Open: Poems (Amichai), 98

Operation Homecoming: Iraq, Afghanistan, and the Home Front in the Words of U.S. Troops and Their Families (Carroll, ed.), 49

The Origin of Species (Darwin), 234, 235

Orwell, George
  "Lear, Tolstoy, and The Fool," 59
  1984, 245, 247
  "Politics and the English Language," 59

O'Sullivan, John, "Annexation," 141

Out of Africa (Dinesen), 98

"The Overcoat" (Gogol), 4, 109, 110–111

Owh! In San Pao (1951) [Davis], 165

"Ozymandias" (Shelley), 24, 29, 30

P

Pacioli, Luca, *On the Divine Proportion* (De divina proportione), 203, 204

Packer, ZZ, *Drinking Coffee Elsewhere: Stories*, 4

Paine, Thomas
  Common Sense, 131
  The Crisis, 131

Pamuk, Orham, *My Name is Red*, 97

Pan: From Lieutenant Thomas Glahn's Papers (Hamsun), 245

"The Pardoner's Tale" (*The Canterbury Tales*) [Chaucer], 188, 190

The Parthenon (447–432 BCE), 25, 26

A Passage to India (Forster), 233

"The Passionate Shepherd to His Love" (Marlowe), 203

Paton, Alan
  Cry, the Beloved Country, 97, 100, 103–105
  Tales from a Troubled Land, 97

Patton: A Biography (Axelrod), 176

Paul Revere (ca. 1768) [Copley], 131

Payne, Robert, *The Gold of Troy*, 48

Paz, Octavio, 74, 76–79
  Eagle or Sun?, 72

Peale, Charles Willson, *Mrs. James Smith & Grandson* (1776), 123, 125

The Pearl (Steinbeck), 164

Peden, Margaret Sayers, *The Old Gringo*, 71

"Peggy-O,"/"The Bonnie Lass o'Fyvie," 5

Péna, Paco, Flamenco guitar music, 246

Pennel, Charles A., "On Introducing Shakespeare: Richard III," 203, 207–210

Pepys, Samuel, *The Diary of Samuel Pepys*, 223

Perrine, Laurence, "Explicating Donne: 'The Apparition' and 'The Flea'," 217–219

"Peter and The Wolf" (Prokofiev), 5

Peter and Wendy (Barrie), 233, 235

"Petrified Man" (Welty), 175

"Phantom Limbs" (Michaels), 24

The Piano Lesson (Wilson), 165

"The Piazza" (Melville), 140

Picasso, Pablo
  Reading at a Table (1934), 246, 249
  Self-Portrait (1907), 59, 60
  The Tragedy (1903), 38
  Young Acrobat on a Ball (1905), 5

The Picture of Dorian Gray (Wilde), 233

Pilgrim at Tinker Creek (Dillard), 176

The Pilgrim's Progress (Bunyan), 212, 214

Pillar of Sundays (1945) [Smith], 176

The Pioneers (Cooper), 140

The Pisan Cantos (Pound), 165, 167

"Plantation Proverbs" (Uncle Remus), 152

Plath, Sylvia, "Tulips," 175

Poe, Edgar Allan
  "Annabel Lee," 233
  "The Black Cat," 4
  "The Cask of Amontillado," 4, 6
  "The Fall of the House of Usher," 140
  "The Raven," 24, 29, 31, 140, 233
  "The Tell-Tale Heart," 4, 6

Poem of the Deep Song (Garciá Lorca), 245, 248

Poems of Black Africa (Soyinka, ed.), 98

Poetics (Aristotle), 37, 38, 48, 52, 54–56

"Poetry" (Moore), 25, 165

Poets with History and Poets Without History (Tsvetaeva), 110

Poggioli, Renato, "Tragedy or Romance? A Reading of the Paolo and Francesca Episode in Dante's *Inferno*," 193–199

Points of View: An Anthology of Short Stories (Moffett and McElheny, ed), 4

"Politics and the English Language" (Orwell), 59

Pollock, Jackson, *Number 28, 1950 (1950)*, 176

Pontormo, Jacopo da, *Deposition from the Cross (Entombment)* [1525–1528], 203, 205

Porcelain plate with design of dragon, Arita (1690s–1730s), 84

Portrait of a Woman (1770) [Wright], 123, 125

Possible Self-Portrait of Leonardo da Vinci (ca. 1513) [da Vinci], 59

The Post Office (Tagore), 83, 85–86

The Potato (1928) [Miró], 246, 249

Pound, Ezra, *The Pisan Cantos*, 165, 167

Poussin, Nicolas, *Et in Arcadia Ego* (ca. 1630s), 213, 216

Power figure, Congo (nineteenth to twentieth century), 99, 101

Preamble to the Constitution and the Bill of Rights, 131

"Preface to *Lyrical Ballads*" (Wordsworth), 59, 223

Primavera (1482) [Botticelli], 203

The Prince (Machiavelli), 203, 204

The Progress of Love: The Pursuit (1771–1773) [Honoré-Fragonard], 223

Prokofiev, Sergei, "Peter and The Wolf," 5

"Promises of Freedom" (Traditional), 153

The Proud Tower: A Portrait of the World Before the War, 1890–1914 (Tuchman), 109

Psalm 96 (King James Bible), 24

Puccini, Giacomo
  "O mio babbino caro" (*Gianni Schicchi*, 1918), 25
  "Un bel di, vedremo" (*Madama Butterfly*, 1904), 25

Purcell, Henry, *Dido and Aeneas* (1689), 49

Pushkin, Alexander, *Tales of the Late Ivan Petrovich Belkin*, 109

Pygmalion (Shaw), 245, 248

Q

Qur'an manuscript, Syria (late ninth to early tenth century), 99

R

Rabelais, Francois, *The Life of Gargantua and the Heroic Deeds of Pantagruel* (Books 1 and 2), 203

Rabelais and His World (Bakhtin), 203

The Raft of the Medusa (1818–1819) [Géricault], 223, 225

Raising of Lazarus, Arena (Scrovegni) Chapel frescos, Padua (after 1305) [Giotto], 189, 191

Raleigh, Sir Walter, "The Nymph's Reply to the Shepherd," 203

The Ramayana (Valmiki), 47, 48, 50–51, 83

Ram's Head, Blue Morning Glory (1938) [O'Keeffe], 165

Raphael
    Madonna, 205–206
    The Niccolini-Cowper Madonna (1508), 203

"Rappaccini's Daughter" (Hawthorne), 140

Rashomon (1950) [Kurosawa, dir], 84, 85

Rashomon and Other Stories (Akutagawa), 83, 87

Raspe, Rudolf Erich, *The Surprising Adventures of Baron Munchhausen*, 223, 224

"The Raven" (Poe), 24, 29, 31, 140, 233

"The Reader" (Wilbur), 25

Reading at a Table (1934) [Picasso], 246, 249

Reagan, Ronald, Brandenburg Gate Address (June 12, 1987), 59, 175

Red Fragmented Figure (1953) [Bourgeois], 176, 178

The Red and the Black (Stendhal), 233, 234

REESWeb: The World Wide Web Virtual Library for Russian and Eastern European Studies, 113

Relief Plaque (Greece, ca. 450 BCE), 49

Remarque, Erich Maria, *All Quiet on the Western Front*, 14, 245, 247

Rembrandt van Rijn
    The Nightwatch (1642), 213, 216
    Self-Portrait at the Age of 63 (1669), 59, 60
    Self-Portrait at an early age (1628), 59, 60

"Remembering Richard Wright" (Ellison), 176, 181–183

Reveries of a Solitary Walker (Rousseau), 234

Rhinoceros (Ionesco), 245

"Richard Cory" (Robinson), 165

Richard III (Shakespeare), 207–210

Richardson, Scott,"The Devious Narrator of *The Odyssey*," 49, 50

Rilke, Rainer Maria
    "Archaic Torso of Apollo," 245
    Letters to a Young Poet, 245

The Rime of the Ancient Mariner (Coleridge), 233

"Rip Van Winkle" (Irving), 140

Rivera, Diego, *The History of Mexico: The Ancient Indian World* (1929–1935), 72, 75

The River Between (Ngugi wa Thiong'o), 97

The Road (McCarthy), 174

"The Road Not Taken" (Frost), 164, 167

Robinson Crusoe (Defoe), 222, 224

Robinson, E. A.
    "The House on the Hill," 165
    "Richard Cory," 165

"Roman Fever" (Wharton), 153, 154–155, 157–161

Romantic Landscape with Ruined Tower (1832–1836) [Cole], 141, 143

Romeo and Juliet (Shakespeare), 37, 38, 39

Roosevelt, Franklin D., First Inaugural Speech, March 4, 1933, 14

"A Rose for Emily" (Faulkner), 164

Rossetti, Christina, "Goblin Market," 233

Rossiter, Thomas Pritchard, *Washington and Lafayette at Mount Vernon* (1859), 131

Rothko, Mark, *Untitled* (1964), 176

"Rothschild's Fiddle" (Chekhov), 109

Rousseau, Jean-Jacques, *Reveries of a Solitary Walker*, 234

Rowlandson, Mary, *A Narrative of the Captivity and Restoration of Mrs. Mary Rowlandson,* 123

Roy, Arundhati, *The God of Small Things,* 83

Rubens, Peter Paul, *The Debarkation at Marseilles* (1622–1625), 213, 216

"The Ruin" in *The Exeter Book* (Anonymous), 189

Rumi, Jalal Al-Din, *The Illuminated Rumi*, 98

Running in the Family (Ondaatje), 58

Rushdie, Salman, *Midnight's Children,* 83, 85, 87

Russia and the Soviet Union: An Historical Introduction from the Kievan State to the Present (Thompson), 109

S

Sachs, Hans
    "The Nightingale of Wittenberg," 203
    Nine Carnival Plays, 203

St. Basil's Catahedral (Moscow, Russia, 1555–1561), 110, 112

St. John de Crèvecoeur, J. Hector, *Letters from an American Farmer*, 131

St. Thomas Aquinas (Chesterton), 189

Salinger, J. D., *The Catcher in the Rye*, 174

Samet, Elizabeth D., *Soldier's Heart: Reading Literature Through Peace and War at West Point*, 49

Sandburg, Carl, "Grass," 165

Saphiro, Iosif, *Hamlet* (1964), 213

Sassoon, Siegfried
    "Counter-Attack," 245, 247
    "The Daffodil Murderer," 245, 247
    "Dreamers," 245, 247
    "The Old Huntsman," 245, 247
    "Suicide in the Trenches," 245, 247

"Saturday's Child" (Cullen), 24

The Scandal of Empire: India and the Creation of Imperial Britain (Dirks), 84, 85

"The Scarlet Ibis" (Hurst), 3, 4

The Scarlet Letter (Hawthorne), 140, 142, 144–148

Scenes from the Life of Buddha (Pakistan or Afghanistan, ca. late second to early third century), 84

Schwitters, Kurt, *Untitled (Oval Construction)* [1925], 246

Scorsese, Martin, *No Direction Home* (2005), 5

Seagram Building, New York City, New York (1957), 176, 178

The Seagull (Chekhov), 109

Seascape Study with Rain Cloud (1827) [Constable], 223, 225

"The Sea of Lost Time" (García Márquez), 71

"Second Inaugural Address" (Lincoln), 58, 62–63

"The Second Coming" (Yeats), 245, 248

The Secret Diary of William Byrd of Westover, 1709–1712 (Byrd), 123

"The Secret Life of Walter Mitty" (Thurber), 4

The Secret Miracle" (Borges), 71, 72–73

Seeger, Pete, "Where Have All the Flowers Gone?," 176

"Seeing" (Dillard), 176

Seize the Day (Bellow), 174

Self-Portrait (1433) [Van Eyck], 59

Self-Portrait (1889) [Van Gogh], 59

Self-Portrait (1907) [Picasso], 59, 60

Self-Portrait (1973) [Bacon], 59

Self-Portrait (1977) [Lawrence], 59, 60

Self-Portrait as the Allegory of Painting (1638–1639) [Gentileschi], 59

Self-Portrait at the age of 13 (1484) [Dürer], 59

Self-Portrait at the Age of 63 (1669) [Rembrandt Van Rijn], 59, 60

Self-Portrait at an early age (1628) [Rembrandt Van Rijn], 59, 60

Self-Portrait with Dark Coat (Matthíasdóttir), 59, 61

"Self-Reliance" (Emerson), 141

The Selling of Joseph: A Memorial (Sewall), 122

Sense and Sensibility (Austen), 233, 235

"Sestina" (Bishop), 175

Sewall, Samuel, *The Selling of Joseph: A Memorial,* 122

Seymour-Smith, Martin, Excerpts from *The 100 Most Influential Books Ever Written: The History of Thought from Ancient Times to Today,* 59

Shaara, Michael, *The Killer Angels,* 14

Shakespeare, William
  Hamlet, 213, 215, 245, 248
  Henry IV, Part I, 203, 204
  King Lear, 213, 215, 245, 248
  The Merchant of Venice, 213
  Richard III, 203, 207–210
  Romeo and Juliet, 37, 38, 39
  Sonnet 29, 203
  Sonnet 30, 203
  Sonnet 40, 203
  Sonnet 73, 24, 29
  Sonnet 116, 203
  Sonnet 128, 203
  Sonnet 130, 203
  Sonnet 143, 203
  Sonnet 146, 203
  The Tragedy of Macbeth, 203
  The Tragedy of Macbeth, 204

Shaw, George Bernard, *Pygmalion,* 245, 248

Shay, Jonathan, *Odysseus in America: Combat Trauma and the Trials of Homecoming,* 48

Shaykh, Hanan al-, *Beirut Blues,* 97

Sheeler, Charles, *Criss-Crossed Conveyors, River Rouge Plant, Ford Motor Company* (1927), 165

Shelley, Mary, *Frankenstein,* 233, 236

Shelley, Percy Bysshe, "Ozymandias," 24, 29, 30

Shokoff, James, "Soul-Making in 'Ode on a Grecian Urn'," 29, 30, 31

Shonibare, Yinka
  Air (2010), 99, 101–102
  Earth (2010), 99, 101–102
  Fire (2010), 99, 101–102
  Water (2010), 99, 101–102

Shostakovich, Dmitri, *The Nose,* 110

Siège de Yorktown (ca. 1836) [Couder], 131

"The Silent Slain" (MacLeish), 165

Simon, Barney, *Woza Albert!,* 98

"Sinews of Peace Address" (Churchill), 59

Singal, Daniel Joseph, "Towards a Definition of American Modernism," 165, 166–167

"Sinners in the Hands of An Angry God" (July 8, 1741) [Edwards], 123, 124

Sir Gawain and the Green Knight (Anonymous), 188, 189

Sister Carrie (Dreiser), 152

Sistine Chapel, ceiling (1508–1512) [Michelangelo], 203

Six Records of a Floating Life (Fu), 84

"A Sketch of the Past" (Woolf), 58

"Skunk Hour" (Lowell), 175

"A Slap in the Face of Public Taste" (Khlebnikov, Kruchenykh, and Mayakovsky), 110, 111

"Sleepy" (Chekhov), 109

"A Small, Good Thing" (Carver), 175

Smith, David, *Pillar of Sundays* (1945), 176

"The Snows of Kilimanjoro" (Hemingway), 164

So Long a Letter (Ba), 97

"Society and Solitude" (Emerson), 141

Soldier's Heart: Reading Literature Through Peace and War at West Point (Samet), 49

Soliloquy Series (Figure in Front of Steps) [1999] (Neshat), 99

"The Solitude of Latin America," Nobel Prize Acceptance Speech, 1982 (García Márquez), 72, 73

"The Solitude of Self" (February 20, 1892) [Stanton], 165

Solzhenitsyn, Aleksandr
  The Gulag Archipelago: An Experiment in Literary Investigation, 109
  One Day in the Life of Ivan Denisovich, 109

"Song: Goe, and catche a falling starre" (Donne), 213, 214, 215

"Song of Myself" (Whitman), 140

Song of Solomon (Morrison), 174

"The Song of Hiawatha" (Longfellow), 47, 48

"Song VII" (Tagore), 83

"A Song of Ch'ang" (Li Bai) [Li Po], 89, 91–93

"A Song of Ch'ang-kan" (Bai), 83
"A Song of Ch'ang-Kan" (Po), 87
Songling, Pu, *Strange Tales from a Chinese Studio,* 83
Songs of Innocence and of Experience (Blake), 223, 224, 226–229
Sonnet 29 (Shakespeare), 203
Sonnet 30 (Shakespeare), 203
Sonnet 40 (Shakespeare), 203
Sonnet 43 (Browning), 233
Sonnet 73 (Shakespeare), 24, 29
Sonnet 116 (Shakespeare), 203
Sonnet 128 (Shakespeare), 203
Sonnet 130 (Shakespeare), 203
Sonnet 143 (Shakespeare), 203
Sonnet 146 (Shakespeare), 203
Sophocles
    Antigone, 37, 38, 39, 41–46, 247
    Oedipus the King, 37, 38, 39
"The Sot-Weed Factor" (Cook), 122
"Soul-Making in 'Ode on a Grecian Urn'" (Shokoff), 29, 30, 31
"The Sound of the Sea" (Longfellow), 25
The Sound of Waves (Mishima), 83
Soyinka, Wole
    Death and the King's Horseman: A Play, 98
    King Baabu, 98, 99
    Poems of Black Africa, 98
Speech to the Virginia Convention (March 20, 1775) [Henry], 131
Spenser, Edmund, *The Faerie Queene,* 203
"Spirit, Substance, Shadow" (Ch'ien), 86
"The Spirit of Liberty" speech at "I Am an American Day" (Learned Hand, 1944), 165, 167
"Spring and Fall" (Hopkins), 233, 235
Standing female figure, Mali (late nineteenth or early twentieth century), 99, 101
Stanton, Elizabeth Cady, "The Solitude of Self" (February 20, 1892), 165
"The Star-Spangled Banner" (Key), 130
The Starry Night (1889) [van Gogh], 25, 26
Steele, Shelby, "The Content of His Character," 176, 177, 181–183

Steinbeck, John
    Of Mice and Men, 14, 164
    The Pearl, 164
Stendhal, *The Red and the Black,* 233, 234
"The Steppe" (Chekhov), 109
Steppenwolf (Hesse), 245, 247
Stevens, Wallace
    "Domination of Black," 165
    "A High-Toned Old Christian Woman," 165
Stieglitz, Alfred, *From the Back Window, 291* (1915), 165
Stoker, Bram, *Dracula,* 233, 235, 236
The Stories of Eva Luna (Allende), 71, 72–73
Storing, Herbert J., *The Complete Anti-Federalist,* 131
"The Story of An Hour" (Chopin), 153, 154–155, 157–161
Stowe, Harriet Beecher, *Uncle Tom's Cabin,* 140
Strange Tales from a Chinese Studio (Songling, ed.), 83
A Streetcar Named Desire (1951) [Kazan, dir], 176, 177
A Streetcar Named Desire (television episode, 1955) [Jordan, dir], 176, 177
A Streetcar Named Desire (Williams), 175, 177
String Quartet No. 15 in A Minor, Op. 132 (1825) [Beethoven], 246
Stuart, Gilbert, *James Monroe* (ca. 1820–1822), 131
"Substance, Shadow, and Spirit" (Ch'ien), 83
The Sufferings of Young Werther (Goethe), 223
"Suicide in the Trenches" (Sassoon), 245, 247
The Summoning of Everyman (Anonymous), 188
The Sunken Bell (Hauptmann), 233
The Surprising Adventures of Baron Munchhausen (Raspe), 223, 224
di Suvero, Mark, *Are Years What? (For Marianne Moore)* [1967], 176, 178
Swift, Jonathan, *Gulliver's Travels,* 222, 224

"The Swimmer" (Cheever), 175
"Swing Low, Sweet Chariot" (Traditional), 153
Symphony in Flesh Colour and Pink: Portrait of Mrs. Frances Leyland (1871–1874) [Whistler], 234, 237
Symphony in White, No. 1: The White Girl (1862) [Whistler], 234, 237
Szymborska, Wislawa, "Conversation with a Stone," 245

T
"Tableau" (Cullen), 164
Tagore, Rabindranath
    The Golden Craft, 83
    The Post Office, 83, 85–86
    "Song VII," 83
"The Tale of How Ivan Ivanovich Quarelled with Ivan Nikiforovich" (Gogol), 109
Tales from a Troubled Land (Paton), 97
Tales of the Late Ivan Petrovich Belkin (Pushkin), 109
Tallis, John, *Tallis's History and Description of the Crystal Palace, and the Exhibition of the World's Industry in 1851,* 234
Tallis's History and Description of the Crystal Palace, and the Exhibition of the World's Industry in 1851 (Tallis), 234
Tan, Amy, *The Joy Luck Club,* 174
The Tao of Pooh and the Te of Piglet (Hoff), 84, 86
The Tao Te Ching (Tzu), 84
"The Tartar Swept" (Kleinzahler), 175
Taylor, Edward, "Upon a Spider Catching a Fly," 122
Tecumseh, Shawnee Chief, "Address to William Henry Harrison" (1810), 141
"The Tell-Tale Heart" (Poe), 4, 6
Tennyson, Lord Alfred
    In Memoriam A.H.H., 223, 224
    "The Lady of Shalott," 25
    "The Lotos-Eaters," 47, 48
Terracotta Hydria (ca. 510 BCE), 25
The Testimony of Contemporary Latin American Authors (Meyer, ed.), 72

The Noé Jitrik Reader: Selected Essays on Latin American Literature (Jitrik and Benner), 72

Their Eyes Were Watching God (Hurston), 164, 166

"Their Finest Hour" (House of Commons, June 18, 1940) [Churchill], 246

The Thief and the Dogs (Mahfouz), 97

Thiep, Nguyen Huy, *The General Retires and Other Stories*, 83, 87

Things Fall Apart (Achebe), 97, 100–101

"This is my letter to the World" (Dickinson), 141

"This Land is Your Land" (Guthrie), 176

Thomas Jefferson's Letter to Benjamin Banneker (August 30, 1791) [Jefferson], 131

Thompson, John M., *Russia and the Soviet Union: An Historical Introduction from the Kievan State to the Present*, 109

Thoreau, Henry David
"Civil Disobedience," 141
Walden; or, Life in the Woods, 141, 142

The Three Musketeers (Dumas), 233, 235

Thunderstorm (Yu), 83, 85

Thurber, James, "The Secret Life of Walter Mitty," 4

Thus Spoke Zarathustra (Nietzsche), 245

Tillich, Paul, *The Courage to Be*, 245

"In Time of Silver Rain" (Hughes), 24

The Time Machine (Wells), 233, 236

"Tintern Abbey" (Wordsworth), 223

"To Daffodils" (Herrick), 213, 215

"To His Coy Mistress" (Marvell), 213, 215

"To His Excellency General Washington" (Wheatley), 122

To Kill a Mockingbird (film) [Mulligan, dir], 15

To Kill a Mockingbird (Lee), 13, 14, 15–16, 18–21

"To My Dear and Loving Husband" (Bradstreet), 122, 123

"To Urania" (Brodsky), 109

"To the Virgins, to Make Much of Time" (Herrick), 213, 215

Today I Wrote Nothing: The Selected Works of Daniil Kharms (Kharms), 109

Tolstoy, Leo
The Death of Ivan Ilyich, 109, 111
"How Much Land Does a Man Need?," 4

"Towards a Definition of American Modernism" (Singal), 165, 166–167

Trading Places: The East India Company and Asia, 1600–1834 (Farrington), 84, 85

"Tragedy or Romance? A Reading of the Paolo and Francesca Episode in Dante's *Inferno*" (Poggioli), 193–199

The Tragedy (1903) [Picasso], 38

The Tragedy of Macbeth (Shakespeare), 203, 204

The Trials of Phillis Wheatley: America's First Black Poet and Encounters with the Founding Fathers (Gates), 122, 124, 126–128

The Tribute Money, Brancacci Chapel, Florence (ca. 1420) [Masaccio], 189, 191

Tripod Bird Bowl (Guatemala, third to fourth century), 72, 75

Trumbull, John, *Declaration of Independence* (1819), 131, 133

Truth, Sojourner
"Ain't I a Woman?" (May 29, 1851), 153
The Narrative of Sojourner Truth, 153

Tsvetaeva, Marina
My Pushkin, 110
Poets with History and Poets Without History, 110

Tuchman, Barbara, *The Proud Tower: A Portrait of the World Before the War, 1890–1914*, 109

"Tulips" (Plath), 175

Twain, Mark
The Adventures of Huckleberry Finn, 152, 154

"The Celebrated Jumping Frog of Calaveras County," 152

Life on the Mississippi, 58

"What Stumped the Bluejays," 152

"The Twelve" (Blok), 109, 111

Twenty Love Poems and a Song of Despair (Neruda and Merwin), 71

Twenty Thousand Leagues Under the Sea (Verne), 233, 235

Twenty Years at Hull House (Addams), 153

Tzu, Lao, *The Tao Te Ching*, 84

U

"Un bel di, vedremo" (*Madama Butterfly*, 1904) [Puccini], 25

Unchained Memories (2003) [Bell and Lennon, dir], 153

Uncle Remus, "Plantation Proverbs," 152

Uncle Tom's Cabin (Stowe), 140

Under The Red Flag (Ha Jin), 83

The Underdogs: A Novel of the Mexican Revolution (Azuela and Waisman), 71

"The Underground" (Heaney), 25, 27, 28

United States Magazine and Democratic Review, 17, No. 1, 1845, "Annexation" (O'Sullivan), 141

University of Missouri-Kansas School of Law, Famous American Trials: "The Scottsboro Boys" Trials (1931–1937), 17

Untitled (1950) [DeCarava], 5

Untitled (1957) [Kline], 176

Untitled (1964) [Rothko], 176

Untitled (1996) [Neshat], 99, 102

Untitled (Oval Construction) [1925] (Schwitters), 246

Up From Slavery: An Autobiography (Washington), 153

Updike, John, "A & P," 175

"Upon the Burning of Our House" (Bradstreet), 122, 123

"Upon a Spider Catching a Fly" (Taylor), 122

Usigli, Rodolfo, The Imposter: A Play for Demagogues, 71

V

Valèry, Paul, "Crisis of the Mind," 246

Valladares, Armando, *Against All Hope: A Memoir of Life in Castro's Gulag,* 72

Valmiki, *The Ramayana,* 47, 48, 50–51, 83

Van Eyck, Jan, *Self-Portrait* (1433), 59

van Gogh, Vincent. *See* Gogh, Vincent van

Vargas Llosa, Mario, 74, 76–79

"Variations on an Original Theme ('Enigma')" (Elgar), 5

Vasari, Giorgio, *Lives of the Most Excellent Painters, Sculptors, and Architects,* 203

Vermeer, Johannes, *Girl with a Pearl Earring* (1665), 213, 216

Verne, Jules, *Twenty Thousand Leagues Under the Sea,* 233, 235

The Vicar of Wakefield (Goldsmith), 223, 225

Virgil, *The Aeneid,* 47, 48, 49, 50

Virginia Statute for Religious Freedom (Jefferson), 130

The Virgin and Child with St. Anne (1508) [da Vinci], 203, 205

A Visit from the Old Mistress (1876) [Homer], 153, 155

"The Visitor" (Forche), 175

"The Visual Artistry of *Romeo and Juliet*" (Black), 38, 39–40

Vitruvian Man (1487) [da Vinci], 203, 205–206

Voltaire, "Micromégas," 223, 224

Vonnegut, Kurt, *Cat's Cradle,* 174

W

Waisman, Sergio, *The Underdogs: A Novel of the Mexican Revolution,* 71

Waiting for the Barbarians or Life and Times of Michael K (Coetzee), 97

Waiting for Godot (Beckett), 245

Walcott, Derek, 74, 76–79

Walden; or, Life in the Woods (Thoreau), 141, 142

Walker, Alice
   The Color Purple, 14, 16
   "Everyday Use," 4

"In Search of Our Mothers' Gardens," 14, 16

In Search of Our Mothers' Gardens, 58

"Walking Distance" (Allbery), 25

"The Wanderer" (*The Exeter Book*) [Anonymous], 189

War Series: The Letter (1946) [Lawrence], 165

"Ward No. 6" (Chekhov), 109, 111

Washington, Booker T., *Up From Slavery: An Autobiography,* 153

Washington Crossing the Delaware (1851) [Leutze], 5, 131, 133

Washington and Lafayette at Mount Vernon (1859) [Rossiter], 131

Wasserman, Dale, *Man of La Mancha* (1966), 213, 215

The Wasteland (Eliot), 245

Water (2010) [Shonibare], 99, 101–102

Watson and the Shark (1778) [Copley], 223, 225

"The Way to Wealth" (*Poor Richard's Almanack*) [Franklin], 131

"We Grow Accustomed to the Dark" (Dickinson), 24, 29, 30, 31–34

We Killed Mangy-Dog and Other Mozambique Stories (Honwana), 97

Wells, H. G., *The Time Machine,* 233, 236

Welty, Eudora
   One Writer's Beginnings, 58
   "Petrified Man," 175

Wharton, Edith
   Ethan Frome, 152
   "Roman Fever," 153, 154–155, 157–161

"What Stumped the Bluejays" (Twain), 152

Wheatley, Phillis
   "An Hymn to the Evening," 122
   "On Being Brought from Africa to America," 122, 123, 126–128
   "To His Excellency General Washington," 122

"When the leaf sings" (Daniel), 188

"When Lilacs Last in the Dooryard Bloom'd" (Whitman), 141

"Where Are You Going, Where Have You Been?" (Oates), 175

"Where Have All the Flowers Gone?" (Seeger), 176

Whistler, James McNeill
   Arrangement in Gray and Black: The Artist's Mother (1871), 234, 237
   Mother of Pearl and Silver: The Andalusian (1888–1900), 234, 237
   Symphony in Flesh Colour and Pink: Portrait of Mrs. Frances Leyland (1871–1874), 234, 237
   Symphony in White, No. 1: The White Girl (1862), 234, 237

Whitman, Walt
   "I Hear America Singing," 140
   "Song of Myself," 140
   "When Lilacs Last in the Dooryard Bloom'd," 141

"Why I Wrote 'The Yellow Wallpaper'" (Gilman), 153, 157–161

"The Wife of Bath's Tale" (*The Canterbury Tales*) [Chaucer], 188

Wigglesworth, Michael, "The Day of Doom," 122

Wilbur, Richard
   "Advice to a Prophet," 175
   "In Trackless Woods," 25
   "Love Calls Us to the Things of This World," 175
   "The Reader," 25

Wilde, Oscar
   The Ballad of Reading Gaol, 233, 235
   The Decay of Lying, 234
   The Importance of Being Earnest, 233
   The Picture of Dorian Gray, 233

"The Wild Honeysuckle" (Freneau), 130

Williams, Roger
   The Bloody Tenent of Persecution, for Cause of Conscience, 122
   A Key into the Language of America, 122

Williams, Tennessee, *A Streetcar Named Desire,* 175, 177

Wilson, August, *The Piano Lesson*, 165

Winesburg, Ohio (Anderson), 164

The Woman Warrior: Memoirs of a Girlhood Among Ghosts (Kingston), 58

Woodworth, Samuel, "The Old Oaken Bucket," 140

Woolf, Virginia, "A Sketch of the Past," 58

Wordsworth, William
 "I Wandered Lonely as a Cloud," 25
 "London, 1802," 223, 225
 "Ode: Intimations of Immortality," 223
 "Preface to *Lyrical Ballads*," 59, 223
 "Tintern Abbey," 223
 "The World is Too Much with Us," 223

The World Is a Room and Other Stories (Amichai), 98

"The World is Too Much with Us" (Wordsworth), 223

Woza Albert! (Mtwa, Ngema, and Simon), 98

Wright, Frank Lloyd, Frederick C. Robie House (1909), 25

Wright, Joseph, *Portrait of a Woman* (1770), 123, 125

Wright, Richard
 Black Boy, 14
 "The Man Who Was Almos' a Man," 175, 177, 180–183
 Native Son, 174

Wuthering Heights (Brontë), 236

Y

Yeats, William Butler, "The Second Coming," 245, 248

"The Yellow Wallpaper" (Gilman), 153, 154–155, 157–161

"'The Yellow Wallpaper' and Women's Discourse" (Ford), 153, 155, 157–161

"Yet Do I Marvel" (Cullen), 164

Yimou, Zhang, *Curse of the Golden Flower* (2006), 84

Young Acrobat on a Ball (1905) [Picasso], 5

"Young Goodman Brown" (Hawthorne), 140

Young Moravian Girl (ca. 1755–1760) [Haidt], 123, 125

Yu, Tsao, *Thunderstorm*, 83, 85

Z

Zakani, Nezam al-Din Obeyd-e, *Ethics of the Aristocrats and Other Satirical Works*, 98, 99

Zhi, Fei, *The I Ching*, 84

Zi'ang, Chen, "On a Gate-tower at Yuzhou," 83